HITLER'S NEST OF VIPERS

HITLER'S NEST OF VIPERS

THE RISE OF THE ABWEHR

NIGEL WEST

FRONTLINE
BOOKS

First published in Great Britain in 2022 by
FRONTLINE BOOKS
an imprint of Pen & Sword Books Ltd,
47 Church Street, Barnsley, S. Yorkshire, S70 2AS

ISBN: 978-1-39908-637-0

CIP data records for this title are available from the British Library

For more information on our books, please visit
www.frontline-books.com, email info@frontline-books.com
or write to us at the above address.

Printed and bound by CPI Group (UK) Ltd, Croydon, CR0 4YY
Typeset by Concept, Huddersfield, West Yorkshire
Pen & Sword Books Ltd incorporates the imprints of Pen & Sword
Archaeology, Atlas, Aviation, Battleground, Discovery,
Family History, History, Maritime, Military, Naval, Politics,
Social History, Transport, True Crime, Claymore Press,
Frontline Books, Praetorian Press,
Seaforth Publishing and White Owl

For a complete list of Pen and Sword titles please contact
PEN & SWORD LTD
47 Church Street, Barnsley, South Yorkshire, S70 2AS, England
E-mail: enquiries@pen-and-sword.co.uk

Or

PEN AND SWORD BOOKS
1950 Lawrence Rd, Havertown, PA 19083, USA
E-mail: Uspen-and-sword@casematepublishers.com

MIX
Paper from
responsible sources
FSC® C013604
FSC
www.fsc.org

CONTENTS

List of Plates ... vii
Acknowledgments ... ix
Author's Note ... xi
Glossary and Abbreviations ... xiii
Reich Security Agency (RSHA) Organisation after 1941 ... xvii
Introduction ... xix
Dramatis Personae ... xxix

Chapter I Pre-War ... 1
Chapter II The Buro Jahnke ... 17
Chapter III Nest Bremen ... 32
Chapter IV GOLFPLATZ ... 57
Chapter V The Front Line ... 105
Chapter VI German Intelligence in the Middle East ... 180
Chapter VII South American Intrigue ... 210
Chapter VIII The Western Campaign ... 223

Appendices
I Abstellen in Germany ... 239
II MI5 Assessment of German Activity in the Iberian Peninsula ... 240
III German Penetration of SOE, SIS and Allied Organisations ... 269

Source Notes ... 295
Index ... 303

LIST OF PLATES

1. Admiral Wilhelm Canaris.
2. Erich Pfeiffer.
3. Thomas Ludwig.
4. Josef Ledebur.
5. Colonel Rudolf.
6. Carl Eitel.
7. Kuno Weltzien.
8. Otto Mayer.
9. Paul Fidrmuc.
10. Gottfried Paul-Taboschat.
11. Nikolaus Ritter.
12. Emile Kliemann and Lily Sergueiev.
13. Bertie Koepke.
14. ISOS.
15. Kriegs Organisation Portugal (KOP).

The Abwehr files . . . deserved more than the attention they got from historians and imaginative writers.

Gerold Guensberg, *Studies in Intelligence* Vol. 21 No. 3 (1977)

The Abwehr is the German equivalent of our own Secret Service. It is a military organisation under the direct control of the German High Command. An Abwehrstelle is a station of the Abwehr.

Major Anthony Blunt to the Prime Minister, MI5 briefing on HARLEQUIN, April 1943

Deception of the enemy is a weapon which is too little employed in the German conduct of war. Our enemies, especially the British, occupy themselves with it and with more success.

General Alfred Jodl, Chief of OKW Operations Staff, 5 March 1945.

ACKNOWLEDGMENTS

The author acknowledges his debt of gratitude to those who have assisted his research, among them the late Bill Williams, Roger Hesketh, David Strangeways, Noel Wild, Juan Pujol (GARBO), Roman Garby-Czerniawski (BRUTUS), Harry Williamson (TATE), Frano de Bona (FREAK), Ib Riis (COBWEB), Dusan Popov (TRICYCLE), Ivo Popov (DREADNOUGHT), Eugn Sostaric (METEOR), John Moe (MUTT), Tor Glad (EFF), Elvira de la Fuentes (BRONX), Lisel Gärtner, Hugh Astor, Len Burt, Christopher and Pam Harmer, Cyril Mills, John Maude, Gerald Glover, Peter Ramsbotham, Tommy and Joan Robertson, Enriquetta Harris, Sarah Bishop, Joanna Phipps, Peter Hope, Jim Skardon, Eric Goodacre, John Gwyer, Dick White, Victor and Tess Rothschild, and Bill Magan. Russell Lee, Michael Ryde, Rupert Speir, Bill Luke, who shared their wartime MI5 experiences; and the late Sigismund Best, Philip Johns, Cecil Gledhill, Nicholas Elliott, Felix Cowgill, Peter Falk, Desmond Bristow, Rodney Dennys, Cecil Barclay, John Bygott, Eddie Boxshall, Euan Rabagliati, Charles Seymour, Andrew King, George Blake, Lionel Loewe, Walter Bell, Kenneth Benton, John Codrington, Lord Tennyson, George Young, Robin Cecil, John Cairncross, who all served in SIS. Also, from SOE, Ronnie Seth, Peter Kemp, Jack Beevor, Brian Stonehouse, Tony Brooks and Peter Wilkinson; Al Ulmer, Bill Hood, Peter Sichel and Hugh Montgomery from OSS, Ken Crosby, formerly of the FBI Special Intelligence Service; Cleve Cram from the CIA and John Taylor from NARA. Finally, Halina Szymanska, Martin and Kim Dearden, Bill Kenyon-Jones, Gunter Peis, Rob Hesketh, Erich Vermehren, David Mure, Jock Colville, and Bill Cavendish-Bentinck, David Kahn, Marco Popov, Roger Grosjean, Ladislas Farago, John Taylor, Jennifer Scherr, Sebastian Cody, Kim and Marton Dearden, Christian Linde, Frederick Solms-Baruth, Kathleen Ritter, Otto Weltzien, Charles Byford, Nicholas Reed, Jim Lee and Christopher Risso-Gill.

ACKNOWLEDGMENTS

AUTHOR'S NOTE

Many of the documents reproduced in this volume originate from official files and have been redacted during the declassification process. Where possible the redactions have been restored, but where this has not been possible the redaction is indicated thus: [XXXXXXXXXXXXXXXX]

The author has retained the convention of printing codenames in capitals but, for ease of reading, has restored capitalised surnames to ordinary lower case.

In the interests of consistency, some American-month / day style dates have been altered to the European day / month convention.

Many Allied and German military ranks have been deliberately omitted as they can be somewhat misleading for the uninitiated as they do not always accurately reflect seniority. In the German system the status of specialist (Sonderführer) was often granted to civilians who had no military background. The five designations (Sondeführer G, Z, K, B and R) were the equivalent, respectively, of an NCO, lieutenant, captain, major and colonel.

AUTHOR'S NOTE

GLOSSARY AND ABBREVIATIONS

@	Alias
104 SCI	Special Counter-Intelligence in Brussels
105 SCI	Special Counter-Intelligence in Paris
AA	Anti-Aircraft
Abt.	Abteilung
ALLIANCE	SIS network in occupied France
Amt	Office
BCRA	Bureau Central de Renseignements et d'Action
BdS	Befehlshaber der Sicherheitspolizei
B9	MI5's Irish section
BISMARCK	B-Dienst HQ
Camp 020	Latchmere House, Ham Common
CIG	Central Intelligence Group
CODAR	FBI counter-espionage investigation
CSDIC	Combined Services Detailed Interrogation Centre
DCI	Director of Central Intelligence
DDO	Deputy Director for Operations
D/F	Direction-Finding
DGII	Dirección General de Informacion e Inteligencia (Chilean secret police)
DNB	Deutsche Nachrichten Buro (German News Agency)
DOPS	Direcao da Ordem Politica e Social (Brazilian secret police)
DORA	I/H West command at Rheda Castle
DSO	Defence Security Officer
FA	Reichsluftfahrtministerium Forschungsamt (Air Ministry Research Office)
FAK	Nachrichten Fernaufklärungs Kompanie (Long-range intercept company)

FAT	Frontaufklärungstrupp (tactical mobile reconnais sance unit)
FHW	Fremde Heere West
Fnu	First name unknown
FSS	Field Security Section
G-2	Irish Intelligence Service
GC&CS	Government Code & Cipher School
GFP	GeheimeFeldPolizei (German Field Police)
GIS	German Intelligence Service
GOLFPLATZ	Abwehr codename for England
GV	German double agent
HAPAG	Hamburg-Amerika shipping line
Hastuf	Hauptsturmführer (captain)
HSSPF	Hoherer SS und Polizei Führer
Ic	OKW intelligence liaison
I/H	Eins Heer
I/L	Eins Luft
I/LTW	Eins Luft Technik
I/M	Eins Marine
INTERALLIÉ	SIS network in occupied France
ISBA	Intelligence Source British Agent ISOS subset
ISLD	Inter-Services Liaison Department (SIS cover organisation in the Middle East)
ISOS	Abwehr decrypts
IVORY	FBI counter-espionage investigation
JIC	Joint Intelligence Committee
KO	KriegsOrganisation
KOBU	KriegsOrganisation Bucharest
KONA	Kommandeur der Nachrichtenaufklärung
KONO	KriegsOrganisation Nehe Orient
KOP	KriegsOrganisation Portugal
KOS	KriegsOrganisation Spain
LRC	London Reception Centre
MA	Military Attaché
MI5	British Security Service
MI6	British Secret Intelligence Service
MIT	Turkish Intelligence Service
MoI	Ministry of Information
MP	US Army Military Police
MSS	Most Secret Sources
ND	Nachrichtendienst
NID	Naval Intelligence Division

NKVD	Soviet intelligence service
NSCO	Naval Security Control Officer
OKH/Chi	Oberkommando der Wehrmacht, Cipher Section
OKM/SKW	Oberkommando der Kriegsmarine, Seekriegsleitung
Ops B	SHAEF deception planning unit
OSS	Office of Strategic Services
OTU	Officer Training Unit
PAIR	Mediterranean theatre codename for ISOS
PCO	Passport Control Officer
PF	Personal File
PPF	Parti Populaire Français
PR	Photographic Reconnaissance
PVDE	Policia de Vigilancia e de Defesa do Estado (Portuguese International Police)
PWE	Political Warfare Executive
RDF	Radio Direction-Finding
ROF	Royal Ordnance Factory
RSS	Radio Security Service
RVPS	Royal Victoria Patriotic School
SABENA	Belgian airline
SABOT	SOE circuit headed by Pierre Bourriez
SAFEHAVEN	Post-war OSS investigation of Abwehr funds
SCI	Special Counter-Intelligence Unit
SD	Sicherheitsdienst
SIM	Servicio de Información Militar
SIME	Security Intelligence Middle East
SIPO	Sicherheitspolizei
SIS	British Secret Intelligence Service
SIS	Italian Speciali Servizio Informazioni
SO 1	SOE's covert propaganda department
SOE	Special Operations Executive
THEODORA	Ast Munster mission
TRIANGLE	ISOS in the Middle East
V-Mann	Verbindungsmann
WIDO	Abwehr nest in Tripoli
X-2	Counter-intelligence branch, OSS
XX	Twenty Committee
Y	Wireless interception
ZbV	Zur besonderen Verwendung ('Special Purpose')
ZEPPELIN	Abwehr headquarters at Zossen

REICH SECURITY AGENCY (RSHA) ORGANISATION AFTER 1941

VI-A Administration

VI-B Western Europe
1. Holland
2. Belgium
3. France
4. Spain
5. Portugal
6. Scandinavia

VI-C Central Europe. Near & Far East
1–2. Russian & Baltic States
3. Ukraine
4–6. Japan
7–8. China
9. Manchuko & Mongolia
10. Thailand & French Indo-China
11. Dutch East Indies & Philippines
12. Iran, Turkey & Afghanistan
13. Arab Countries

VI-D United Kingdom and the American Continent and British Empire
1. Canada
2. United States
3. Mexico
4. South America
5. United Kingdom

VI-E Italy, Switzerland & Balkans

VI-F Training

VI-G Documentary. (Falsification of documents, photography, copying, etc.)

VI-H Greece and Balkans

VI-I (Function unknown.)

VI-S: Special Enterprises. (Training of agents, W/T operators and saboteurs.)

V1-Z: Russia and Africa. Perhaps also India and China

VI-Wi: Economics. (Wirtschaft.)

7: Transportation Section. (Fahrbereitschaft)

Department Function

Amt VIA	Organisation
Amt VIB	West Europe (neutral, Allied and occupied countries)
Amt VIC	Russia, Near East, Far East (including Japan)
Amt VID	Western Hemisphere, Great Britain, Scandinavia
Amt VIE	Southeast Europe (including Allied and Occupied areas)
Amt VIF	Technical Support
Amt VIG	Scientific-Methodic Research Service
Amt VI Wi/T	Economics and Technology
Amt VIS	Sabotage
Amt VI Kult	Non-scientific Domestic Acquisition Service
Amt VIZ	Military Counter-espionage and Personnel Checks
Abwehr	Civilian Counterespionage and Personnel Checks

INTRODUCTION

> Our knowledge of the German Intelligence Service, its organisation, its personnel and its activities against the Western powers and in the Balkans is very imperfect from 1939 to 1940, adequately representative from 1940 to 1943, and from 1943 to 1945 probably complete. (Our knowledge of its activities on the Russian Front is less satisfactory.)
>
> SHAEF Report, December 1945

Modern historians have consistently condemned the Abwehr and the Sicherheitsdienst as incompetent and corrupt organisations. However, even the most recent analysts have not had the benefit of newly declassified MI5, CIA and US Counter-Intelligence Corps files which shed a very different light on the structure, control and capabilities of the German intelligence machine in Europe, South America, the Mediterranean and the Middle East.

The quantity of German records seized during the Allied occupation was immense, literally tons of military files and the entire Foreign Ministry archive which dated back to 1870. However, between 1958 and 1962 the US Government sponsored a declassification programme which transferred the material onto film and concluded with the return of the documents to the Federal Republic for permanent storage. But according to the CIA's Paul Hartman, who worked on this project,

> The exploitation should have taken place sooner and with, a greater sense of urgency. When the sheer mass of captured paper is taken into account, it is to the credit of the armed forces, OSS, CIC, and CIA that the documents were exploited to a fairly high degree. The early exploitation was done by the OSS Cl War Room in London. Later came efforts by the CIC, ONI, G-2, and others. Allied powers also began their exploitation, and the Soviets were not excluded from access in the very early post-war period.

> The biggest flaw in these early efforts was that the records were not examined systematically. In 1956, then DDO, Frank Wisner obtained approval from the then-DCI Allen Dulles to have the Cl Staff conduct a systematic analysis. All but a small portion of this study was concluded by 1964, and work on the remaining segment, continuing at a slower pace, was concluded in 1967. Each captured record deemed to contain intelligence data was summarised, indexed, and included in the records of the Directorate of Operations. Much of the same information was also fed into appropriate computerised data banks. Items of interest to other US agencies or certain foreign governments were forwarded to them. As a result of this effort, more than 1,250,000 names of persons of intelligence interest – including all of the names on the filmed index of Nest Bremen – were recorded in the DDO's Main Index.[1]

Altogether, some sixty-five reels of microfiche, amounting to the entire wartime existence of the Nest Bremen, subordinate to the Ast Hamburg, which had been captured by the US Navy in 1945, was accidentally retained, and discovered in a facility in Alexandria, Virginia, when transferred to the National Archive, to be copied by an assiduous researcher, Ladislas Farago.

This windfall discovery, which did not undergo declassification until December 1976, formed the basis of Farago's *The Game of the Foxes*, perhaps the first history of wartime intelligence operations to be based on officially-released documents.[2] Initially Farago took his apparent treasure-trove at face value, but his publishers alerted him to plans by the Yale University Press to produce a sanitised version of Sir John Masterman's account of *The Double Cross System of the War of 1939-45*,[3] which revealed that some of the most active spies run by Ast Hamburg, including Wulf Schmidt, whose mission lasted from his insertion by parachute in September 1940 and continued until the German collapse, had actually been a double agent controlled throughout by MI5.[4] Similarly, a spy codenamed EDDA in Iceland, who transmitted nearly 400 reports between May 1942 and June 1944, was actually Ib Riis, a double agent better known to MI5 as COBWEB.[5] Most importantly, Farago asserted that he had acquired a key index which had enabled him to link individual Abwehr codenames to code-numbers, and then to the real names of agents.

In the light of these revelations, Farago hastily amended his manuscript to accommodate the hitherto secret information, but nevertheless provided a somewhat self-congratulatory perspective on the Abwehr's performance. He took the view that if Nest Bremen's reach, as far as the United States and the Middle East, was indicative of operations conducted by the organisation's other sub-branches, the

Abwehr had been grossly underestimated. He took as an example S-2118, codenamed TURCO, who submitted forty-four reports in 1940 and more than a hundred in 1941, mainly from the ports of Istanbul, Alexandria, Port Said and the Suez Canal. Farago disclosed that this hitherto unknown spy was actually Tekin Saygin, a Polish Jew, born Liehtenthal, who had moved to Turkey, converted to Islam and in 1938 volunteered his services to the Abwehr.

Farago's uncritical approach attracted much adverse comment from the US intelligence community, represented by Gerold Guensberg who, contributing to *Studies in Intelligence* in October 1977, pointed out that the Farago cache may have included payment and reporting files, but not the operational material. While he had broken through the protection designed to conceal true identities, the Nest had destroyed the associated message copies, thus making a balanced judgment more difficult.

The few Allied intelligence officers who gained access to the post-war interrogation reports of their captured adversaries soon came to realise that the enemy had constructed a huge organisation which had been largely underestimated. For example, in November 1945 the American captors of Erwin Lahousen, a senior Abwehr officer and one of Admiral Canaris's closest supporters, who had only narrowly escaped the Gestapo's ruthless purge after the 20 July plot by being wounded on the Russian Front a couple of days before the attempted putsch, noted that

> The Abwehr was not weak and ineffective because of corruption, defeatism, personal politics and superannuation, but that even before the war it was a principal center of opposition to the Nazi Regime with the aim of sabotaging a German victory. On this basis our views of the German Intelligence service, and specifically of the failures and inertia of the Abwehr need serious revision.[6]

In November 1946 MI5's Klop Ustinov made this very compelling appeal for his cooperation while questioning Richard Kauder, a key figure, in an attempt to solve one of the war's remaining mysteries, relating to the infamous MAX–MORITZ radio traffic in the Balkans: 'As you will realise, the Allied victory over Germany has been so complete that not only every single official and in many cases unofficial German document, but also all the persons connected with those documents who are still alive have fallen into Allied hands.'[7] Ustinov's tactic, which almost always worked, was to spell out to prisoners that the Nazi defeat had been so comprehensive that it was in the interests of individual prisoners to give their full assistance to their captors as obfuscation and obstruction was bound to fail.

In the decade following the German surrender British and American intelligence agencies were preoccupied by the Cold War and the retention of records became an administrative nuisance. While the CIA catalogued some of its holdings for future exploitation and put the rest into long-term storage, the British seem to have mislaid large quantities of paper records, and made little effort to preserve them. In the absence of any external pressure, such as the Public Record Act, which was not enacted until 1958, the files of Security Intelligence Middle East were squirreled away in Nicosia, and documents entrusted to the Colonial Office were consigned to Hanslope Park, an isolated secure facility in the Buckinghamshire countryside. This was an era in which the term 'declassification' hardly existed and sensitive security and intelligence issues were not considered suitable for public debate.

In February 1956, in preparation for awkward Parliamentary Questions in the House of Commons concerning the 1951 defection of Guy Burgess and Donald Maclean, the Home Secretary Gwilym Lloyd George was briefed by officials that 'we now know from captured German records that the number of German agents operating against the United Kingdom during the war was 201. And the number detected and arrested by our Security Service was 200.'[8] But was this really true, or another example of the unjustified hyperbole associated with the victors' view of their vanquished opponent?

By the outbreak of war MI5 had accumulated some knowledge about the Abwehr, mainly from information acquired from the interrogation of a small number of spies arrested within their jurisdiction, such as Hermann Goertz and Mrs Jessie Jordan; reports from foreign liaison partners, such as the French Service de Renseignements and Deuxième Bureau; and the American FBI; and early operational experience developed during the management of double agents, among them the pilot Christopher Draper, the Welsh businessman Arthur Owens, and the reluctant co-opteee, Hans George. Additionally, MI5 had run some penetration agents against the German embassy in London, including the anti-Nazi diplomat Wolfgang zu Putlitz and the Austrian *agent provocateur* Lisel Gaertner, to learn more about German espionage methodology.

As hostilities began in September 1939 both sides were unprepared for the conflict. MI5 had established an elaborate counter-espionage programme involving the creation of an entirely new organisation, the Radio Security Service, which was intended to monitor the airwaves and detect the tell-tale illicit transmissions of enemy spies equipped with wireless sets. As it turned out, the only illegal traffic to be monitored was that of double agents operating under MI5's control.

Evidently the Germans had learned the lessons of the First World War by reading about British success in the COMINT field and had learned the necessary lessons.[9]

The inescapable weakness of any intelligence network, as the Germans fully understood, was the requirement for spies to deliver their messages in sufficient time for the information to be acted upon. Surface mail addressed to an intermediary in a neutral country was a lengthy and unreliable conduit, but the use of even miniaturised transmitting apparatus was almost bound to attract unwelcome attention. Accordingly, most of the agents active in England during the summer of 1939 were withdrawn before hostilities commenced, leaving behind a single clandestine transmitter and a very busy wireless in the German legation in neutral Dublin.

Whereas the Abwehr's British target did not have a large pool of pro-Nazi sympathisers to engage in espionage, the story was very different in the United States and much of South America. The spy-rings headed by Guenther Rumrich and Frederick Duquesne, which consisted mainly of German émigrés, demonstrated that the Hamburg and Bremen Abstellen enjoyed the full support of the government which had exercised influence on the management of the transatlantic shipping lines to facilitate the networks' couriers.

By the end of hostilities the Allied security and intelligence services had learned vastly more about their adversaries, and had exploited four sources in particular that had not been available previously: intercepted radio traffic exchanged between headquarters and the various outstations spread across the globe, captured documents, defectors, and prisoner interrogation.

The wireless messages revealed a complex spider's web of individual agents, transmitters operating from commercial, diplomatic and consular premises, usually linked to major regional hubs such as those located in Madrid, Sofia and Istanbul, and a further network of smaller, subordinate stations which maintained regular contact with the mainline centres.

The study of captured documents began in earnest during the Battle of Britain, when enemy aircrew often flew on their missions in possession of manuals and other supposedly restricted material. There were plenty of other 'pinches' too, such as the seizure of Enigma codebooks during the brief occupation of the Lofoten Islands in March 1941, and the tragic raid on Dieppe in August 1942 which yielded a copy of *Das Brittische Kriegheer*, the first solid evidence that the Allies' strategic deception campaign to exaggerate its military strength was really working.

As for high-level defectors, they were as a commodity something of a double-edged sword, as those with a current knowledge of intelligence activities were likely to compromise Allied deception operations. Some were deterred (such as ARTIST, in April 1944, when he unintentionally jeopardised several controlled double agents), while others were accepted, among them Erich Vermehren, Hans Ruser, Willi Hamburger, Hans Zech-Nennwich, Georg Kronberger, Richard Wurmann, Otto John, Josef Ledebur, Herbert Berthold, Peter Schagen and Carl Marcus.

The final source was the reporting from captives who underwent intensive interviews in an effort to build a comprehensive picture of the enemy's intelligence activities, to identify the personalities involved, and to validate data already on file. Most of the prisoners were very cooperative, mainly because they acknowledged the scale of the defeat, and hoped to win their freedom by manifesting candour. They must also have realised, from the sophisticated nature of the questions put to them (despite a strict rule not to refer to especially sensitive sources), that there was little point in concealment. Too many of their colleagues had talked already and the jointly-coordinated Anglo-American interrogations followed a pattern which was based on the triangulation technique, comparing each assertion to the statements of others. Prisoners, uncertain of the likely length of their captivity, saw the futility of obfuscation and abandoned any inhibitions about describing their personal experiences and providing personality profiles of their colleagues, which were filed and cross-referenced by the MI5 – Section V – OSS X-2 counter-intelligence War Room in London. As each dossier was created, the relevant passages were duplicated into the existing Personal Files which had been built on intercepts, double agent reports and defector debriefings. What emerged, overall, was a thoroughly comprehensive analysis of the enemy's order-of-battle, solving the puzzles of codenames and alias identities, together with offering opportunities to tie up the thousands of loose ends left after the surrender.

Some of these sources, such as the senior defectors, would remain unknown for decades, their information attributed to codeword-protected sources such as PRECIOUS, JUNIOR, COLOMBINE, JIGGER and DICTIONARY. Similarly, even after the first disclosures about MI5's programme of controlled enemy agents, managed by the XX Committee, the true identities of the individual double agents remained secret, although TRICYCLE, ZIGZAG, TREASURE, COBWEB, BRUTUS, MUTT and GARBO chose to write about their experiences.[10]

The full picture of Nazi Germany's intelligence structure, and its scale and scope, only began to emerge after the study of the Abt. IIIF records for the period 1935–9 captured in Thuringia at Bad Blankenburg and the Abwehr administrative archive retrieved from Bad Sulza. Both collections were flown to the US Army's intelligence training depot at Camp Ritchie in Maryland. Abt. III was the counter-intelligence branch, and the 'F' stood for Fremde ('enemy'), and its operations had been among the Abwehr's most secret.

Initially, it appeared that the Germans had done a typically efficient job at destroying their intelligence records, as was described by an SD officer, Eugn Steimle, who was interrogated in December 1945.[11] He recalled the first major file-destruction operation which was conducted at Camp WALDBURG that took place in January 1945 as the Red Army approached Frankfurt an der Oder. A repetition of the housecleaning of the files was completed at the end of the month at Lauenstein, with another conflagration at Rottach-Egern. Finally, the very last card-indices and notes relating to the most important current cases were incinerated at Lufer, near Salzburg.

The surviving files were important because so much had been deliberately obliterated by the Germans, or fallen into Soviet hands, in the last days of the war, and the other major eradication of Ast Hamburg files, ended up at the British Army Records Centre in Hayes, where they were shredded from April 1958, leaving just 3,000 personal and subject files, which were incinerated in 1960. Ironically, there survives in MI5's records a large file containing the correspondence exchanged between MI5's organisation in Germany, the British Services Security Organisation, and MI5 in London which itemises the collection, listing such intriguing titles as *The Manufacture and use of Counterfeit Currency by the RSHA* and *German Intelligence Service – Use of Deception as an Aid to Military Operations.* In retrospect, from a historian's viewpoint, this destruction amounts to wanton vandalism.

Study of the files created immediately post-war, by the very few officers authorised to access them, showed that initial assessments of German incompetence, especially in the counter-intelligence sphere, needed to be revised, as MI5's Ian Wilson minuted in August 1945, referring to the Bad Blankenburg archive

> While we are well informed about almost all activities of the German Intelligence Service in the latter stages of the war, we have still very little knowledge of their counter-espionage work before and at the beginning of the war

> It is slowly becoming apparent from captured documents and elsewhere that the German counter-espionage service at this period was far more efficient than other activities of the German Intelligence Service. It is clear that III/F was controlling a number of British agents and was engaging upon an ambitious policy of deceiving this and other countries by feeding false information through such double agents and through other channels.[12]

In many ways III/F was of particular interest to its declared targets, Allied intelligence agencies. It had been headed by the genial 'Uncle Richard' Protze, one of Canaris's closest colleagues, who was later succeeded in 1939 by Joachim Rohleder. The Abt. was divided into geographic sections, III/F-1 (England, Holland, Belgium and Denmark); III/F-2 (France, Switzerland and Sweden); III/F-3 (Czechoslovakia and the Soviet Union); and III/F-4 (Balkans and later the Soviet Union). Upon reorganisation in 1944 the entire III/F would become Mil Amt's VI/Z under Georg Hansen and Walter Schellenberg.

Other useful material that fell into Allied hands included an Abt. II telephone directory for the ADOLF internal communications system dated October 1941 and recovered from France in 1944, containing over a hundred names and their departments; an Abwehr headquarters telephone directory dated March 1943 seized in Wiesbaden in April 1945; an alphabetical list of Abwehr officers in France in June 1942, together with their ranks, seniority and postings, recovered in Paris in September 1944; and a complete set of agent reports from Ast Dijon from between late 1942 and 1944, discovered in Stuttgart. Other valuable contributions were the Kassel staff roster, captured in April 1945, and a photo album of the Abwehr's senior staff.

An Allied summary of reports and interviewees dated February 1945 listed some of the highlights, with ten items allegedly selected arbitrarily:

(i) Reports on Weber, Aberle, Eppler and Sandstede: These give an account of the Abwehr work in Libya and Egypt.

(ii) Reports on Gottfried Müller and the MAMMUT undertaking. These describe an Abw. II expedition against Iraq and Persia.

iii) Reports on Mirko Rot and Andre Gyorgy. These deal with the Abwehr's chief source of operational intelligence from Russia and the British Mid-East area, i.e. the Luftneidekopf Sofia of Richard Kauders @ KLATT. As KLATT is under interrogation, these reports may soon be replaced by his information; also Oberst Wagner @ Dr Delius, who was head of KO Bulgaria from 1941-1944, should throw further light on the subject.

(iv) Report on Willy Goertz. This gives details of the Abwehr's stations in Vienna and Budapest and of the technical/military (IH/t.) section of Abwehr HQ.

(v) Report on Hens Salzinger. Salzinger was an officer in the Abwehr's CE section for Scandinavia (III F. 6). He gives a full list of the important officers at work in this period.

(vi) Reports on Meisstueffen and Poils. Those two men were agents of Nest Cologne and give details of its personnel and activities.

(vii) Reports on Delgrande, D'Hooghe, Hagemann, and Werner Unversagt. These reports, taken together, give a complete picture of the activities of Ast Brussels in the period. Werner Unversagt is the only officer among them and is probably the most reliable. He was an I/H specialist and he covers military espionage cases. Hagemann deals mainly with Ast Brussels' station in Paris. D'Hooghe was a naval specialist and describes Ast Brussels' coastal network. Delgrande is useful for his list of personnel.

(viii) Reports on Kliemann, Cloeren and Speck. This is a selection of reports covering Abwehr activities in France during this period. They are all officers of the Abwehr. Kliemann covers the work of I/Luft in Paris, Cloeren of I/H. at Angers and Speck of III/F also at Angers.

(ix) Report on the German deserter Luipold Haffner. Haffner was employed by the I/M section of KO Spain and gives details of its Gibraltar reporting services as well as of its main: personalities.

(x) Reports on Christensen @ Lucassen; Engels @ ALFREDO; Ottokat Mueller, and Walter Napp. These four were the Abwehr's chief agents in Brazil in 1941-42. Their stories properly belong to the early war years, but they were not rounded up and interrogated until 1942. Christensen was an agent of Ast Kiel I/N; Engels, by far the most important and dangerous of the batch, represented the economic espionage department (I/Wi) of Abwehr headquarters. Mueller and Napp were part of Ast Hamburg's network run by [Friedrich] Obladen and described by [Herbert] Wichmann.

Two other sources are available for this period. The first is the information given by the deserters Vermehren and Hamburger on the work of the Abwehr in Turkey and the Near East. Their evidence greatly expands Ludwig's story which is restricted to counter-espionage.

Vermehren also discusses the decline of the Abwehr in these years and Hansen's efforts to arrest it. His information on this aspect of the Abwehr supplements that of Ledebur and Kuebart. The second source for this period, which does not fall into the class of ordinary interrogations, is the commentary made on the Abwehr by several officers of the Italian intelligence services who surrendered in

> September 1943. The best accounts are given by Major Nani on the Abwehr's work in Tripoli and Tunisia, Colonel di Carlo on the Abwehr in Spain and Spanish Morocco, Major Vaciago on work of Abwehr II and Max Ponzo on Abwehr I/M.[13]

The analysts who collated the files were astonished to discover that the Abwehr employed a staff of more than 20,000 and was a much larger and more complex organisation than had been hinted at in previous MI-14 assessments. The new evaluations also had the benefit of the interrogation reports completed after lengthy interviews with key personnel, principal among them Walter Schellenberg, Erich Pfeiffer, Laurentius Ludwig (Belgrade), Carl Eitel (Berlin), Otto Meissner (Oslo, Angers and Paris), Herbert Wichman and Nikolaus Ritter (Hamburg).

As well as these interviewees, there was supporting testimony from Wurmann (Athens, Berlin, Biarritz and North Africa); Hans Scharf (Spain); Hans Kautz (Berlin and Paris); Ernst Behrens (Hannover, Warsaw and Kassel); Peter Schagen (Lisbon and Paris); Wilhelm Leisner and Ernst Kleyenstuber (Madrid). What emerged from their accounts would change post-war perceptions of the conflict, although few outside the intelligence community would ever be indoctrinated into the full details.

Nigel West

DRAMATIS PERSONAE

Walter Aberle	Abt. II saboteur in Iraq
Donald Adams	Pre-war Abwehr spy in England
Gerhard Addicks	Pre-war Abwehr agent in England
Henry Addicks	South African Abwehr spy in London in 1935
ADOLPHE	I/H stay-behind agent in Marseilles
Heinrich Alhrichs	Pre-war Etappendienst agent in England
Sigurd Alseth	Abwehr spy landed at Lerwick in March 1941 to join SOE
Mori Aoki	Japanese intelligence officer in Ankara
Alfredo Aruajo	PVDE agent, Lisbon
ANCHUR	Norwegian spy for the SD in 1942
Armando Annes	Abwehr, Lisbon
Pierre Arend	Belgian pilot codenamed FATHER
ARMOUR	Luigi Alassi, SIM officer and Abwehr stay-behind agent in Rome
ARTHUR	Abwehr codename for DOLEFUL
ARTIST	MI5 codename for Johannes Jensen
ATOM	Stay-behind agent
Marc Aubert	French naval officer executed January 1939
Prince Karl Adolph Auersperg	Resigned from the Abwehr in Berne in 1944
AUGUSTA	Abwehr spy in Lisbon Renato Roque Laia
Robert Baheshy	Abwehr candidate for MAMMUT II
Norman Baillie-Stewart	British officer imprisoned in 1933
Louis Bakos	Iraqi candidate for MAMMUT II
BASKET	MI5 codename for Joseph Lenihan
Friedrich Baumeister	Leiter, Ast Paris, alias Colonel Rudolf

Johannes Becker	SD Chief in South America
Kurt Beigl	Abwehr defector in Istanbul in August 1944
Captain Benson	NCSO, British Embassy, Lisbon
Herbert J. Berthold	Abt. II deserter in Paris codenamed JIGGER
Ahmed Bey	SIME double agent DOLEFUL
Bibire	Pre-war Abwehr spy in England
Johannes Bischoff	Abwehr officer at Nest Bremen
Ludwig Bischoff	Abwehr cut-out in Dallas
BISCUIT	MI5 double agent Sam McCarthy
BLACKGUARD	SIME double agent Hamdi Khaqqay alias Mirz Khan
Wolfgang Blaum	Alias Friedrich Baumann, head of Abt. II in Madrid until February 1945
BLAZE	Stay-behind agent in Munchen-Gladbach
Gunther Blume	SD officer and member of ANTON captured in Tehran in August 1943
Anthony Blunt	MI5 officer
Corneille Boehme	Dutch spy for the Abwehr detained at Camp 020 in January 1942
Carl Boemelburg	SD Paris
Paul Borchardt	Ast Munich V-Mann arrested in New York in December 1941
Pierre Bourriez	SOE agent arrested in January 1943
Juan Brandes	I/H KOP
Gertrud Brandy	Pre-war Abwehr spy in Dublin
Arthur Breuer	Abwehr agent landed in the US by U-boat in 1941
BRIZO SENIOR	Abwehr codename for Georg Hansen
Harald Bruhn	Abwehr agent detained in August 1940 on meteorological reporting mission
BRUTUS	MI5 codename for Roman Garby-Czerniawski
Erich Buecking	I/M Lisbon
Roberto Buenaga	Spanish officer and Abwehr agent
Karl Burger	Pre-war Abwehr spy in England
CABANON	I/H stay-behind agent in Toulon
John Cairncross	SIS Section V desk officer
Joachim Calca	Abwehr agent, Lisbon

CAMOUFLAGE	Stay-behind agent
Francis P. Campbell	Pre-war Abwehr spy in England
Joachim Canaris	I-H KOS
Wilhelm Canaris	Abwehr Chief until February 1944, codenamed GUILLERMO
CARELESS	MII5 double agent Edward Ejsymont
Goesta Caroli	Abwehr spy parachuted into Cambridgeshire, September 1940
Mathilde Carré	SIS wireless operator codenamed VICTOIRE
Jean Carrere	SD double agent in Paris codenamed KEEL
CELERY	MI5 double agent Walter Dicketts
CHARLIE	MI5 double agent Charles Eschborn
CHEESE	SIS/SIME double agent Renato Levi
Charles Cholmondeley	MI5 officer
COLACO	SIS agent, Lisbon
Axel Coll	Abwehr spy detained in August 1940 while on meteorological reporting mission
COSSACK	Stay-behind agent
COSTA	Abwehr codename for British double agent, a member of PESSIMISTS
Jose Costa	SIS agent, British Consulate, Lisbon
Fritz Cramer	Alias of Ludwig Kramer von Auenrode, Chief, KOP
Mrs Crookes	Pre-war Abwehr spy in England
CROW	Norwegian SD agent arrested in 1942
CRUDE	Turkish businessman and SIS double agent in Iraq
DARIEN	British double agent in Lisbon
G.H. Darragh	Pre-war Abwehr spy in England
DAVIT	French double agent in Paris stay-behind group
Françoise Deeker	Abwehr spy landed in Scotland in September 1940
Jose Antonio Del Campo	German spy in Madrid
DEPUTY	SD stay-behind agent in Antwerp
DERRICK	Stay-behind agent in Bruges
de Renzy	Pre-war Abwehr spy in England
Charles de Salis	SIS Section V in Lisbon

DESIRE	Albert Gabas, double agent in France, 1944
DICTIONARY	Abwehr defector Carl Marcus
Otto Dietergaertner	Abwehr agent arrested in Ireland July 1940
Friedrich Dohse	SD Bordeaux
DOMINANT	SD stay-behind agent in Antwerp
DOMINO	Abwehr codename for DOLEFUL
DOLEFUL	Ahmed Bey, ARTHUR to the Abwehr
DON PEDRO	Bertie Koepke, Nest Barcelona
DOOLITTLE	Polish airman and double agent, recruited by MI5 in October 1940
DRAGOMAN	X-2 codename for double agent Jean Frutos in Cherbourg
DRAGONFLY	MI5 double agent Hans George, codenamed KILLIAN by I/L
Christopher Draper	MI5 double agent terminated in January 1933
Frederick Duquesne	Abwehr spy arrested by the FBI in New York in June 1941
Bernard Durrant	Pre-war Abwehr spy in England
ECCLESIASTIC	Olga Zemanova, SIS agent in Lisbon
Gunnar Edvardsen	Abwehr saboteur arrested in Scotland in October 1941
John Eikens	Stay-behind agent in Cherbourg codenamed PANCHO
Carl Eitel	I/M Lisbon, codenamed ELLERMAN by OSS
Edward Ejsymont	Polish pilot codenamed CARELESS by MI5
ELLERMAN	OSS codename for Carl Eitel
Heinz Engelhorn	Abwehr officer implicated in the 20 July plot
Vera Erikson	Alias of Vera von Schalburg, Abwehr spy landed in Scotland in September 1940
My Eriksson	Abwehr spy detained in London in September 1939
Charles Eschborn	MI5 double agent codenamed CHARLIE

Arnold Evinsen	Abwehr spy posing as Norwegian refugee landed at Lerwick in January 1943
FAN	French double agent and former Fascist
FANK	SD stay-behind double agent in Brussels
Massud Farzad	Persian interpreter on ANTON mission
Waldemar Fast	SD in Istanbul
FATHER	MI5 double agent Pierre Arend
FEDERICO	Abwehr codename for Friedrich Knappe-Ratey in Madrid
Mario Ferreira	Abwehr agent, Lisbon
Paul Fidrmuc	Czech fabricator in Lisbon codenamed OSTRO
Ulrich von Finkenstein	Abwehr agent on meteorological reporting mission, detained in August 1940
FISH	Stay-behind agent
FOREST	Lucien Herviou, French stay-behind agent
FORGE	SD stay-behind agent
FRANK	SD double agent in Brussels
Richard Frauedorf	Etappendienst agent expelled from London in 1938
FREELANCE	Three parachute agents
Jean Frutos	X-2 double agent codenamed DRAGOMAN
Engelbertus Fukken	Abwehr spy, alias Jan Willem Ter Braak, parachuted into Buckinghamshire in November 1940
Lisel Gaertner	MI5 double agent codenamed GELATINE
Alfred Gaessler	SIS radio operator, defector to the Abwehr
GANDER	MI5 codename for double agent Kart Goose
GAOL	Stay-behind agent in Paris
Roman Garby-Czerniawski	Polish SIS agent codenamed WALENTY and BRUTUS
Hans Otto Gast	Czech spy in the Abwehr

GAT	French-controlled stay-behind agent
Ludwig Gehre	Abwehr Abt. III
GELATINE	MI5 double agent Lisel Gaertner
Wilhelm Gessmann	Alias Alexander, German spy in Lisbon
GILBERT	BCRA codename for André Latham
Karel van Gils	Belgian seaman detained at Camp 020
GIRAFFE	MI5 double agent Georges Graf
GIRRANT	Stay-behind agent
Hermann Giskes	III/F in Paris, The Hague and Brussels
Tor Glad	MI5 double agent codenamed JEFF
GLASS	Stay-behind agent
Hermann Goertz	German spy arrested in England in 1935
Willy Goetz	Hungarian journalist in Istanbul and SME detainee in November 1944
GOLD	I/H source in Istanbul
GOLDFLAKE	Stay-behind agent in Marseilles
Karl Goose	MI5 double agent codenamed GANDER
Hans Graepe	Member of the FRANZ mission to Iraq in March 1943
Georges Graf	MI5 double agent codenamed GIRAFFE
Georg Grille	SD member of the FRANZ mission to Iraq in March 1943
Martin Grimaldi	MI5 B1(a) officer
Carl Grundell	Swedish seaman and I/M agent arrested at Gibraltar in February 1945
Andur Gross	Abwehr agent and SIME detainee in 1943
GUILLERMO	Abwehr codename for Admiral Canaris
GULL	Abwehr spy Elie Haggar, sent to Egypt December 1942
Viktor Guryevich	GRU illegal codenamed KENT
John Gwyer	MI5 officer
Andre Gyorgy	Alias of Andur Gross
Werner von Haeften	Aide to Colonel Count von Stauffenburg
Luipold Haffner	Abwehr defector in Madrid, August 1945

Elie Haggar	Abwehr spy in Egypt codenamed GULL
Jawad Hamada	Abwehr spy captured on the *U-572*
Mahmoud Hamada	Abwehr spy codenamed ROMEO in Syria
Willi Hamburger	Abwehr defector in Istanbul
Georg Hansen	Chief, Abwehr Abt. II, codenamed BRIZO SENIOR
Kurt Hansen	Danish Abwehr agent detained in August 1940 on meteorological reporting mission
Kurt Harbers	SD radio operator for the ANTON mission captured in Persia in March 1944
HARDY	Abt. II saboteur Wilhelm Hoffmann
Hans Harnisch	SD representative in Argentina
HATCHET	MI5 double agent Albert de Jaeger
Osmar Hellmuth	Argentine envoy arrested in Trinidad
HELMUTH	SIME double agent SCEPTIC
Lucien Hervious	Stay-behind agent codenamed FOREST
Stephen Hill-Dillon	Allied Counter-Intelligence Chief Mediterranean
Otto Hinrischen	Abwehr, Bilbao
HITTITE	MI5 double agent recruited by the German consul in New Orleans
Wilhelm Hoffmann	Abt. II saboteur in Iraq codenamed HARDY captured in July 1943
Dr Holm	Czech spy in the Abwehr, alias Paul Thummel, arrested in March 1942
Hans Holzapel	Radio operator on the FRANZ mission to Iraq in March 1943
HOSIERY	SIME codename for Willi Hamburger
HOST	Stay-behind agent
HOSTESS	Stay-behind agent
Gerhard Huntemann	III/F in The Hague and Brussels
Jack Ivens	SIS Section V, Madrid
JACQUES	I/M stay-behind agent in Marseilles
JAEGER	Abwehr codename for Otto John
Adolf Jaeger	Pre-war Etappendienst agent in England, expelled in 1938

Albert de Jaeger	Belgian detainee at Camp 020 codenamed HATCHET
Kurt Jahnke	German intelligence officer
Dietrich Jakobs	Pre-war Etappendienst agent in England
Josef Jakobs	Abwehr spy parachuted into Huntingdonshire in March 1941
Ralph Jarvis	SIS Section V, Lisbon
JEANNOT	I/H stay-behind agent
Johannes Jebsen	Abwehr officer codenamed ARTIST by SIS
JEFF	MI5 codename for double agent Tor Glad
Paulino de Jesus	SIS source on the Abwehr in Lisbon
JIGGER	Herbert J. Berthold, Abwehr NCO in Paris
Invald Johansen	Abwehr spy landed at Lerwick in March 1941 to join SOE
Otto John	Abwehr defector codenamed WHISKY by SIS and JAEGER by Berlin
Otto Joost	Abwehr spy arrested in Nairn in October 1940
Franz Jordan	Abwehr agent arrested in Brazil in 1942
Jessie Jordan	Abwehr postbox in Dundee arrested in March 1938
Leon Jude	Belgian Sabena pilot and Abwehr spy detained at Camp 020, June 1942
JUNIOR	SIS codename for Abwehr defector Hans Ruser
Joe K	Kurt Ludwig
Ernst Kaltenbrunner	SD Chief
Otto Kamler	Amt. I, KOP
Richard Kauder	Abwehr officer alias Fritz Klatt
KEEL	Jean Carrere, SD double agent in Paris
KELLER	Stay-behind agent
Joseph Kelly	Pre-war Abwehr spy in England
KENT	GRU illegal Viktor Guryevich
KEYNOTE	Stay-behind agent
Mizra Khan	I/M agent codenamed SHAROCK
Charles van der Kieboom	Abwehr spy landed in Kent in September 1940

Bernie Kiener	MI5 double agent codenamed RAINBOW
KILLIAN	I/L spy Hans George codenamed DRAGONFLY by MI5
KINGPIN	MI5 double agent
KISS	Double agent Mohamed Salmassi
Fritz Klatt	Alias of Richard Kauder
Karl von Kleczkowsky	Abt. III defector in Istanbul
Stella von Kleczkowsky	Abt. III defector in Istanbul
Ernst Kleyenstuber	Leiter KOS from September 1944
Emile Kliemann	I/L Paris
Friedrich Knappe-Ratey	Abt. I officer in Madrid, codenamed FEDERICO
Simon Koedel	Ast Hamburg agent arrested in New York in March 1945
Ernest Kondgen	Abt. II wireless operator on ANTON mission, arrested in Tehran in August 1943
Georg Konieczny	Abt. II saboteur captured in Iraq in June 1943.
Karl Korel	Abt. II wireless operator on ANTON mission to Iraq in 1943
Ludwig Kramer von Auenrode	Leiter KOP, alias von Karstoff, codenamed LUDOVICO
Georg Kronberger	SD defector in Greece in September 1944
Wilhelm Kuebart	I/H Berlin
KUPPER	I/H source in Istanbul
Martin Kurmes	Leader of ANTON, committed suicide in March 1944
Josef Kuvett	SIS double agent codenamed MIMI
Ernst Lahmann	Etappendienst agent expelled from London in 1938
Erwin Lahousen	Chief, Abt. II until 1944
Fred Lang	Abwehr spy convicted September 1945
Ilya Lang	Associate of General Turkul
Alfred Langbein	I/M agent delivered to the US by the *U-213* in May 1942
LARK	Norwegian SD agent Herluf Nygaard
Andre Latham	BCRA double agent codenamed GILBERT

Joseph Laurenssens	Belgian seaman detained at Camp 020
LAZY	Stay-behind agent in Munchen-Gladbach
LEAGUE	Stay-behind agent
Josef Ledebur	Abwehr defector in Madrid
LEGION	Abt. III stay-behind agent
Wilhelm Leisner	Leiter, KOS until September 1944, alias Lenz
LENA	Abwehr operation to support 1940 invasion
Joseph Lenihan	MI5 double agent codenamed BASKET
Renato Levi	Codenamed CHEESE by MI5 and ROBERTO by the Abwehr
Renato Roque Liai	Portuguese spy in London
LIBERATORS	Abt. II mission to Iraq
Gerard Libot	Abwehr spy arrested in Plymouth in September 1940
Cecil Liddell	Head MI5's Irish section, B9
Guy Liddell	Director, MI5's B Division
LITIGANT	Stay-behind agent
Robert Lochner	I/M KONO
Walter Lohrey	Abwehr agent arrested in New Jersey in November 1944
Peter Loxley	Foreign Office Under-Secretary
LUC	I/L stay-behind agent in Dragignan
Kurt Ludwig	Abwehr spy 'Joe K' arrested in the United States in December 1941
Legwald Lund	Abwehr saboteur arrested in Scotland in October 1941
Graham Maingot	SIS in Lisbon
Richard L'Estrange Malone	Pre-war SIS double agent
MAMMUT II	Abt. II mission to Iraq
Maria Marek	MI5 double agent codenamed THE SNARK
Carl Marcus	Abwehr defector codenamed DICTIONARY
MARCHAND	I/H stay-behind agent in Grenoble
Hans Marschner	Alias adopted in Eire by Gunter Schutz
Otto Mayer	Abwehr officer captured in Yugoslavia
Franz Mayr	SD officer captured in Iraq in September 1943

Sam McCarthy	MI5 double agent codenamed BISCUIT
MEADOW	SD line-crosser
Albert Meems	Animal dealer and I/H Hamburg agent
Carl Meier	Abwehr spy landed on Kent coast in September 1940.
Rogerio de Menezes	Portuguese diplomat arrested in London
Merckl	Abwehr officer in Lisbon
Friedrich W. Meyer	Pre-war Abwehr spy in England
Cyril Mills	MI5 officer
MIMI	Josef Kuvett, SIS double agent in Istanbul
MINT	SD stay-behind double agent
MODEL	Stay-behind agent
John Moe	MI5 double agent codenamed MUTT
MONARCH	Stay-behind agent
MONOPLANE	Paul Jeannin, stay-behind agent in Marseilles
MONTAG	Abwehr agent in Spain. Employee of the German-French Mining Co.
MONUMENT	Stay-behind agent in Paris
Ludwig Moyzisch	SD representative in Ankara
MULETER	Stay-behind agent
Gottfried Müller	Abt. II saboteur in Iraq codenamed TIGER, captured in June 1943
MURAT	Abwehr codename for Otto Mayer
MUTT	MI5 codename for double agent John Moe
Dietrich Niebuhr	Abwehr representative in Argentina
Willem Niemayer	SIS agent arrested in Holland in 1942
Fritz Noak	Abwehr agent arrested in Brazil in January 1942
Henry Obed	Abwehr agent arrested in Ireland in July 1940
Daniel Ocana	Detainee at Camp 020
Martin Olsen	Abwehr spy arrested in September 1941
Waldemar Othmer	Abwehr spy arrested in Trenton, New Jersey in July 1944
Arthur Owens	MI5 double agent codenamed SNOW

PABLO	Leiter, Nest Barcelona
Vaclav Pan	Head of Czech intelligence in Lisbon
PANCHO	John Eiikens, double agent in Cherbourg
Heinz Pannwitz	Alias of Heinz Paulsen
PASCHA	Spaniard in Cairo represented in Istanbul by Guelfo Zamboni
PASTURES	MI5 codename for a German spy who arrived from Lisbon in June 1941
Gottfried Paul-Taboschat	Leiter, Nest Barcelona
Heinz Paulsen	Sonderkommando ROTE KAPELLE, alias Heinz Pannwitz
PEDRO	Alberto Koepke, I/H Barcelona
Jean Pelletier	SIS radio operator alias Lacoste and Abwehr spy arrested in London in April 1942
PENKNIFE	Stay-behind agent
PENNANT	Stay-behind agent in Paris
PERCY	Stay-behind agent
PERRIER	Stay-behind agent
PESSIMISTS	British-controlled network of double agents
Waldemar von Petroff	Chief agent of the Buro Jahnke
Robert Petter	Abwehr spy landed in Scotland, September 1940
Erich Pfeiffer	I/M Bremen
Kim Philby	SIS officer in Section V, then Section IX
PIE	Ferdinand Rodriguez-Reddington
PIGEON	British double agent in Lisbon
Isabel Pilderit	Abwehr agent in Valparaiso
PIP	Finnish seaman double agent
Kurt Pirwanko	SD radio operator for the ANTON mission captured in Persia in March 1944
POGO	MI5 codename for Miguel del Pozo
Sjoerd Pons	Abwehr spy landed on the Kent coast in September 1940
Dusko Popov	MI5 double agent codenamed TRICYCLE
Walter Praetorius	I/Wi Ast Hamburg
PRECIOUS	SIS codename for Erich Vermehren

Willi Preetz	Abwehr agent interned in Ireland in July 1940
John Price	British double agent in Lisbon codenamed WASHOUT
Juan Pujol	V-Mann 319, codenamed GARBO by MI5, IMMORTAL and BOVRIL by SIS, ALARIC by the Abwehr
PUMPKIN	SIS agent in Lisbon
QUALITY	Abwehr stay-behind officer in Kaiserslautern
QUEASY	Stay-behind agent
RAINBOW	MI5 codename for Bernie Kiener
Nafti Rashid Ramzi	Iraqi interpreter arrested in July 1943
Percy Rapp	London taxi driver and Abwehr spy
Heinrich Reimers	Abwehr agent in Valparaiso
Karel Richter	Abwehr spy parachuted into Hertfordshire in May 1941
Gene Risso-Gill	SIS, Lisbon
Jose Rist	Abwehr spy in Union City, New Jersey
T.A. Robertson	Head of MI5's B1(a) section
Werner Rockstroh	SD member of the FRANZ mission to Iraq in 1943
Ferdinand Rodriguez-Reddington	SIS agent codenamed PIE
Kurt von Rohrscheidt	Leiter, Amt III, KOS
William Rolph	Ex-MI5 officer, committed suicide in May 1940
George Romanov	General Turkul's assistant
ROMEO	Mahmoud Hamada
Gustav Ronning	Abwehr spy arrested September 1941
Renato Roque Laia	Abwehr spy in Lisbon codenamed AUGUSTA
Rudolf Roser	Etappendienst agent expelled from London in 1938
ROSIE	Stay-behind agent
Mirko Rot	Yugoslav spy for the Abwehr, arrested in London in December 1943
Gunther Rumrich	Abwehr spy arrested by the FBI in February 1937
Hans Ruser	Abwehr defector codenamed JUNIOR by SIS
Gilbert Ryle	Radio Security Service cryptanalyst

Olaf Saetrang	Abwehr spy landed at Reykjavik in September 1941
Charles de Salis	SIS Section V officer in Lisbon
Mohamed Salmassi	Double agent KISS
SCEPTIC	Notional double agent known to the Abwehr as HELMUTH
Peter Schagen	Abt. II defector in Madrid
Vera von Schalburg	Abwehr spy alias Vera Erikson
Fritz Scharpf	Pre-war Etappendienst agent in England, expelled in 1938
Walter Schellenberg	Chief, Amt VI
Gottfried Schenker-Angerer	I/L Istanbul
Ernst Schmidt	Abwehr, Oporto
Wolf Schmidt	MI5 double agent TATE, alias Harry Williamson
Gunther Schallies	Etappendienst agent expelled from London in 1938
Aloys Schreiber	I/H, then Leiter KOP
Erich Schroeder	SD Chief, Lisbon
Wilhelm Schulze	German journalist and Abwehr agent in London until August 1939
Berthold Schulze-Holthus	I/L stay-behind agent in Persia, freed in prisoner exchange
Gunter Schutz	Abwehr agent arrested in Dublin in March 1941
Heriberto Schwartau-Eskildsen	Abwehr agent arrested by the FBI in October 1941
Otto Schwerdt	Radio operator of the FRANZ mission to Iraq in March 1943
Stanley Scott	Pre-war Abwehr spy in Southampton
Duncan Scott-Ford	British seaman and Abwehr spy executed in England
SHAROCK	Mirza Khan
Mario Shumann	Abwehr officer, Lisbon
SILBER	I/H source in Istanbul
Juan da Silva Purvis	Abwehr spy arrested in New Jersey in 1943
Arnold Silver	US Army interrogator
Ernesto Simoes	Portuguese spy arrested in England
Walter Simon	Abwehr agent expelled from England in March 1938, interned in Ireland in June 1940

SISYPHUS	SIS agent in Lisbon
SKULL	Double agent Jean Senouque in Cherbourg
THE SNARK	Maria Marek, a Yugoslav domestic servant and MI5 double agent
SNOW	MI5 double agent Arthur Owens
Robert Solborg	OSS Chief in Lisbon
Thorleif Solem	Abwehr spy landed at Lerwick in March 1941 to join SOE
SOMER	Abwehr codename for Leiter, KOS
Dante Souza	SIS agent, British Consulate, Lisbon
George Speich	I/M officer
STANDARD	Stay-behind agent in Rouen
Claus von Stauffenburg	Failed assassin and 20 July conspirator
Florent Steiner	Dutch seaman and Abwehr spy arrested in Liverpool in December 1942
Michel Stockmann	I/M Paris
Richmond Stopford	SIS station commander, Lisbon
Adolf Striepe	Abwehr spy arrested in Jackson Heights, New York in September 1945
STRIPE	MI5 double agent
Theodor Struenck	Abwehr officer implicated in 20 July plot
SUMMER	MI5 codename for Goesta Caroli
TATE	MI5 codename for Wolf Schmidt
Jan Willem Ter Braak	Alias of Engelbertus Fukken
THISBE	Ast Paris agent arrested in London in July 1941
Hans Thost	Pre-war *Volkischer Beobachter* correspondent in London
Paul Thummel	Alias of Dr Holm
Theodore Tietz	Pre-war Abwehr spy in England
TIGER	Abwehr codename for Gottfried Müller
Alphonse Timmerman	Belgian hanged in London in July 1942
Herbert Tributh	Abwehr agent arrested in Ireland in July 1940
TRICYCLE	MI5 double agent Dusko Popov
Anton Turkul	White Russian at KOBU
Robert Ulshofer	I/L Istanbul
Werner Unland	I/Wi Ast Hamburg spy in Dublin from August 1939 until arrested in April 1941

Klop Ustinov	MI5 agent U.35 alias Mr Johnson
Jack Verlinden	Belgian spy detained at Camp 020 in January 1942
Erich Vermehren	I/H defector in Istanbul, codenamed PRECIOUS
VICTOIRE	Mathilde Carré
VIPER	SIS double agent at the Hotel Aviz in Lisbon
Eduard Waetjen	Abwehr defector in Switzerland in 1944
Otto Wagner	Leiter Ast Sofia, alias Dr Delius
José Waldberg	Abwehr spy landed on the Kent coast in September 1940
WALENTY	Roman Garby-Czerniawski
Helmik Wallem	Abwehr spy posing as Norwegian refugee arrested in Scotland in May 1941
Werner Wälti	Abwehr spy landed in Scotland in September 1940
Ludwig Warschauer	Abwehr agent in London interned in 1940
WASHOUT	British codename for John Price
Erwin Wassner	Pre-war German naval attaché in London
Waldemar Weber	Abt. II spy in Iraq
WEASEL	Dr Hilaire Westerlinck, Belgian ship's doctor and MI5 double agent
Kuno Weltzien	Abwehr, Lisbon
Hilaire Westerlinck	MI5 double agent codenamed WEASEL
WHISKY	SIS codename for Otto John
Gerth van Wijk	Abwehr spy landed at Whitchurch in April 1941
Tarleton Winchester	Pan Am representative in Lisbon
Rita Winsor	SIS in Lisbon
Herbert Winterstein	Abwehr spy arrested in Brazil in January 1942
William Wishart	Pre-war Abwehr spy in England
WITCH	Stay-behind agent
Bruno Wolf	SD in Istanbul
Friedrich Wolf	SD in Buenos Aires
YODLER	SIS double agent in Switzerland
Edgar Yolland	Abwehr spy in OWI Istanbul
Kurt Zaehringer	I/M Istanbul
Guelfo Zamboni	Italian journalist in Istanbul
Olga Zemanova	ECCELSIASTIC in Lisbon

Chapter I

PRE-WAR

> My [Eriksson] is an extremely clever woman, a brilliant actress and a consummate liar.
>
> Richard Butler, MI5, 20 June 1941[1]

Prior to the outbreak of war in September 1939 there were at least four German intelligence agencies operating with a measure of independence, in parallel with each other, collecting intelligence mainly against France, the United Kingdom and the United States. Their efforts consisted of sending individual agents on short-term missions, and the recruitment of disaffected or disadvantaged military personnel.

During this period MI5 learned of thirty German agents or potential recruits that experienced an approach or 'pitch'. Of these, twenty-one were British, and most made no attempt to pass on intelligence of any value to the Germans, but did relay insignificant items in a bid to obtain maximum reward for minimum effort. Typically, they received no training, and half the cases involved people who were never in a position to procure anything that could be construed as valuable information. Among the thirty were four ex-officers, four businessmen and four members of the armed forces; most of them reported the approach to the authorities immediately, and their accounts were quite similar. In many cases the targets had responded to small advertisements in the newspapers, explicitly aimed at ex-officers, businessmen and specialists with technical knowledge seeking jobs. This methodology was adopted from 1936 by the Hamburg Abwehrstelle in particular, involving twenty-six of the thirty known cases. This represented a very considerable escalation of activity, but the Abwehr appeared to channel their communications through just three 'post-drops', one each in England, Scotland and Ireland. These same addresses were also employed for suspect correspondence from the United States and France.

Eleven of the thirty supposed recruits informed MI5 about the German approach; nine were exposed by mail intercepts, five were denounced by private individuals whose suspicions had been aroused, one was reported by an immigration officer, one was denounced by an anonymous informant, and the other two were uncovered by accident. Of the eleven agents who reported they had been recruited, who would probably have escaped detection, six had been contacted in person.

One of those ex-officers who was sounded out about becoming an agent was Major Christopher Draper, a well-known air ace who was propositioned while attended a Munich air show in July 1933 by Dr Hans Thost, the London correspondent of the Nazi newspaper *Volkischer Beobachter*.[2] Thost's work permit was not renewed in November 1935 so Draper had been instructed in February 1936 to send his reports to 'Postfach 629, Hamburg', an address that was then monitored by MI5.

The interception of mail to the Hamburg address revealed that the same postbox was the recipient of correspondence from Jessie Jordan, a 51-year-old hairdresser of Kinloch Street, Dundee. The widow of a German soldier killed during the First World War, Jordan had spent most of her adult life in Germany and had returned to Dundee to open a small business. At the age of 16 she ran away from her mother (she never knew her father) and found a job as a domestic servant. Four years later she had met a German named Jordan in Scotland and returned with him to Germany where they were wed. After the war she had married again but had subsequently obtained a divorce from her second husband. Eventually she had returned to Scotland, partly in disgust at the anti-Jewish treatment she had witnessed, although she was not herself a Jew. Apparently, the name Jordan, a name she had readopted after the failure of her second marriage, had Jewish significance. By the end of 1936 MI5 had established that not only was the hairdresser receiving an unusual amount of mail, but she was posting a great deal too, and the bulk of her post went to America. She also received letters from Holland, France, Germany, Sweden and South America.[3]

MI5 intercepted Jordan's mail and learned that she was acting as a postbox for the Abwehr, so at the end of January 1937 the Deputy Director of MI5's B Division, Guy Liddell, went to Washington, D.C. and explained to the Director of the FBI, J. Edgar Hoover, that Mrs Jordan had been in communication with a 'Mr Kron' in New York. Hoover checked the address and established that 'Herr Kron' was Günther Rumrich, a Sudeten German who had become a naturalised

American. His record showed that he had served seven years in the Army and had been sentenced for desertion and embezzlement of mess funds from Fort Missoula in Montana. The FBI kept Rumrich under surveillance so the Jordan postbox could be monitored but on 16 February 1937 he was arrested by detectives from the Aliens Squad after a tip-off from the State Department. Rumrich had been taken into custody after a bizarre attempt to obtain a quantity of blank American passports by impersonating a senior State Department official, Edward Weston, an Under-Secretary of State.

Apparently Rumrich had been instructed by Karl Schleuter, a steward on the SS *Europa,* to obtain fifty passports for the Abwehr. Just as the FBI were being told about MI5's suspicions concerning Rumrich, the State Department's New York Passport Office had asked the Aliens Squad to investigate a phoney request for fifty blank passports which were to be delivered to the Taft Hotel.[4]

After his arrest Rumrich confessed that after he had read Colonel Walter Nicolai's memoirs he had written to the Berlin *Volkischer Beobachter*, the major Nazi daily, offering his services. He asked that if the Germans were interested in the information that 'a high official in the United States Army' could pass they should place an advertisement in the *New York Times*. It was to read: 'Theodor Koerner – Letter received' and give an address where he could contact the Abwehr. In the event the Abwehr had instructed him to reply to 'Sanders, Postbox 629, Hamburg 1, Germany'. The announcement duly appeared on 6 April 1936 and 'Herr Kron' and Rumrich went into action. He operated for 20 months between May 1936 and February 1938 and succeeded in passing a considerable amount of intelligence back to Hamburg via 1 Kinloch Street, Dundee.

Under interrogation Rumrich revealed that apart from Mrs Jordan his contact with the Abwehr had been by a courier, Karl Schleuter, employed as a steward on the *Europa,* and his girlfriend, Johanna Hofmann, an American from Queens but born in Dresden, who was working on the same liner as a hairdresser. Hofmann was promptly arrested by the FBI which pursued numerous other leads. Among the suspects incriminated in the spy-ring were Erich Glasser, a soldier based at Mitchell Field, Long Island with the 18th Reconnaissance Squadron; William Lonkowski, an aircraft mechanic from Silesia who had worked in various American aircraft factories until an incident with US Customs in September 1935; Eleanor Boehme, apparently an occasional courier, resident in Long Island; Werner Gudenberg, a young engineering draughtsman; Otto Voss, who worked for the Sikorsky factory at Farmingdale, Long Island;

Johann Steuer, an inspector at the Sperry Gyroscope bombsight factory in Brooklyn; Johann Koechel, of the Kollmorgan Optical Corporation, engaged in the manufacture of submarine periscopes; Dr Ignatz Giebl, a First World War artillery officer, graduate of Fordham University and a US Army Reserve physician in the Medical Corps; and Theodor Scheutz, a steward of the SS *New York* who disembarked in Havana as soon as the arrests were announced. A Grand Jury investigation was started and the Abwehr officer at the centre of the operation, Erich Phieffer (alias 'N. Spielman', 'Dr Erdhoff' and merely 'Herr Doktor') was identified as the major conspirator, based at Wilhelmshaven.

Mrs Jordan was arrested on 2 March 1938 and when her house was searched the police found a rather amateurish sketch map of Fife and a list of Coastguard stations between Montrose and Kirkcaldy. Jordan admitted her espionage and confirmed she had received various small sums for her service to the Abwehr. Accordingly, on 15 May 1938 she was sentenced to four years' imprisonment, which she served at Perth prison. Liddell felt strongly that MI5's hand had been forced prematurely by the FBI's precipitate intervention, but he was powerless to influence Hoover. Instead, he prevailed upon the American authorities to exercise discretion over references to the Hamburg postbox so as to avoid alerting the Germans to the double role played by Draper, who was described as a patriotic Englishman who should not be compromised. MI5 also engaged in some deliberate distraction by briefing the press that Jordan's unusually heavy foreign mail had alerted her local postman who had reported his suspicions to the authorities. In reality, of course, she had fallen victim to the domino effect of related cases. Furthermore, although there was a theoretical need to protect Draper, his utility was long over because of MI5's inability to keep him supplied with information that was of any value to the Germans. In short, it simply had not been possible to continue fobbing them off with worthless material, a fundamental flaw in the organisation's ability to manage double agents.

Draper's termination, or perhaps the suspicion that he had come under British control, may have been a factor in the Abwehr's change of strategy which manifested itself in July 1935 with the arrival of Hermann Goertz, a respected Hamburg lawyer who, based in a rented furnished bungalow in Stanley Road, Broadstairs, had undertaken a sketch and photographic survey by motorcycle of RAF airfields in southern England ranging from Launceston in Cornwall to Mildenhall in Suffolk. On this mission he was accompanied by his 19-year-old secretary, Marianne Emig.

Goertz would be arrested in Harwich in October 1935 as he returned to England on the basis that some incriminating documents had been found at his rented home where his landlady had reported a stolen motorcycle, thereby triggering a police search of the property. Goertz, a pilot in the First World War and an interrogator of Allied prisoners, was an experienced intelligence officer and was sentenced to four years' imprisonment for breaches of the Official Secrets Act, and was deported in February 1939.

MI5's investigation of Goertz, which only really concluded after his suicide in Ireland in May 1947, decided that, at best, the airman had been a probationer who had been attempting to re-join the Luftwaffe, and that his self-appointed mission had not represented a change in the Abwehr's methodology or policy. This view would later be confirmed by post-war interviews which showed that Goertz had not been a deliberately stubborn recipient of Colonel Edward Hinchley-Cooke's methods of interrogation, but he genuinely knew nothing about the Abwehr.[5]

British knowledge of the organisation would remain almost non-existent until July 1938 when SIS's station commander in Prague, Archie Gibson, circulated a comprehensive eight-page organisational analysis which had been acquired by the Czechs and shared by Colonel Frantisek Moravec. The document, entitled *Organisation of Military Counter-Espionage*, was dated 13 November 1937 and had been compiled from a memorandum which had been drafted after an Abwehr III conference held on 20 October.

At that time Moravec had the benefit of two Abwehr sources. The first, Hans Otto Gast, had been rejected by the Hamburg police academy and in an act of revenge had volunteered to spy for the Czechs. However, he was tracked down by an III/F officer, Heinz Schmalschlaeger, and persuaded to become a double agent. The second source was Dr Holm, alias Paul Thummel, the holder of a Nazi Party gold badge who had volunteered to pass information to the Czechs in 1936, and who would be arrested in Prague in March 1942 by a Gestapo officer, Willi Abendschoen, imprisoned, but never prosecuted.

The fallout from the FBI's arrest of Rumrich was considerable, and led to his brother Gustav, then a student at Teplice in Czechoslovakia. When he was detained for questioning, he was found to be in possession of the address of Mrs Gertrud Brandy at 14 Willow Terrace, Dublin, which turned out to be the Abwehr's second mail-drop. Clandestine examination of her correspondence showed that she was receiving accurate and therefore dangerous intelligence messages from a French merchant navy officer, Ensign Marc Aubert, who was arrested at the end of 1938 and shot in January 1939. When news of the execution reached Ireland, Mrs Brandy fled to Germany, unhindered by the Irish G-2 which had kept her under surveillance at MI5's request.

The third Abwehr mail-drop to be identified by MI5, inadvertently compromised by Gustav Rumrich, was Mrs Duncombe of 90 Broadhurst Gardens in north London. Accordingly, in July 1937 she became the subject of a Home Office warrant to intercept her mail, an expedient which revealed her instructions the following month to pay a German visitor, Walter Simon, the sum of £5 upon application. Coincidentally, Simon was also the subject of a report from MI5's source inside the German embassy, U.35, who disclosed that Simon had approached the embassy for financial help, a request that had been rejected, but clearly had been the cause of some consternation and communications with Berlin.

Investigated by MI5, Simon turned out to be a figure of some importance, having visited England three times, in July via Harwich, September via Folkestone and finally via Harwich in October 1937. Born in Elberfelde in December 1881, he had joined the Kaisermarine in 1904 and had been captured at sea in 1914, causing him to be interned in Australia throughout the First World War, and could easily pass as an Englishman. He was placed under observation by the police and seen to take notes at an RAF barrage balloon site in Kidbrooke, Kent, in February 1938, and to sketch Hendon aerodrome. These incidents prompted his arrest in London on a charge of having failed to register as an alien, which resulted in a prison sentence of five months, served at Wormwood Scrubs, and his deportation from Grimsby in July 1938. In spite of the overwhelming evidence of his espionage, Simon was not prosecuted under the Official Secrets Act, which would have involved a much longer sentence, most likely because of the need to protect MI5's continuing valuable sources inside the German embassy, the existence of whom might have been at risk of disclosure in any trial.[6]

Examination of Simon's diary and notebooks, and an interrogation conducted by MI5's Edward Hinchley-Cooke, revealed that his mission had been to complete a reconnaissance of various airfields, and to interview nine individuals who apparently were candidates for recruitment as agents. They were a Hungarian journalist, E. Abel of 43 Porchester Square, who would be deported in January 1939; William A. Garner of 8 King Street and 17 Havelock Road, Oxford; George Billings of 86 St Mary's Road, Tunbridge Wells; Bernard Durrant of 310 Southbourne Grove, Westcliff-on-Sea; E. Gregory of 1-2 New Street; F.C. Gorenson of 7 Edeline Avenue; Norbury; Reveoz of 47 Coram

Street; Frank Smith, an unemployed engineer of 2 Webster Gardens, Ealing; and a Mr Gardner of 1-3 St Paul's Church Road. London.

MI5 tried to trace all nine suspects and cleared some of them, apart from Reveoz and Gardner, who could not be found, and Bernard Durrant who turned up in Egypt where he surrendered himself and was detained for the duration. An attempt was made by Security Intelligence Middle East to establish contact with his Abwehr controllers, but when this failed he was sent back to England.

Under interrogation Simon gave an account of his recruitment, and independently named 'Dr Rantzau' (later identified as Nikolaus Ritter) as the Abstelle leiter in Hamburg who had assigned him his mission. His information would be corroborated by another agent, My Eriksson,

Simon would later turn up in Ireland in May 1940, and be arrested a month later and interned for the remainder of the war. His London contact Mrs Duncombe was also investigated by MI5 and was revealed to be a 49-year-old widow of German origin. Born Else Schmidt, she had married a Somerset-born electrical engineer, William Duncombe, in Chelsea in 1931, when she was a divorcee, but she took her own life on 3 March with an overdose of aspirin, three weeks after Simon was arrested.

Simon was also in contact in January 1938 with My Eriksson, a woman who arrived in Southampton in February 1930 to be employed as a cook and housekeeper in Roehampton by a Major and Mrs Macphie, and in a succession of large homes. From 1936 she worked for Lord Derwent, Lady Elveden, The Hon Mrs Freddy Cripps, and Sir Walter Windham. Although she invariably described herself as a Swedish widow, she was actually a German, born in Kassel in 1892, and a divorcee, having left her husband Erik in 1926. She was arrested as she attempted in December 1939 to leave Gravesend for Rotterdam and was interrogated by Edward Hinchley-Cooke. She was convicted in January 1940 of various immigration offences, served three months' imprisonment, and then was interned at Holloway and on the Isle of Man. At her trial Lord Derwent, then serving as an honorary attaché at the British embassy in Berne, gave her a character reference.

MI5's investigation of Eriksson, conducted by Richard Butler, confirmed that as well as Simon, she had been in contact with two other agents, one of whom, the Duchesse de Chateau-Thierry, she had introduced to Dr Rantzau. The other, Vera von Schalburg, was a spy who would land in Scotland in September 1940 accompanied by two other Abwehr agents.[7] Evidently Eriksson had cultivated a wide circle of domestic staff, many of them foreign-born, who were employed by the higher echelons of London society, such as the artist Sir Timothy Eden, Lady George Cholmondeley, and the Viscount Elveden, an heir to the Guinness dynasty. Among those befriended by Eriksson was Olive Scott, then working as a maid at 10 Downing Street. Although Eriksson admitted her connections with the impecunious, Dutch-born Duchesse de Chateau-Thierry, who played the role of hostess at her regular *salon* in Mayfair, she resolutely refused during her internment to reveal the identity of two other of Rantzau's agents, even when she had been offered inducements by MI5's Jock Whyte and threatened with dire consequences.[8]

Mathilde Claudius was another example of Rantzau's tradecraft of establishing long-term agents in England. Born in Hamburg in January 1872 she had married a German, Carl Krafft, who owned a coconut plantation in Fiji.[9] He had naturalised British in 1872 but died in 1918, and three years later his widow moved to England and in 1922 bought a large detached house in Clifton Road, Bournemouth where she adopted a daughter, Editha Dargel who eventually moved to Copenhagen.

In September 1940 an MI5 double agent, codenamed SNOW, began to receive payments in cash of £25 in £5 notes delivered in the mail in handwritten envelopes addressed to 'T Wilson, 9 Norbiton Avenue, Kingston', which had been posted in Bournemouth, Southampton and London, respectively.[10] Through some impressive sleuthing, the banknotes were traced back to Mrs Krafft who came under surveillance until she was detained in July 1941. She had also acted as a paymaster for Eugene Horsfall-Ertz, a pro-Nazi journalist and broadcaster of German extraction who, under interrogation, identified Mrs Krafft as a woman she had met by appointment in Southampton railway station in November 1939 who had handed him £18 to pay for his travel to Berlin via a neutral country.[11] On this evidence Krafft was detained for the remainder of the war, but she resolutely refused to incriminate herself.

As Guy Liddell would later acknowledge in 1943, while addressing an audience of MI5 officers, 'this double agent saved us from absolute darkness on the subject of German espionage'.[12] SNOW would become the foundation of MI5's double cross strategy and transform MI5's counter-intelligence doctrine, an innovation that would literally provide the key to ISOS, and give access to the Abwehr's communications, as Dick White would later explain to an audience of Security Intelligence Middle East staff officers in February 1942, during a talk in which he referred to ISOS by its local designation, TRIANGLE:

> The creation of TRIANGLE began with the handing-over by a double agent of the instructions the enemy had given him for W/T communications with them. From this the Radio Security Service was able to identify and study the Hamburg station that controlled him; and from that beginning it had succeeded in disentangling the W/T traffic of Hamburg and other Abwehr controls. The importance of TRIANGLE could be illustrated by the fact that it has enabled us to capture 30 spies and a German U-boat and had saved two British ships from sabotage. Moreover, largely as a result of this revolutionary source of intelligence the MI6 counter-espionage staff in London has grown from 3 to over 100.[13]

Because hitherto SIME personnel had not been indoctrinated into ISOS, the conscientious guardians of which had been the Cairo SIS station, this disclosure must have been quite a revelation, and an explanation for the exponential increase in Section V's staff (to the extent that this development might have been visible in Egypt), and the loss of the *U-372* off Haifa in August 1942 when it had been ambushed by four Royal Navy destroyers. White's reference to the sinking of the enemy submarine and the capture of its entire crew might have struck a chord with some SIS officers, as the episode had been orchestrated in Cairo as a means of infiltrating an agent to Palestine whose principal task was to deliver badly-needed funds to CHEESE.[14]

By way of background, White addressed a SIME conference held in Beirut in February 1943 attended by all the regional Defence Security Officers (Syria, Turkey, Palestine, Persia and Iraq), and sketched out how MI5 intended to exploit its ISOS advantage by adopting a policy of active penetration against its adversary, a very dramatic change in the organisation's conventional counter-espionage posture.

> Our objective is the neutralization of the enemy's intelligence activities. As our experience has grown, it had become the policy to have less recourse to immediate arrest, and more to the nursing of suspects in order to penetrate their organisation more effectively. In the last war the technique of Security was to round up and arrest suspects with all speed. But we had become more subtle. As Colonel White remarked, it was now the security policy to treat the captured enemy agent or suspect primarily as a source of information to be exploited for further penetration of an enemy organisation, and not to dispose of him prematurely.

White's exposition of the ambitiously aggressive policy towards the Abwehr was well received by his audience, which welcomed what he represented as an opportunity to turn the tables on the adversary, while still acknowledging its considerable prowess, pointing out that

> as a servant of the German General Staff it was frequently called upon at a moment's notice to carry out large-scale commitments in the interests of some strategic plan; thus it had little opportunity for steady, long-term work and the sometimes extraordinary incompetence of the enterprises against us discovered both at home and in the Middle East was to a large part caused by this. Where the Abwehr had more time at its disposal, as for example in connection with obtaining intelligence for the war at sea, they showed much better results. In any case it was a mistake for British counter-espionage services to underestimate their enemy. Technically the Abwehr was well-equipped, e.g. the German W/T sets supplied to Abwehr agents were certainly the best in existence. Moreover, they had established a technically proficient observation service on the Southern coast of Spain which did considerable damage to our naval interests in the Mediterranean. The Abwehr commandos too had scored successes, while the counter-espionage division of the Abwehr (Abt. III/F) had a record of achievement which was formidable.

White's presentations to selected audiences, usually intelligence officers in associated security organisations, often stressed that because MI5 had only been able to afford to devote just two officers (Edward Hinchley-Cooke and Tommy Robertson) pre-war on German counter-espionage duties, the full picture would not emerge for some years, but the evidence, such as it was, would appear to suggest that while the Abwehr had possessed a quite extensive peacetime network in the British Isles, the organisation had never developed a deep-cover stay-behind spy-ring. Indeed, it would later emerge that some key players had slipped through the net and disappeared abroad in September 1939. As examples, White referred to two agents, Paul Borchardt and Ludwig Warschauer.

Born in Berlin in July 1886 and of Jewish origin, Borchardt was a geographer who had attended London University and participated in several expeditions to North and West Africa.[15] He pioneered aerial photography and was thought by one of his British colleagues, the celebrated author and desert explorer W.J. Harding King, to be likely a German spy. During the First World War he acted as an Arabic interpreter in Mesopotamia and was attached to the German Military Mission in Constantinople. Having been dismissed by the Nazis from his teaching post at Munich University because of his Jewish heritage he was detained at Dachau concentration camp in November 1938, but was released a fortnight later through the intervention of Hans Oster and a member of Ast Munich, Franz Seubert.

Sponsored by the Quakers, Burkhart, who was a member of the Royal Geographical Society, had arrived in England as a refugee in early 1939 and undergone the usual screening process.[16] Once cleared, he applied to join the War Office and then the Admiralty but, having been rejected, moved in December to New York where he would be arrested as part of the Kurt Ludwig espionage organisation in December 1941, and sentenced in March 1942 to 20 years' imprisonment at Fort Leavenworth.[17] In his defence Borchardt claimed to have acted under duress, in return for his release from Dachau, an assertion denied after the war by Seubert.

Warschauer's experience was not dissimilar. A 41-year-old Jewish electrical engineer from Posen employed by Siemens but recruited by the Abwehr in 1938 for a mission to Poland, he was instead sent to England in June 1939, accompanied by his assistant Elisabeth Kohsen, who became his wife, ostensibly to represent the Mannesmann recording equipment through his firm WAF & Co. Ltd. During the First World War he had been commissioned into 234 Flight of the air force and then served as an intelligence officer on the Western Front.

Upon arrival in London Warschauer contacted various government departments to sell his patented apparatus, but MI5's industrial espionage section, designated B4(b), intervened to prevent any purchases and in 1940 Warschauer was routinely interned as an enemy alien at Hutchinson Camp on the Isle of Man. It was not until August 1942 that Warschauer finally admitted to his persistent MI5 interrogator, John Noble, to having been sent on an espionage mission, and made a lengthy confession, in which he confirmed having communicated with the Abwehr through a cover-address in Stockholm, but the precise details would remain unclear until the end of hostilities. Warschauer was kept in custody, mainly in Brixton, until December 1945 when he was deported to Germany.

In his fifty-page statement Warschauer incriminated the only contact he had made in England, who had been Max Bertram, the pre-war Lufthansa assistant manager at Croydon Airport since 1935.[18] This lead turned out to be a dead-end as Bertram had returned to Germany in August 1939. He would later be posted to Oslo, but fled to Sweden where he claimed asylum in October 1944.

Quite demonstrably, several Abwehr spies had been withdrawn as war loomed, and Werner Unland, resident in London since 1929, moved with his English wife to Dun Laoghaire until May 1940 when they rented a flat in Dublin's Merrion Square.[19] Unland's role as an I/Wi agent only became apparent in March 1941 when a recently-arrived German parachutist, Gunter Schutz, had been arrested near Taghmon, County Wexford, by the Gardai and found to be in possession of Unland's address, his photograph, and a suitcase transmitter.[20] Unland was arrested in April and the following month was interned in Mountjoy Prison for the next five years, being released in October 1946.

According to his Ast Hamburg controller, Dr Praetorius, Unland had been in contact constantly between 1938 and August 1939 through a cover-address in Copenhagen, and had received a monthly salary. Scrutiny from April 1940 of Unland's mail which, unknown to the Abwehr, had been routed through the postal censor in London, had revealed his twice-weekly unsigned correspondence with an addressee named Schutz at the Majestic Hotel in Barcelona, and an investigation by MI5 linked Schutz to a flat in Highgate which had been abandoned by the tenants, Wilhelm Schulze and his wife Anna, who lived with their American-born son Herbert and German maid Emma Balzer. The gist of one strand of the Unland-Schutz correspondence was concern about the Schultzes' possessions seized by their landlord. At the very least, this was proof of some past connection between the German fugitives, and MI5 interpreted obscure references to 'a bridge party' as implying that Unland had four agents under his control.

At the time of his arrest in Ireland, Schutz had already acquired a large MI5 file as in February 1940 RAINBOW had identified him as his recruiter. A dance band pianist, they had both roomed at the same lodgings in Ealing in 1938, and shortly before his departure Schutz had revealed his role as an industrial spy, and identified his controller in Germany as a 'Dr Praetorius'. RAINBOW had reported this episode, somewhat belatedly, to MI5. A case summary compiled in March 1943 described his background and friendship with Schutz, detailing his birth in London:

> His father, who is Portuguese, is still living in England but his mother, a German, married again soon after RAINBOW's birth to a German subject who took RAINBOW back with him to Germany. He was educated in Silesia and spent seven years working with various firms in Hamburg and Berlin. In 1936 his employers sent him to England, where soon after his arrival he married a Rumanian girl to whom he had been engaged for some time. A year later an old school-friend of RAINBOW's, Gunther Schutz, arrived in England, ostensibly the representative of a Hamburg chemical firm, but in fact, on an espionage mission. Schutz left suddenly for Germany about a week before the outbreak of war, and RAINBOW heard nothing more of him until January when Schutz wrote to him from Antwerp and proposed a meeting there. RAINBOW, who had previously refrained from denouncing Schutz on account of their friendship, now explained the position to the authorities, fearful lest he himself should come under suspicion, and it was then arranged

> that he should make the journey as requested. He left for Belgium on 8 February 1940 and returned a week later, having been given instructions regarding the work which he was to undertake in England by Dr. Huckreide of Eins Wirtschaft Ast Hamburg, who had come specially to Belgium to meet RAINBOW. He was given a good invisible ink, a sum of money and a cover-address. Instructions from the Germans were to be sent to him in the shape of micro-photographs on full stops after the date in otherwise innocuous letters. In April paid a further short visit to Antwerp and received three more cover-addresses.
>
> RAINBOW's original mission was to report any developments in aviation of air defence, the effects of air-raids and details of transport in the United Kingdom. He wrote several secret letters to one of his cover-addresses along these lines but by January 1941 he had received no fresh instructions from the Germans. Contact was however renewed in due course new cover-addresses and small sums of money. His questionnaires by now relate almost entirely to industrial and economic matters and are fairly high standard.
>
> His real and supposed position in 1941 was that of pianist in a dance band in Weston-Super-Mare but at the end of that year he received instructions from the Germans to obtain work in London with the promise that if he did so they would not allow him to suffer financially. They agreed to pay him £1,000 for a year's work, and in December 1941 made this good to the extent of sending him £300 through TATE and a further £500 by the same means in July 1942. They have recently enquired whether he would prefer them to reserve him marks in Germany. In February 1942 RAINBOW obtained work at Gillette's factory where he is still employed, and this fact, together with his dual nationality, has furnished the Germans with a reason for his not having been called up.[21]

When Schutz was arrested on the day of his arrival, he was carrying alias documentation in the name of 'Hans Marschner' but when his South African passport photograph was shown to RAINBOW he was recognised instantly, and the identification was passed by MI5's Cecil Liddell to G-2 in Dublin, although Schutz did not finally admit his true name until May 1942.

Schutz had come to London in June 1938 from Holland as a student to attend the German Commercial School in Ealing, and had led a very busy social life centred around the Linguists' Club in Kingsway. Born in Hamburg, he had also acted as the representative of a German company, Remy & Co, supposedly a chemicals firm, which later turned out to be an Abwehr front. His friends described him as wealthy, generous and ascribed his popularity with women to his ownership of a German-registered Adler sports car. Although his chemicals import business operated from shared premises at 78 Queen Victoria Street, he rarely visited the office. When MI5's John Marriott began to trace his many acquaintances it was learned, with some embarrassment, that they included an SIS secretary, Pamela Hall, to whom he had proposed marriage. Reportedly he had asked her to introduce him to her influential circle.

Under interrogation by G-2, based on a questionnaire supplied by MI5, Schutz eventually acknowledged his true identity, and claimed to be a reserve officer of the 50th Artillery Regiment, but he made no meaningful admissions and his exchange of letters with his fiancée in Hamburg gave nothing away. In February 1942 he escaped from custody by climbing out of the prison at night dressed as a woman, with the assistance of another detainee, Jan van Loon, a Dutch naval deserter and scaled the perimeter wall, but was recaptured ten weeks later, at the end of April, at the home of a well-known IRA supporter, Mrs Caitlin Brugha, during a police raid intended to arrest her daughter.

MI5's attention then turned to Unland's other connection, and travel records showed that Wilhelm Schulze was a 40-year-old Hamburg-born German journalist who had arrived in England from New York in August 1937 to represent Ullstein Publishing in replacement of his Jewish predecessor. His secretary, Hildegarde Schlattau, who was thought to be Unland's mistress, lived nearby in Highgate, also departed for Germany suddenly in August 1939. Further research by MI5 revealed that Hildegarde shared her flat with a typist employed at the German embassy.

MI5 came to suspect that a hitherto unknown Ast Hamburg-directed spy-ring, involving Schlattau, Schulze, Schutz and Unland, had been operating in north London for some years before the war. However, when interrogated by the Irish G-2, Unland made no admissions, although he did fall for an ingenious ruse which led him to believe that, while interned at Mountjoy Prison, he was in clandestine contact with the Irish Republican Army (IRA). In reality, Unland had been duped and the correspondence was intended to entrap him into disclosing information about his espionage role. Unland never learned of the deception, and upon his release from internment spent fruitless weeks trying to re-establish contact with the elusive IRA.

The issue of the supposedly covert channel to the Dublin legation was highly relevant, although Schutz never knew it, because it was the source of great friction amongst the detainees, to the point that Willi Preetz had accused Schulz of treachery, the charge being the compromise of a cipher, and Walter Simon had threatened to kill him. On one occasion the mutual hostility had descended into a 'three-cornered fight' between Schulz and Herbert Tributh clashing with

Walter Simon, in which Schulz and Simon were injured. The internees at Mountjoy (later moved to the Athlone Barracks) amounted to the largest assembly of Abwehr captives living together anywhere, and the atmosphere was toxic, exacerbated by the fake messages fabricated by G-2 with the intention of undermining the group's discipline and isolating potential informants.

Whereas the other dozen German spies caught in Eire were deported at the end of the war to face Allied interrogators (with the exception of Goertz who committed suicide), the Irish authorities found themselves in a dilemma regarding Unland who apparently had broken no laws, lived under his own name and moved to Ireland openly and legitimately. Naturally, MI5 was anxious to question him, but after much effective lobbying by his wife, Unland was granted permanent residence in Ireland.

After his release from detention and deportation in May 1947 to Frankfurt, Schutz was interrogated by the US Army's Arnold Silver in Ludwigsberg in August and became cooperative, giving a detailed account of his escape from gaol, which he had accomplished without outside help. He had acquired a list of likely Republican sympathisers in Dublin from other prisoners and had approached Mrs Brugha at her home in Temple Gardens who had hidden him for the entire period he was a fugitive. His intention had been to have the IRA buy a boat with funds provided by the legation and sail to France. Schutz remained bitter that he had not received any support from the German minister, Eduard Hempel, and was still unaware that an apparent channel of communication from inside Mountjoy to the German legation in Dublin had actually been another G-2 scheme. During his apparently very incomplete statement to Silver, which omitted to mention his recruitment of RAINBOW, Schutz described his initial attempt to reach Ireland by sea from Antwerp in February 1940, posing as a Jewish refugee. His failure to secure a passage had led to Ast Hamburg's decision to insert him by parachute. Under interrogation at CSDIC, Dr Praetorius had expanded on this, explaining that his original intention had been to post anther I/Wi officer to support Unland in Dublin with a transmitter by appointing someone under consular cover, but the Irish government had refused permission to expand the legation staff.[22] Interestingly, Praetorius also named Eischborn 'as a likely recruit, wrote to him, and travelled with Huckrede of the ARPA Verlag to meet him in 1940.' Of Schutz he recalled:

> His mission was to contact Unland in Dublin; Praetorius thought that Unland, as a sensible businessman, would be a suitable partner to Schutz who could then operate as his W/T operator more than as an independent agent. No specific orders were given to Scheutz about working with his friend Eischborn but Praetorius regards it as probable that he would try to use Eischborn as an information source whose reports he would receive by letter quickly from the UK and then send by W/T to Hamburg: it would be reasonable, Praetorius considers, for Scheutz then to give his microscope to Eischborn so that he, Eischborn, having no W/T, could receive his instructions by the microphoto process.[23]

While Schutz exercised discretion with his American inquisitors, Praetorius was uninhibited at Bad Nenndorf and disclosed details of an agent who had gone undetected, a merchant navy officer named Simonsen who had been recruited originally by I/L and sent to Ireland by U-boat to contact Unland. Allegedly 'Praetorius heard later in 1940 that Simonsen had been arrested for irregularities in his passport'.

The reference to another Ast Hamburg spy represented a further loose end which would never be satisfactorily resolved. Additionally, there supposedly was an agent resident in London's Maida Vale, perhaps a medical student, who was the intended recipient of Schutz's transmitter, and these leads were pursued with enthusiasm by MI5 case officers anxious to take control over Hamburg's network. Given the asymmetry between the two adversaries, the vast resources devoted to developing Abwehr networks in the United States, Eire and Great Britain, and the unpreparedness of MI5 and the FBI, it is remarkable that the British agencies were sufficiently nimble to mount counter-intelligence operations with double agents, and gain a breakthrough into the ISOS traffic. Combined, both these two strategies would yield extraordinary dividends.

Chapter II

THE BURO JAHNKE

The whole project was majestic.

Winston Churchill, *Closing the Ring*[1]

Kurt Jahnke is one of the more remarkable intelligence officers of the twentieth century, yet little has been written about him, outside of classified files. Born in Born near Gnese (now Gniezno, Poland) in February 1888, Jahnke was the son of a Pomeranian landowner. After joining the Imperial German Navy, he served in the International Customs Service in Peking and then returned briefly to Europe before emigrating to the United States where he enlisted in the US Marine Corps, which posted him to San Francisco, Pearl Harbor and the Philippines before he contracted malaria after just ten months' service and was discharged on medical grounds. Jahnke then moved to San Francisco where he ran a successful shipping company trading in Mexico and Asia. Upon the outbreak of the First World War, Jahnke volunteered to help the German Admiralty's Nachrichtenabteilung, which accepted his offer and employed him to collect information about American munitions production and send it on to Germany. In June 1915, he was in contact with the German consul-general in San Francisco, Franz von Bopp, although ostensibly he was employed by the Morse Patrol, a nightwatchman service. On 10 February 1916, he reported to the Federal authorities in San Francisco that he had overheard a plot to blow up the US Navy Yard at Mare Island. No notice was taken of him, but soon afterward the site's magazine was destroyed in a huge, unexplained explosion. Jahnke escaped all suspicion, although at the time he was closely associated with von Bopp and his principal saboteur, Lothar Witzke.

Jahnke would also be implicated in the massive explosion in July 1916 at Black Tom Island and the sabotage of some fourteen American cargo vessels carrying war materiel to Europe. A series of diplomatic communications intercepted and decrypted by British Admiralty cryptanalysts revealed his role: a message dated 12 November 1917 from the German minister in Mexico City addressed to Berlin, routed through Madrid, linked Jahnke to the Nachrichtenabteilung in Antwerp. After the war and a brief period in Mexico, Jahnke returned to Germany in January 1921 and reportedly two years later participated in more sabotage during the French occupation of the Ruhr. Between 1925 and 1927 he served as a deputy in the Prussian Diet, and he then established his own independent intelligence agency, selling information to the Reichswehr and the Soviets. His role as an unofficial conduit between Berlin and Moscow for the exchange of intelligence became widely known, and would be mentioned by a GRU officer, Walter Krivitsky, when he defected from his post as illegal *rezident* in The Hague in 1937. According to Krivitsky, who was interviewed by MI5 in January 1940, Jahnke had become an intermediary in 1927, and had been the channel for the delivery of stolen British documents of the highest importance, such as papers from the Foreign Office, the Committee of Imperial Defence and even top secret diplomatic intercepts designated 'BJs'. As soon as MI5 learned of the leak, Herschell Johnson of the US embassy in London was alerted and an investigation was initiated, although in the absence of more than hearsay evidence, it quickly stalled.[2] In November 1944 the Abwehr defector Carl Marcus (later codenamed DICTIONARY) would mention, independently, that before the war Jahnke had 'tried to recruit a foreigner on account of his political connections and then tried to use the man for pure espionage rather than for his political face value. Some time in 1937 or 1938 Jahnke was in touch with one of [Sir Robert] Vansittart's "men" and Hitler had agreed to see him when Ribbentrop intervened and stopped the affair.'

> Before the war and up to March 1940 Jahnke obtained copies of reports etc. prepared by American diplomats from the UK. DICTIONARY can remember having seen the following types of reports, etc. in Jahnke's files:
>
> a) A good number of American diplomatic reports typewritten (top copy) on thick paper. DICTIONARY cannot remember what headings were on the paper.
>
> b) Thin violet blue carbon copies of American diplomatic reports from England.
>
> c) DICTIONARY can remember only one photocopy of a report and cannot remember it's subject.[3]

The mystery of Jahnke's sources, and his relationship with his principal agent, a mysterious Russian, Waldemar von Petroff, would endure for years, and never be fully cleared up. When pressed, Marcus recalled that Petroff,

> now furnished with a South American passport, is the son of a Czarist General who migrated to Japan where he made many friends in the Japanese Intelligence Service, and from there came to Germany. He was attached to Knochen as technical adviser and was taken by the latter to Paris, still in an adviser capacity. Through Petroff, whose vast influence Source conceivably over-rates, it is possible that Amt VI maintains some relation with the Japanese Intelligence service.[4]

The quality of Petroff's reporting, and Jahnke's apparent access to high-level American diplomatic reports, would preoccupy Anglo-American molehunters for years, particularly because he had been identified as a GRU asset by Walter Krivitsky in January 1940 when the defector had been brought to London to be interviewed by MI5. At that time Krivitsky had described Petroff as having been on the staff of the Japanese embassy in Berlin between 1921 and 1929, and as a spy designated '401'. Significantly, Krivitsky had recalled that he had noticed a suspicious similarity between 401's reporting and newspaper articles published under the pseudonym 'Augur' in *The Times*. When challenged, Petroff had denied any connection with Augur, who was actually the London-based journalist Vladimir Poliakoff, a Russian-born Jew who had sold the Parisian émigré newspaper *Pariser Tageblatt* in 1939 to Nazi interests.[5]

Poliakoff died in June 1956, but it seemed likely that the Jahnke Buro had been penetrated at an early stage by the GRU in the person of Petroff. At the end of the war MI5 remained interested in Petroff because Krivitsky had asserted that Moscow had 'considered him a most valuable agent for British colonial matters' and when asked, Walter Schellenberg recalled him as

> a high grade professional intelligence agent who came from the Jahnke Bureau, with which, [Walter] Schellenberg believes, he maintained his connection to the end. Prior to this he is alleged to have worked for many years for the Japanese Intelligence Service. Through a Jagdscheutz company he had succeeded in maintaining direct contact with [Reinhard] Heydrich and his adjutant, a Major Pomme and received from that source a salary which continued to be paid to him even when he was with [Helmut] Knochen, under whom he worked in Paris for two or three years.

> Schellenberg had the impression that in Paris he lived well and led Knochen by the nose. He paid one visit to Spain on a mission for Knochen.
>
> Some time in 1941 he paid a visit to Rome where he visited an old V-Mann who was alleged to have some connection to the American Intelligence Service. The Italian police intervened and arrested this agent. An awkward situation then arose for Schellenberg because the Amt. VI representative in Rome, Dr Groebel, was involved, and SD espionage in Italy had been forbidden by Hitler. Consequently Schellenberg sacked Groebel.
>
> Petrow frequently visited Schellenberg, bringing political information, the last occasion being the late summer of 1944, shortly before he left for Switzerland, where he was going after first having made short visits principally for reasons of his own safety. He was to undertake a mission for [Ernst] Kaltenbrunner, to whom he had been introduced by Scheidler, and who for a long time told everybody Petroff was working for him in Switzerland. From remarks which Scheidler accidentally let fall, Schellenberg gathered that he must have had a large sum of money paid out to him for the execution of this mission. As he had no means of communication of his own from Switzerland to Germany, however, he relied in Switzerland on Daufelt, who had to forward his post to Schellenberg.
>
> Formerly Petroff had brought quite good political reviews, but his reports from Switzerland latterly smacked of deception material. Schellenberg had the impression that he was a double agent (although possibly not a conscious one), but had no idea for whom he was primarily working, if for anyone. Whenever he was pressed about his sources and connections he became reticent. Schellenberg had repeatedly commissioned VI Z to make an investigation in Switzerland, but there was never any result. He had a wide circle of acquaintances, and his principal sources were mainly South American diplomats. A typical Petroff report was 25 pages and was based on gossip heard in Switzerland or France. He possessed a Chilean passport and a very rich Jewish-Swiss mistress. Fastnacht, who lived on his estate near Berlin and speaks French, German, Russian and probably Spanish.[6]

Krivitsky's evidence showed that von Petroff had been a GRU agent, suspected of collecting at least some of his information from *The Times*, while Schellenberg apparently regarded him as a loyal German agent and did not suspect he was also working for the Soviets.

Although Jahnke would become an anti-Nazi, he associated himself with Rudolf Hess and the SA founder Franz ('Pan') Pfeffer von Salomon, who found his information useful. While he maintained an office next to Pfeffer's in Berlin's Williamstrasse 64, and a country estate in Mecklenburg-Pomerania, his files were kept separately in his villa at Sedanstrasse 26 in the south-west suburb of Steglitz, managed by Jahnke's secretary, Fraulein von Hartmann, and his assistant, von Selle. Hartmann's husband, Max Deichmann, travelled regularly to London and was connected to Schroeder's Bank. Among his other associates was an American friend from Mexico, Federico Stallforth, who owned a silver mine, and a Canadian, Victor Drury. Stallforth's brother Alberto, formerly the German consul in Parral, had been indicted in 1917 as a German agent linked to the notorious Franz von Rintelen. Another important contact was Erich von Salemann, employed in London since March 1930 as a journalist for the *Frankfurter Zeitung* but known to have links to suspected Soviet and Japanese intelligence couriers. By 1935 he was submitting weekly reports through Admiral Erwin Wassner, the German naval attaché, and had recruited his daughter, Elspeth McQueen, who typed his reports, as a sub-agent. Also involved was his Austrian maid, Theresa Mirnig. When questioned in Holloway prison in June 1941, Mrs McQueen identified a dozen of her father's informants, among them a radical Roman Catholic journalist, William J. Teeling; Edward O'Brien, of the British Council's press section; the controversial Whitehall commentator Kenneth de Courcy; and George Edinger. Others were listed as Joseph Wasserman, described as a pro-Nazi Jewish banker; Michael Lorant, a British journalist working for Hungarian newspapers; a White Russian, Vladimir Korostowitz; and the well-known writer on aviation, Lady Grace Drummond-Hay. Another suspect was Major Leadlay, a member of SO1's staff later 'dismissed for unreliability'. McQueen's MI5 interviewer observed that she was 'so vehement in her denials of knowing anything about her father's activities that I am convinced she was lying throughout'. He concluded that 'She was not the slightest bit ashamed of her father's activities and would, I am sure, have felt very proud to have called him a spy.'

When in 1940 Augusta ('Gulla') Pfeiffer was interviewed by MI5 during her internment as an enemy alien, she recalled seeing a large British Foreign Office file on Jahnke's desk. Another of Jahnke's staff was Hans Christian Daulfeldt who in 1937 enrolled as a student at the London School of Economics and lodged in Ealing at the home of a well-known artist, Leslie Holland.[7] On that occasion he was accompanied by his fiancée, Hedwig Gut, and had visited the German embassy frequently to collect mail and money. On a second visit he was accompanied by a Swiss girlfriend, Julie Corraux. He also had access to the ambassador, Joachim von Ribbentrop, which attracted the attention of two MI5 sources reporting from inside the building: the former press attaché Klop Ustinov and his successor Wolfgang zu

Putlitz. In May 1937 Ustinov, codenamed 'U.35', reported 'Daulfedt has been rather active lately. He frequently visits the embassy and Ribbentrop. It will, according to P[utlitz] be very difficult to find out much about his activities as he always fetches his letters himself at the embassy. There is not the slightest doubt that he is a close collaborator of Himmler's and the Gestapo.'[8]

Daulfeldt returned to Berlin in November 1937 and later he would be appointed head of the British desk in the SD's Amt VI after having worked as a saboteur in Czechoslovakia and undergone training at Bad Tolz in Bavaria. During this period Jahnke was also working for the Abwehr, and was especially close to its chief, Admiral Canaris, who directed him to target Britain. According to the defector Carl Marcus, Jahnke's successes included: a ten-page photocopy of a typewritten report on German factories; a photocopy of a typewritten report on the Reichswehr; an RAF contingency plan of Belgium, with maps; a British Intelligence report on German émigrés and their links to the Soviet Union, mentioning two individuals, Meugel as resident in England and Otto Strasser in Prague; an eight-page report on the possible use by German Intelligence of refugees; an agent report on the Royal Navy and British naval bases; and copies of a quantity of US diplomatic reporting from London. Under interrogation, Marcus claimed that the top two DNB representatives in London were on Jahnke's payroll. Another key source reportedly was a man of Russian origin named Petroff (alias Petersen and Peters), based in Paris, who in March 1940 would be transferred to Reinhard Heydrich's control.

Jahnke's influence over the way the wartime Abwehr would develop and his role in mounting counter-intelligence operations against Great Britain were immense, and can be traced back to his enthusiasm for an opportunity that had presented itself in the form of Vinzenz Kraft, a former British SIS agent who had been active during the First World War. He had re-established contact with SIS through the Passport Control Office (PCO) in The Hague where a veteran staff member, Adrianus Vrintern, re-employed him. A retired police detective, Vrintern ran his own credit reference agency and worked as an 'outside man' for the PCO, conducting enquiries that might have compromised the British personnel. In 1940, when the PCO was hurriedly evacuated in the face of the German invasion, Vrintern carelessly discarded a batch of reports, including some that implicated Kraft in playing a double game against Jahnke. This material fell into the hands of 'Stelle-P', a III/F mission to monitor the British organisation in Holland, which arrested Kraft and had him sentenced to six years' imprisonment.

The concentration on the British network in the Netherlands, initiated by Jahnke, began with a card index created by Willy Piert who drew a wiring diagram of SIS's structure, based on the penetration agents deployed against the PCO and on interrogation reports emanating from interviews conducted with the PCO himself, Major Richard Stevens, who would be abducted by the SD while attending a rendezvous on the German frontier at Venlo in November 1939. Thereafter, SIS's activities across the Low Countries became known in detail to III/F. Stevens' companion, and fellow prisoner, Sigismund Best, revealed himself to be the head of a separate, parallel SIS network which had been directed from London and had acted as a check on the PCO.[9]

Another important source, managed from Ast Hamburg, was headed by Richard Protze, assisted by Major Rohleder and Adolf von Feldman who recruited two *Erkunder* penetration agents. One was Gordon W. Perry, a London-born executive of the Batavian Oil Company who had been dismissed by SIS. Of Irish extraction, and originally employed as an interpreter by the League of Nations in the Saarland, Perry moved to The Hague for Royal Dutch Shell and then was recruited in 1935 by the Abwehr, for whom he later travelled to Bucharest. According to his version of events, disclosed during an interrogation in Hamburg in 1945, Perry had applied for a job at Thomas Cook, and was later interned at Thost. In reality, he had continued to operate as an *agent-provocateur* in Brussels for III/F.[10]

The other main penetration agent was Hans Pottel, a German unterofffizier who had been thrown out of the Wehrmacht, but there were others too, as von Feldman later described when questioned at Bad Nenndorf in September 1945: Leo Hermans, a Dutch sales representative from Ijmegen; a pharmacist in The Hague named Leon; a German porter named Johansen at the Hotel Wilhelmina in Amsterdam; and a Dutch Communist 'with connections at the Internationaler Seemansklub'. In addition, von Feldman recalled three active double agents, being Friedrich Book of the Blohm & Voss shipyard in Hamburg; an employee of Dusseldorf's Rheinmetall works named Glanz; and Schubert, a German soldier who was in touch with the French Deuxième Bureau in Belgium. Critically, von Feldman revealed that his star penetration agent was a former PCO staff member, Jack Hooper.

The PCO in The Hague had a sorry history of debacles, dating back to the appointment of Hugh Dalton who had shot himself in September 1936 after he had been caught in a routine audit embezzling fees paid by Jewish refugees for visas to Palestine. Also implicated were his subordinates Hooper and a man named Taylor, who were sacked by the new PCO, Monty Chidson. Short of money, Hooper had sold out to the Abwehr in Cologne in 1938. Although he was no longer employed by SIS, he knew all the PCO personalities and introduced von Feldman to Percy. Although suspicious that Hooper was attempting to regain SIS's trust and go back on the payroll, von Feldman did not challenge him and accepted his information. Indeed Hooper's plan worked, and he was able to worm his way back into SIS and after the station's evacuation to England then transferred to MI5.[11]

According to von Feldman, Hooper had identified several of his former colleagues at the PCO, and mentioned that Harry Hendrik, operating in Scheveningen, had a weakness for women. This had led Ast Hamburg to recruit an agent of Russo-German background named Nina to befriend Hendrik and pump him for information. Allegedly this scheme worked well until Vrinten became jealous and reported Hendrik's behaviour. A post-war investigation, based on information from von Feldman and his III/F supervisor Hermann Giskes, resulted in his dismissal for a second time, and both he and Parry only narrowly escaped prosecution.[12]

The realisation that Hooper had acted for the Abwehr before the war came as a bitter blow to both MI5 and SIS, even if there was no evidence that he had been in contact with the enemy during the war. His final damage assessment blamed him for the exposure of SIS's star German agent, Otto Krüger, who had sold highly-valued German naval secrets to SIS since 1915. Krüger had been arrested on espionage charges but had committed suicide while in prison, unaware of how he had been betrayed.

* * *

Much of the information accumulated about Jahnke originates with Marcus who crossed the French lines in a Wehrmacht uniform in November 1944, on Jahnke's instructions, to make contact with the Allies. Born in November 1911 in the Saarland and qualified as a lawyer after attending the universities of Bonn and Cologne, he underwent military service in 1938 and was transferred to the Brandenburger Regiment in 1940 to specialise in sabotage.[13]

When questioned in Paris in December 1944 by 105 SCI, Marcus identified Hans Daufeld, whom he disliked, as the head of Amt VI's British section and described six of his pre-war sources:

a) A German businessman interviewed at the Prinz Albertstrasse.
b) A contact in Scotland.
c) Baillie-Stewart went straight to Daufeldt on his arrival in Germany.
d) Daufeldt claimed to have close connections to a man in BUF group.
e) The series of other connections enumerated by Daufeldt do not merit record.[14]

After the war had started, Daufeldt's sources of information supposedly had consisted of:

a) Federico Stallforth, whom he had taken over from Jahnke.
b) Connections with USA journalists, particularly 'Bales' (phonetic).
c) A network of W/T sets in the South American states from which agents were run into the US
d) Frank Ryan, who died.[15]

Some of these individuals were instantly recognisable to MI5. Stallforth, of course, had been active since the previous war, and was thought to know President Roosevelt personally, and 'to have been well in with the editors of *Life*'. Norman Baillie-Stewart was an army officer had been convicted of passing classified information to the Germans in 1933 and resettled in Germany on his release from prison in March 1937.[16] The former IRA leader Frank Ryan, freed from a Spanish prison by German intervention in 1940, had died of pleurisy in Dresden in June 1944.

Marcus also said that Daufeld had supervised three missions to the United States, all of which had been captured. They had involved seven men sent by U-boats, two infiltrated from Mexico and an estimated further five by submarine. When in June 1942 Daufeldt was posted to Lausanne under consular cover he had been succeeded by his protégé, Schueddekopf. His staff included his deputy, *Ostuf* Niklaus, and two advisers, Dr Krieck, who had been a pre-war newspaper correspondent in London, and Dr Hamann, who had a great knowledge of Liverpool and Manchester.

When asked to name particularly effective officers, Marcus listed Maiwald, who lived in Lisbon with his English wife, and the senior VI representative in Portugal, Hans Vollbrecht. He also gave a summary of SD operations, past and current, in Hungary, Romania and Greece, as well as at various dienststellen within the Reich.

In January 1945 Peter Mason of SIS's Section V flew Marcus into England with Czech papers under the alias Marienfeld to undergo interrogation, during which he explained that the SD's internal organisation had been structured on advice from two NKVD officers, one named Krasinsky, who had been sent to Germany as advisers. It later emerged that a senior Gestapo officer, Kunowski, had been recruited at this time as a Soviet spy.

In detailing the background and components of Amt VI, Marcus explained that it had been accommodated at Zossen between February and April 1944 when it briefly returned to its original premises in Berkuerstrasse, and then moved to the Schloss Baruth. The British espionage branch, Amt VI D, had been headed by Hans Daufeldt until April 1941 when Dr Graefe of VI C had taken over until his death a year later. The third wartime chief had been Schueddkoff.

> The department was divided into sub-sections ranging from A to F, each of which deals with some aspect of English life.
>
> Schellenberg employs Peters, the dean of the faculty of foreign studies at Berlin University who interviews agents for VI/D.7. He also employed Hauptsturmführer Pfeffer who has written a blue pamphlet and a certain Bunzing of VI/B Italy who has certain contacts of value.[17]

According to a DICTIONARY interrogation report dated April 1945, Daufeldt 'had certain useful connections in England in the business world and also with women, in particular with a daughter of a Colonel in MI5'. He also recalled that Daufeld had recruited 'a Swedish consular official named Schmitt-Lemere and his wife Else who provided Daufeld with reliable information from the UK. Another connection through Sweden was with the Warner Bros film company. Irish diplomatic circles in Berlin also had their uses.' Convoy information was acquired 'from an officer named Berthold who was sent out to South America'. He also 'obtained intelligence about English war production' and a Swiss or English woman employed by the Red Cross in Geneva supplied information about social conditions in England. The most valuable of Daufeld's schemes was the use of 'Dutch soldiers going over to England' and he also had some success with 'certain Irish cloth merchants who had been working in Courtrai in the early months of the war and later travelled back to Ireland and thence to England'.

> Source has already spoken of the Dutch officer on Prince Bernhadt's staff who provided Amt VI with invaluable information. Dr Henge, a member of Seyss-Inquart's staff, in the Netherlands, also made valuable contributions through his English connections.[18]

Much of the pre-war espionage directed against Britain was planned in Hamburg where Dr Messerschmidt cultivated commercial contacts and Dr Guttjahr developed good links to certain students with 'Edinburgh University having been penetrated with special thoroughness'.

In April 1940, on Hitler's personal orders, the Jahnke Bureau was transferred to the SD's Amt VI, and in 1942 Daufeldt was posted to Lausanne under consular cover, where he remained until March 1945 when he was expelled and returned home, accompanied by his wife and child, to Bad Toelz in southern Bavaria where he was arrested in May by the US Third Army Counterintelligence Corps and interrogated. Daufeldt's cross-examination was complicated unnecessarily by two problems. Firstly, there was confusion with his brother Helmut, also a SD officer, who had worked in Copenhagen and had been implicated in the dispatch of two missions to Iceland, resulting in detailed accounts from the spies involved of their German handler who was misidentified. This muddle was eventually resolved, but the second issue would be more long-lasting, and had a wider impact. From the outset Daufeldt's veracity was in doubt as he consistently sought to minimise his role and denigrate his organisation's activities. Of course, he was unaware of the ISOS source which exposed, for example, his role in Switzerland in running local sources, handling huge sums of money and his frequent travel to Milan. The ISOS intercepts revealed his participation in various networks and his plans to develop a stay-behind structure in France, but he was never challenged in a way that might have compromised COMINT, which would remain protected for another 30 years. Daufeldt's efforts to play down his own contribution and omit certain key moments in his career would be replicated by many other SD prisoners in their post-war interrogations, and to some extent this strategy coloured subsequent assessments made by outsiders about the Abwehr's innate inefficiency, incompetence, internal rivalries and corruption. In reality, this was a narrative driven by self-preservation that suited those implicated.

In September 1935 Pfeffer's sister-in-law Gulla Pfeffer arrived in London undertake post-graduate studies at the London School of Economics. An academic whose expertise was the languages of West Africa, Gulla also travelled to Ireland and, according to an SIS report, took an interest in the Irish Republican Army during a visit to Ireland in October 1935. On 18 February 1940 MI5's Guy Liddell recorded in his diary;

> Jock Whyte has brought me the case of Gula Pfeffer. It seems that this woman was at one time in close touch with a certain Charles Fletcher of the Foreign Office whom she, in talking to her solicitor, said she had

> blackmailed. Fletcher in a written statement says that in 1935 he went to Berlin with the knowledge of his department where he met Pfeffer's relations. These include Captain von Pfeffer, whom I believe to be identical with the notorious Captain Pfeffer of the German secret service. It now transpires that Fletcher is employed in the GC&CS. It seems not altogether improbable that he may be the man in the Foreign Office who has been supplying Jahnke with SIS reports and Committee of Imperial Defence policy reports. He might also be the person giving the contents of Ambassador Kennedy's telegrams to President Roosevelt.

Five days later Liddell attended a meeting with SIS and GC&CS senior management, accompanied by MI5's Richmond Stopford, to discuss Fletcher, an Arabic scholar.

> I attended a meeting at SIS in order to discuss the case of Charles Fletcher of the GC&CS. The SIS Chief, Valentine Vivian, Felix Cowgill, Alastair Denniston, Richmond Stopford and myself were present. From Denniston's description of Fletcher it is obvious that he has a kind of secret service kink. He has never been very content with his ordinary cipher work and has always been trying to get into something more exciting. He likes to imagine himself as a kind of cloak and dagger man, and is given to relating hair-raising stories about himself which have absolutely no foundation in fact. There was a curious incident at the outbreak of war. Colonel Vivian received a letter in a foreign handwriting from a woman. She stated that Mr Fletcher had told her at the time of the 1938 crisis that his life would be in great danger and that if she wanted to know about him she should communicate with Colonel Vivian at Room 46, Foreign Office. On this occasion Fletcher was sent for, confronted with the letter, whereupon he became as white as a sheet and almost hysterical. He wanted to know whether he was going to be sacked. He was told that he had behaved in an extremely indiscreet way by giving Colonel Vivian the kind of publicity which he did not in the least desire and if he did anything like that again his services would probably be dispensed with. The letter was then torn up and the incident closed. My impression of Fletcher from what was said is that he is the kind of fellow who must be in the limelight at all costs, and that if he is the source of the leakage this is more likely to be his motive than money. It was generally agreed that the odds were about 60-40 against him and that very careful enquiries should be made about his habits and associations before any action was taken. There is really nothing to interrogate him on since he has very carefully covered himself in his association both with Gula Pfeffer and with Captain von Pfeffer. It seems also from an earlier report that he met Jahnke on at least one occasion. We are going to try and get a look at his banking account though I doubt whether this will disclose anything much.

Although Fletcher was interviewed by Stopford and his MI5 colleague Desmond Vesey, and again in May 1940 for five hours by SIS's Felix Cowgill, this matter would remain unresolved until Gulla Pfeffer's version of events was obtained. According to Fletcher, he had met Jahnke in May 1935 while on an expenses-paid visit to Berlin with his wife. During the trip he had also been introduced to Pan von Pfeffer, General Walter von Reichenau and the Deputy Führer, Rudolf Hess. He also acknowledged that in July 1937 he had been visited by Gulla Pfeffer.

On 26 January 1945, Liddell noted a further meeting concerning Jahnke and his subordinate Carl Marcus, who had been dispatched on a mission the previous November to make contact with the British:

> I went to see C this afternoon to ask him about the case of Carl Marcus. He told me that in November last Marcus had come through the lines as a *Volkssturm* deserter. He had been interrogated by the French but said that he wished to see the British. The French, either because they did not want to pass him to us or more probably through sheer negligence, left him more or less loose in Paris. We eventually heard about him through the Chinese military attaché who informed our military attaché. Marcus's story was that he came with a special mission from Jahnke who is now working in close touch with Walter Schellenberg. Jahnke might conceivably be getting out to Switzerland for consultation about a plan to dislocate industry at the moment of the British invasion of Germany. Frank Foley was sent over to Paris to interrogate this man and said that he had a lot of valuable information about the SD and should in any case be brought to this country. A flap then started in SIS as they felt it was necessary to get the Foreign Office, if not the Prime Minister's sanction for bringing a man to this country who was prepared to cooperate with us in a plan of this kind. Somehow or other it seems to have got associated in people's minds with a peace proposal. There is no reason as far as I can see why the case should not have been treated in a perfectly normal manner. However, the authorities of both Eden and the Prime Minister, the later rather reluctantly, was obtained. The French then said they would only allow the man to come here if he was accompanied by a French officer who should be present at all interrogations. It was under these conditions that Marcus was brought over. C, I think, had taken it for granted that we had been told about the whole thing but in any case made no mystery about it and was perfectly willing for us to be given copies of all papers. I then pointed out to him that there might be a rather interesting tie-up with the old case of Jahnke and Fletcher. I also reminded him of Krivitsky's association with Jahnke. C then told me that in order to avoid any possibility of the Russians getting to hear about this and thinking that we were entering into peace

> negotiations a wire had been sent to Cecil Barclay in Moscow instructing him to inform the NKVD that we would give them copies of all reports obtained. C thinks that it is probably too late to get in touch with Jahnke but he is going to see if anything can be done. He would not, I think, be averse to our seeing Marcus if any useful purpose would be served. We would have to do so however in the presence of Vaudreuil. Marcus is technically a French prisoner of war. It appears that Marcus also has details of the progress of the atomic bomb with the names of certain professors. C says it is not a big bomb. His view is that Marcus is quite possibly a plant by the SD to scare us and if possible to draw us into some arrangement which will reveal to the Germans the date and place of our next attack.

During the course of his extended interviews, all conducted by SIS, Marcus made some important disclosures, one of which concerned SD operations in France involving an F Section agent, Robert Benoist, who had been recruited in the field in 1942 and hitherto widely regarded as one of SOE F Section's great heroes:

> A certain Benoit *(sic)* formerly of 47 Avenue Brocard, Paris, worked for the Germans and denounced to them the well-known racing driver Grover Williams, who was parachuted into France in 1942 and was working under Gestapo control in May 1943. He also denounced two British parachutists Mackenzie and Howard.
>
> Benoit is further stated to have disclosed to Amt VI the link in Holland who was involved in receiving British sabotage material parachuted somewhere south of Groningen. Benoit received this information from the de Gaullists whom he was double crossing with the Germans. Source urges this information be used with the greatest discretion, since it would appear that there is a bad leakage of information in the Deuxième Bureau to the Germans and that members of the de Gaulle government may still be in touch with the enemy. Source further stated that Grover Williams was now in Germany.

This was an allegation which, if true, was of the utmost gravity, and a strong indication of Marcus's veracity, so SIS was informed that SOE's Major Warden was already in Paris looking into the Benoist case. As for William Grover-Williams, he had been arrested by the SD in August 1943 during the PROSPER disaster, having been parachuted into the CHESTNUT circuit at the end of May 1942. He had then recruited his old friend and fellow Grand Prix driver, Robert Benoist, to operate as an agent in the Rambouillet area. Grover-Williams had been incarcerated at Sachenhausen concentration camp, where he was executed in March 1945. Benoist was arrested in Paris by the Germans three days after Grover-Williams, but managed to escape to England and undertake a second mission in March 1944 to the SEBASTIEN circuit near Nantes. However, he was caught on 18 June and murdered at Buchenwald three months later.

The results of Warden's enquiries are unknown, as is the Dutch Intelligence investigation into leaks from Queen Wilhelmina's staff where her secretary, the unpopular and controversial former police commissioner in The Hague Francois van t'Sant, came under suspicion.

Two days after this claim, Marcus was interviewed again by SIS Section V's Michael Wallace-Hadrill and Peter Mason who probed the prisoner about his motives for deserting. He then went on to make further allegations, this time about a spy in the top levels of the Dutch government-in-exile, a source supposedly close to Queen Wilhelmina, and described as 'a regular officer of the rank of major, known to the Germans as FREDERICKS who came to the UK in 1940. He is described as of Spanish type. He sent messages in secret writing to Ireland and those were relayed by W/T from the German Legation. Something may have happened to this agent as he was not heard of after 1943.'[19]

These were all intriguing counter-intelligence leads requiring full investigation, but Marcus's own knowledge was limited, with the key obviously in the hands of Jahnke himself. However, it seemed that when Jahnke's home in Berlin had been bombed out, he had moved to his estate in Pomerania where he had been arrested and interrogated by the Soviets. Further research suggested that he had been executed in 1945, leaving a legacy of suspicion about his extraordinary career and casting a shadow over his many mysterious contacts. What remained undeniable was his unrivalled contribution to the development of German Intelligence.

Chapter III

NEST BREMEN

The war will be won or lost on the beaches.

Field Marshal Erwin Rommel, 31 December 1943

Theoretically subordinate to Ast Hamburg, Nest Bremen acquired a special status within the Abwehr because of its unparalleled experience in foreign intelligence collection, and the energy of its first commander who commenced operations in 1935 to exploit the city's worldwide sea links. Uniquely, Nest Bremen did not accommodate elements of Gruppe II or Gruppe III, leaving the staff to concentrate on the business of espionage.

The Nest's charismatic leader was Erich Pfeiffer who had originally worked in Wilhelmshaven collating naval information acquired from his waterfront contacts. By the end of 1934 his scope had extended to:

1) Contacts in Belgium and Holland who had undertaken to supply written reports on such information as could be gleaned in the ports of Antwerp, Rotterdam and The Hague.
2) Suitable informants recruited from the many regular business travellers registered at the Bremen Aussenhandelsstelle who supplied material regarding foreign defences and naval and shipping construction, collected in the normal course of their travels.
3) Merchant Navy captains and officers whose ships were based in the port of Wilhelmshaven.
4) Stewards on ships plying between Germany and New York who obtained shipping publications and technical journals of all types in New York and reported to Pfeiffer the results of their own observations of shipping, etc. In addition, these men acted as couriers for (5) below.
5) Germans resident in New York who had volunteered their services and were asked to obtain details of military and air force, as well as naval, developments in the USA and to send reports to Pfeiffer by the couriers mentioned above.[1]

In April 1935 Pfeiffer was visited by his Chief, Admiral Canaris, who agreed that the Nest should relocate to Bremen, and in October Nebenstelle Bremen was formally established with a staff of four, including Pfeiffer's secretary, chauffeur and a shipping expert, Hans Bendixen. In March 1942 Bendixen would be transferred to Lisbon where his 24-year-old mistress, Inge Szelinski, was a secretary in the KO's I/M section.

Pfeiffer, who in July 1940 had been transferred from Bremen to head a newly-established Ast Brest, would be taken into custody at the German consulate in Istanbul in September 1944. Under interrogation, he acknowledged that he had been transferred from Brest to Paris in February 1942, and then in May 1943 had served in Berlin before being posted to Turkey in May 1944 to lead KONO.

Pfeiffer's replacement as Nest leiter was Hans Karl, a naval reservist who had been a pre-war director of the Bremen shipyard. In early 1944 he was moved on to Marseilles and succeeded by Adolf Driesen.

To expand their collection activities, Pfeiffer established contact with the NordDeutscher Lloyd shipping line and obtained the board's consent to actively recruit among its crews. By 1936 he was focused on France, exploiting contacts in the Rhine and Ruhr valleys, and began to manage a 24-year-old French naval volunteer, Marc Aubert, who sold him high-grade documents, having originally approached the German naval attaché in Paris. Anxious to support the cost of his womanising, and designated A-2009, Aubert's first delivery of documents weighed 95lbs and over a period of three years he produced more than a hundred classified documents, some of which he removed from his training ship, the cruiser *Jeanne d'Arc*.[2]

> From travellers to England came reports on UK ports, ships and the British Navy while from his merchant marine informants Pfeiffer received excellent material dealing with shipping and defences the British colonies, Japan and Russia.
>
> It is of interest to learn from Pfeiffer that he welcomed reports on Russia obtained through that country's placing of contracts with German firms in the Ruhr. It was not until 1937 or 1930 that it was decided that intelligence from Russia did not fall within the aegis of Nest Bremen.
>
> In the autumn of 1937 Pfeiffer was instructed to expand his work of espionage against the United Kingdom, from which country any type of intelligence was to be sought, and to facilitate the implementation of these instructions the Stelle was considerably expanded, new officers being appointed to initiate I-H and I-Luft sections.[3]

Heading I/M was Hans Alter, then Leutnant Klaps. I/H was in the hands of Major Augener and I/L was run by Hauptman Wenzlau. Augener's principal role was the management of an exceptionally productive agent, Albert Meems, who was based in Tilburg, Holland, but operated in England, Eastern Europe, Malaya and India. A middle-aged livestock dealer, he acquired exotic animals in the Far East and sold them to circus and zoo proprietors across Europe. He and his brother Aikne, who lived in New York, also traded as wholesalers in canaries and other pets. A post-war investigation into Meems's espionage revealed that he had visited London, where he had stayed in the Grafton Hotel four times after the outbreak of war and his last departure had been in April 1940. The handling of Meems, who was married to a German woman and gained German citizenship, would be passed by Augener and Klaps to Johannes Bischoff, formerly a PoW of the British during the First World War when he had been held at a camp near Chester.[4] Meems was never caught during the war, and travelled extensively, especially to the United States. He had also managed his own networks of sub-sources that also went undetected.[5]

Recruited by Pfeiffer in 1938 after two years' travelling in the United States, Latin America and Great Britain, Bischoff operated in Bremen under a genuine commercial cover, Seevag, as a cotton trader, and as well as being a successful businessman was responsible for the recruitment of many agents, among them Juan Frutos in Cherbourg; Hermann Rullhusen in Bogota; and in 1940 he sent Hans Holl and Frank Jordan to Rio de Janeiro. When quizzed after his arrest, Rullhusen mentioned that he had known two other agents in Bremen, Erich Hermann and a man named Richter, who subsequently had been posted to Shanghai, thus extending the Nest to the Far East where a KO was planned under the leadership of Curt Remmicke, alias Richter, a trainee who had spent more than a decade in England and become a naturalised citizen.

Often Bischoff used Ludwig, his American cousin in Dallas, as a cut-out to relay messages and deliver money. One of those incriminated by receiving his payments was Simon Koedel, designated A-2011, who would be arrested in New York in October 1944 for tax evasion before being convicted with his daughter Marie of espionage in March 1945.[6] Bischoff also set up a network in Lisbon, run by Hans Grimm, Hans Kassner and Hans Scholz, which extended across the Peninsula, North Africa and the United States. Yet another was based at St Jean de Luz, the resort on the French side of the Spanish frontier, where a stay-behind centre ('Residenten-Netz' or R-Net) was established in anticipation of the need for emergency communications with Spain if all German residents were expelled and as a contingency in case of an Allied invasion in the region. Eventually, in September 1944 this funkstelle, commanded until May 1944 by Werner Roepke, would be evacuated to Bilbao.

As the Nest Bremen network expanded, so did the staff, and in 1942 it was joined by Kapitan Koenig, an insurance broker who had spent years in London representing his father's business, and therefore spoke perfect English. He was followed by Carl Lohmann, a former officer on the SS *Bremen*, on which the photographer, Hoeffig, had conducted a comprehensive photographic survey of Southampton for Pfeiffer while the ship docked in 1937. In 1940 Hoeffig would be put in charge of the Nest's photographic and secret-writing branch.

The Nest Bremen boasted its own training facilities at the Schloss Schierensee, known as the 'Seehof', and a radio station in the Nachtatstrasse, and this was where an American of German descent, Walter Lohrey, was taught the skills of micro-photography before he returned to the United States in April 1940. His espionage role was discovered when his home in New Jersey was searched by police investigating a local burglary. The FBI would not become involved in the case until November 1944 when his significance was eventually realised.[7] Born in San Francisco to a German father, Lohrey was a former soldier in the US Army who had become a Hitler Youth organiser in California and then travelled to Germany on the SS *Hansa* in July 1939, the journey having been arranged by an acquaintance, Kurt Ludwig. He underwent wireless training in Bremen and in February 1940 returned to the United States on the SS *Conte de Savoia* on a mission to report shipping movements on the Delaware River and from Philadelphia. When interrogated in June 1945 Lohrey named as fellow spies his friends John M. Kessler,[8] who had sailed back to the United States separately in September 1939 on the SS *Vulcania*, and John M. Joslin in April 1940 on the SS *Volandia*.[9]

Ludwig would be implicated in the 'Joe K' case in 1941 when his correspondence in secret writing with compromised cover-addresses in Europe was intercepted in Bermuda, sparking an FBI search for a German spy. Eventually the Ohio-born Ludwig would be arrested in Washington, D.C. in August 1941. In March 1942 Ludwig, together with his co-conspirators Helen Mayer, Karl Mueller and Hans Paget, would receive long prison sentences.

Other spies later identified by Bischoff[10] included Paul Mulak, sent on a mission to Canada in 1940; Waldemar Othmer, a former German-American Bund leader arrested in Trenton, New Jersey, in July 1944; and Carl Grundell, a Swedish electrical engineer recruited in 1944 but arrested in Gibraltar on 23 February 1945 when his vessel, the Red Cross ship SS *Tamara*, was on a voyage from Piraeus to St John, Newfoundland. Aged 26, Grundell had appeared in four ISOS messages and under interrogation at Camp 020 confirmed what the intercepts had already disclosed, that he was an ideologically-motivated spy who had been cultivated in Salonika in September 1944 by the SD upon the production of a written recommendation of an American acquaintance, Harald Arrowsmith. As well as the ISOS evidence, there was an incriminating document recovered from the SD's office at 129 Queen Sophia Street when the city had been liberated by British troops in November 1944.

In his confession Grundell described his military service in Finland, as an infantryman fighting the Red Army, and a visit to the United States where he had studied at Cornell University. When he had volunteered to join the Waffen-SS he was instead recruited into the I/M under the codename ROBERT. He was detained until the end of August when he was deported to Sweden.[11]

While Grundell was incarcerated at Camp 020 Mulak was traced and arrested in Canada in August 1945 on the basis of Bischoff's interrogation, and immigration records showed that he was an engineer who had first arrived in Ontario in April 1930, and acquired British citizenship by naturalisation in June 1937. He had returned to Germany in 1939, as an enthusiastic member of the Deutsche Bund, and had been recruited as an agent by Nest Bremen. In May 1940 he sailed from Genoa on the SS *Washington* to New York and crossed over at Niagara Falls into Canada where he was interned until October 1944, and then released, only to be rearrested in January 1946. When pressed by his interrogators he reluctantly admitted a version of the truth which somewhat corresponded to his file as A-2022 in Bremen. In the absence of any concrete proof of espionage, no further action was taken against him.[12]

During the summer of 1940 Bischoff, newly promoted to replace Pfeiffer on his transfer to Brest, travelled to Genoa with Bendixen to develop contacts in the port with a view of deploying agents to the United States and South America. While in Genoa they recruited Hans Grimm, recently returned from Honduras, and Erwin Schatz, a German Jew who had acquired Hungarian citizenship. Bischoff also recruited his own firm's local representative Carl Eitel, and two stewards, Richard Koepf and Hans Kassner, to act as transatlantic couriers on the SS *Manhattan*.

Grimm would become the foundation for a network in Portugal codenamed GIOVANNI which began with Hans Scholz in Lisbon, operating independently of the KO; Hans Uhse in Madeira; Johann Majewitz in Funchal; and Klein and Franz Lackner in Angola. However, their organisation would be handicapped in late 1942 by the arrest of Grimm and Scholz on charges of having attempted to recruit local Portuguese, and this embarrassment meant the rest of the network would be absorbed by the KO. Persistent official representations from the German embassy on their behalf eventually obtained their release in May 1943. By then Grimm and Kassner had turned their attention to the United States by recruiting Adolf Striepe, a 33-year-old resident of Jackson Heights, Queens. He would be run by an intermediary, Fred Lang, who would be convicted of espionage in September 1945 and sentenced to seven years' imprisonment. In turn, the FBI learned, Striepe had recruited John da Silva Purvis, a Portuguese arrested in Newark, New Jersey and imprisoned in November 1943.[13]

The Nest's organisation in Madeira included Umberto de Freitas and Candida Lacombe Raposo who collected shipping information. Raposo then recruited Antonio de Silva Peralta to cover Portuguese Guinea, where a spy named Lochner was active, and the Azores. Lochner's mission also extended into the Belgian Congo. An attempt to infiltrate an I/M agent into South Africa during the winter of 1941/42, with a radio link to Le Havre, was unsuccessful, as was a plan to send a team of three agents to Dakar, but the trio was withdrawn after they reached Madeira. A further effort to send a ship's doctor, Hilaire Westerlink, accompanied by his wife, to the Belgian Congo, failed in May 1942 when he was detained in London.[14]

The Nest's expansion into South America had originated with Franz Jordan's mission to Brazil in 1942 but, operating under the alias Frank Walter, he was arrested after his illicit wireless signals had been detected and he was sentenced to 15 years' imprisonment.[15]

Bischoff would be arrested with a colleague, Gerhard Addicks, by First Canadian Army troops in the village of Edewecht in April 1945 and detained to a PoW camp at Deventer. When taken to London and questioned at Camp 020, Bischoff proved entirely cooperative. Specifically, he named Jose Rist as one of his protégés, based in Union City, New Jersey; Herbert Winterstein and Fritz Noak, spies arrested in Brazil in January 1942; and Isabel Pilderit and her husband Heinrich Reimers, based in Valparaiso, who were compromised by the arrest in the United States of Heriberto Schwartau Eskildsen in October 1941.

The Nest's organisation in South America was particularly strong in Colombia where Hans Kolbe, employed by the exporters von Griebheim & Barranuilla, reported for I/M until 1942, having been recruited by Herman Rullhusen who also enrolled Georg Parczyck. Rullhusen, who had worked for Bischoff before the war, was an experienced wireless operator and had been assigned the task of basing himself in Bogota and building a network across the continent, linked by radio.[16]

A Kriegsmarine officer, he also turned out to be a compliant prisoner and described his role in the Nest as an agent recruiter, denouncing two of his V-Men as Albert Meems and a man named Geitje.[17]

Like Bischoff, his colleague Nikolaus Bensmann was already well known to Allied counter-intelligence.[18] In November 1944 one of his recruits, Alfred Langbein, had given himself up to the Royal Canadian Mounted Police in Ottawa, confessing that he had worked at the Nest Bremen for Bensmann for two years before he had been delivered to Canada by the *U-213* in May 1942. In his statement he disclosed that he knew of two other German spies. One, Arthur Breuer, had been landed on the Atlantic coast of the United States in the spring of 1941, and another, named Hartmann, had been reporting regularly from Newport News, Virginia. The FBI had launched two investigations, codenamed CODAR and IVORY respectively, but failed to trace either man, although it was suspected that 'Hartmann', also referred to as MAURICE, may have been Waldemar Othmer. Langbein also recalled a dentist, Karl Kraeutzer, whom the Bremen Nest intended to send to Addis Ababa.

While under interrogation Bischoff was challenged about the true identities of several of the as-yet unidentified agents thought to have undertaken a course at the Nest's Seehof. One such student was described as a Dutch colleague, Willem Kuiper, as 'the son of a British admiral wounded in this war' whose cover-name was WELLINGTON. Aged 22, and from Denmark, he had ended his course prematurely and was thought by a couple of the students to have been 'liquidated'. Where there were gaps in Bischoff's memory, they were filled in by his long-serving secretary, Margarethe Sick, who before the war had worked for American Express. She turned out to have an encyclopaedic recollection, and easily identified almost all of the Nest's agents, their cover-names, aliases and V-Mann numbers. Further corroboration was also provided by Walter Fricke, the Nest's paymaster, who had kept meticulous records of his financial transactions with individual agents.

Nest Bremen developed extensive assets in Spain and Portugal where it was represented by Theodor Schnoele who worked under commercial cover as an employee of NordDeutschen Handelgesellschaft GMBH; Hans Scholz, who had been active for I/M in Angola before the war, until he was expelled in 1939; Erich Maier, ostensibly representing the Bremen firm of Maierform; and Hans Uhse of I/H who operated in the Azores until his arrest in April 1943. He was released to return to

Bremen six months later. Also caught in the Azores at the same time was Johann Majewitz, a Deutsche Atlantisch Linien engineer who had been reporting for I/M. Similarly, Franz Lackner was arrested in July 1943 in Luanda, but was later released.

In March 1946 the War Room circulated a short monograph to cover Nest Bremen's history, based on post-war interviews conducted with Erich Pfeiffer, Johannes Bischoff and Nikolaus Bensmann:

I INTRODUCTION

Aussenstelle Bremen, nominally an out-station of KIM Hamburg, was perhaps unique among Abwehrstellen in the degree of independence which it possessed in the number of countries, to which its agent networks extended, and in its long history of activity.

From its inception in 1935 until the absorption of the Abwehr into the RSHA in 1944, the Bremen organisation was a Nebenstelle. Since the only practical effect on Nest Bremen of the Abwehr's re-constitution into Mil. Amt was its change of nomenclature, the Nest being thereafter known as an Aussenstelle of KIM Hamburg, and since a description of the stelle's activities during the Mil. Amt phase would provide a totally inadequate picture of its interests and achievements, this report will comprise a brief account of the Bremen Stelle from its inception until its final dissolution, a division being made into pre-war and wartime activities.

Throughout its existence the Bremen Stelle comprised Gruppe I elements only; at no time was it concerned with Gruppe II activities, and although before the outbreak of war the Nest was expanded to include I/H and I/L sections (which later disappeared) and interested itself in economic intelligence whenever propitious, the main concern of the Stelle throughout its history was with I/Marine interests.

Nest, later Aussenstelle, Bremen, must not be confused with the Iwi stelle situated in Bremen, known alternatively as Reterat Rolland and Stelle Frisohnuth, and sometimes loosely named Stelle Bremen. The latter was an entirely separate organisation, bearing no relation to Nest Bremen and responsible only to Abt. I in Berlin.

II ORIGINS

In 1934 Erich Pfeiffer was working in Wilhelmshaven as a Nachriten-offizier for the Abwehr, then in its infancy. He was occupied with the task of forming what cannot be rated higher than an information system to bring dividends from all parts of the world in the shape of reports in foreign shipping and naval matters. To this end Pfeiffer had established the following sources of information:-

1) Contacts in Belgium and Holland who had undertaken to supply written reports on such information as could be gleaned in the ports of Antwerp, Rotterdam, and The Hague.
2) Suitable informants recruited from the many regular business travellers registered as the Bremen Ausenhandelstelle, who supplied material regarding foreign defences, and naval and shipping construction, collected in the normal course of their travels.
3) Merchant Navy captains and their officers whose ships were based on the port of Wilhelmshaven.
4) Stewards on vessels plying between Germany and New York who obtained shipping publications and technical journals of all types while in New York, and also reported to Pfeiffer the results of their own observations of shipping, et. In addition, these men acted as couriers for (5) below.
5) Germans resident in New York who had volunteered their services, and who were asked to obtain details of military and air force, as well as naval, developments in the USA, end to send reports to Pfeiffer by the couriers mentioned above.

It should be understood that at this stage Pfeiffer had not asked for any actual espionage to be undertaken on his behalf; informants were urged not to draw attention to themselves by unlawful or dangerous 'snooping'. Nevertheless, from these sources, and from other individual informants too numerous to mention here, Pfeiffer had begun to build up a great deal of valuable material for the use of the naval and military authorities and was laying the foundations of an extensive intelligence organisation which was to prove extremely valuable in later years.

It is amusing to learn that Pfeiffer was an admirer of Max Ronge, the Austrian 'Master-Spy' of the 1914-1918 war, whose methods influenced his own approach to intelligence work.

By the beginning of 1935 Pfeiffer found the closed area of Wilhelmshaven and the limited scope offered to him there, irksome and obstructive, and began to work more and more in the Bremen area, which as a world-wide shipping base offered more opportunities. Consequently, after making representations to Canaris during the latter's visit to Wilhelmshaven in April 1935 Pfeiffer was authorised to transfer his office to Bremen and was promised full facilities for conducting and expanding his work there. After he had submitted a scheme for the Bremen Stelle to Abwehr headquarters, it was officially agreed that Pfeiffer should concentrate on the obtaining of marine intelligence and should seek information on worldwide, as well as North Sea, traffic.

III NEST BREMEN 1933–1939

The Stelle was opened officially with the title Nebenstelle Bremen in October 1935. Its staff of four consisted of Pfeiffer as Leiter, assisted by the shipping expert Hans Bendixen, one secretary and one chauffeur.

The Nest was conducted on the same lines as those previously pursued by Pfeiffer and enjoyed complete freedom of action. Bendixen proved an asset to Pfeiffer, immediately proceeding with the recruitment of informants from among merchant marine officers based on Bremen, thereby building up a vital source of information from all quarters of the globe.

At this time and subsequently, both before and after the outbreak of war, Pfeiffer exploited personal contacts in the directorate of the Nord-Deutscher Lloyd Shipping Company for the purpose of recruiting agents and couriers from among crews on the company's vessels, and the company collaborated with Nest Bremen to the extent of presenting likely recruits for employment as agents or officials of the Nest.

In 1936 Pfeiffer commenced to explore the possibility of obtaining reliable intelligence regarding France's navy and defence systems.

Profitable sources of such material were contacts made in Rhine and Ruhr construction firms undertaking contracts in France. A second valuable source was a French naval officer, Marc Aubert, who volunteered his services as a German agent, and provided extremely high grade material.

From travellers to England came reports on UK ports, shipping and the British Navy while from his merchant marine informants Pfeiffer received excellent material dealing with shipping and defences in the British colonies, Japan and Russia.

It is of interest to learn from Pfeiffer that he welcomed reports on Russia obtained through that country's placing of contracts with German firms in the Ruhr. It was not until 1937 or 1938 that it was decided that intelligence from Russia did not fall within the aegis of Nest Bremen. In the autumn of 1937 Pfeiffer was instructed to expand his work of espionage against the United Kingdom, from which country any type of intelligence was to be sought, and to facilitate the implementation of these instructions the Stelle was considerably expanded: new officers being appointed to initiate I/H and I/Luft sections.

One of the most important undertakings of Major Augener, the newly-appointed I/H officer, was the recruitment, training and control of all agents in Holland, Albert Meems, who until the outbreak of war was productive of material from the UK, Western Europe, India and Malaya, all of which countries he visited under business cover.

Pfeiffer controlled a number of agents in the Nest who provided shipping intelligence from the Bosporus and Dardanelles area, and later from Syrian ports.

Pfeiffer meanwhile continued to expand his existing sources, and was highly satisfied with results, until early in 1938 when to his surprise and dismay a major catastrophe befell his agents in the USA, the majority of these being apprehended by the FBI. This disaster was followed very shortly afterwards by the arrest in France of Marc Aubert who had been providing useful information regarding French coastal defences and naval construction.

The denouement in America caused criticism of Pfeiffer, not only within the Abwehr but also by Norddeutscher Lloyd officials since the arrests, which included that of a hairdresser, Johanna Hoffmann, of the SS *Europa,* brought disrepute to the shipping line. However, Pfeiffer managed to excuse himself to Canaris who indeed showed considerable restraint and understanding by explaining that the rounding-up of his group of agents had been due to the careless and confused behaviour of one of the couriers, Karl Schleuter, who entirely without Pfeiffer's knowledge, had been utilised simultaneously by Ast Hamburg, and had also become involved in Nazi Party organisations in the United States. Canaris accepted this explanation, which was in fact legitimate and Pfeiffer continued to enjoy both Canaris's confidence and the same degree of independence as hitherto.

During the same year of 1938 Pfeiffer had enlisted the services of two men who were to remain with Nest Bremen throughout the war and who maintained and developed the Nest's resources with considerable energy and enterprise, namely Johannes Bischoff and Nikolaus Bensmann. The former, cotton merchant, had business connections in England, and during the frequent visits which he made to the UK, up to the outbreak of war he produced information on industrial and aircraft developments in that country. Bensmann, an expert in the oil industry, with innumerable contacts in Europe and America, was able to recruit agents who supplied intelligence regarding oil storage and refining plants in many countries. Bensmann was also responsible for creating a secret writing and photographic laboratory in Bremen.

At the time of the Czechoslovak crisis of 1938 Nest Bremen, in common with all Abwehrstellen responsible for offensive espionage in the West, was instructed to report on preparations for war on the part of Great Britain and France.

During 1938 the Nest was used as a training school for I/M officials from other Stellen, evidence of the high regard which was held at Abteilung headquarters for Pfeiffer's efficiency and achievements. Pfeiffer himself was anxiously engaged in constructing a new network of agents to operate against the USA. Convinced that, but for the utilization without his knowledge of certain of his agents by Ast Hamburg, his previous methods would have continued to bring successful results, he proceeded along similar lines, first recruiting two stewards on a New York-Germany shipping route, and secondly gladly accepting an offer of services received shortly afterwards from Simon Koedel, a German in New York, whom he instructed to report on military matters and on shipping in New York.

In January 1939 Pfeiffer attended a special course for Abt. I officers in Berlin which was directed by Brasser, Gruppenleiter I/Luft, and which consisted of detailed instruction in aircraft recognition and technical aviation matters.

During the succeeding nine months, Nest Bremen received an increasing number of enquiries from headquarter regarding ports and shipping in the Levant, but was unable to achieve satisfactory results in this direction.

Pfeiffer, who had for some years been convinced of the inevitability of war, and who now realised its imminence, painstakingly brought his dossiers up to date from official and unofficial naval publications obtained from his own sources, considering that statistics and charts issued by Abt. I/M were inaccurate. He thus was able to construct a plan of campaign in respect of naval intelligence, rendered himself independent of, or unlimited by, directives issued by the Kriegsmarine, and was ready to get the altered demands which he anticipated when war was declared.

IV NEST BREMEN SEPTEMBER 1939 – JUNE 1944

Immediately after the outbreak of war Nest Bremen was given the priority assignment of obtaining detailed intelligence regarding foreign shipping in Northern European waters. To Pfeiffer's disappointment, he found that the majority of his contacts lapsed into silence and he received very little intelligence from pre-existing agents. It therefore became a vital and urgent necessity to activate new sources. To this end Nest Bremen officials toured the Low Countries and Denmark, recruiting agents mainly from amongst Bensmann's business contacts, among these were agents who provided information regarding the RAF and the aircraft industry in Britain. Meanwhile, Bischoff, following the tradition established by Pfeiffer, opened a new channel of communication with agents in the United States. The agent Grimm was established in Milan with the task of recruiting and controlling members of crews of US ships calling at Italian ports. Grimm was assisted in this work by Carl Eitel who before the arrests early in 1938 had been a steward on the SS *Bremen,* utilised as an agent courier by Pfeiffer. These sub-agents acted as substitutes for the couriers on the Bremen-New York liners used before the war to bring material from the USA. They were also utilised as couriers for Bensmann's USA contacts, the exploitation of whom enabled Nest Bremen to keep au fait with the latest American technical developments. By the end of 1939 Pfieffer was receiving from this channel excellent reports on shipping and Army training methods from a pre-war agent in New York.

Further contacts of Bensmann proved useful agents in Romania, and through yet another friend of Bensmann with good connections in Chile, a network of informants was created in South America. Heinz Rhilhausen, an agent of Bischoff dispatched to Colombia via Italy in 1940, was instructed to set up a W/T station there and by building up a sub-agent network in South America, another source of information on developments in the USA was established.

Activities on behalf of Nest Bremen in China are evidenced by the presence in 1940 of at least one agent, Remmicke, in Shanghai with whom the W/T station in Colombia made contact, while an agent dispatched to the USA in the spring of that year dispatched reports to Bremen via cover-addresses in Shanghai, Switzerland and Milan, and probably communicated also by W/T via the Colombia station.

A further important development in the early part of 1940 was the establishment of agents in France.

The spring of 1940 saw an attempt to expand the Nest's resources in the Western Hemisphere by the dispatch of an agent named Mulak to Canada; however, although the agent reached Canada via the USA, and successfully evaded detection, by the US and the Canadian authorities, no reports were received from him.

At this Bischoff undertook the task of contacting through the Bremen Chamber of Commerce persons entering and leaving the country. These travellers were discreetly interviewed prior to their departure after their return, and while spectacular results were neither achieved nor expected, a certain amount of useful information was thus obtained. This interrogation was carried on under the cover-title of the 'Seeverkehrs-Navigationsbuero', and the work was known as the 'intelligence service'.

An 'interview facility' was formed by other Nest Bremen personnel who primed and interrogated ships' captains and crews. These two methods of seeking intelligence were abandoned in 1942; however, throughout the war the Nest continued to interrogate German nationals returning from abroad, both to obtain intelligence and with a view to selecting possible agent recruits. This work was described latterly as Ruckwanderbefrangersdienst.

In May 1940 Pfeiffer left Nest Bremen, taking charge of an Einsatzkommando which accompanied the German Army in its advance through the Low Countries and France, and was replaced as Leiter by K.Lt Carl who from the outbreak of war until this date had been Leiter of I/p (Presse) Nest Bremen, a section formed to deal with the extraction of intelligence from foreign publications received in the Nest from all sources. Carl had been assisted in this work by Scf. Schierrenbcck, and by Bischoff. The latter specialised in material from the UK, Eire and the USA, and also in the collection of economic material on South America, which last task he performed on behalf of Abteilung I/Wt, sending the results of his labours to Berlin headquarters. Most of the material derived from South America was received by Bischoff from Grimm in Milan who subscribed to all important South American publications.

From the time Pfeiffer left the Nest the prominent figures were not, as might be expected, the subsequent Leiters, but Bischoff and Bensmann. Little is known of Carl's personal ability as Leiter, but much has merged regarding the activities of these two subordinates who continued in the traditions of their recruiter and first Leiter, Pfeiffer.

In the summer of 1940 an attempt was made to dispatch Albert Meems to India, after careful training had been given in secret-writing and micro-photography. This agent failed to advance beyond Belgrade and eventually returned to the Nest for re-employment elsewhere. No evidence has been received of any agents successfully operating from India during the war.

In this year also a W/T-trained agent was placed in Antwerp to report on Channel shipping.

In addition to the above, by the end of 1940 Nest Bremen was receiving reports on Allied and neutral shipping from the following sources:

1) Officers of German cargo vessels based on Bremen, Bremerhaven and Emden;
2) German Merchant Navy vessels in Baltic ports;
3) Agents in Swedish ports;
4) An agent in Istanbul;
5) German merchant shipping still plying in the Mediterranean (reports from these being mostly dispatched to Bremen via Istanbul).

As a preliminary experiment in the autumn of 1940 Bischoff had sent two agents to Portugal to set up a Lisbon branch of a Bremen firm with whom one of them was connected. When the branch had been established in Lisbon one agent, John Osmers, returned, leaving Johann Kassner to continue recruiting, and for six months sending economic and naval intelligence in secret writing to Bischoff. By the spring of 1941 it had been decided that more serious attention should be given to the exploitation of the Iberian Peninsula as a base for the obtaining of naval and shipping intelligence, and therefore Grimm, in whom Bischoff placed great confidence, was recalled from Milan and after instruction and preparation in Bremen was sent to Lisbon to construct a large-scale agent network in the Peninsula, and to establish a W/T station for the rapid transmission of intelligence to Bremen through the Hamburg W/T stelle.

In June 1941 Carl attempted to supplement the existing sources of intelligence in France in particular by the establishment of agents on the Riviera coast. Negotiations with Ast Paris, however, fell through and after the frustration of successive attempts Carl ceased to pursue this aim.

No major developments followed during the winter of 1941/42. It is of interest, however, to note that, always in search of fresh fields, Nest Bremen dispatched two agents to Africa. The first was sent to Portuguese West Africa, where it was intended that he should establish himself with a W/T transmitter. He was also instructed to recruit a sub-agent to operate in South Africa and both were to collect shipping and economic intelligence for transmission to Hamburg. Abteilung I/M and Ast Le Havre co-operated in arrangements for the agent's dispatch. He was arrested shortly after landing in Africa, and no reports were ever received from him.

The second agent, a Belgian national named Westerlinck, who had spent many pre-war years in the Belgian Congo and was recruited by Ast Antwerp, was trained jointly by the Antwerp Stelle and by Nest Bremen, was sent to Lisbon en route for the Belgian Congo where he was to establish W/T contact with Hamburg and to transmit intelligence of an economic and general nature. While in Lisbon, this agent was entrusted to the care of Grimm. The agent failed to reach the Belgian Congo, being arrested on arrival in England, in which country he had hoped to procure a visa for the Congo.

In April 1942 a second agent, Alfred Langbein, was dispatched to Canada, this time by submarine. However, although the agent had been trained and controlled by Nest Bremen officials this mission was directed by Abteilung I/M.

During the same year Frank Jordan was dispatched by Bischoff to South America; this agent was directed to settle in Rio de Janeiro and shortly after his arrival he established W/T contact with Bremen, transmitting shipping intelligence which proved of little value.

V GIOVANNI ORGANISATION IN PORTUGAL

By the summer of 1942 Grimm had established a large network of agents in Lisbon, Madeira, the Azores and Portuguese Africa from where he received excellent shipping reports. The whole network, which probably comprised at least two dozen agents, was known as the GIOVANNI organisation. Through the recruitment of members of the crews of Portuguese vessels, Grimm organised a courier system of communications with outlying agents.

In 1942 Bensmann trained three or four Moroccans for an I-network which he planned to establish in the Dakar neighbourhood, but while en route in Madeira these agents behaved irresponsibly and were sent back to Germany.

In the autumn of 1942 in view of the possibility that Spain would decide to deport German nationals, it was decided, firstly, that a number of Spanish nationals should be trained as W/T agents, and secondly that a courier service should be formed to convey letters by hand from the

Franco-Spanish frontier to Bremen. This second aim was accomplished by the recruitment of links in Paris, Tilburg and Groningen. Unfortunately for the first part of the plan, however, November saw the arrest in Lisbon of Grimm and his chief assistant who would have carried out the work of recruitment before such progress had been made and a few weeks later eight more of the GIOVANNI network were arrested by the Portuguese. In spite of repeated offers by Bischoff he never succeeded in fully re-establishing the R-net in Portugal. However, after a number of visits and representations to KO Portugal, Bischoff succeeded in procuring the release of Grimm and his assistant early in 1943, the majority of the network continuing to be held under arrest.

An Aussenstelle of Nest Bremen was set up experimentally in France in January 1943. This amounted to little more than a W/T post. Two others were sent by Bischoff to St. Jean de Luz, where they installed a transmitter and established contact with Bremen. The purpose behind this move is not clear but, as far as is known, the Stelle was utilised mainly as a long-distance practice station, to which qualified Nest Bremen agents and operators were sent for short periods and from which daily traffic was exchanged with students at the Bremen Stelle. Grimm was in charge of this funkstelle until May 1944 when he was replaced by Werner Ruepke.

Appointment of Driessen as Leiter

In March 1943 Carl was transferred to Marseilles and Adolf Driessen was promoted to take his place as Nest Leiter. Driessen proved to be an apathetic and ineffectual leader and was content to allow Bischoff and Bensmann to take the initiative in the Nest's enterprises.

Agent Network in the Iberian Peninsula

Throughout 1943 abortive attempts were made by Bischoff to re-establish and strengthen the GIOVANNI organisation in Portugal and to build up a network of W/T agents in Spain. Finally Grimm was sent to Madrid in this connection, but he probably had little success.

Switzerland

Another hunting-ground for intelligence was Switzerland, which Nest Bremen officials and agents visited from time to time throughout the war generally under cover of personal business. A not inconsiderable quantity of material was amassed in this manner, the intelligence thus obtained being largely of an economic nature.

North Africa

In the summer of 1944 in the light of the termination of campaigns in North Africa, I/M Sued considered it desirable to create an intelligence network in that country and since Homann, an official of Nest Bremen, was in touch with Arab circles in Syria and Iraq it was decided that Nest Bremen should undertake this task. Dr Otto Homann was ordered to investigate the possibility of recruiting Arabs in France and North Africa through these contacts. A number of Arabs were interviewed by Bensmann in France but none was considered suitable for recruitment as an agent and, although the effort to find eligible recruits was sustained until the summer of 1944, the project had finally to be abandoned.

France

In January 1944, further unsuccessful attempts were made to obtain intelligence regarding Mediterranean shipping through the establishment of agents along the south coast of France.

Egypt

In the spring of 1944 a single agent, Josef Farraoq @ JUPP was trained for a general intelligence mission in Egypt, but he was killed en route and was not replaced.

AUSSENSTELLE BREMEN JUNE 1944-45

The absorption of the Abwehr into the RSHA appears to have effected little practical change in the Bremen Stelle. While its activities and staff gradually dwindled, there were no drastic alterations in function or administration.

Preparation to meet the Allied Invasion of Germany

In the summer of 1944, a half-hearted attempt was made to establish stay-behind agents in the south of France, who would report by wireless on the progress of the Allied Forces advancing from the south; no satisfactory results were achieved.

At this time a scheme known as Unternehmen Sued was devised by KDM in anticipation of landings on the north coast of Germany. This undertaking involved the assembly of a fleet of Dutch fishing vessels and their disposition along the coast. Carefully selected W/T operators were placed on each vessel with instructions to report any signs of an approaching Allied seaborne invasion force. Nest Bremen participated in this operation to the extent of inspecting and servicing the W/T transmitters on these vessels and at the controlling station in Delfzijl, Bischoff supervising this work.

This plan exemplifies the desperate and ineffectual attempts of the RSHA to prepare for the Allied invasion of Germany. Such a scheme could never have produced any results, for the low grade agents selected as operators would almost certainly not have had the courage to betray themselves to the enemy by transmitting had they in fact found themselves overtaken by an invasion fleet.

In September, in view of the progress of the Allies in France, an attempt was made to transfer the St Jean de Luz Stelle to Bilbao, but shortly after his arrival in Bilbao the W/T operator was expelled from Spain by KO Madrid, objection being taken to his unheralded arrival in Spain.

An attempt was made in November to obtain information concerning activities on the Western Front, and about the current situation in France by the formation of a stay-behind network of W/T agents to which end Bensmann visited the neighbourhood of Baden-Baden. This project was found impossible of fulfilment and had to be abandoned.

By the end of the year, with the occupation of Germany and the end of the war in sight, only three senior officials remained in Aussenstelle Bremen, namely Bischoff, Bensmann and the Leiter Driessen. Bensmann found himself without work and devoted his attention for the remainder of the war to the oil industry, joining a subsidiary firm under the Speer organisation. Bischoff directed his energies to the establishment of stay-behind agents in the area for which Aussenstelle Bremen was responsible. The organisation of stay-behind networks in Wehrkreis X was directed by KDM Hamburg, and Bremen's area of responsibility in the Wehrkreis was bounded by the Dutch frontier in the West, a line passing through Eaden, Leer; Oldenburg and Bremen in the North, the river Weser in the East, and the Wehrkreis boundary in the South. The agents were to operate only beyond a depth of 50 kilometres from the fighting front, the intervening 50 kilometres being the responsibility of the Frontaufklärungs organisation. By January 1945 Bischoff's stay-behind agents numbered about sixteen, and were apparently considered by KDM Hamburg to be satisfactory, although Bischoff himself admits that he was unable to obtain recruits of any calibre, and that the majority were apathetic and had no intention of operating after the Allied occupation. Each agent was trained in code and in Morse, and was equipped with a transmitter. As far as is known, not a single agent made contact with his control station.

VI COOPERATION WITH ABWEHR AND MIL. AMT. HQ & NEIGHBOURING STELLEN

In addition to the activities conducted on its own behalf, from time to time Nest Bremen applied agents, recruited and trained by Nest Bremen officials, for missions directed by Abteilung I/M from Berlin. For example, in the summer of 1941 I/M Sud Ost transferred an agent of Nest Bremen, Hans Georgiades to Athens, whence he was dispatched on an I/M mission to Alexandria. A second example, previously mentioned, is that of Alfred Langbein, sent to Canada by submarine in 1942, on a mission directed by Abt. I/M.

Nest personnel also frequently assisted other I/M Stellen, notably Ast Antwerp and Nest Brest, the latter Stelle being in origin an offshoot of Nest Bremen, although subordinated to Ast Paris.

VII SUBORDINATION

a) October 1935-1937: During this initial phase in its history Nest Bremen was subordinated administratively to Ast Wilhelmshaven, operationally to Abwehr HQ Berlin.

b) 1937-June 1944: In 1937 the Nest became subordinated administratively (for discipline, postings and transport) to Ast Hamburg while operationally it remained under the direct control of Abwehr HQ, which also dealt with Nest's finance and promotions.

c) June 1944-April 1945: During the Mil. Amt phase Aussenstelle Bremen was entirely subordinated to KDM Hamburg, all orders issued by the Mil. Amt being directed to Bremen through the I/M Leiter.

It is reiterated, however that the Stelle enjoyed throughout its existence a unique degree of independence. Ast Hamburg exercised virtually no control over the Nest's activities, while such directives as were received from Berlin were those resulting from general changes in policy. Constructive or practical advice on methods of operation were apparently seldom given, and the successes achieved by Nest Bremen were due entirely to the ability of its officers and cannot be regarded as reflecting credit on the Abwehr as a whole.

VIII TRAINING ESTABLISHMENTS OF NEST BREMEN

W/T School: This school was established at the beginning of the war under the charge of Sdf. Schierenbeck in the Wachtstrasse offices of the Nebenstelle. In March 1943 Schierenbeck left Bremen and was replaced by Ogefr. Langner and the W/T school was transferred for a few months to Hamburg. Towards the end of 1943 it was again set up in Bremen with Bischoff as its controlling officer. Instruction was given to agents in Morse code, W/T transmission and construction; but the training of important agents was frequently supplemented by a course in the Hamburg W/T school. The Hamburg Funkstelle exercised close control over the Bremen school and regular supervisory visits were paid by I/i officials of the Ast Hamburg training school. A number of agents controlled by other Stellen were given full or supplementary training in the Bremen W/T school. Stellen known to have used the school for the training of their agents include Ast Wiesbaden, Ast Netherlands, Ast Brussels, and Ast Stettin.

The I/i section's functions comprised agent-training and the equipment and servicing of agents' transmitters only. No W/T communication was conducted with other Stellen, or with Nest Bremen overseas, whose traffic was handled by the Ast Hamburg W/T station.

In September or October 1944 the school was evacuated to Lübeck.

(2) I/g Section: The Leiter of I/g in 1939 was Lt Estorf, He probably left in 1940, the work being continued by his assistant Waiter Hoefig. The office and laboratory was situated in the Haus des Reiches. In addition to the training of agents in secret writing a large part of the work done by this section consisted in the development of films of defences, armaments, buildings etc, brought in by agents returning from abroad, Hoefig specialised in the preparation of micro-photographs and the training of agents in this subject.

IX THE ST JEAN DE LUZ FUNKSTELLE

Leiters: April 1943 – May 1944: Hans Grimm
May 1944 – July 1944: Werner Hoepke

Address: Transportuebarwachunsstelle, Nano Sohokoa
Rue Vonbau, St Jean de Luz

The function of this outstation has been described above. In addition the personnel were able to facilitate the frontier-crossing of Nest Bremen personnel wishing to enter Spain. In August 1944 the office was closed and all equipment destroyed, the personnel leaving for Bilbao.

X OFFICES USED BY NEST BREMEN

(1) Haus des Reiches, Herdentowall, Bremen – Pfeiffer's offices in 1939 (identical with (2) below)
(2) Kriegsmarine Lienstelle, Haus des Reiches, Richteweg 9, Bremen. Head offices and 1g laboratory of Nest Bremen.
(3) 'Seevag' offices – Seevericers-und-Navigationbuero, Wachtstrasse 27-29, Bremen – Bischoff's offices and W/T school. (Formerly Bischoff's business premises.)
(4) Interfraco (Internationale Frachtkontor Ludendorfstrasse 32, Bremen (bombed early in the war) and Postfach 237, Bremen.

Offices used by Grimm in Lisbon
Cia Comoorcio Iberio – Ultramarine Lda (OIBUL)
Rua Eugenio dos Santos 27-30, Lisbon

Offices used by Grimm (under alias Sr Don Harold Grasshof) in Madrid
Calle de Rafael Calvo 42-1°, Madrid.
Telephone Number of 'Nest Bremen – 29216.
Feldpostnummer of Nest Bremen – 33039

XI NUMBERING OF NEST BREMEN AGENTS

Agents controlled by Nest Bremen were allotted identification numbers in the following series:

2300 – 2399; 2600 – 2699; 4800 – 4899

XII APPRECIATION

Nest Bremen's achievements were undoubtedly considerable during Pfeiffer's term of office as leiter although the ultimate value of the intelligence procured cannot be judged. Pfeiffer avowed great initiative, was extremely industrious, and sustained considerable enthusiasm for his work. The succeeding Leiters lacked inspiration and indeed most of the good qualities shown by Pfeiffer and Dreissen in particular gives the appearance of being entirely apathetic towards his duties.

The development of agent networks after Pfeiffer's departure in May 1940 was achieved largely by virtue of the extensive business connections possessed by Bensmann and the industry and intelligence which Bischoff brought to his work, but both these officers lacked the authority and experience of Pfeiffer. Had they possessed these qualities, and had Bensmann been less pre-occupied with his own business interests, they would no doubt have been able to carry out the various projects, notably in France and the Iberian Peninsula, with a greater measure of success.

Another factor which handicapped the Nest's undertakings was the poor standard of its agents, a disadvantage reflected in the majority of the Abwehr and Mil. Amt undertakings. Many of the agents possessed a low degree of intelligence, and almost all worked for mercenary rather than ideological motives. As more and more men became incorporated in Germany's armed forces the choice of recruits available to the Nest became increasingly smaller and the recruits were not of the type to make enterprising or loyal agents.

The history of Nest Bremen shows a gradual but continual decline in success and enterprise which dates from the autumn of 1942, when the GIOVANNI network was liquidated by the Portuguese.

Nevertheless, in its primary function, that of collecting naval and shipping intelligence on behalf of Abteilung I/M, Nest Bremen, conspicuous among Abwehrstellen operating against the Western Allies, achieved results of value and won considerable credit for its leaders.

This War Room analysis was intended to give Allied counter-intelligence staff a somewhat superficial briefing on the background, activities and personnel of what was arguably one of the Abwehr's most important Nest, even if theoretically it was administratively subordinate to Hamburg, which also had been running foreign collection operations pre-war. Headed from May 1940 by a naval officer, Herbert Wichmann, who succeeded Joachim Burghard, Ast Hamburg had three particularly energetic officers, Hans Dierks, who would be killed in a drunk-driving car accident in December 1940, Dr Walter Praetorius who had studied at Southampton University and had cousins in Dundee, and Nikolaus Ritter. All three men would recruit, train and dispatch numerous agents to England and the United States, and it was estimated that this trio handled up to forty-two agents. Under interrogation at Camp 020 Wichmann gave an account of all of them, of which thirty-five were already known to MI5, but seven could not be immediately identified.[19]

Some of these agents, of course, were familiar to MI5 because they had been turned and then run as double agents. Others, having posed as refugees, had confessed their clandestine missions and had described the Abwehr personnel they had come into contact with, often giving a detailed account of their course at the Ast's training school at the Schloss Schierensee, near Kiel.

Ast Hamburg also managed a large radio station at Wohldorf where some forty-four naval transceivers were in contact with agents across the globe. Although most other Abstellen had their own communications, much of the long-range traffic was routed through Wohldorf because of the staff's skill and efficiency. For instance, the station routinely acted as an intermediary between Ast Cologne and its agents in Argentina.

Ast Hamburg's Friedrich Obladen specialised in developing networks in Latin America where, according to Wichmann,

> He had some 5/7 agents in South America. Three of them operated wireless sets in Rio de Janeiro, Buenos Aires and Valparaiso. Another, without a set, was in Pernambuco. They set out news on shipping either by means of these W/T sets or by means of the post, as the Lufthansa operated to South America until the USA entered the war.[20]

In addition, Hamburg played roles before the invasions of Norway and then Holland, mainly monitoring local shipping movements with fishing boats, and was selected to plan an Abteilung in September 1940 which was intended to become Ast London after a successful invasion.

Because of its reputation for professionalism, Ast Hamburg was also assigned other special tasks, such as training a kommando for deployment in Greece, and advising on agent recruitment in Turkey and Denmark. At the conclusion of Wichmann's interrogation in August 1945 MI5 drew up a summary of his interviews:

> In general, very little guidance or information came from the Oberkommando der Kriegsmarine nor did they produce questionnaires or summaries of work required at that time. Officers had to work out for themselves what was wanted and sort out the details to send in from the information passing through.
>
> Foreign newspapers and periodicals were studied and much technical information was taken from such papers as *Rudder*, *Yachting* and *The Navy*, which proved of interest to the Konstructionamt of the OKW.
>
> All the captains of merchant ships were enlisted to furnish reports on harbours and installations all over the world wherever they might put in. This was pursued actively by Kapt. Lt. Mueller, and provided much information. Having been at the Zontral Hotel with the Gen.Kdo since 1935 he moved into Stella Haus, Roedingsmarkt.52, in the harbour area. Here he had an office named Internationaier Schiffersdienst Ernst Moeller.
>
> Much purely organisational work was done by I/M for Amts-Gruppe Ausland IV. It was a question of dealing with the many business representatives scattered abroad, who in case of war would have to ensure supplies of fuel, water and provisions to German war and merchant ships.
>
> The work in France was mainly organised and run by [Hans] Dierks who employed an agent called FRANZ. This man in turn employed a number of informers, of whom Wichmann can remember the following cover-names: LEHMANN, HECHT, LOGENBRUDER, and a Spaniard whose real name was Vilar.
>
> These people were all established in either France or Spain, but connection with them ceased in 1939 or 1940 and as far as Wichmann knows has never been resumed.
>
> Wichmann saw reports on the following subjects supplied through FRANZ:-
>
> a) The harbours of Marseilles, Toulon, Bordeaux; Brest, Caen and Fecamp.
> b) The shipyards of Toulon, Brest, and Caen.
> c) The smaller Breton harbours like Quimper etc,
> d) The trials of new flotilla leaders (Mogador, Fantasque).
> e) Submarine repairs
> f) The technical co-operation between destroyer and submarine flotillas.
> g) Forecast of the building programme of the French Navy.

Dierks also employed a few individuals who travelled to France now and then. There was a Swede known as the Professor, who brought back several interesting reports in the years 1937 to 1939 from the circles in which he moved. Dierks told Wichmann that this man died just before the outbreak of war. Another agent called FLUNKI produced nothing of interest during this time.

Nebenstelle Bremen was nominally under the control of Ast Hamburg at this time but in fact was quite independent. The Leiter was Korv-Kapitan Pfeiffer who had a fair measure of success in France, but Wichmann goes on to say that he also had some bad luck with a group of agents in the USA. Apart from the rather general statement Wichmann is unable to provide any further details of the activities of Nest Bremen or Pfeiffer at this time.

ACTIVITIES AGAINST ENGLAND:

Wichmann states that all attempts to spy on England were disappointing and that in spite of their efforts the Germans achieved nothing. He mentions that Admiral Canaris who was himself most displeased in 1939 with the results of two years' work. This was not confirmed to the I/Marine section or Ast Hamburg, but applied to the whole I section of the Abwehr generally. Wichmann states that he continued in the methods initiated by Burkhardt. This last officer, when Leiter I, sent a man, unknown to Wichmann, to try to win over some members of the crews of the British steamers sailing weekly to Hamburg; this had no success.

A young Dutch art dealer, named Reich, made two trips, to England in 1938 to try to recruit agents who might supply information, but he fared no better. If there had been any correspondence he would have used his own address in Holland, to which to have the letters sent. Wichmann met this man once in Dusseldorf.

Newspaper advertisements were studied, both German and English (*The Times*); the German ones for firms or individuals who had connections in England who travelled to this country and who might be willing to accept missions. *The Times* was read for similar advertisements asking for people who might have German connections.

Firms were set up in Hamburg to answer the advertisements. They did no trade whatever, and merely had a single room with a doorplate. Their names and addresses will be found later in the appropriate section.

Wichmann remembers receiving one report from a man called Frick (now deceased in Germany) which came from Alexandria. This gave information on the harbour, oil installations, and the coastline from Alexandria down to Mersa Matruh.

Dierks received one report from Britain. It came from an agent called Jessie Jordan, whom Wichmann has never seen and concerned storage tank installations in the Firth of Forth. This woman lived, Wichmann

> thinks, near Dundee, and was later arrested. Wichmann also knows that Dierks received one report on Sheerness, from a man whose name Wichmann never knew, and who travelled to England.
>
> Dierks this time used several postboxes in Holland for receiving information from various sources. The people at the places used were unaware of the contents of the mail, and the real identity of the persons using them. He liked to use newspaper kiosks, this provided him with an uncontrolled mail delivery. These functioned well until the spring of 1940, and Dierks used to collect a regular packet of mail.[21]

Though Wichmann often pleaded a poor memory, what he did remember must have reassured MI5, especially when he was cross-examined on his Ast's pre-war activities.

> Hauptmann Ritter @ von Rantzau recruited one agent by answering an advertisement. Wichmann does not know this man's name but he was referred to as 'der Kleine', He furnished information on the state of the air industry.
>
> Ritter also ran an agent called DICK, an English airman in the last war. This man stayed in Hamburg for a few days in 1940, passing through on his way from Portugal, and then returned to Portugal again. Nothing further was heard of him although he should have made contact with Ritter again, either in Portugal or Germany.

As both DICK and 'der Kleine' had been MI5-controlled double agents, Walter Dicketts and Arthur Owens respectively, Wichmann's evidence was reassuring. Most of the cases to which he alluded, such as Jessie Jordan and the 'English airman', were instantly recognisable for the. latter was Dicketts, known to MI5 under the codename CELERY.[22] The implication was that Ast Hamburg had failed in its task to successfully deploy spies undetected into the British Isles, but this complacent assumption would prove to be very mistaken.

Chapter IV

GOLFPLATZ

> So far as I know Brandenstein put only one agent in England (Enterprise FRITSCHEN) during the whole period of his stay in Paris . . . I believed him to be a double agent for the English Intelligence Service.
>
> Erwin Lahousen interrogation, 1945[1]

In the six years before the outbreak of hostilities in September 1939 the Abwehr embarked on a very large-scale espionage offensive against the British Isles. At the time MI5 did not fully appreciate the true nature of the escalation, nor even know the word 'Abwehr', and it was not until March 1942 that B Division and SIS's Section V reviewed their files and began to comprehend what had happened. When gathered, the statistics were eloquent and suggested that the annual number of German spies detected were:

1933	1
1934	0
1935	3
1936	6
1937	7
1938	10
1939	2

These figures implied a gradual increase in espionage after the Nazis took power, with a relatively concerted effort in the two years before the war was declared. They should be compared with a second set of statistics, illustrating the number of definite German agents now known to have operated in the United Kingdom:

1933	1
1934	0
1935	3
1936	8
1937	10
1938	17
1939	10

These numbers[2] indicated an even greater effort on the part of the Abwehr as war approached, and an MI5 summary listed the individual cases chronologically and disclosed their duration:

> Christopher Draper (August 1932 – January 1933); Captain Pye-Smith (February 1936 – February 1938); Henry Addicks (April – September 1935); [XXXXXXXXXXXXXXXX] (April 1935 – January 1938); Hermann Goertz (October – November 1935); Else Duncombe (July 1936 – April 1938); S.P. Gray (August 1936 – September 1937); Morrow (August 1936); Mahon (August 1938); Battye (August 1938); McCartney (August 1936); Kurt Wheeler-Hill (March 1937 – May 1938); Jessie Jordan (July 1937 – February 1938); Walter Simon (July 1937 – February 1938); My Eriksson (August 1937 – September 1939); Francis P. Campbell (August 1937 – April 1938); Gertrud Brandy (August 1937 – November 1938); G.H. Darragh (September – December 1937); Percy W. Rapp (January – August 1938); James Cohn (May – October 1938); Stanley Scott (June 1938 – September 1939); Friedrich W. Meyer (June 1938 – September 1939); Bibire (August – December 1938); Karl Burger (August 1938 – September 1939); Donald Adams (October 1938 – June 1939); de Renzy (September 1938 – ?); Theodore Tietz (November 1938 – September 1939); William Wishart (December 1938 – September 1939); Mrs Crookes (March – April 1939); Joseph Kelly (December 1938 – April 1939); Bernard Durrant (May – September 1939).

Some of these cases had common denominators. For example, six (Pye-Smith, Morrow, Mahon, Battye, Darragh and McCartney), were unemployed ex-military officers seeking work through the columns of *The Times* who were contacted by Ast Hamburg. S.P. Gray, a commercial traveller, had also been approached after advertising in the same newspaper, and had attended an interview in Amsterdam. Henry Addicks was a German-born South African who had been recruited by Erich Pfeiffer of Ast Bremen to spy on French coastal defences. De Renzy was a Nazi sympathiser in New Zealand. Investigation of Else Duncombe showed her to be employed by Herbert Campbell and linked to Walter Simon who was found to be carrying Bernard

Durrant's address in his notebook. While on his mission to England in May 1937, Simon received money from a domestic servant, Mrs My Eriksson, who was arrested as she attempted to leave the country in September 1939. Under interrogation she implicated her former London employer, the Duchesse de Chateau-Thierry, and her paying-guest Vera Eriksson.

A young German student, Kurt Wheeler-Hill, was living in Dublin in 1937 when he was compromised by receiving money from the same Hamburg bank, the Nederlandsch-Ostfreische Hypotheekbank, that had been identified as paying Gray. Wheeler-Hill, whose brother Axel would be arrested in the Duquesne case in New York in 1941, attempted to recruit his language pupil, Francis Campbell, who reported the matter to MI5 while on a visit to London in April 1938.

Most of the pre-war cases of German espionage came to MI5's attention either by information supplied by the individual concerned or by the repeated use of already compromised cover-addresses, a lapse in tradecraft that was exploited by the GPO's Letter Interception Unit. Comparison of the examples, usually linked to Hamburg or Cologne, showed most to be low-level, without the danger of jeopardising British secrets, although two manifested counter-intelligence objectives. In October 1938 Friedrich Meyer, a German engineer living in London, was invited to Hamburg and instructed to collect information on the British Intelligence Service, and a month later a South African, Karl Burger, had the same experience and also reported it to MI5. Indeed, because of the failure of some agents to fully disclose some aspects of their espionage, MI5 came to suspect Percy Rapp, employed as a London cabbie, and Stanley Scott, a van driver from Southampton, as acting as triple agents, having been directed by their handlers to approach the British authorities with a rather abbreviated version of their story.

The counter-intelligence dimension should have been a cause for concern, for this was a bold strategy indeed, and suggested that hostile penetration was on the German agenda. Another potential anxiety should have been the unexpected appearance of a pair of 'inspectors' working under official Board of Overseas Trade cover, who visited London in July 1935 to check up on the poor performance of Henry Addicks. The concept of deploying street investigators into hostile territory to conduct integrity tests on suspect sources was innovative and troubling.

Another tactic adopted by Ast Hamburg was to advertise in *Aeroplane* magazine for aeronautical engineers to undertake apparently innocent translation work, and in October 1938 just such a qualified reader, a draughtsman working in an aircraft factory named Bibire, responded and attended a meeting in Rotterdam at which he was invited to collect technical data for a book supposedly to be published on the subject of modern aircraft. Bibire promptly alerted MI5 to the 'pitch'.

Although MI5 successfully concluded more than thirty pre-war German espionage investigations, there were nevertheless several indications that other as-yet undiscovered networks had been active. For example, interception of mail addressed to Theodore Tietz in Hamburg from November 1938 found handwritten espionage reports, probably from a woman, but she was never identified. Similarly, retrospective study of Rapp and Scott strongly suggested that they had engaged in unreported work for their German contacts, communicating to undeclared cover-addresses. In the case of an ex-soldier, William Wishart, who travelled to Hamburg from Grimsby in January 1939, MI5 was suspicious, when he was arrested on the outbreak of war, that he had been paid by his contacts and equipped with several hitherto unknown correspondence cover-addresses, but allegedly had never sent any information.

A couple of the pre-war cases were self-recruitments, involving a visit to German consular or diplomatic premises easily monitored by MI5. Thus the London taxi-driver Percy Rapp offered his services to the embassy, as did Mrs Crookes who was employed as a cook by the Admiral Superintendent of the Portsmouth Dockyard. Similarly, Joseph Kelly, a labourer in the Royal Ordnance Factory (ROF) at Euxton, wrote to the German consul in Liverpool.[3] These *ingénue* were too unsophisticated to anticipate MI5 surveillance in the form of routine mail and telephone covers, or even the possibility of a penetration agent already on the premises.

When war was declared, only six known German agents were at liberty (the ROF labourer Kelly and a horse-racing journalist, Donald Adams[4] having been convicted and imprisoned already) so My Eriksson, Stanley Scott, William Wishart and Karl Burger were detained. This left Tietz's unknown source and a single active, MI5-controlled double agent, Arthur Owens, codenamed SNOW.

In assessing their adversary's tradecraft, MI5 analysts noted that the Germans had adopted a preference for postal 'cut-outs', apparently in an effort to evade mail interception, and accordingly no less than three women with German backgrounds, Else Duncombe, Jessie Jordan and Gertrud Brandy, had acted as 'live letter-drops' by receiving and forwarding letters and packages. The flaw in the arrangement, of course, was the danger of contaminating other correspondents once the clandestine postmistress had come under surveillance. However, no onward addresses were ever linked to Mrs Brady, leaving the possibility that she depended on couriers employed on ships calling at Irish ports. As often as not, MI5 was unable to exercise much control over these cases because other overseas correspondents were invariably at the mercy of foreign agencies, such as the FBI or Deuxième Bureau.

In concluding its study of the pre-war German espionage cases, the 1942 MI5 report observed, with some complacency and self-congratulation, that

> out of 24 agents recruited or approached by the Germans during 1933-36, (this figure excludes recruiters and postboxes) 13 of them reported the matter to us, either at its very inception or some time during the course of the case and some of them went on working for the Germans, under our instructions, for periods varying from a month to three years.[5]

However, MI5 did acknowledge a very serious handicap relating to the management of double agents, which would be resolved by the creation of the XX Committee in January 1941:

> The chief difficulty in running these double cross agents in peacetime was the problem of supplying them with information that was both innocuous and at the same time satisfying to the Germans; for all the elementary information they might need was to be had in England, simply for the asking and the Germans were not content for long to receive handbooks which could be bought at any bookstall.[6]

The key to successful manipulation of controlled enemy agents is a juggling act of several competing, contradictory factors, one of which is to retain the interest of the principal sponsoring party. Unless the profit-and-loss account appears to demonstrate a healthy credit balance, an unproductive well will be abandoned, but few armed services, in time of war, are given to compromising their secrets without good reason. The XX Committee, technically a sub-committee of the Chiefs of Staff Committee, enjoyed the necessary authority to approve schemes that would deter lesser mortals, and thereby provided a mechanism for sanctioning, on a weekly basis, items that would excite the enemy without causing apoplexy in Whitehall. At a stroke, the inhibition which had ruled out the engagement of double agents in the First German War, and undermined the credibility of the inter-war agents, was replaced with an ingenious structure designed specifically for the purpose, and sanctioned at the very highest levels of command. However, by June 1940 the Security Service possessed only one covert channel, a mercenary Welsh nationalist and his small group of supporters, with which to communicate with its German counterparts. From the Axis perspective, the strategic position in Western Europe had been transformed, and the British Isles unexpectedly became a very real candidate for invasion and occupation.

* * *

The Abwehr's reaction to the new map of Europe, in response to demands from the Kriegsmarine, Wehrmacht and Luftwaffe, was to develop, at short notice, a veritable espionage offensive against GOLFPLATZ, the Abwehr's codename for Great Britain. From Berlin's perspective, this had been a secondary consideration, with Czechoslovakia, Poland, France and Belgium being higher priorities.

The burden for planning, agent selection, training and operational support for the British target fell almost entirely on Ast Brussels, staffed largely by personnel posted from Hamburg and Bremen. Supervising the operation codenamed LENA was Walter Sensberg, a 44-year-old officer from Bavaria who had been commissioned in 1915 and discharged from the army in 1919 to work for a travel film company that went bankrupt. In 1934 he had re-joined the Wehrmacht to become Leiter Eins at Ast Kassel, moving on to Ast Wiesbaden in 1936 and then Ast Brussels in May 1940.[7] Although based at the Ast's headquarters in the rue de Loi, Sensberg maintained a villa in Le Touquet where he entertained his agents, among them José Waldberg whom he had known in Wiesbaden.[8] He also oversaw a training school at 4 rue Stein and in August 1940 he supervised the training of Charles van der Kieboom,[9] Sjoerd Pons[10] and Carl Meier[11] who were dropped onto a beach near Dymchurch in Kent by a fishing boat on 3 September. Three days later a Swede, Goesta Caroli,[12] landed in Cambridgeshire, to be followed on 19 September by his Danish friend Wulf Schmidt[13] who also arrived by parachute. In the meantime, on 7 September a Spanish journalist, Miguel Piernavieja del Pozo,[14] flew in from Madrid, having been sponsored by the British ambassador, Sir Samuel Hoare. Soon after he touched down at Whitchurch he was compromised by SNOW's nominee G.W, a retired Welsh policeman and supposed Welsh nationalist, but MI5 took no action against him apart from a surveillance operation codenamed POGO. Del Pozo returned home in February 1941, apparently unaware of the interest in him. Coincidentally, he had flown into England on the same airliner as a Portuguese engineer, Renato Roque Laia, who was also on an espionage mission, and was kept under observation until he flew home in early November, his activities having been monitored through ISOS.[15]

On 23 September the MV *La Part Bien* docked in Plymouth with a Swedish skipper, Hugo Jonassen, his two Belgian crew, de Lee and Gerard Libot, and a pair of innocent passengers. When questioned, the trio admitted having been recruited by the Abwehr in Brest.[16]

Next to arrive was a party of three, Vera Eriksson, Karl Drucke (alias François de Deeker) and Robert Petter (alias Werner Wälti), rowed ashore from a flying-boat in Scotland on 30 September.[17] This brought the total number of Abwehr spies sent to Britain during the month to thirteen, a record for the entire war, and eloquent proof of the renewed interest in GOLFPLATZ.[18]

Then, Kurt Goose (GANDER)[19] landed in Northamptonshire on 3/4 October, and was followed on 2 November by Engelbertus Fukken whose parachute was found near Haversham in Buckinghamshire. He was never apprehended, but shot himself in a Cambridge bomb shelter in March 1941 when he ran out of ration coupons.[20]

Later in the month, on 25 October, two Norwegians, Gunnar Edvardsen and Legwald Lund, accompanied by a Saarlander, Otto Joost, were all arrested in Nairn, Scotland.[21] The trio claimed to be refugees who had escaped across the North Sea in the fishing-boat *Boreas* but under interrogation at Camp 020 confessed to having been delivered on an Abt. II sabotage mission by a Luftwaffe amphibious aircraft. Finally, on 12 November, the MV *Josephine* was detained at Fishguard and eight men were taken into custody. The Dutch master, Cornelius Eveertsen, quickly admitted to the police that he and his voyage had been sponsored by the Germans, as did his crew, Peter Krag and Arie Vandam, and his five Cuban passengers Silvio Robles, Pedro Hecheveria, Nicolas Pazos-Diaz, Theophil Jazequel and Juan Martinez then admitted their guilt.[22]

By the end of the year the Abwehr had inserted four agents by parachute, eight by boat, and infiltrated a further seven by posing as legitimate travellers. In this last category were a Belgian fighter pilot, Pierre Arend, Cyril V. George and Dusan Popov, who all arrived independently from Lisbon in December. Others from the Peninsula included the Czech soldier Georges Graf (codenamed GIRAFFE) on 29 September; STRIPE in October, with DOOLITTLE on 11 October); and KINGPIN on 29 October. Then there was Albert de Jaeger (HATCHET) on 4 October, with Karl van Gils and Joseph Laureyssens soon afterwards, with SISYPHUS too.[23]

In the new year of 1941 the unprecedented 'assault', as described by MI5, continued in January when an established double agent, Hans George, codenamed DRAGONFLY, returned from Lisbon with a radio transmitter concealed in a gramophone. Born and brought up in England by German parents, George had been living in The Hague in 1939 when he had been recruited by the Abwehr. Upon his return to London in April 1940 he had reported his clandestine contact with the enemy to MI5 and had become a double agent. In November 1940, at MI5's suggestion, he had travelled to Lisbon, ostensibly as a not very successful wine importer, but actually to receive instructions from his I/L handler, Emile Kliemann. Significantly, as one of only two Abwehr transmitters active in England, George was put in touch with the Belgian fighter pilot, codenamed FATHER by MI5, to send his messages.

DRAGONFLY was soon followed by Josef Jakobs[24] who parachuted into Huntingdonshire, and in March by the MV *Volga* which may (or may not) have delivered more German spies. A 38-year-old Dutch cheese exporter based in Madrid, Gerth Van Wijk,[25] arrived from Lisbon on 5 April but, having been compromised by ISOS, signed a 36-page confession in which he detailed his espionage mission. In August 1941 Dick White wanted to 'treat him like a reference library' and described him as 'one of our principal sources of information on the German Intelligence Service in Spain'.[26]

Then two more Norwegians, John Moe[27] and Tor Glad,[28] rowed ashore in Scotland from an amphibious aircraft, and a few days later the *Taanevik* docked and produced a further four: Henry Torgersen, Hans Hansen, Bjarne Hansen, and Johan Strandmoen.[29] On 10 May Karel Richter dropped by parachute into Hertfordshire on an assignment which included delivering some wireless crystals to TATE.[30] In June PASTURES arrived from Lisbon. In Shetland on 6 July the *Hernie* was found to be carrying three Norwegian refugees, Helmik Wallem, Ingard Nilsen and George Lunda. Compromised by ISOS, Wallem confessed to espionage at Camp 020, while his companions were freed as having innocently supported his cover story.[31] Florent Steiner, a Dutch seaman who successfully entered the country at Glasgow in June 1941 as a ship's engineer on the Panamanian-registered freighter SS *Csarda,* would not be tracked down for a further eight months, when he was denounced by Jack Verlinden and arrested at his brother's home in Mossley Hill, in Liverpool. Under interrogation Steiner admitted having been recruited by the Abwehr's George Hoffman in Lisbon, but denied having maintained contact with the Germans since his arrival.[32]

Also, Edward Ejsymont (codenamed CARELESS) arrived from Lisbon on 15 July, with Joseph Lenihan (BASKET) being parachuted into Eire on a mission across the border in Ulster, followed by the Yugoslav domestic servant Maria Marek (THE SNARK) on 24 July, and THISBE on 30 July. The Belgian seaman Alphonse Timmerman[33] was arrested in London on 1 September and the Norwegian Olaf Saetrang, off the *Hornfjelll*, at Reykjavik, followed from Oslo on 13 September (but hanged himself in his cell at Camp 020 before he could be interrogated).[34] A fortnight later, on 26 September, Ast Oslo sent over two further spies, Gustav Ronning and Martin Olsen. The relevant MI5 B1(a) report, dated June 1942, noted that 'Saetrang seems to have been intended to penetrate either the SIS or SOE Norwegian organisations. Ronning and Olsen may have had some similar mission or may only have been sent to observe ship movements in northern waters since it was apparently expected that the boat on which they came (as ostensible traders) would be allowed to return to Norway.'[35]

The scale of the Abwehr's concentration on GOLFPLATZ was quite extraordinary, and was all the greater if the Irish missions are included, for they consisted of two deliveries by submarine, the *U-38*, of Willi Preetz and Walter Simon in June 1940; three arrivals on a yacht, the *Soizic*, in July 1940, of an anti-British Indian, Henry Obed, and a pair of South African students, Herbert Tributh and Otto Dietergaertner.[36] Two others, Hermann Goertz and Hans Marschner, were dropped by parachute in May 1940 and March 1941 respectively. All had been directed to join a network created by Werner Unland, who had fled London with his English wife Muriel Dugarde just as war was about to be declared, but was arrested at their flat in Merrion Square, Dublin, in April 1941. Previously unsuspected of espionage, the 49-year-old Unland, who had been born in Hamburg, had been compromised by receiving funds from a bank on MI5's watch-list because of its link to Ast Hamburg. Unland was also identified as a German spy by the recently-arrived parachutist Gunter Schutz (alias Hans Marschner).[37] Evidently Unland's mission, devised by Dr Praetorius, had sent him to England in April 1939, where his presence had gone undetected.[38] Having arrived as a student, he ran several unsuccessful businesses, including one representing German textile manufacturers, and another selling shoes. However, he would not be the subject of an MI5 investigation until long after he had left the jurisdiction.

More evidence of the Abwehr's operations was provided by eleven others who were intercepted at sea before they could land in Britain. The first group was found in King Oscar's Fjord, off the coast of Greenland, aboard the *Vesle Kari* on 18 August 1940, consisting of Hoel,

Giaever, Hannestad and Axel Coll.[39] Their mission had been chiefly meteorological, and their Abwehr role was not discovered until it appeared in ISOS, leading to internment on the Isle of Man for Coll and two of his companions, both radio operators.

The second vessel was the trawler *Hinrich Freese*, found off Jan Mayen Island, carrying its leader, Ulrich von Finkenstein, together with his subordinate, Harald Bruhn, and a Dane, Kurt Hansen.[40] There was also a civilian crew of five others, all supposedly engaged on weather reporting. The mission had left Trondheim on 2 November 1940 but had been intercepted by the light cruiser HMS *Naiad* on 16 November. Von Finckenstein and Hansen remained at Camp 020 until July 1945, when they were transferred to Diest, while Bruhn was killed when the Luftwaffe bombed Kingston Hospital where he was receiving treatment. All the rest of the *Hinrich Freese*'s crew underwent internment until the end of hostilities.

The British had responded to the German strategy, which had resulted in the deployment of several dozen spies, by recruiting many of them as double agents, among them the first three parachutists, SUMMER, TATE and GANDER. At the time, during the critical 'invasion summer' of 1940, the Abwehr possessed only three sources in England, and all were run by MI5. SNOW[41] was equipped with a transmitter, and had created a network which included the retired Cardiff policeman codenamed G.W.; and an Anglo-German, Charles Eschborn, one of three brothers from Cologne. Codenamed CHARLIE, Eschborn was a Manchester photographer who had been recruited by the Abwehr in 1938 while on a visit to see his family, but had reported the incident to the police and then to MI5, two days after the outbreak of war. The other members of SNOW's ring was Sam McCarthy, a petty criminal codenamed BISCUIT, and a former RAF officer, Walter Dicketts, codenamed CELERY.

One of SNOW's associates, introduced by MI5, was William Rolph, the proprietor of Hatchett's restaurant in Piccadilly. Rolph himself had been a Security Service officer during the First World War, and therefore had appeared a suitable nominee to place close to SNOW, but in May 1940 he attempted to sell information to the Abwehr using SNOW as a somewhat reluctant intermediary (or so he later claimed). When his scheme was discovered by MI5, Rolph committed suicide by gassing himself in his office in Dover Street.

Apart from this group, the only other Abwehr asset in England was Bernie Kiener. Codenamed RAINBOW, he was a piano player in a jazz band working in Brighton. In December 1941 three MI5 officers, Charles Cholmondeley, John Gwyer and Martin Grimaldi, assessed the situation in a paper entitled *The Objectives in England of the German Secret Service.*

1. Information about the objectives in this country of the German Secret Service can be derived from three sources of varying reliability: first, documents found on captured enemy agents; secondly, the instructions which these agents admit under interrogation to having received; thirdly, the supplementary questions which certain established agents are known to have been asked since their arrival. Of these, the first source is clearly the most reliable. If, for example, an agent arrives with maps only of northern Scotland in his pocket, it seems safe to assume that he was intended to work exclusively in that area. The second source is more open to question since an agent may have some interest in lying or concealing the exact nature of his instructions. One is not, therefore, on absolutely safe ground except in those cases where an agent brings an actual written questionnaire with him. The third source is subject to a different qualification. No question arises of the agents having lied. On the other hand it is clear that no one can expect an agent to carry out exactly the instructions which he has received. The physical situation in which he finds himself, his own character and a number of chance circumstances must make it easier for him to obtain one type of information than another. An agent originally sent to report on troop movements may find himself better placed to report on aerodromes and do so exclusively. It is then probable that most of the questions subsequently asked him by the Germans will concern aerodromes, since they know that he is likely to be able to answer them; and this might be so even if information about troop movements were of more immediate interest. We have therefore based this report on primary questionnaires and other documents carried by agents on their first arrival. The deductions which we have been able to make from this material have been to a considerable extent enlarged and modified in the light of an analysis of the supplementary questions. We have not, however, anywhere based a deduction solely on the evidence of supplementary questions.

2. We have attempted in this review to cover the whole period between the outbreak of war and the end of September 1941. It is, however, 'noticeable that (if we except Mrs. Krafft and her circle) no enemy agents are known to have arrived in this country before September 1940 – that is a year after the outbreak of war. This is certainly a curious circumstance. It would have seemed more natural, perhaps, for the Germans to have taken advantage of the nine months lull following the outbreak of war – when they might have expected conditions of control to be less strict – to filter agents into this country against the time when they would really need their services. One must therefore consider the possibility that enemy agents of whom we know nothing did in fact reach this country during the first year of the war. Against this there are, however, two things to be remembered. In the first place, we know that the Germans did make every effort in the period immediately

before the war to build up an espionage organisation in England. It is possible to distinguish at least four separate groups of spies, centring respectively round SNOW, RAINBOW, Walter Simon and My Ericksen [*sic*]. So far as the Germans knew, all these groups remained active at least for some time after the outbreak of war; who they believe still to be active. It is not possible to say exactly at what point in the Germans' opinion this pre-war organisation broke down, an investigation of it is still in progress, but no definitive report has yet been issued. In default of this one can only say that the Germans may have remained in ignorance of the collapse of their organisation for some months after the outbreak of war, but cannot have remained ignorant for as long as a year. It is therefore evident that there must have been some period of time during which, if no other agents entered the country, the Germans were dependent for their information mainly upon SNOW and RAINBOW. This information would, of course, have been supplemented through diplomatic channels by the German organisation in Eire, of which very little is known, and possibly also by the German industrial espionage system. It is, however, noticeable that the Germans seem to have aimed before the war at establishing contact points in England for future use, rather than recruiting actual agents. So far as we know they have not since attempted to put these contacts to any use, except in one instance to which reference will be made below.

Secondly, there is independent evidence which suggests that the German organisation, large though it now is, is not yet large enough to devote its full energy to more than one front at a time. It may be that during the period when its principal purpose was to gather information in France, it was obliged, for reasons of organisation and capacity, to ignore England almost completely. This view is to some extent supported by an analysis of the questions known to have been asked during the first year of the war. Very little can be derived from an analysis of RAINBOW's traffic, since no complete record of it has been kept. Several points are, however, clear from SNOW's traffic. In the first place, the geographical area about which he was asked for information contracted noticeably after September 1940. Before that date he had been asked for information about specific places in almost the whole area of southern England as far west as Dorset, Wales and, to a lesser extent, south Yorkshire. After September 1940 this area contracted and can be seen to have divided itself fairly accurately into three smaller districts: the London area, where SNOW himself was living, South Wales and the Manchester-Liverpool area, where he was known to have sub-agents placed. Moreover in the first year of the war the majority of questions asked of SNOW were of a very general nature, such as 'Find out all that you can about aircraft production'. After September 1940 the questions became far more particular. This certainly suggests that during the earlier period SNOW was the Germans' main source of information about England, and that there were not, in fact, other agents of whose existence we are ignorant. It can also be observed that the area covered by SNOW did not coincide at all accurately with the main industrial areas of England. Broadly speaking, it would even be true to say that he was asked more questions about non-industrial than about industrial areas. This would bear out the suggestion that the Germans considered themselves to be well served by a system of purely industrial espionage. Further evidence in support of this view can be found in an analysis of a questionnaire brought back by BISCUIT in August 1940, which asked for information about a particular list of firms and factories, all of which were, we understand, engaged on the work described at the outbreak of war but many of which had since gone out of business or changed the nature of their work.

3. With the fall of France the situation changed abruptly. Since then there has been a fairly steady flow of enemy agents into this country who have arrived either by parachute and seaplane or on some legal pretext. So far as can be determined all these agents (with one possible exception) were despatched under the control of the same organisation, that is the Abwehr. They have, however, come from a variety of Stellen – Oslo, Hamburg, Brussels or Brest, Paris, Madrid and Lisbon – as well as direct from the Berlin headquarters. One can trace a certain family resemblance between the agents from any particular Stelle. It is natural that the methods by which they arrive and the purpose for which they come should be conditioned by the position of their controlling Stelle and in order to interpret the signification of an agent's arrival correctly it is necessary to know first something of what these differences are.

Oslo

Oslo itself, or the Bergen Stelle which is under Oslo's control, has sent in all approximately ten agents to this country between 21 September 1940 and 13 September 1941. In addition, various meteorological expeditions have been dispatched to Greenland, Spitzbergen and other northerly points and we know from independent information that Oslo is much preoccupied in gathering weather reports from all available sources. But it is to be observed that, with one exception, none of the agents sent to England has been asked to give weather reports or provided with the means to do so. The exception is the MUTT and JEFF expedition of 7 April 1941. Their original instructions are said to have included the sending of weather reports (a business of which one of them had some slight knowledge); but at that time it was also apparently assumed that they would be operating in Scotland. In fact they settled near London and did not send and were not asked for weather reports. From this it seems safe to assume that although Oslo's work is so largely meteorological, their interest is only in the extreme north, any reports coming from further south than Scotland (at the most) being dealt with by other stations.

The second noticeable point about Oslo is what appears to be its total lack of interest in Service matters. Of all the agents sent only MUTT and JEFF have to our knowledge been equipped with any means of sending back reports to Norway. A study of the MUTT and JEFF traffic has further shown that Oslo up to date has not asked any questions directly relating to Service matters, except in one instance when a passing interest was shown in troop concentrations in Iceland and another when MUTT and JEFF volunteered a certain quantity of information about a forthcoming British landing in Norway. Otherwise, the staple of the traffic has been general information about conditions in England, with particular relation to the food position, rationing and so on. It is particularly remarkable (in view of our experience with other Stellen) that at no time has Oslo asked for or received any information on Air Force matters.

These conclusions are borne out by a study of the instructions of other Oslo agents. In at least five out of the ten cases noted there has been some hint of penetration in one of its many forms. Joost, who arrived on 25 October 1940, has said that he was told to enter one of the Free Forces, discover what he could about its organisation and, on the occasion of the German invasion, report to the nearest German officers. As he had no means of communication, it seems that his main utility would have been in fifth column work within the Free Force. Joost's companion Lund has given no very coherent account of his instructions. Edvaardsen, who also arrived on the same date, says that he was instructed to do general sabotage of a minor character in Scotland.

Next came MUTT and JEFF, likewise instructed to do minor sabotage in Scotland, though this time against specific objectives. It was also proposed to them as an alternative or second string that MUTT should seek a post in the Norwegian Government and JEFF in the Free Forces. In that event it was apparently contemplated that they would have to dispose of their transmitter, thereby also reducing themselves to the status of fifth columnists. Finally, there is some suggestion that JEFF was intended to penetrate the Intelligence Service and return to Norway as a British agent.

On 6 March 1941 the MV *Volga* arrived, and may or may not have had a German agent on board. She was followed on 27 April 1941 by the *Taanevik*, which certainly brought an agent, of whose objectives we are, however, ignorant. Then came the *Hernie* on 8 July 1941, an acknowledged IIIF or counter-espionage undertaking with the apparent purpose of penetrating either the British service or some escape organisation. Finally, on 13 September 1941, Saetrang arrived in Iceland with, so far as can be seen, the object of planting false information on the military.

In sum it would seem that Oslo (apart from its meteorological interest) is very largely concerned with counter-espionage of which the offensive aspect, which mostly concerns this country, is the running of double agents of a resident or fifth columnist type. Apart from this there were two attempts at sabotage (Edvardsen and MUTT and JEFF); of these the former will be seen to take his place in the natural sequence of events observable in other Stellen.

The Peninsula

The two Peninsula Stellen, Lisbon and Madrid, (of which the latter is probably the controlling station) sent sixteen agents to England between September 1940 and September of this year. They came at their thickest in October 1940, the Peninsula providing exactly half of the ten agents who arrived in that month. The significance of this date is further discussed below.

It is possible to distinguish four main strands in the information required by Lisbon and Madrid: Service matters; the flow of armaments and raw materials from America; questions of food supply, rationing and public morale; shipping intelligence. Up to a point the collection of information in each of these categories is assigned to different types of agents. For example, four agents, de Jaeger on 4 October 1940, Van Gils and Laureyssens later in the same year, and Timmerman on 1 September 1941, have been sent as seamen to collect information about ship movements and damage in ports. They were asked, broadly speaking, only such questions as could be answered by an observant man employed in coastwise shipping or ashore for short periods in port. Apart from strictly shipping matters, a few questions were included about the volume of supplies from America and the public attitude towards the war. No questions were asked about specifically naval matters except what was directly observable in ports, e.g., warships under repair, position of minefields, etc.

The next group is of six agents mainly or wholly concerned with Air Force matters: GIRAFFE on 29 September 1940, STRIPE in October 1940, DOOLITTLE on 11 October 1940, KINGPIN on 29 October 1940, FATHER (who should probably be classed as a Peninsular agent) on 20 June 1941 and CARELESS on 15 July 1941. There are not very many comments to these questionnaires; but it is worthwhile to remark on the carefully selective basis on which these agents were recruited. For example, GIRAFFE, who had passed through the Czech Military Academy, was told to confine himself to a report on the AA defences of London. DOOLITTLE, FATHER and CARELESS, all trained Air Force officers, were given questions directly concerned with types of aeroplane, aircraft production, and the arrival of aircraft from America. On the other hand, STRIPE and KINGPIN, who had no such specialised training, were given more general questions to answer including references to the food situation or public morale.

Next there are four agents – SISYPHUS in October 1940, G.W. who re-opened contact with the Germans through a Spanish diplomatic channel on 6 October 1940, PASTURES in June 1941 and the SNARK on 24 July 1941 – who were provided with general questionnaires which covered between them Army, Navy and Air Force matters, political questions and questions of public morale and details about aircraft production and supplies from America. There are certain points worth noticing. First, there is again evidence of careful recruiting. For example, PASTURES, who collects his information from the gossip of travellers in Lisbon and the SNARK, who is a domestic servant in London, both had questionnaires very well adapted to their position. Secondly, both the Naval and political questions are more frequent and specific than can be noted from any other Stelle. Thirdly, G.W.'s military questions referred to a specific area in the south Midlands, the significance of which will be discussed below.

Hamburg

The German pre-war organisation, to which reference has already been made, was so far as we know wholly under the control of the Hamburg Stelle. Apart from that Hamburg has despatched or acquired eleven agents: G.W. in October 1939, BISCUIT on 18 May 1940, SUMMER on 6 September 1940, TATE on 19 September 1940. Walti, Eriksson and de Deeker on 30 September 1940, Ter Braak (probably) on 2 November 1940, Jakobs on 31 January 1941, CELERY in February 1941 and Richter on 12 May 1941. This is not so large a total as the Peninsula; nor on the whole have the agents brought so much specialised knowledge to their tasks. Nevertheless, there seems no doubt that Hamburg is the Stelle principally concerned with work against this country. This conclusion, which can be reached from independent evidence, is reinforced by an analysis of Hamburg agents' traffic, which shows an astonishingly high proportion of domestic questions, that is questions essential to the running of agents, e.g., about identity and ration cards, travel control, whether gas masks are carried and so on.

Beyond this, there are certain distinct characteristics which can be noted in Hamburg agents. In the first place, they are predominantly, sometimes almost exclusively, concerned with Air Force matters. Their questions under this heading concern the position of aerodromes and aircraft factories, new types of aeroplane, AA defences, predictor equipment and indeed the whole range of Luftwaffe interests; they are expressed with far greater detail and precision than similar questions emanating from other Stelle. Questions concerning the army are fairly frequent, but subject to the geographical limitations discussed below. Questions relating to the navy are conspicuous by their absence. They only occur in two connections. One or two questions were asked about the movements of certain ships, such as the *King George V*, apparently from a Luftwaffe point of view. SNOW was asked a certain number of questions about shipping at Liverpool during the period when he was known to have a sub-agent working in Manchester.

Secondly, almost all Hamburg agents (excepting RAINBOW and G.W. who do not use wireless) have been instructed to send regular and sometimes daily weather reports, no matter in what part of the country they are settled. It would seem, therefore, that on the meteorological side Hamburg is concerned with immediate weather conditions over England, rather than with longer term weather forecasts of the type with which Oslo deals.

Thirdly, all Hamburg agents other than those established before the war, have been given specific geographical areas in which to work. When the pieces of the jig-saw puzzle are put together, it appears that Hamburg has a special interest in a Midland area bounded by London, Oxford, Birmingham, Northampton and London. In addition to this, Hamburg has displayed marked interest (either in agents' instructions or in supplementary questions) in three outlying areas: South Wales, Liverpool and Manchester, and East Anglia. The first of these is easily explained by the fact that G.W., a sub-agent of SNOW's, was resident in South Wales, though it is worthwhile to note that SNOW was specifically instructed to recruit a Welshman. The Manchester-Liverpool area is similarly explicable, but apparently more importance was attached to it since the Germans did once attempt (unsuccessfully) to drop an additional agent in that area. East Anglia is more interesting. Hamburg has despatched three agents, TATE, Ter Braak and Jakobs, instructed or equipped to work round Cambridge, that is, on the extreme eastern fringe of the main area. In addition, they have sent four agents, Walti, Eriksson and de Deeker and Richter, who all carried either maps of East Anglia or a list of objectives in that area. It seems, therefore, that they have a special interest in the coast between the Wash and London and its hinterland. It is also interesting to notice how persistent this interest is, extending (with Jakobs and Richter) beyond what is usually thought of as the invasion period, although information from that area would be, above all, of immediate operational importance in the event of a German landing, Moreover, the Germans' persistent efforts to place an agent in the Cambridge area have not been wholly unsuccessful, since TATE is still active, though in the southernmost point of his district. But their efforts in East Anglia have been uniformly failures; yet, since Richter's arrival and arrest, no further attempt has been made to our knowledge. One must speculate why, if the Germans still required information from that area in May of this year, they should, apparently, have ceased to require it thereafter. Finally one must also point out that with the exception of agents specifically destined for East Anglia, no Hamburg agent has ever been asked a question relating to this area; this even applies to SNOW during the period September 1939 and September 1940.

One other curious point about Hamburg agents is worth remarking. According to SNCW's pre-war information the Hamburg Stelle is divided into three sections; an Air Force section, presided over by Dr. Rantzau, a naval section, and an army section presided over by Dr. Lorenz, alias Hans Luders. This information has been to some extent confirmed since. With each of the Hamburg agents referred to above (who shew a predominant interest in Air Force matters), it has been possible to trace a direct connection with Dr. Rantzau. We are also aware of two occasions before the war on which Lorenz recruited agents: F.P. Campbell in Dublin and [Percy] Rapp, the taxi-driver, in London. Both of these received military questionnaires exclusively concerned with information about the army of a detailed and specific kind. Further confirmation is afforded by the analysis of SNOW's traffic during the first year of the war, which shows geographically a remarkable blind spot in the Salisbury Plain-Aldershot area. It is interesting to speculate why Lorenz has not apparently attempted since the outbreak of war to run any agents into this country.

Brussels

Brussels, so far as we know, has sent only two expeditions to this country: Meier, Pons, Kieboom and Waldberg who arrived together by boat on 3 September 1940 and GANDER who arrived by parachute on 3 October 1940. The original party of four, who were equipped with (like GANDER) wireless transmitters, were clearly intended to report on coastal defences in the district between Margate and Folkestone with particular reference to the Dungeness peninsula, with subsidiary objectives on the Military Canal and the Dover-Canterbury railway. It is interesting to notice that Waldberg, by far the most experienced agent of the four, was also given instructions to report on the coastline from Aldeburgh to Cromer and, if possible, to return and deliver this report in person.

The second arrival, GANDER, was dropped near Wellingborough with instructions to send daily weather reports and to report on civilian morale (with particular reference to evacuation) and road obstructions in an area between Bedford and Liverpool, including the towns of Leicester, Birmingham and Coventry. It seems that the information which GANDER would have given in these circumstances would, like that of the previous party, have been mainly of immediate operational interest. The evidence is admittedly scanty, but the general impression left is that Brussels is an advanced base for espionage, more closely linked than other Stellen with the operational staff of the army.

Brest

This Stelle also has to our knowledge sent only two expeditions to England: the fishing boat *La Part Bien* on 23 September 1940 and the party of Cuban saboteurs who were landed at Fishguard on 11 January 1940.

Of the former expedition we know very little. The master of the boat was instructed to sail from Brest to Le Touquet, there to pick up two agents who were then to be landed on some part of the English coast where a small boat would come out to meet them. Instead, the master brought *La Part Bien* direct to England from Brest. It seems just possible, since the objective was apparently to contact established agents, that this expedition should be connected with the earlier venture of Pons, Kieboom, etc.

The Cuban saboteurs (of whom there were three) have said that their instructions were to find work in some factory near Bristol for the purpose of sabotage. Against this, it is noticeable that their equipment (two or three bombs each, explosives, detonators, fuses and ammunition) suggests immediate action rather than the more insidious sabotage that a regular employee in a factory might indulge in. Their training, which included the wrecking of high tension cables, had the same tendency. It is also very probable that one should connect the Cubans with the three saboteurs whose reception in South Wales G.W. had been asked to prepare in the previous August. This view is supported by the fact that the Cubans had with them a Hamburg cover-address for use should they later succeed in leaving England for a neutral country. When the Cubans actually arrived, however, G.W. was not asked to cooperate. Presumably, then, they were not after all intended to contact G.W.'s reputed sabotage organisation in the neighbourhood of Cardiff but to work in some other area. One's final impression, therefore, is that they were probably intended to work at large in an area of which Bristol was the most westerly point. This will be seen to fit in fairly well into the general chronological picture discussed below.

Paris

Paris has so far been responsible only for three agents: DRAGONFLY who was recruited during November of 1940, BASKET who was dropped in Eire on 19 July 1941 and THISBE who arrived in this country on 30 August 1941. DRAGONFLY received instructions (which he since carried out) to send regular weather reports from the London area and to send general information, including army and Air Force but excluding naval and shipping matters on which it was said that the Germans were already sufficiently well posted.

BASKET was sent with the main purpose of setting up a meteorological station in Eire, to which end he had received fairly extensive training in Paris. He had the secondary objective of reporting on civilian morale and the effect of air raid damage in England.

THISBE is the single case – referred to in the introduction – of an agent possibly not controlled by the Abwehr but by some other organisation. He was not by his own account in touch with the German personnel at any of the offices previously known to us in Paris. His questionnaire was mainly of a general political type, with a supplement of detailed questions on naval anti-submarine devices. It appears that this supplement was not the work of THISBE's normal control but of a naval officer imported from Nantes for the purpose. Moreover, THISBE would in fact have been incapable of answering any of the questions asked, though it is possible that certain incidents in his earlier career mislead the Germans on this point.

Of this evidence it is not possible to say very much, except that it is consistent with Paris being in the nature of an advanced GHQ Paris, meteorological interests appear to be the same as those of Hamburg though conceived on a more professional basis. It should be emphasised that weather reports from the west coast of Eire are absolutely essential for an accurate short-term (24-36 hour) forecast of weather over central England.

Berlin etc.

There are only three agents known to us who are controlled directly from Berlin: TRICYCLE and his attendant sub-agents BALLOON and GELATINE. Of these GELATINE has never received a regular questionnaire, but has simply been instructed to report on political matters of interest as they come to her knowledge. TRICYCLE and BALIOON's traffic is more illuminating; it is an excellent example of the extent to which an agent's traffic can be conditioned by the relative value of his answers to earlier questions, TRICYCLE received his first questionnaire on 15 September 1940. It covered army, naval and Air Force matters in a fairly general way, the RAF questions being the most detailed and the army the weakest. Questions about raw materials and supplies were particularly detailed, no doubt in view of TRICYCLE's status as a business agent. In the course of the next few months TRICYCLE answered a high proportion of the questions given to him, but was strongest on the RAF. His naval questions were not answered so fully and it appeared subsequently that the Germans were distrustful of his naval contact. Accordingly, his next questionnaire in February 1941 showed an increase in detailed questions about the RAF, a heavy increase in the aircraft industry, a slight increase in army questions and a distinct falling off in naval questions. General questions about the food situation, etc. had almost disappeared. This was answered in the same way as before. His third questionnaire in April 1941 was wholly confined to service matters with particular relation to detailed questions about the RAF. TRICYCLE's final questionnaire in August 1941 was handed on by him to BALLOON, who had been the source of much of his earlier information. It consisted of nothing but detailed questions about the RAF, aircraft production and AA defences. Apart from this there is very little comment to be made on the TRICYCLE questionnaires except to say that the questions generally are of a type that one would expect to come from headquarters rather than an outlying Stelle. They show, for example, a high proportion of specific questions about the organisation of the RAF and a number of questions which do not occur in other questionnaires about the supply of particular raw materials such as ferro-vanadium or molybdenum.

We have to consider two other agents as probably controlled from Berlin, or at least assignable to no other particular Stelle; HITTITE who was recruited in America during October 1940, and YODLER who has been operating in Switzerland since June 1941. Of the purpose of the former we know little or nothing. The latter has been asked a number of questions about the army and British oil supplies – very reasonably, since he derives his information from the Swiss general staff. He has also been asked, more surprisingly, for detailed information about the system of food rationing in England. It is hard to know what, if anything, to deduce from this.

Chronological Analysis

1. We have annexed to this report a chart showing month by month the number of questions asked by the Germans on various subjects. Like all statistical documents it is in some respects misleading. For each entry we have shown two totals, the first representing the number of questions asked in primary questionnaires, the second the number of supplementary questions. We have not, however, been able to show how many different agents or different questionnaires are represented in a given total. Thus the forty-one questions relating to aircraft production in February 1941 were in fact extracted from a single questionnaire given to TRICYCLE. It is more than probable, had TRICYCLE been a wireless agent, that these questions would have been spread over a period of months and so shown a different result on the chart. Similarly, certain of the subject headings are necessarily vague. For example, food in this context includes both the location of food dumps and the price of rationed foods, which might in an ideal analysis have come under different heads. For these reasons the chart can only be read with safety in its broadest indications; but, subject to this qualification, it gives, we think, a fair picture of German activity over the period

2. It does appear that the fluctuation in the number of questions asked by the Germans about, say, the RAF, does bear a direct relation to their operational plans. What is, perhaps, the best example of this is not unfortunately shown on the chart. Between August and October of 1940, when the Battle of Britain was at its height, the majority of questions directly relating to aerodromes were concerned with the position and defences of fighter aerodromes. Conversely, by August 1941, at the opening of the British air offensive on the continent, interest had swung over to bomber aerodromes, and the landing grounds from which bombers operate. This high level of interest has not, however,

been maintained in recent months, a fact which lends itself to one of two inferences. Either the Germans have not found British bombing so damaging as they had at first supposed that it would be or they know that they would lack the means to use the information even if they had it.

3. A number of similar indications can be drawn from the chart. In the first place, it shows broadly speaking three peak periods: during September and October 1940; between February and April 1941; and lastly a fairly steady general rise dating from June or July 1941. With regard to the first period, the rise can be seen to begin in August, attain a flat peak at some point during September and October; and then die away abruptly and completely during November. The two months September and October are also, as one would expect, the peak months for the arrival of new agents. It is noticeable that, whereas September's entry was made up mainly of Hamburg agents, October's came very largely from the Peninsula. This is presumably to be accounted for by the fact that Hamburg agents arrive by air but Peninsular agents largely by sea, taking longer on the journey, and would be consistent with the view that the actual order to obtain more information about England was issued some time fairly late in August. This would mean – allowing for the length of time that it takes to establish an agent – that the Germans expected to have their organisation working at its maximum by, say, the last week of October or the first week of November. No new agents arrived (until right at the end of the year) after the three Cubans on 11 November, and we have reason to think that that party had been considerably delayed. It seems therefore safe to assume that for whatever reason by the first week in November at the latest the German espionage offensive was over.

4. From the chart German interests during this period appear to have been fairly general; but a closer analysis shows that they were in fact concentrated on information of immediate operational value. During the first part of the period (which coincided with the height of the Battle of Britain) their questions were largely concentrated on AA defences. Slightly later their curiosity expanded to include the south coast defences (SNOW had been asked for a general, preliminary report on coastal defences in August), coastal defences in East Anglia, troop dispositions, the location of aerodromes, types of aircraft in service with the RAF, air raid damage and public morale, the aircraft and armaments industry and the location of food dumps. In short, it appears that they were anxious to discover how great had been the effect of their air attack, what specific resistance an invading force would meet and to what extent such a force could maintain itself in the country after its arrival. This interest, as we have already noticed, ceased abruptly in November when, we may presume, the German invasion plan was cancelled.

5. During the second period, i.e. between February and April 1941, it will be seen that interest was concentrated almost entirely upon the three Services and aircraft production. The type of question asked on these subjects had also changed considerably. The Germans seemed predominantly interested in the organisation, equipment and current strength of the RAF and to a lesser degree of the Army and Navy. It is, however, worthwhile to remark that the level of Army and naval questions was distinctly above the average and proportionately at least as high as that of RAF questions. As we pointed out above, no agent has come to light since the outbreak of war instructed to report mainly or wholly on the Army, though there have been several reporting almost exclusively on the Air Force.

6. This second period covers the months during which the Germans must have been mainly engaged in planning and mounting their Russian offensive. It is to be noticed that the type of question asked is consistent with their having attempted to estimate simultaneously the current offensive strength of Great Britain and therefore the weight of the assistance which they might expect us to give to Russia either on the Eastern or some other front.

7. The last period – from June of this year to the present time – is more difficult to comment on, for the questions asked cannot yet be related to any event or change of policy which we know to have taken place. But certain general indications can be observed. The most obvious point – apart from the interest in bomber aerodromes which we have already noticed – is the steady rise in the number of questions about supplies (particularly aircraft) from America. This, as we noted above, is a particular preserve of the Peninsular Stelle, but in recent months agents from elsewhere seem also to have taken an increased interest in the subject. Secondly, the number of questions about food supplies and prices has shown a marked rise and has in fact reached a higher level even than during the first period. Moreover, the type of question has altered. The Germans seem no longer to be interested so much in the physical location of food dumps as in the total amount of food in the country and the machinery by which it is rationed and distributed. This, taken with the noticeable rise in the number of naval (and shipping) questions and the increased interest in supplies from America, suggests that during this summer the Germans were settling down to a long term blockade of this country and were using their agents largely to obtain a day to day estimate of its results. The rise in the number of purely political questions and questions about morale and the nature of these questions is also consistent with this view.

8. We have not, for obvious reasons, been able to push our detailed analysis much beyond September. We can only remark generally

that, whereas naval and shipping questions have not on the whole maintained the same high level, questions about food, politics and public morale have been fairly consistent. Very recently there has also been an increase in questions directly relating to the army and in particular to the organisation of the AA command, the training and strength of parachute troops. Questions on these two subjects seem to show a direct opposition of interest, since the state of preparedness of our parachute force is a reliable index of our capacity for offensive action on the Continent, and the organisation of the AA Command a mainly defensive matter. In neither case are the questions inconsistent with the general trend of the war situation, though it is scarcely possible to say what particular development they indicate in the future. Indeed, the whole problem of forecasting the future from indications in the current traffic is not an easy one. Looking back over a period it is easy enough to distinguish the general trend of questions and relate it to the known facts of the war; but the present is necessarily more formless. There are, however, certain sign posts to be used. One can, for instance, detect very rapidly any variation in the normal behaviour of a particular Stelle. Thus even a single naval question asked of a Hamburg agent or a military question asked of an Oslo agent would stand out at once as remarkable and significant. For example, the threat of a British landing in Norway immediately produced from Oslo a number of questions on military dispositions (in which they are not normally interested) and the offer of a reward for further information on the same subject. In the same way any marked alteration in the geographical area covered by agents generally could be observed and interpreted immediately.

9. In this context it is perhaps interesting to attempt to forecast the general nature of German espionage during the next few months, so that this may later be compared with the reality as that gradually reveals itself. In the first place it seems perfectly clear that the German interest in the volume of supplies from America will continue on a fairly high level. It is perhaps unlikely that it will actually increase, since a great part of German energy in this respect will necessarily be focused on the Southern Atlantic route. Secondly, one would expect a maintenance of interest in naval and shipping matters but (in view of our northern supply route to Russia) with an increased emphasis on arrivals and departures from northern ports. Thirdly, a revival of interest in strictly military matters appears likely, particularly in respect of any units about to proceed overseas. Fourthly, during the remainder of the winter it is probable that the present close watch on questions of food supply and public morale will be maintained. Lastly, one would expect, at any rate from the early spring of next year, a much increased interest in those ports at which British raiding parties or a possible offensive force might be expected to embark.

10. All this, translated into terms of Stellen, would mean almost certainly an increased activity on the part of Oslo and the Peninsula, particularly the former. It would also mean a distinct alteration in the type of information asked for by Oslo, for it is reasonable to suppose that espionage in northern ports would fall largely to their share. There seems no reason to expect many new arrivals from Hamburg, the less so since most of their agents have come by parachute – a method which we have reason to think that the Germans now regard (with reason) as unsatisfactory. On the other hand, one would expect the established Hamburg agents to enlarge the scope of their enquiries a little and take in (as they have already done) questions of food supply and public morale and also perhaps an increased number of purely military questions. Brest and Brussels one would not expect to show much activity unless and until the possibility of a German invasion is once more imminent. As for Paris and Berlin there seems no reason to expect any special variation in their behaviour, in respect either of the number of agents sent or the instructions given to them. Finally, it is interesting to speculate – in view of the German preoccupation with British food supplies – whether the comparatively newly established sabotage organisation in the Peninsula will extend its activities to an attempt to run saboteurs into this country, perhaps through Ireland.

11. These speculations are merely based on the assumption that what appears to be the current trend in German activities continues. Needless to say, none of the forecasts given may be justified in the event. On the other hand, if the general outline of the [corrupt] is not radically altered within the next few months and German espionage activity nevertheless deviates noticeably from the lines suggested, that will be a clear indication that some move is in progress of which the traffic, at any rate, has so far given us no hint.

<u>Geographical Analysis</u>
We have said something above, under the heading of the Hamburg Stelle, about the activities of SNOW and RAINBOW between the outbreak of war and September 1940. Both of them were certainly Hamburg agents. SNOW was clearly working under I Luft – the Air Force Section of the Stelle's Operational Branch – and RAINBOW was apparently recruited by I Wi – the section responsible for economic espionage. The nature of his original instructions, which were to report on factories – particularly those manufacturing AA guns – supports this view.

Up to September 1940 both SNOW and RAINBOW were to the Germans' knowledge living in or near London. At the end of that month RAINBOW reported that he had moved to Brighton. Both of them were, however, assumed to travel to some extent in search of material for their reports; but in German eyes SNOW was incomparably the more important. He was well paid, in almost daily wireless communication with Hamburg and was supposed by his employers to have sub-agents or contacts scattered broadcast over England. RAINBOW on the other hand appears to have received no money, little encouragement and no fresh instructions between his visit to Antwerp in April 1940 and January of the following year. No complete record of his traffic during this period has been preserved. It is therefore difficult to say whether he was ignored because the Germans considered his reports incompetent or for some other reason, but it seems a fair assumption (as the Germans have since employed him actively) that the Section I Wi did not feel the need during 1940 to foster an agent in RAINBOW's position. This may have been due, as we suggested above, to the circumstance of their having been well served from other sources.

At the beginning of 1940 SNOW was equipped with three specific sub-agents – G.W in Cardiff, Eschborn in Manchester and BISCUIT in London. He himself was living at Richmond. It is possible, as we have already shown, to calculate the approximate geographical area that he was required to cover at this period. When those of his questions which have a direct geographical context are plotted on a map they are seen to cluster most thickly round London and the district immediately to the south. Few or no questions were asked about any place in southern England further west than Dorset, and there was a noticeable blind spot in the Salisbury Plain-Aldershot area. The general area of the South Midlands was also well, but not quite so well, covered. A number of general questions were asked about Wales late in 1939, and it was at the Germans' particular direction that the Welshman G.W. was then recruited. There is no doubt that at that period the Germans were hoping to plan with the help of the Welsh Nationalist Party some substantial insurrection. By the beginning of 1940, however, this scheme had been dropped, largely perhaps on the advice of SNOW himself; but German interest in South Wales has nevertheless persisted.

Except for one specific question about the Glasgow neighbourhood, SNOW's work did not usually take him further north than Liverpool. (Eschborn was established in Manchester by January 1941). It is, however, very noticeable that the Germans do not seem to have been particularly interested in general information about industrial installations in this very industrial area. Rather one is left with the impression that they were using SNOW's services to fill the gaps in a knowledge already fairly complete. Eastwards SNOW's area took in, though on a reduced scale, the general district of southern Yorkshire but conspicuously avoided the East coast. But one can trace few questions relating, for example, to Lincoln and none at all for the whole of the East Anglian coast between the Wash and Southend or its immediate hinterland. Yet this, as later events proved, was an area deeply interesting to the Germans.

This broad dispersal of SNOW's efforts did not continue after September. From that moment onwards other agents began to arrive who took over from him sections of what had previously been his district. This process reached its climax in the fortnight following 10 October 1940, when the Germans must have supposed themselves to have had a minimum of fifteen agents actively at work in England. It is interesting to follow in detail the process by which events were brought to this point.

At the beginning of August RAINBOW gave unsolicited a general report on public morale. On the 14th SNOW was asked to report on the exact location of a number of Ministries and headquarters. Two days later he was asked about air raid damage in Odiham and Farnborough. Then came a further request for the whereabouts of important headquarters and a particular order to discover the exact position of a GHQ reported to be at Maidenhead. The following day G.W. was instructed through SNOW to prepare a house in Swansea for the reception of three well-equipped saboteurs, due to arrive presently. At about the same time SNOW was also told that a South African (of whom nothing more has ever been heard) had been dropped by parachute, with orders to work somewhere in southern England. Before the end of the month SNOW had been asked further questions about a factory in Chester, air-raid damage at Hendon and the aerodromes at Feltham, Heston, Denham, Maidenhead, Milton and Benson.

By the end of August, therefore, one can say that the Germans were evidently taking steps to strengthen their organisation in England. On the whole the focus of their attention appeared to be moving south. Evidently South Wales was also still occupying their attention.

On 1 September SNOW was asked to report on an anti-aircraft factory in Chichester. On the 3rd, Pons, Meier, Kieboom and Waldberg arrived by boat on the south coast, with instructions to report on defences in the neighbourhood of Dungeness and the Dover-Canterbury railway. Waldberg was also to report on the coast from Aldeburgh to Cromer and, if possible, to return and make his report in person: a reasonable precaution seeing that all four agents had only one-way wireless sets and could not, therefore, be asked to supplement their reports. One of them did in fact succeed in sending two messages before his capture. This fact and the obviously immediate nature of their mission must have combined to make the Germans aware of their capture very shortly after it took place. It is, therefore, not surprising to find that by the 7th SNOW was also required to report on coastal defences between Margate and the Isle of Wight. In the meantime Eschborn had been asked (through SNOW) for a report on the Liverpool docks and SUMMER had lighted on the Midlands with instructions to work the area Oxford-Northampton-Birmingham during the short time that he actually remained in this area SUMMER was asked only for a general report on air-raid damage. On the 12th SNOW was asked to make a personal report on Manchester. On the 19th TATE arrived with orders to work in the quadrilateral London-Bedford-Cambridge-Colchester. At about the same time TRICYCLE in Yugoslavia was receiving his first questionnaire which contained, from the geographical point of view, one or two interesting items:

> Details of coastal defences from Wash to Southampton.
> What importance have light signals from Wash to Birmingham in parallel lines, also large lighted quadrangles?
> Have anti-aircraft guns undergone any trials and what are results on south coast?

It will be seen that interest was beginning to concentrate itself on the two vital invasion areas; the south coast and the East Anglian coast, with apparently a subsidiary-objective in the Manchester-Liverpool area. The strengthening of the German organisation forecast in August had begun to take effect, and SNOW had been relieved of responsibility for two considerable districts. South Wales had temporarily dropped out of the picture. The first stirrings of interest were visible in the districts on the route between East Anglia and Liverpool.

On 22 September SNOW was asked for an urgent report on the defences of the Royal Military Canal between Hythe and Appledore. Evidently the Germans were taking the idea of a Dungeness landing seriously, for this Canal would be the first natural obstacle in the path of an invading force.

At about the same time *La Part Bien* should have arrived with two further agents, presumably for the southern coastal area. On the 28th GIRAFFE arrived in London with instructions to report on the strength and disposition of anti-aircraft defences in London and the location of the SOBAC and Ministry of Aircraft Production headquarters. Two days later SNOW was again asked for an urgent report on the Military Canal, this time with reference to the defences between Hythe and Ruckinge. On the same day Walti, de Deeker and Vera Eriksson landed from a seaplane on the Scottish coast. The objects of this expedition must always remain obscure: no coherent story was ever extracted from its members, of whom two are now dead. However, it has been assumed, from the comparative importance of de Deeker in the German organisation (and the possibility that he was only a substitute for the more important von Wedel), that the expedition was intended primarily to pick up existing German contacts in England. Walti carried maps of Scotland and East Anglia; Vera Eriksson and de Deeker a list of aerodromes covering the coastal area between Grimsby and Southend. Presumably, then, the three members of this party were intended to work in East Anglia, though they may (especially Walti) have had additional objectives elsewhere.

From this it would seem that by the end of September the Germans were paying at least as much attention to the East Anglian coast as to the Dungeness peninsula. They had sent in all four experienced agents to work in the district and (if we include TRICYCLE) had asked on three separate occasions for a report on its defences. Moreover, TATE had been working in the area immediately to the west, where he was to the end of September reinforced by SUMMER. SUMMER had been, since shortly after his arrival, notionally in the care of BISCUIT (acting under SNOW'S instructions), since the Germans believed him to be suffering from the effects of having spent a fortnight in the open. On his supposed recovery he was instructed to work the district Oxford-London-Colchester-Southend. The first arrival in October was GANDER, with instructions to report on the district between Bedford and Liverpool, including the towns Leicester, Birmingham, Coventry with particular relation to road obstructions and evacuee population. At about the same time Laureyssens must have been writing his first reports on shipping and the western ports. The next arrival was DOLITTLE, who reached London on 10 October with instructions to report on London AA defences and various aspects of the RAF. On the following day SNOW was told to report on the aerodromes at Cardiff, St. Athan, Llanwit and Briton. (A week later these instructions were corrected, Pontardawe being substituted for St. Athan and Llaitwit.) At approximately the same time both STRIPE and SISYPHUS were supposed to arrive in London with the fairly general questionnaires referred to above. On 18 October SNOW was told to report on the Colt factory in Birmingham and the Hispano-Suiza factory at Grantham. Three days later he was despatched to Tolworth in Surrey. On the same day G.W. received independently a set of fresh instructions, which asked among other things for a report on troop movements in the area Berkshire-Birmingham-Oxford-Bedfordshire-Northampton-Salisbury-Aldershot. Simultaneously RAINBOW was despatching (by post) an unsolicited report on the Brighton defences. On the 23rd SNOW was asked about the propeller factory at Lostock Junction near Bolton. On the 24th he was again asked for a report on the location of various important headquarters and on air raid damage in Glasgow.

By the following day TATE and SUMMER were sending weather reports from their respective areas, the latter from his new area. Lund, Joost and Edvardsen had arrived and were presumably pursuing their dark activities in Scotland. On the 26th SNOW was told to report on air raid damage in Birmingham and Coventry and the position of two more headquarters.

We have now reached the peak period of German espionage activity and by the same token have come very close to the invasion date. One would expect the geographical situation to have clarified itself and in fact it has done so. As far as the Germans knew their position was as follows:

London Five agents were working in the London area – SNOW, BISCUIT, GIRAFFE, STRIFE and DOOLITTLE. Of these the last three were making (by letter) reports which need not necessarily have involved them in much travel. The first two were in wireless contact and were expected and required to travel widely.

Midlands G.W. (who was in indirect wireless communication through SNOW) was reporting on troop movements in Berkshire, Buckingham,

Oxford, Bedfordshire, Northampton, Salisbury and Aldershot. GANDER (with his own wireless set) was reporting on the district between Bedford and Liverpool, including Leicester, Birmingham and Coventry. In this area SNOW was to some extent reinforcing GANDER's activities.

Manchester and Liverpool Eschborn was reporting on the Manchester neighbourhood. The suggestion that he should be reinforced by another agent was first made at the end of August, though it did not come to a head before November, apparently for some administrative reason.

South Coast The Pons-Kieboom expedition had failed. SNOW and BISCUIT were in a position to provide alternative reports and had done so. RAINBOW was in Brighton, though communicating only by letter. His report on the coastal defences had not yet been received. TATE, who had a wireless set, was however aware of RAINBOW's London address and could at a pinch be put in touch with him.

East Anglia Waldberg's expedition had failed. Walti, Vera Eriksson and de Deeker had arrived on 30 September. It is not clear whether by the end of October the Germans necessarily supposed them to have been captured. True, they carried a wireless set, though that may not have been intended for their own use. If, as has been assumed, they were intended to pick up existing contacts in England and in some sense organise an English Stelle, then no immediate report may have been expected from them. But this in its turn would almost seem to imply the presence of an already established German agent in East Anglia, the area for which they were apparently destined.

Cambridgeshire and Essex TATE was operating in the area London-Bedford-Cambridge-Colchester; SUMMER (also with a wireless set) was operating in the area Oxford-London-Colchester-Southend.

South Wales G.W., who was reputed to have some small organisation of his own in South Wales, was still awaiting in Swansea the arrival of the three saboteurs.

Scotland On 25 October Lund, Joost and Evardsen had arrived and, as far as the Germans knew, were still at large. They each had some ill-defined objective in Scotland, connected, in the case of the last named, with sabotage. None of them appears to have had any means of communication.

Coastal Shipping Laureyssens and perhaps some other seamen had begun to send in their reports.

From these indications it is possible to reconstruct at least to some extent the German invasion plan. Five danger points had been clearly indicated:

1. The south coast and in particular the Dungeness peninsula;
2. East Anglia, especially the coast line between Aldeburgh and Cromer
3. Manchester and Liverpool.
4. South Wales in the neighbourhood of Cardiff and Swansea;
5. Southern Scotland.

It seems clear that of these the first two were the main military objectives; the last two in the nature of diversions on a more or less serious scale. The position of the third objective (Manchester and Liverpool) is more ambiguous. Clearly this was an important area simply from the bombing point of view and merited considerable attention on that ground alone; but that is an insufficient explanation in itself of the Germans' desire to reinforce Eschborn and the additional interest shown by SNOW in the district. Moreover, it is interesting to notice that GANDER's district covers the route between East Anglia and Liverpool (also referred to in TRICYCLE's questionnaire and in certain questions addressed to SNOW) and that he was instructed to give information of a type particularly valuable to a rapidly advancing force.

It is therefore reasonable to assume that two landings were in fact intended, one in Kent and one on the Norfolk coast. The southern force was clearly intended to strike at first due west, since enquiries had been made about the immediate obstacles which would have confronted such an advance.

At a point not further west than Aldershot this attack would have turned north with the object of encircling London from the south. This may be deduced from the nature of the enquiries made through G.W., the original area allotted to SUMMER and the noticeable thinning out of questions relating to places further west than Aldershot.

It is possible that the Norfolk landing was intended to be the heavier of the two. Certainly it was meant to have the higher proportion of armoured fighting vehicles, which would in any case have found the country more congenial in East Anglia than on the south coast. The espionage arrangements in the Norfolk area were on the whole the more elaborate, and there seems no doubt, in view of GANDER's and Eschborn's positions, that a part of the force must have been intended to strike northwards in the direction of Liverpool. The other arm of the attack would presumably have turned south to effect a junction with the other invading force. Such a plan, which seems clearly indicated by the evidence, would have necessitated a heavy landing in keeping with the comparatively elaborate espionage network in that district. On the other hand, it is worthwhile to remark that the considerable cluster of agents in and around East Anglia was composed, as far as we know, wholly of men working under I Luft. Their principal dominant interests were therefore in aerodromes and bomb targets. The Germans, in considering how best to provide fighter support for their two invading forces, may well have decided that the southern arm could always be

> protected by fighters based on northern France, whereas the northern arm (in view of the greater distance) would have to acquire landing fields of its own at an early stage. This may have been a sound explanation in itself of the greater concentration of agents north of London. It would at least be proper to add to the other possibilities an airborne attack on flying fields in East Anglia. The view that such an attack was intended to take place is supported by both the list of aerodromes carried by de Deeker and the persistent interest which the Germans have since shown in possible landing grounds in this neighbourhood.
>
> Lastly, there is the question of the two diversions or side-shows in South Wales and Scotland respectively. The former was undoubtedly intended to take the form of extensive sabotage and the same is probably true of the latter. The enquiry to SNOW about Welsh aerodromes and the Scottish agents' apparent lack of any means of communication also suggest that in each case the diversion would have been supported by a feint landing on a small scale.
>
> We are further inclined to believe that the Germans originally intended something in the nature of a rising in Wales, supported presumably by a larger landing force, but later abandoned this idea as impractical.
>
> We have not continued our geographical analysis beyond what we consider to have been the invasion period. It was at that time, as one would expect, that the Germans' careful disposal of their agents was most clearly visible. Since then there has been no evidence that the Germans were marshalling their forces from a geographical point of view in one way more than another, except that their interest in the immediate hinterland of East Anglia has persisted strongly. If, however, an attack on this country became imminent once more, it is reasonable to expect the arrival of a fresh supply of emergency agents and a careful re-allotment of geographical areas in parallel with the activity of September 1940. It should be possible, by comparing these individual dispositions with the previous ones, to form a very clear idea of the extent and nature of any alteration in the German invasion plans.[42]

Demonstrably, the B1(a) analysts believed there was much to be learned from the discernible shift in Abwehr behaviour and conducted a forensic study of all the detected cases of German espionage. Their underlying purpose, of course, was to ferret out any evidence of surviving pre-war spies, or the existence of undetected agents.

A second B1(a) report, dated June 1942, reflected the information that can be gleaned from an enemy intelligence questionnaire, and was competed at a time when the XX Committee was still in its relative infancy. All the participants were finding their way and at that stage the concept of strategic deception, as already practised in the Middle East by CHEESE, was but a distant horizon. In the absence of confidence about a comprehensive grip on the Abwehr's sources, and the lingering fear there might be undetected spies at liberty, MI5 was vulnerable to the kind of contradiction that occurred when in 1941 ALARIC, then operating independently in Portugal, received a questionnaire duplicated to BALLOON. At that stage ALARIC, as he was known to Madrid (before he was taken on by MI5 as GARBO), was a mere fabricator, submitting some quite outlandish reports, whereas BALLOON, as part of TRICYCLE's network, was acting as a part of a wider, organised matrix, and his army background, and detailed knowledge of weaponry, gave him an elevated status in terms of reliability. A conflict between answers provided by ALARIC and BALLOON was to be avoided.

The issues were revisited on 1 June 1942 by the same three analysts when they took the opportunity to update their findings in a report entitled *The Objectives in England of the German Secret Service, 1 October 1941 – 15 April 1942.*

> In our last note on this subject (dated 27 December 1941) we suggested that in the ensuing months the main subjects of interest to the Germans would probably be: first, the volume of supplies reaching this country from America; secondly, naval and shipping intelligence with particular relation to the northern supply route to Russia; thirdly, the strength and equipment of the British Army, especially of units which were about to go overseas or which might form part of an offensive force on the continent; fourthly, the food-supply of Great Britain, rationing and price levels. We forecast that an interest in these subjects translated into terms of espionage would mean an increased activity on the part of the Oslo and Peninsular Stellen, little or no activity from Hamburg, Brussels or Brest, and continued activity on the same level and of the same type from Berlin fold Paris. We also speculated whether the Peninsular Stellen might not attempt to run saboteurs into this country, perhaps through Eire.
>
> Up to a certain point these predictions have been borne out by events, Oslo has certainly been active, though not perhaps to the degree which we had expected. Of the seven known German agents who have arrived in this country since September 1941 three have come from Oslo; Saetrang on 13 September 1941, Ronnig and Olsen on 26 September 1941. It is not yet entirely clear what was the objective of either expedition. Saetrang seems to have been intended to penetrate either the SIS or SOE Norwegian organisations. Ronning and Olsen may have had some similar mission or may only have been sent to observe ship movements in northern waters, since it was apparently expected that the boat on which they came (as ostensible traders) would be allowed to return to Norway. Contrary to our predictions the Peninsular Stellen have not been active; as far as is known they have sent only two agents to this country within the period, the seaman Timmerman, who arrived on 1 September 1941, and the WEASEL, who reached this country on 5 May 1942. Timmerman's

instructions were substantially the same as those previously given to Laureyssens and others, i.e. to report on the position of minefields, the arrival or departure of convoys, the condition of ports and similar matters. The WEASEL was despatched to this country by the Section Eins Marine in Lisbon with a questionnaire which dealt largely with the constitution of convoys and ports used by them, the position of mine barriers and other coastal defences and similar subjects. He is a Belgian who was originally destined for work in the Congo; but while he was still in Lisbon he was called up by the Belgian Government for military service, and this opportunity was seized by the Germans to give him a fresh assignment in England. His arrival must therefore be regarded to some extent as fortuitous. We were apparently correct in saying that Hamburg, Brussels and Brest would show little activity and in fact no agents are known to have arrived from any of these Stellen within this period. The same is true of Berlin headquarters. On the other hand we were seriously wrong with regard to Paris, which has shown considerable activity of a particular type. The last two of the seven new agents, who arrived in February and April 1942 respectively, were both under the control of this Stelle. They were both British agents who had been captured and induced to work for the Germans. Their orders were to contrive to be sent back to France as British agents with fresh instructions, so that they might assist in the capture of further British agents and give, through their wireless traffic, advance information of impending British operations on the Continent. In addition to these two agents a third person, Stella Lonsdale, arrived from France on 5 November 1941.[43] It is not yet certain that she came as a German agent, though it is very probable that she did. If so her instructions were no doubt similar to those of the two known agents. In all, therefore, if we include THISBE who arrived in not dissimilar circumstances on 30 October 1941. Paris has dispatched a possible total of four such agents or penetrators within the last eight months. We know from other sources that the Paris Stelle also seeks every opportunity of running captured wireless transmitters for double cross purposes. Moreover apart from the sending of agents direct to this country the Germans have recently been increasing their efforts to gain shipping and naval intelligence by the use of boats at sea disguised as fishing or trading vessels. It would appear that these enterprises are largely or wholly under the direction of Eins Marine, Paris. It is clear, therefore, that we had underestimated the potentialities of this Stelle which would seem now to have taken the place of Hamburg as the Stelle most directly concerned with work against this country. This is, of course, entirely consistent with Paris being, as we suggested in our last report, in the nature of an advanced GHQ of the Abwehr.

There has recently been a marked change in the methods used by the Germans to introduce agents into this country. Between September 1940 and May 1941 direct methods, almost of assault, were attempted and a large number of agents landed by parachute or boat. So far as we know, no illicit landing of this type has taken place since 12 May 1941. All agents since that date have arrived on some quasi-legal pretext, as traders or neutral travellers, as ostensible refugees, or even as persons attached to a neutral Embassy or as accredited British agents. It is clear that the present emphasis is almost wholly upon the use of double-cross agents of one type or another. In one sense this is strongly to our disadvantage since such spies, besides being more than usually difficult to detect, rarely carry those detailed instructions and questionnaires which have proved useful in the past. In another sense this change in German tactics may be to the good. The use of double agents is almost wholly defensive tactic, since its scope is limited by the material which the enemy is willing to supply. The general deduction to be drawn from the change of tactics, is that, whereas at the end of 1940 and the beginning of 1941 the Germans were principally concerned with what they were going to do to us, their main preoccupation at the moment is what we may be expected to do to them.

The instructions given to new agents (so far as we know them) and general developments in espionage elsewhere, suggest an over-riding interest on the Germans part in two of the four subjects mentioned in our last report; naval and shipping intelligence with particular relation to northern waters, and more especially the possibilities of British offensive action on the Continent. With regard to the second point the distribution of the new agents (three from Oslo, two or possibly three from Paris) suggests that the Germans are evenly divided in their minds between the possibility of an attack on Norway, and the possibility of an attack on France. A comparison of dates would support the theory that at the end of 1941 the Germans considered an invasion of Norway as the more probable but have recently been concentrating their fears on France. Very little reliance can, however, be placed on this inference as the actual date of an agent's despatch is usually governed by considerations which have little or nothing to do with strategy. This is, of course, particularly true of double-cross agents.[44]

By the time Cholmondeley, Gwyer and Grimaldi came to undertake their second study in June 1942, they were in a position to recognise a dramatic change in Abwehr tactics, involving two distinct phases of behaviour patterns, referring to 'the revolution that has taken place between the two periods of German strategy against this country'.

Eins Luft

During the current period questions relating to Air Force matters have been asked of agents from the Peninsula, from Brussels, from Hamburg, from Paris and from Oslo. The interest shown by the last-named Stelle is remarkable, not because the number of questions asked has been high but because before September 1941 Oslo took next to no interest in Service matters. This change seems to imply that MUTT and JEFF (the only Oslo agents now working) who came originally as Abteilung II agents, are now being turned over to Abteilung I reporting work in the same way that G.W. was turned over earlier. In the earlier period between September and December 1940 the majority of Air Force questions naturally related to air raid damage. Such questions no longer occur. The next most striking change is the comparative lack of interest which is now shown by the Germans in the organisation of the RAF. During the earlier period there were constant messages about squadron numbers, the location of particular squadrons and the allocation of the squadrons to groups and commands.

Within the current period this type of question has only been asked upon one occasion. In December 1941 BALLOON was instructed to give a report on the type of machine used by the 219th squadron, the location of the 10th fighter group and the 28th group.

The last item is significant in the light of the great interest which the Germans have shown in other details of our night fighter defences, most of these questions have naturally been addressed to FATHER, himself a fighter pilot, whom the Germans suppose to be well placed for acquiring technical information. BALLOON has also been questioned. In December 1941 he received a careful questionnaire headed 'British UHF night fighting devices'. It asked whether the device used infrared or UHF waves, what frequency it operated on, what was the shortest range at which it was effective and whether it gave its signals optically or acoustically. In the same month FATHER was instructed to give information about the locating apparatus used by night fighters and about a form of anti-aircraft defence using rockets with trailing metal cables.

In March FATHER was asked to send 'news of utilisation of lance-flammes' apparently on aircraft. It is possible that this may have referred to the use of searchlights by night fighters. Later in the same month FATHER was instructed to send information about the Marconi TFG 10 fixed locating station on the south coast. The answers which FATHER gave to these questions excited great interest and provoked an immediate response in the shape of further questions. Finally he was asked to escape to France in a night fighter of the latest type, but has so far not found a suitable method of doing so. It may be that this spate of questions was simply the result of the Germans' belief that they had an excellent informant in FATHER. It is, however, true that questions about the position of anti-aircraft guns and balloon barrages have been fairly constant throughout the period and on the whole more frequent than before.

Indeed as will be seen below German interests in every detail of anti-aircraft organisation has been continuous and striking. This, taken in conjunction with their interest in night fighter devices, must mean that during the past few months they have been making the most careful review of our air defences.

During the early period there was a large number of questions about the exact position of certain named factories such as the Hispano-Suiza factory at Grantham, the Colt factory at Birmingham and so on. Such questions are now rare. During the past six months the Germans have frequently asked in general terms for the position of new aircraft and munition factories or aircraft assembly shops with particular attention to the last-named. Only on a few occasions have they asked for the location of particular factories. In November 1941 they asked TATE for further details of the Nestles factory on which he had reported some months earlier. In December they asked BALLOON for the location of a factory producing Sunderland aircraft which was thought to be in Scotland. In the same month they also asked TATE for a report on a new Vickers factory said to be near Ruthin and on a factory in Birmingham producing Semape fuel tanks. Finally in April TATE was instructed to investigate 'aeroplane factories and aerodromes at Cranfield (13 km. south west of Bedford) and Sywell (10 km. north east of Northampton)'. He was told to report on the number, size and position of workshops, the size of the staff and the types of aircraft built or assembled. In at least three of these cases there may be some reason to suppose that the Germans knew of the position of the factory concerned before they asked the question. It is therefore possible that these questions should be discounted as being merely minor test questions put to the agent concerned. On the whole one must say that the Germans during the current period have shown themselves either much less interested than they previously were in specific industrial targets or else much less well informed on this subject. The second is perhaps more likely to be the correct inference, for the total number of questions on industrial plants has not fallen off noticeably. This view is also supported by the BISCUIT questionnaire of August 1940 (referred to in our last note) which seemed to suggest that the Germans were ill-informed about changes in the aircraft and munitions industry which had taken place since the outbreak of war. Moreover the Germans' insistence on the location of assembly shops and one series of questions to BALLOON in January 1942 about the effects of dispersal on industry suggest that they have been finding it necessary to revise their list of bombing targets considerably. Broadly speaking, the current indications are decidedly against a resumption of large-scale bombing, at least on industrial targets.

On the whole German interest in the supply of aircraft from America has been consistent since the end of 1940. The general level of questions is rather higher now than it was in the earlier period. Questions have also become noticeably more specific and the emphasis is of course now on aircraft from the USA and not from Canada. In the earlier period the most usual form of the question was 'give the numbers of aircraft reaching England from Canada and from the US', now agents receive more detailed questions. In October 1941 CARELESS was asked to give information about the transportation of American planes with reference to whether they were sent by boat or flown direct. In December BALLOON was asked to find out the reason why several aircraft on the transatlantic route had crashed in the previous August and what was the type of machine principally involved. In March FATHER was told to give information about the arrival of American aircraft in England, how many planes of what type were sent monthly, how were they transported and what was the exact site of the assembly shops. He was also asked how soon these machines were brought into service and in what number, and how many American pilots were now available for service in the UK and Ireland. In the same month he was asked what English planes were equipped with American engines and what was the number and make of the engines concerned. One may say, therefore, that, although the total number of questions has not greatly increased, the detailed nature of the questions now asked shows a rising interest in American aircraft production. Curiously enough, however, during the past six months there have been only two questions (CARELESS in October and DRAGONFLY in December) relating to the export of aircraft from this country either to Russia or the East. It is not clear whether this implies that the Germans do not yet consider the volume of exports sufficiently high to be worth investigation or whether it merely shows that they believe themselves to be better served by a reporting service at the point of delivery.

During the earlier period there was a fairly constant flow of questions about devices on British aircraft, in particular the Beaufighter. This interest appears now to have lapsed. The only question remotely of this type during the past six months was one to FATHER in March 1942 'nature of method of acceleration of Blenheim type. Is there a regulated control?' Apart from this there have been one or two single questions of some interest. In December 1941 CARELESS was asked to report on the shortage of air screws and air-cooled engines which was alleged to have developed. In the following March FATHER was asked to say what English firms were manufacturing the Fahy American incendiary bomb. He was also asked for 'technical documents about regulated propeller blades, Fairey-contra', to report on the extent to which the use of the Lips 1900 lb bomb might be expected and to give details of the Norden Bomb sight. This was in some ways a curious question for, during the Duquesne trial in America last year, it emerged that the Germans had claimed to have been in possession of the Norden bomb-sight for some while, and therefore deprecated an attempt on the part of one of their American agents to obtain it.

Eins Wirtschaft

As in the earlier period the majority of economic questions continued to refer either directly or indirectly to the aircraft industry. These questions have already been dealt with above under the heading of Eins Luft. Apart from the aircraft industry the Germans' main preoccupation in the current period has been, as we forecast, the food and rationing position. Questions upon this subject have been more or less continuous. In October 1941 SWEET WILLIAM was asked for a general report on morale and the rationing situation with particular reference to the possible moral effect of food shortage upon the army. In November the SNARK was asked to give a full report on current food prices especially of meat, flour, sugar and milk. She was also instructed to describe the rationing system in force with notes of the principal shortages and to report upon the position with regard to clothes and fuel. In December BALLOON was asked what stocks were held of the main foodstuffs, where food dumps were situated and how much food was imported from America. In January the same questions were put to TATE, this time with particular reference to the position of cold-storage equipment and of food depots in 'bulkhead areas'. In the same month BALLOON was again asked to report on the exact location of food depots and refrigerating plants and to assess how far the dispersal of food stocks about the country had progressed. In February TATE was instructed to report on the current prices of meat. In March he was again told to give the location of 'National Pantries' or food depots. In short, in every month throughout the period there have been one or more questions on the subject, which is clearly a matter of the highest interest to the Germans. The exact form of the questions is harder to explain, for it is not clear why the Germans should be so interested to know the exact location of food depots. It may be for the purpose of bombing, since they would no doubt regard a food dump as a legitimate and profitable target. On the other hand, such dumps are hard to locate and harder to destroy, since so much of the material in them is incombustible. It may be, therefore, that it is sabotage and not bombing which lies behind these questions, (in this connection we should point out that the only saboteurs of whose intentions we have full knowledge – MUTT and JEFF and G.W., – were all instructed to pay attention to food stores.) Alternatively it may simply be that the Germans find that the location of food dispersal points and auxiliary depots is a convenient method of assessing the total food stocks of the country.

At all events whatever the motive may be their interest is undoubted and far keener than it was in the earlier period. Then three agents – HATCHET, STRIPE and TRICYCLE – were all asked in September 1940 to report on the food situation and the location of food depots, but except in this one month questions upon this subject did not occur. There have also been within the current period one or two questions not directly relating to food supplies but of a similar nature. Thus in December BALLOON was told to report what harbours had been put out of commission and which emergency harbours were in use. He was also asked for information about soap rationing (which had not yet come into force) and the stocks of mineral oil in the country. In January RAINBOW was asked for a general report on any shortages observable in vital supplies. In April MUTT and JEFF were asked a number of questions about the mining of British harbours and similar subjects which are referred to below more fully under the heading of Eins Marine. The general impression left by these questions about food is that the Germans are now concerned mainly or wholly with the long-term operation of the blockade. The questions suggest that although they are keeping a close watch upon price levels they do not expect any particular shortage at least in food supplies to develop in the near future. The food questions have been distributed among agents from the Peninsula, Hamburg and to a lesser extent Oslo. Neither Brussels nor Paris has been represented, the former no doubt because their only agent FATHER has been fully occupied in dealing with technical Air Force questions. The lack of questions from Paris is more strange, since their only agent DRAGONFLY is supposedly employed by a Food Office and should therefore be an excellent informant in these matters.

Apart from the questions dealing either with food supplies or with the aircraft industry, the economic questions have been rather miscellaneous, A few questions have been asked about tank production; of BALLOON in January in some detail and of TATE in March. On two occasions (RAINBOW in October, BALLOON in January) questions were asked about the supply of clockwork fuses. There was one question to CARELESS in October about the production of poison gas. In contrast to the earlier period comparatively little interest has been shown in specific raw materials. RAINBOW was asked in October about aluminium supplies and in January in more general terms about the position with respect to raw materials and manpower.

In the same month BALLOON received a questionnaire asking in great detail for information about current iron and steel production as compared with that for the period 1939-41. There was, however, nothing comparable to TRICYCLE's questionnaire of September 1940 which asked for detailed figures of the supply of a long list of essential minerals – lead, copper, tin, zinc, ferro-vanadium, etc. Lastly there has been a fairly considerable interest in the production of anti-aircraft guns and ammunition. The Germans appear particularly interested in the quantity of ammunition, especially AA ammunition, which is still imported. In October RAINBOW was asked to assess how much anti-aircraft ammunition was imported and in December this question was repeated to CARELESS, In March MUTT and JEFF were told to report whether 4.5 AA guns were manufactured in mobile form, what were the measurements of its barrel and what was its life in numbers of rounds. Presumably these questions were only another reflection of the Germans' intense interest in every detail of our anti-aircraft organisation, which is discussed below under the heading of Eins Heer. It seems however curious that they should still be seeking information about the 4.5 gun which figured in previous questionnaires as early as 1937 and 1938.

Eins Heer

During the earlier period at the end of 1940 nearly all the strictly military questions referred obviously to the Germans' impending invasion. For example in September SNOW was instructed to report on troop dispositions and coastal defences between Margate and the Isle of Wight. In the same month TRICYCLE was asked for a report on the coastal defences between the Wash and Southampton and for the Home Forces Order of Battle. All the subsequent questions followed very similar lines. In the current period however a great change has taken place. No questions whatever have been asked about coastal defences and only on two occasions have any detailed questions been asked about troop dispositions. In December BALLOON received a curious questionnaire asking him to confirm the location of a number of named headquarters, none of which was accurately placed. Our information suggests that this represented a report turned in by some other agent which BALLOON was being asked to check. Little significance need therefore be attached to the questions which must primarily have been given to test the bona-fides of the other unknown agent. In April 1942 MUTT and JEFF were asked to give an account of troop dispositions on the south coast and the position of anti-aircraft batteries. It is not clear what was the significance of these questions but it seems probable that the Germans wished to know whether any offensive force was massing in that area. Apart from these few questions the Germans' main interest in military affairs has been concentrated on the organisation of our anti-aircraft defences and the training and strength of our parachute and airborne troops. In November CARELESS was asked for a report on the organisation of AA Command and also for details about the 20 mm. AA gun. He was also asked for information about parachute troops and airborne infantry. These questions were repeated in an almost identical form to TATE in the same month. In January 1942 FATHER was asked for details about the latest model of anti-aircraft gun. In January CARELESS was again asked about parachute troops and the methods by which they were trained and transported. In February TATE was asked for a report on troop-carrying gliders which were said to have come into service and MUTT and JEFF were instructed to give a report on the organisation of anti-aircraft command. In March 1942 TATE was asked in some detail for information about parachute troops and airborne infantry, their organisation and equipment. In the same month FATHER was asked to give information about the new 3.9 anti-aircraft gun. In March also TATE was again asked for information about parachute troops and airborne infantry the type of aircraft which they used and the position of their headquarters and training centres. In the same month MUTT and JEFF were asked for a report on the 4.5 AA gun and the use of the Kerison predictor with the 4 cm Bofors gun. In April they were asked urgently and in great detail for a report on the organisation of anti-aircraft command, how many corps were included in it, how many brigades formed a normal anti-aircraft division, whether the personnel was drawn from the Royal Artillery or also from the Royal Engineers and whether there were still anti-aircraft battalions and companies attached to the REs. At the same time they were also asked for information about light and heavy searchlight units. It may be that part of this flood of questions was produced by the fact that MUTT is now ostensibly in the Army and in a good position to acquire this type of information, but the persistent recurrence of the same question put month after month to different agents does imply a very high level of interest on the part of the Germans. Presumably the questions about parachute troops and airborne infantry implies some fear on the behalf of the Germans of our offensive intentions. This view is supported by the fact that TATE's questions on this subject in November were specifically directed to discovering whether parachute troops were being trained for service overseas, especially in the Middle East. The questions were marked 'Urgent'. The Germans' intensive interest in anti-aircraft organisation is less easy to understand. One would have expected it to have been combined with questions suggesting a renewal of their bombing offensive in this country but, as we have seen above, this is not so.

There has been a fairly steady flow of questions about the movement of troops overseas or British offensive intentions on the Continent. For example, in December 1941 TATE was asked for a report on a number of invasion barges which were alleged to be being transported from Liverpool to Gibraltar for use in landing operations against Italy or North Africa. In January he was asked for a general report on any troops known to be about to go overseas. In the same month BALLOON was asked in considerable detail for information about reinforcements to the Middle and Far East. He was instructed to report how many divisions had been or were about to be shipped at what date and from what port. He was also told to report whether any of a list of some ten named vessels were to be used as transports. These questions are in part to be accounted for, like the earlier questions about the Home Forces Order of Battle, by a previous report from another agent which BALLOON was being asked to check, and, as in that case, the information embodied in the questions was largely inaccurate. In February DRAGONFLY was asked for a report on some troops alleged to be leaving for Singapore. In the following month he was asked specifically to visit Brighton and report upon the first Canadian division which was said to be stationed there and to be about to move. He was to discover its destination which was thought to be somewhere overseas. This question was based upon fact in so far that the Canadian Division was actually stationed near Brighton though it was not due to go abroad. Presumably therefore DRAGONFLY was being used to check some report already received, perhaps from a Canadian source. In March also MUTT and JEFF were asked urgently for details of British landing intentions in Norway, where such a landing would take place, what units would be involved and in what strength, how large a naval force would accompany the expedition, etc. This question was repeated again later in the month. In April MUTT and JEFF were asked whether there were rumours in official circles of an impending English or American attack against the Azores, Cape Verde, the Canary Islands or the west coast of Africa. In sum, it is clear that during the past six months the Germans have been very seriously exercised at the possibility of a second front being opened in the West.

The remaining military questions have not been of any great significance and have usually been called forth by some particular incident. In December BALLOON was asked whether the reserves of 1920, 1921 and 1922 had yet been called up, and if so what proportions of them had been allocated specifically to the Army. In January DRAGONFLY was asked for a report on RAF motorised units and the RAF armoured car corps. This question apparently arose out of a newspaper report which had come into the Germans' hands; they were anxious to discover how the RAF mechanised units fitted into the general organisation of armoured formations. In March MUTT and JEFF were asked about new types of service gas mask; and in the same month TATE was asked what bases were being used in the UK by American troops and DRAGONFLY to what extent troops were now being trained abroad as, for example, in Canada or the USA. Lastly there has been a more or less regular influx of questions about tanks and tank production. In January DRAGONFLY, who had recently given some information about new types of tanks, was congratulated and asked particularly to discover how heavy the armament of these tanks was. In the same month BALLOON received instructions to report on the monthly output of tanks and to give further details about the Valentine, the infantry tank Mark III and light tank Mark VII. The Germans wished to know what works had gone over to the production of Valentines, how many workers were employed, what other types of tank were turned out by the same factories and what was the actual monthly output of Valentines. TATE was asked also in the same month for a report on the tank factories of Great Britain, their position, the types they manufactured and their monthly output with, if possible, rough details of the total British output.

Military questions were distributed among agents from all the Stelle concerned, that is to say, the Peninsula, Brussels, Hamburg,

Paris and Oslo. The Oslo questions were no doubt dictated by MUTT's present position as a soldier, but are nevertheless interesting because, as we remarked above, up till September 1941 Oslo took so little interest in Service matters. Evidently the Germans have been eager during the last six months for military information. For example, the agent GELATINE who was recruited, exclusively to report political information and, in so far as she has reported anything, has always done so, was specifically asked in January to take up whatever military contacts she could and report in future on military rather than political affairs. Reference to the graph will show to what extent the Germans' demands for military information from England have increased recently. The general trend appears to be to concentrate on the possibilities of British offensive action. There is no indication whatever in current messages that the Germans are contemplating an invasion, even in the distant future. A comparison of current traffic with that of the period September – December 1940 when invasion was imminent shows clearly to what extent they have changed their tactics

Eins Marine

As will be seen from the graph, there has been within the current period a slight revival of naval questions, but the volume of these questions for either period has been so low that no effective comparison between the two periods is possible. In the last six months questions on these subjects have been distributed among agents from the Peninsula, Hamburg, Paris and Oslo. This is in itself interesting for, as we pointed out in our previous report, neither Oslo nor Hamburg had up till now taken any interest in naval matters. No particular trend is discernible in the questions themselves, but on the whole they appear to derive mainly from some aspect of the Germans' submarine campaign. In November RAINBOW was asked for a report on some new torpedo nets which were alleged to have come into use. This question appears to have been based upon some particular report which reached the Germans about that time, for we understand that they were also seeking the answer to the same question in rather more specific terms among travellers in Lisbon. In the same month BALLOON was instructed to report what emergency harbours were in use and what existing harbours had been damaged. In January both TATE and BALLOON were asked about the sending of transports and convoys overseas in the terms already referred to above. In February DRAGONFLY was asked to confirm a report that two battleships had sailed for Singapore, and in the following month was given a short but more detailed questionnaire about harbour installations, ship traffic in harbours and the arrival and departure of convoys. Curiously enough these questions reached him in the same message in which he was asked to report on the Canadian Division at Brighton. It appears at a first reading of the message as if the questions about harbour installations etc. must have referred to Brighton, but it seems scarcely possible that this should be so. Later in the same month DRAGONFLY was instructed to find out from what ports U.S. troops and supplies destined for this country were leaving. In April MUTT and JEFF were asked in some details to describe the effect of the mining of British harbours, the use of torpedo nets in ports, the system of convoying in force, the public reaction to the sinking of merchant ships and the extent to which shipping losses were being made good. As will have been seen, the agent who received most naval questions during the period was DRAGONFLY who works under the control of Paris. This is consistent with the recent development of Eins Marine, Paris, to which we referred above. Presumably the questions put to MUTT and JEFF (who work under Oslo) were intended to have reference principally to arrivals and departures from northern ports.

Abteilung II

One cannot isolate from the current period any questions which must necessarily have been the concern of Abteilung II. Indeed it is noticeable that there have not been, as there were during the earlier period, any requests, for example, for propaganda material. Towards the end of 1940 questions about rationing and food supply were very often accompanied by other questions about public morale and reactions or even, as in TRICYCLE's questionnaire of December 1940, direct questions about the type of propaganda most likely to be effective and the classes of the population most susceptible to it. Such questions no longer occur, presumably because the Germans do not think that any immediate capital is to be made from the present situation. For the rest Abteilung II is represented, if at all, by the questions already referred to under the heading Eins Wirtschaft about the location of food depots and refrigerating plants. As we pointed out above, it is possible that what lay behind these questions was an intention to sabotage food depots as being a more convenient method of destruction in this case than bombing. We must point out, however, that we have been given no other indication that sabotage is intended, and indeed we know that, while he was still working, G.W., who had been recruited primarily as a saboteur, was discouraged from undertaking any work of this sort.

By the same token, although a successful act of sabotage apparently restored the Germans' confidence in MUTT when it was severely strained in October and November of last year, he has not since received, perhaps fortunately, any marked encouragement to repeat his effects. Similarly the agent GARBO recently suggested to his German control that he should recruit saboteurs when he was in England and was specifically instructed to use such men, if he found them, only as reporting agents and not in any other capacity. On the whole therefore it would be fair to say that there has been little or no evidence of Abteilung II interest

> in this country during the past six months. This may well be due to the fact that Abteilung II prefers to work through some existing subversive movement or minority group and that, since their failure with the Welsh Nationalist Party, they have come to the conclusion that no such group exists effectively in England.[45]

In the six months since their previous report, the B1(a) analysts had demonstrably gained confidence and seen the double cross system develop under XX Committee control, albeit with the benefit of ISOS. An example of the continuing pressure from the enemy materialised in July 1942 when a demobilised French fighter pilot, Paul Morel, made contact with Ken Benton, the Section V officer in Madrid, to declare his sabotage mission for the Abwehr and to offer his services as a double agent. With Benton's approval, Morel was smuggled into Gibraltar and flown to London where he performed poorly during routine interviews at the LRC and so was transferred to Camp 020. Aged 28, and born in French Morocco, with his wife held hostage by the Germans, Morel was thought to be a little too enthusiastic to work as a double agent, so he was detained for the duration and deported to France in August 1946. However, after his release some Abt. III/F documents were recovered by French security officers in Germany, dating from June 1942, and referring to him as V-Mann F.7129 which appeared to support Morel's narrative.

> Concerning F.7129
> On the 20 June 1942, F.7129 was sent to the English Consulate in San Sebastian, with instructions to get to England either by getting into the Intelligence or Sabotage Service.
> F.7129 travelled officially with a French pass, a German pass, and a Spanish visa. He received his pass from the French Prefect of Police, as an author.
>
> F.7129 received the following accurate instructions:
>
> (1) To find out and report on the expedition at the British Consulate in San Sebastian, as well as the Transport route to England, and the port of arrival in England.
> (2) To report on the manner of training and development in England, the training personnel, and the training centres, and further partakers therein.
> (3) To report on the general living conditions in England, the morale of the people, as well as the behaviour of the individual, the one to the other, and the feeling between the English, the Scots and the Irish.

For I/H and I/Luft (air). F-7129 received further instructions as follows: (a0; – I/H.

To get information on;

(4) How the Union of Foreign Troops (the Norwegians, Poles, Dutch, Belgians and Czechs, etc.) are banded together, and equipped, the state of their morale and discipline, and where they are stationed.

(5) The exact strength and divisions, division numbers, training progress and the arming of USA troops in Great Britain.

(6) If the USA troopships use 'tactical' signals, and which belongs to which division, and, if so, to give exact descriptions of and report on which 'tactical' signal for which division.

(b) – I/Luft.

(7) Air Power question (Contingents)

(8) How many Hurricanes would be delivered to Russia, where and whether from the home country or overseas, or from the Middle East.

(9) Are there underground factories in the aircraft industry – and where?

(10) Parachute troops, and airborne troops.

(11) What is the Air Force in the districts doing, and how are they placed together?

(12) Where are the night-fighters stationed? On which airfields? How many? Where are they trained?

In case F.7129 should be sent to England by a sea route, he should likewise undertake to report on anything of interest to I/M.

F.7129 received instructions to concentrate on getting information and particulars of English spying and sabotage training, and to get just as much as he could for I/H. and I/Luft. without committing himself.

His principal work is to get in with the English Intelligence Service in France, get installed there, and with the addresses gained eventually from the English, proceed to get in contact at once with the H.Q. (German).

In case Sdf Scheise should not be there any more, or that F.7129 by his contact with German authorities, should be arrested, F.7129 had instructions to get in contact with Hotel Lutetia, Apparat 349, under his cover-name of Miller, or to call the (German) Service Centre (HQ).

In case of an arrest, then the German HQ would instruct whether F.7129 should be given the chance to escape, or keep up the straightforward camouflage, in case of arrest with others with whom he had travelled to Paris.

F.7129 had 2 people to whom he could turn in England.

F.7129 is acquainted with the French Col. LEHMANN, who lives in Paris, Rue de Sevres, is of Alsatian origin, speaks good German, and who was with the now English General Ingersoll, as German prisoner, in the [First] World War.

Col. Lehmann had given F.7129 verbal recommendations to General Ingersoll, his stay in England to be fixed first.

Mrs. Ricard Fair, nee Blanche Fiault.

F.7129's sponsor, and his mother's niece, has been 22 years in England and East Africa, employed by Sir Alexander Harding (Private Secretary to the King) as governess. His address, and also where Mrs. Fair lived, was Spring Grove, Wharncliffe Side, Near Sheffield.

The contact between F.7129's family and Mrs. Fair, during the time of these activities, was quite straightforward.[46]

Although there were many doubts about Morel, and his interrogators took a negative view of his trustworthiness, J.C Masterman recommended his employment as a double agent, but he was overruled. With the benefit of hindsight, Morel proved to be a missed opportunity, and the German evidence in his favour only came to light months after he had been released from Camp 020.

In taking stock of the new situation MI5's Dick White revealed in a lecture in September 1942 that since the outbreak of war '73 enemy agents have been apprehended or identified in this country, while another 45 have been apprehended or identified in British possessions or British controlled territory abroad'.[47]

Perhaps more significantly, the B1(a) counter-intelligence specialists had spotted a distinct change in the Abwehr's attitude towards the British Isles, summed up in the casual remark, that in 'the beginning of 1941 the Germans were principally concerned with what they were going to do to us, their main preoccupation at the moment is what we may be expected to do to them'. In retrospect, it can be seen that this would turn out to be as accurate an observation as Winston Churchill's about Allied victories before and after El Alamein.

Chapter V

THE FRONT LINE

> The efforts of the SD to set up an organisation in Spain were persistently check-mated by the rival organisation which considered itself to hold the monopoly of German espionage in the peninsula.
>
> Interrogation of Marcel Schunke, Diest, August 1945[1]

The London War Room counter-intelligence's final analysis of the SD's activities in the Iberian peninsula was illuminating, but was incomplete because so many of the staff wanted for interview by the Allies had avoided expulsion and were therefore in 1946 still beyond the reach of the interrogators. Nevertheless, the draft summary relied on interviews with fifteen SD figures directly involved.

> The importance of neutral territory to Amt VI work in Western Europe has already been mentioned in dealing with Referat VI B 3 and Switzerland. This importance was considerably greater in the case of the Iberian Peninsula. Switzerland, though neutral, was surrounded by countries entirely under German domination; further, Switzerland attempted to maintain strict neutrality and was not disposed to grant any special facilities to Germany. In both these aspects the Peninsula offered much greater facilities; it had a seaboard, and the number of contacts which could be established with the outer world was thereby greatly increased. Moreover, agents earmarked for despatch to enemy territory, or to other neutral territories abroad, could be sent through Spain, while actual entry into Spain had been greatly facilitated after the French armistice, when German occupied France and Spain had a common frontier of a few miles near the Atlantic coast. Spain also offered an important observation post in the Western Mediterranean, and a base for operations against North Africa in view of the Führerbefehl operative in Italy.

Secondly, unlike Switzerland, Spain, though a neutral country, was closely bound to Germany, and its exploitation thereby considerably facilitated. Spain therefore occupied a unique position among the neutral countries in the war as Sweden, the only remaining neutral country in Europe apart from Switzerland (and of course Eire) was greatly restricted in its communications with the outside world, and in any case its normal volume of trade did not cover the same wide field as that covered by the Iberian Peninsula. It is not surprising therefore that Spain became the cockpit of espionage in the course of the war, and the fruits would fall to that country able to exploit its possibilities to the best advantage. It is hardly necessary to point out that this advantage lay very heavily on the German side; but even then the course of Amt VI activity in the Iberian Peninsula, especially in the initial stages, was not altogether smooth.

The roots of German activity in Spain go back to the Spanish Civil War. The Condor Legion which took part in that campaign contained elements of the GFP, and several of the subsequent Amt representatives in Spain had seen service with the Condor Legion, a typical example being Stubaf Mosig Jost during his period of service as Leiter of Abteilung 111/3 of the SD Hauptamt had paid official visits to Spain in 1938 to foster liaison between the Spanish and German police services, and it was under this liaison that Amt VI developed its first penetration of the Peninsula. The facilities afforded, however, were not entirely favourable to Amt VI. The best cover would of course have been through the Foreign Office, but that department was throughout hostile to Amt VI activities in Spain, as elsewhere. It was therefore Amt IV which held chief sway in Spain through the powerful position of the Polizei Attaché, who, though not officially acting as an Amt IV representative abroad, was in fact recruited from Amt IV, as were most of his staff. In Spain the Polizei Attaché from 1939 until late 1944 was Kriminalrat Paul Winzer.

The position of Winzer in Spain was especially strong; he had been attached to the German Embassy in Madrid as early as 1936-37, and returned to the capital in 1938 where he enjoyed the special support of Heydrich himself. He remained throughout a special protégé of Mueller, Amtschef IV, as Mueller regarded the Polizei Attachés as an extension of his functions into foreign territory. Winzer was on very good terms with the Spanish police and with the Falange, and in the circumstances was not likely to welcome any activity on the part of the new Amt VI into territory over which he ruled in the interests of the RSHA. Winzer was killed in an air crash over French territory in September 1944 and was replaced by Kriminal Kommissar Ernst Hammes, who had until then worked in Barcelona as an Amt IV representative under Winzer.

The pattern of Amt VI activities in Spain differs from that in other countries because of its comparative complexity. There was latterly no single Amt VI station through which Amt VI conducted its affairs.

As explained in para. 2, the Polizei Attaché remained the chief RSHA representative in Spain and the Amt VI official representation functioned under his control. This system had disadvantages for Amt VI and in 1943 Mosig was sent under camouflaged cover in the Sofindus firm so as to work independently of the Polizei Attaché – the Grille organisation. Thirdly, the Sonderlinien of Schellenberg operated in Spain as in Switzerland in the persons of von Hohenloe and Grafin Podewils. Finally, Oberführer Bernhard, the most important figure in Spain for Amt VI, was neither an Amt VI officer nor agent, but worked both for Amt VI and the Abwehr, and his activities covered economic as well as intelligence spheres. These separate developments were of course a gradual evolution.

While the GIS started with an enormous initial advantage in Spain, this was not true of Amt VI, which entered too late into the field. In Spain, as in other countries, the same difficulties were encountered. The Foreign Office was resentful and unsympathetic, the Abwehr suspicious and uncooperative, while an added complication was the strength of the Polizei Attaché, Winzer, who considered himself the sole representative of the RSHA and covering the interests of the SD. The general weakness of Jost and the poor quality of his Beauftragter were not likely to triumph over such difficulties, and the first period of Amt VI activities was, as elsewhere, a failure.

Jost's first appointments to the Iberian Peninsula were Hastuf Plath to Spain and Hastuf Fast to Portugal. Plath took up his appointment in Madrid shortly before the outbreak of war where he soon came into conflict with Winzer who insisted that Plath could only work under him and submit his reports through him. This early did the Polizei Attache impose his ascendancy over Amt VI, an ascendancy which was maintained nominally until the end. Plath was a failure and was recalled in the Spring of 1940 before being sent to the Eastern Front (in company with Zschinke of VI B 2) where he was killed in action. Plath was in turn succeeded by Hastuf Pfisterer, who remained a short spell before being transferred to VI F. Pfisterer was replaced in 1941 by Ostuf Singer who remained until the end.

It was with the advent of Schellenberg that Amt VI activities in Spain and Portugal developed along vigorous lines. The importance of the Peninsula was not lost on Schellenberg and his changes involved both the Referat and the representatives in the countries themselves. The changes in personnel in the Amt were not of course confined to the Spanish Referat; Schellenberg's general policy was to introduce into Amt VI some of the officers with whom he had been connected in Amt IV. Among these was Stubaf Mosig, who served for a spell as Referent for Spain before going there in September 1943 on a special assignment. He had replaced Ostubaf Keinert, and on his departure to Spain was in turn replaced for a short spell by Ostuf Neuburg. Neuburg was succeeded by Stubaf Fendler who remained as Referent until the final collapse.

Side by side with these changes within the Amt itself was Schellenberg's intensified direction of activity within itself. The most important development was his relationship with Oberführer Bernhard. Bernhard was a prominent shipyard owner in Germany who lost most of his money in the early 1930s. Later he established contact with Franco in Morocco and acted as intermediary between Franco and Goering regarding the provision of transport planes for Franco's troops. Thanks to this early and invaluable service to Franco, Bernhard subsequently became the most influential German contact between the German government and Franco's government, and personally enriched himself as head of the Sofindus firm.

This firm represented the controlling agency of German economic interests in Spain, arranging in particular for the import to Germany of valuable raw materials such as wolfram and tungsten. The facilities for espionage offered by Sofindus were obvious, and the firm was exploited both by the Abwehr and by the SD. It was only with the advent of Schellenberg as Amtschef VI, however, that VI B exploited Sofindus to any extent.

The relationship between Bernhard and Schellenberg has been reported as a close and personal one though this has not been confirmed; in any case it is certain that Bernhard extended the facilities afforded by Sofindus to Amt VI, whether on a personal or official basis. Bernhard's personal contacts were of course invaluable. It was through Bernhard that contact was established with Ramon Serrano Suner, Franco's minister for Foreign Affairs until 1943.

Suner was a most important source on the political trends of the Franco government itself. Other valuable high-level contacts established through Bernhard were Carcellar, the Spanish Minister of Economy, Bau, the former Minister of Commerce and Shipping, and Muycos Grandez, Franco's adjutant and former commander of the Blue Division. Another good source of information, though to a great extent an unwitting one, was General Arda, the leader of the Spanish opposition party. Bernhard covered of course a very wide field in intelligence and economics, and Schellenberg soon realised that Sofindus offered better scope for Amt VI work than did the official representative who was subordinated to the Polizei Attaché, Ostuf Singer, in Madrid.

Plath had been eventually replaced by the permanent representative, Ostuf Singer, probably by the end of 1941. Singer's connections in Spain had gone as far back as the Civil War, when he had been a member of the Condor Legion. He took up his appointment as a member of the German Consulate in Madrid where he was attached to the Polizei Attaché, Winzer, but the hold of Winzer over Singer was however not so strong as it had been over Plath. Singer was responsible to Winzer on matters of discipline only and his reports were sent direct to the Amt. Singer's assignment was to maintain contact with those members of the

Spanish police and the Spanish Foreign Office with whom contact had been established by Amt VI, while he likewise acted as paymaster and communications officer for Amt VI agents in Spain. Singer had as his assistant Hastuf Krueger, who acted independently and was responsible for recruiting and running the important agent, Schwarz von Berg, who specialised in Spanish military circles. Singer in his capacity was able to make contact with minor officials in the Spanish Foreign Office from whom details of records in the Spanish Foreign Office were obtained. These records contained accounts of visits from foreign representatives. He also succeeded in contacting the Spanish police and the Spanish Military Intelligence.

The disadvantages in Singer's work from the point of view of Schellenberg was his continued subordination to Winzer. The position in the first place was too open, and secondly Amt VI activities were by the nature of things known to the Polizei Attaché. In order to circumvent these two difficulties, and at the same time to exploit more fully the facilities afforded by Bernhard and his Sofindus organisation, Schellenberg sent Mosig in September 1943 on a special assignment to Spain. Mosig together with three or four agents recruited from the Lehr-Regiment Kürfürst set up their organisation MadHans Weiss, known as the Organisation Grille, having its own W/T station controlled by Mosig's secretary, Fraulein Brueckner.

The special assignment given to the Organisation Grille was the exploitation of the Sofindus firm in social and commercial circles, and further to maintain the contacts initiated by Bernhard, and enumerated in para. 2 above.

Mosig's subordinates in this work were Lackner, Holting, Ewald Kruse, Hans Weiss, Erich Dietel, Paul Anger and Franz Staudinger, all with appointments in various branches of the Sofindus organisation. In this way Amt VI was able to operate independently of Winzer.

The third line of development in Amt VI activities in Spain was through Schellenberg's personal 'Sonderlinien'. These were two in number, Prinz von Hohenloe and Grafin Podewils. Hohenloe was an influential businessman in Spain with extensive and excellent contacts in Spanish social circles. His reports, which were passed to Schellenberg via Singer, represented his own summary of political trends in Spain based on his contacts in political, business or military circles. Grafin Podewils also had good social connections and was friendly with Suner. Her reports dealt with the results of her conversations with representatives of foreign missions in Spain.

By 1944 the change in the general war situation enabled the Allies to bring pressure to bear on the Spanish government regarding the expulsion of German nationals known to be carrying on espionage activities in the country. Owing to the influence of Bernhard only a few minor personalities were expelled, but it became apparent to Schellenberg that provisions would have to be made to meet a threatening situation. Attempts were made therefore to send more Amt VI officers to the Peninsula in case Allied pressure on the Spanish government should become effective. It is uncertain whether in fact any new replacements were sent though it is known that Gumprecht, who joined VI B 4 late in 1944, did go to Spain soon afterwards; he returned however after a short stay. It is believed that Gumprecht returned however to Spain early in 1945 in company with Hastuf Kreuger, Singer's assistant; and a certain Hastuf Schumann who is otherwise unknown.

Arrangements were likewise made in 1944 for the organisation of I-Netze in Spain and Portugal. Spain offered of course favourable conditions though the Sofindus organisation especially in the transfer of sufficient funds to support the I-Netz for time. Arrangements were left to Mosig, but details of his work in this connection are still unknown. In Portugal Vollbrecht and Nasserstein failed to achieve any results, though the latter is thought to have succeeded in penetrating a Brazilian firm for the purpose. Both in Spain and Portugal, however, one overriding consideration prevailed; the I-Netze had been planned on the assumption that some form of central authority would remain functioning in Germany itself, and as this condition was nullified by the German collapse, the I-Netz, even if they were successfully organised, were organised to little purpose.

Probably connected with the organisation of the I-Netze was the mission entrusted in the Autumn of 1944 to a certain Meyer, who had previously been the W/T technician for Amt VI in Tangiers. Meyer was sent under cover of the Allgemeine Eléktrische Gesellschaft to recruit Spanish born W/T operators. The network was meant to operate in the event of a diplomatic break between Spain and the Allies or when Allied pressure succeeded in having German representatives expelled from Spain. It is not thought however that Meyer met with any success in his mission as it was undertaken at too late a date. Gumprecht too who has been mentioned in paragraph 6 above, had been given the assignment of recruiting some fifty Spaniards from a Spanish camp, in the Tyrol, who were meant to be sent to Spain as intelligence agents. The agents were in fact recruited, but training was not undertaken owing to the speed of the Allied advance. The selected agents were assigned in the end to fighting units.

Karl Arnold worked independently in Madrid through Singer. Although stationed in the Peninsula, Arnold was in fact a VI D representative and operated on behalf of that Gruppe in the organisation of a courier service to South America. His activities, together with those of Meywald, also a VI D representative, are dealt with in the War Room Publication on VI D.

Early activity against Tangiers had come under the control of Hastu Schmuck alias Schmeidow, who was attached to the German Consulate in Tetuan in 1940. Schmuck's special assignment was to submit reports on public opinion in French Morocco, for which purpose his chief agent was the notorious John Dollar. Schmuck remained in Tangiers until January 1942 when he returned to Germany, being eventually sent to Portugal in February 1944 to work under Erich Schroeder. Subsequent activity in Tangiers were under the control of Ustuf Schulze with his assistant, Criminal Assistant Seidel. Schulze established contact with the Arab nationalist leader Yasssani from whose entourage he claimed to have recruited some fifty agents for operations in Spanish Morocco. He made extravagant claims regarding his operations, and when the Consulate in Tangiers was closed in May 1944, he had great difficulty in explaining away the large amounts of money which had been expended by him for so little result. He was eventually dismissed from the Amt and later worked for the DNB. His assistant, Seidel, was expelled at the same time from Tangiers and later worked in Seville.

Doehring has already been referred to under VI B 2 in his capacity as a member of the Dienststelle of BdS, Frankreich. In Paris Doehring had specialised in French North Africa, a subject in which Nossek too had shown considerable interest. During his period of service in France Doehring had made several visits to Spain with a view to establishing a channel through Spain for the despatch of agents into French Morocco. His plans for a network however were cut short by the invasion, and after the retreat from France Referat VI 134 (Parseval) was formed with Doehring as Referent and having as his assistants Ostuf Wiedemann, Oschaf Schnell and Hans Seidel, referred to in paragraph 2 above. Details of enterprises undertaken by Parseval are still lacking. In the early part of 1945 however Doehring was attached to Leitstelle Walter.

Hermann Kallab had the important assignment of acting as VI B 4 representative at Hendaye on the Franco-Spanish frontier, where he carried out his work under cover of the Sofindus organisation. Kallab's function was to facilitate the passage of VI B agents from France into Spain, as well as documents and equipment which could not be sent openly to the country. He was assisted in this type of work by Paul Anger who specialised in the smuggling of important material such as tungsten out of Spain.

Information on Amt VI activities in Portugal is even less complete than that on its activities in Spain. Jost's first representative in Portugal was Ostuf Fast who is almost certainly identical with Waldemar Fast, the HVIO representative in Turkey at present under arrest. Fast was replaced in 1941 for a short spell by Ostuf Schoenbeck who had previously been Amt VI representative in Finland. Latterly under Schellenberg the two Amt VI representatives were Stuba Nasserstein and Stuba Vollebrecht

The general situation in Portugal differed from that in Spain in two respects. Firstly there was no Polizei Attaché as Schroeder, who took up his appointment in Portugal in October 1941, was only recognised as a Polizeiverbindungsführer. His position was not so strong as that of Winzer in Spain, but nevertheless his relations with Amt VI representatives were never cordial. Secondly, the general attitude of the Portuguese government was not so well disposed towards Germany, as that of the Spanish government.

During the period 1942-43 Kurt Foerster had acted in the interests of Amt VI, but was expelled in March 1943 as a result of an unfortunate attempt at recruitment of an agent which ended in failure. Foerster was replaced by Vollebrecht who remained in Portugal from August 1943 onwards. Nasserstein acted in the dual capacity of VI B 4 and VI D representative as his duties involved specialisation on South American matters. It is not possible on available evidence to assess the work of Vollebrecht and Nasserstein. It is significant however that Schellenberg considers both as complete failures in their work.

In assessing the work of Gruppe VI B in the six years of its history it should be remembered that it is more than a little inaccurate to say that Amt VI evolved out of the old SD-Hauptamt III/3. The extension of SD activity from security operations to offensive operations and from the domestic to the foreign field was in fact a step which broke new ground. It was really only in Eastern Europe that the old SD Hauptamt laid any good foundations for the work of the new Amt VI. Gruppe VI B, therefore, dealing with Western Europe, was faced with a difficult task, as only in the case of Switzerland was there any previous SD work which it could further exploit. For the Gruppe to have been successful therefore in its initial stages it would have required both energetic direction from the Amtschef combined with sympathetic cooperation from other organisations. Neither of these conditions were in fact fulfilled in the first two years of Amt VI activities in the west. Generally speaking therefore Gruppe VI B did not succeed in overcoming the difficulties with which it was faced. It failed almost dismally in France, Holland and Belgium: it did not achieve the success it might have done in the case of Switzerland, while Italy represented a case of lost opportunity, but for reasons not attributable to the Gruppe itself. But the failures in these countries were due not only to the opposition of other Amter in the RSHA, to the hostility of the Foreign Office, nor to the lack of cooperation with the Abwehr, but also to the inefficiency and lack of imagination on the part of most of the leading personnel in the Gruppe. The results achieved were meagre in comparison with the effort expended. Only in the case of the Iberian Peninsula is it likely that the final assessment will reflect favourably on the work of Gruppe VI B, and while the final assessment is not yet possible in this connection, it would not seem that Amt VI took full advantage of the very favourable circumstances which existed in Spain.[2]

Whereas the Allies would have the benefit of access to the German intelligence personnel in Lisbon, who were repatriated at the end of the war by the Portuguese authorities, Franco's regime in Spain did not inflict such indignities and allowed a large number of intelligence targets relative freedom, with only voluntary participation in post-war interviews. Inevitably, there would be plenty of loose ends to be addressed, and information relating to the SD was particularly scarce. However, the SD's Friedrich Dohse had been arrested post-war in Denmark where he recalled that Paul Winzer had been killed in October 1944 when his aircraft had been shot down over Lyon, and had explained the scale of the SD's parallel organisation in Spain:

> Winzer was in charge of 55 – 40 men, who were stationed at various Spanish towns, at the German Consulates. Officials were stationed at Barcelona, San Sebastian, Bilbao, Santander, Saragossa, Pamplona, Algeciras, Valladolid, etc. 2 or 3 men were stationed at each place, and all of then came direct from the Gestapo. Most of the men were former clerks from the German offices during the Spanish Civil War. They co-operated with Spanish V-Manner, especially from the Spanish police. Winzer in Madrid reported information obtained in Spain to Bömelburg in Paris, in so far as the information concerned German interests in France. Other information was sent direct to Berlin by courier post. The whole organisation, as well in Spain as in other countries, ranged under Abt., IV N in RSHA, Berlin, and the head was Obergruppenführer Müller or Gruppenführer Schellenberg. The detainee can only remember two other names, viz, the head at Barcelona was Kriminalkommissar Shaeffer, and the head at San Sebastian was Untersturmführer Kriminalsekretär Konnecke. Winzer had connections in Spain and Portugal, and in the countries in South America, where Spanish was spoken. Schroeder at Barcelona had connections in the countries where they spoke Portuguese. The work was mainly turned against the Allies and by help of the Spanish police, prisoners were exchanged between Gestapo in France and the police in Spain.[3]

* * *

In contrast to the SD's relative impotency in the Peninsula, the Abwehr had been well established in Madrid and Lisbon over many years, and the War Room counter-intelligence analysts at Oberursel were able in August 1946 to interview two key witnesses, Wilhelm Leisner[4] and Ernst Kleyenstuber, who both had headed the KOS. Following an early interrogation of Leisner, a reassuring summary was sent to London:

In 1937 Leisner was posted to the Legion Condor in Spain, owing to his knowledge of Spanish, and became Leiter of Abw Ausaenstelle Algerciras. With the dissolution of Legion Condor in May 1939 he remained in Spain and became Leiter of KO Spain.

There are details of the building up of the Abwehr organisation in Spain after the outbreak of war, and the methods of reporting information.

Very close watch was kept on Gibraltar and shipping in the Straits.

Attempts were made to recruit seamen going on long voyages to report their observations. This became increasingly difficult, due to British security measures at Trinidad.

Those seamen did not show much inclination to bring back papers and periodicals from abroad; also the transportation of wireless sets was impossible, owing to the difficulty of hiding them aboard ships.

It was not possible to vet Spanish V-Men employed by the Germans with the Spanish authorities. Eventually it became increasingly difficult to employ Spanish V-Men, and it was known that there was an order prohibiting this with the Falange.

Main task of I/H was reporting on troop movements in France.

A Spanish V-Mann was employed for this purpose, who was supposed to have a good network in France; it was later found that many of the messages were false.

England also came under the jurisdiction of l/H. Prior to the war, KO Spain had not worked against England, therefore considerable difficulty was experienced in overcoming England's insular position. As far as Leisner recollects the England/Referent of l/H managed to send a Pole, who was in transit, as V-Man, who sent a few reports about troop positions in England.

After further efforts a Spaniard was sent to England, who according to his reports had a small network in Southern England, reported on troop movements. He employed a 'Red' Spanish W/T operator, who thought he was reporting to a 'Red' station in Spain. These reports were viewed with some doubt in Berlin. Up to the time of the end of Leisner's appointment as Leiter, this W/T communication with England was taking place.

Apart from those contacts, there were no other communications with England, Ireland or the Empire.

The plans and installations of Gibraltar were known in Berlin, and any changes were obtained by long-distance photography from Algeciras.

Berlin was mainly interested in reports from America. Leisner states that before commencement of war against the USA it was strictly forbidden to work against this country. As in the case of England, it was impossible to overcome all the difficulties, owing to the lack of preparation. Navicerts and shipping facilities were unobtainable, therefore no V-Men could be sent from Spain.

Main task of l/T Lw of KO Spain was to obtain information on Allied Radar equipment. This was unsuccessful, particularly since the personnel was continually fluctuating.

There was no wireless contact with the USA.

The work of Gruppe II was mainly directed against enemy shipping in Gibraltar – the idea being to blow holes in ships; this appears to have been rather ineffective. Abw II withdrew from Tangier in the spring of 1944.

Abw III dealt with counter-espionage, i.e. the enemy in Spanish territory. This was fairly successful, except difficulties was created, because other Abw Stellen from in Germany etc, sent V-Men to Spain without notifying the KO.

At the beginning of 1944 an R-Net was started in case of an Allied landing in Spain.

The Spanish authorities tolerated the GIS in Spain.

Short paragraph re Canaris' dislike of Hitler, Himmler and Ribbentrop, and his disapproval of their methods. Apparently he often sent non-Aryan officers to Spain.

Short paragraph on English list presented by Spanish authorities to the Germans.

List of Abwehr officers in Spain.

V-Leute employed by KO Spain were mostly insignificant people.

It was impossible to use people in Spanish government because of the training that would be needed.

One V-Man's name Leisner remembers is UTRILLAS.

In England the V-Men used numbers in the 200s, probably between 212 and 219. The 'Red' Spanish W/T expert was probably directed by 212.

Details of Spanish officers etc., with whom Loissner was in communication. He complains that Spanish government were un-co-operative, since they could have informed of Allied landings and the conference in Casablanca.

Some of the V-Leute employed were from the Falange organisation. There were a number of agents in Tetuan, also working for Spain, so that their messages may not have been authentic.

The KO had no V-Leute in Spanish regiments.[5]

Somewhat undiplomatically, MI5 expressed dissatisfaction with this joint statement, signed off by Leisner and Kleyenstuber, as it rather looked as though the two officers had tried to minimise the KOS role, and it appeared to MI5 that the American interrogators were less interested in the KOS wartime operations than in the tracing the Abwehr's funds, an OSS investigation codenamed SAFEHAVEN.

Kleyenstuber, who had replaced Leisner in Madrid in July 1944, was a naval aviation expert specialising in aerial minelaying operations who, born in Kiel in 1912, had joined the Kriegsmarine in 1931 to train as a naval pilot. His only previous intelligence experience had been as a liaison officer with the Luftwaffe's II Fliegerkorps in the Mediterranean. Then, in January 1944, he had been posted to the Abwehr in Berlin to head Amt I/L. His subsequent transfer to KOS was unusual in that Leisner remained in Madrid as Kleyenstuber's subordinate. Upon his repatriation to Germany he had been held by the US CIC at Asperg.

Leisner's interrogators regarded him as unimaginative, whereas they were quite impressed with his I/L successor, Kleyenstuber:

> In the course of the re-organisation of Section 1 of the Abwehr Department carried out in the spring of 1944 the hitherto existing division of groups was dropped. In April or May Chief I, who was then simultaneously Abwehr departmental head, told me of his intention to entrust me with the conduct of the KG in Spain. The command was to be limited to approximately 6 months. After that my Abwehr activity would be concluded, my service in that Abwehr department then reached a total of 2 years. I was then to be re-transferred to the Luftwaffe (I had repeatedly requested combat service in the Luftwaffe as the ministerial deskwork at the Department did not suit my taste).
>
> Through Colonel Hansen the predominance of the military sector of work in the Abwehr department over the economic and technical sector had greatly increased. Furthermore, the influence of the ICs of the Wehrmacht branches (army, navy and Luftwaffe) on the work of the Abwehr departments were strengthened (IC – reconnaissance of enemy's situation – Feindlagebenarbeitung). Colonel Hansen himself as well as all his newly-appointed group chiefs, and some of their collaborators from IC positions. As I had IC experience in the Mediterranean theatre of war he evidently considered me the right man to personally influence the KO in Spain in the direction of utilising their intelligence material in accordance with his wishes and reflection.
>
> The immediate reason was the depreciation of the relations between the German Embassy and the KO in Madrid. The main questions of controversy were the numerical size of the KO and the site of its office. Shortly before he was removed from his office, Admiral Canaris had held a meeting with members of the Madrid embassy at which he had to agree to wholly withdraw his service out of the embassy, thus giving up diplomatic protection. In this Colonel Hansen thought the admiral had gone too far. As I was a former group chief and former General Staff officer, he expected me to take a firmer stand toward the embassy and to protect the vital pre-requisites of the military intelligence service.

Affix
stamp
here

Pen and Sword Books
c/o Casemate Publishers
1950 Lawrence Road
Havertown, PA 19083

Admiral Wilhelm Canaris. Appointed to head the Abwehr in 1935, Canaris established a reputation for ambiguous loyalty to the Nazi government and unwavering support for politically risky operations conducted in the United States and Great Britain. He was credited with having provided the Wehrmacht with the vital military intelligence that made possible the swift 1940 victories in France, Belgium and the Netherlands. However, a series of defections in Istanbul precipitated his suspension in February 1944 and, following the 20 July plot, his arrest. He would be executed in April 1945.

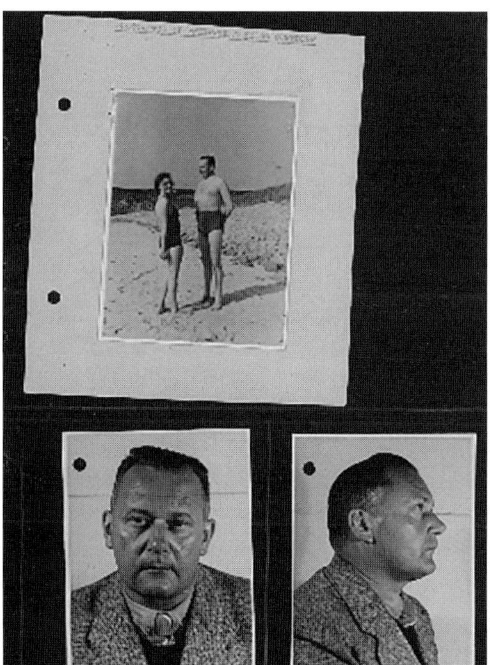

Erich Pfeiffer. The architect of Ast Bremen's pre-war espionage offensive in England, Pfeiffer was transferred to Brest in 1940 and then posted to Paris before being appointed to head KONO in Istanbul, where he was detained by the Allies in September 1944. Under interrogation he cooperated with his captors and provided vast amounts of information about the Abwehr's activities.

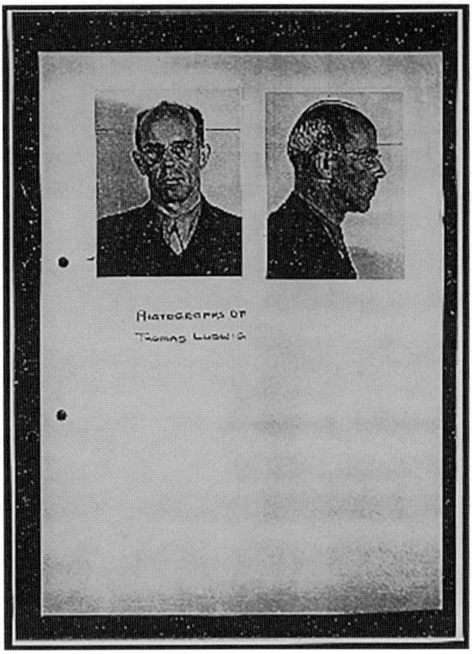

Thomas Ludwig. The Abwehr's spymaster in Belgrade and then Istanbul, Ludwig was detained in May 1945 when the *Drottningholm*, the liner repatriating German diplomats. docked at Liverpool, thus giving MI5 the opportunity to interrogate him at Camp 020 where he identified all his wartime agents.

Josef Ledebur. A senior Abwehr defector in Madrid in August 1944, Ledebur was brought to London by SIS and interrogated by MI5 from November. His information resulted in an 86-page report, with a further 100 pages of appendices, 'every word of which has been of value'.

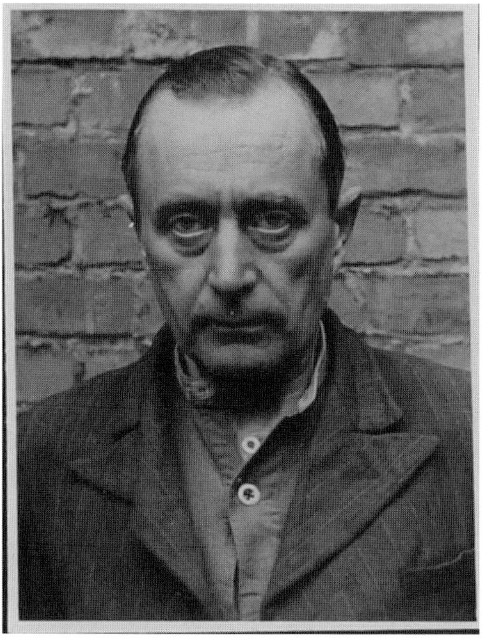

Colonel Rudolf. The chief of Ast Paris, Rudolf was the alias adopted by Friedrich Baumeister. He was imprisoned in 1944 by the Gestapo for complicity in the 20 July plot and was interrogated by MI5 in November 1945. Under cross-examination Baumeister disclosed details of operations he had directed against France and Great Britain dating back to 1933.

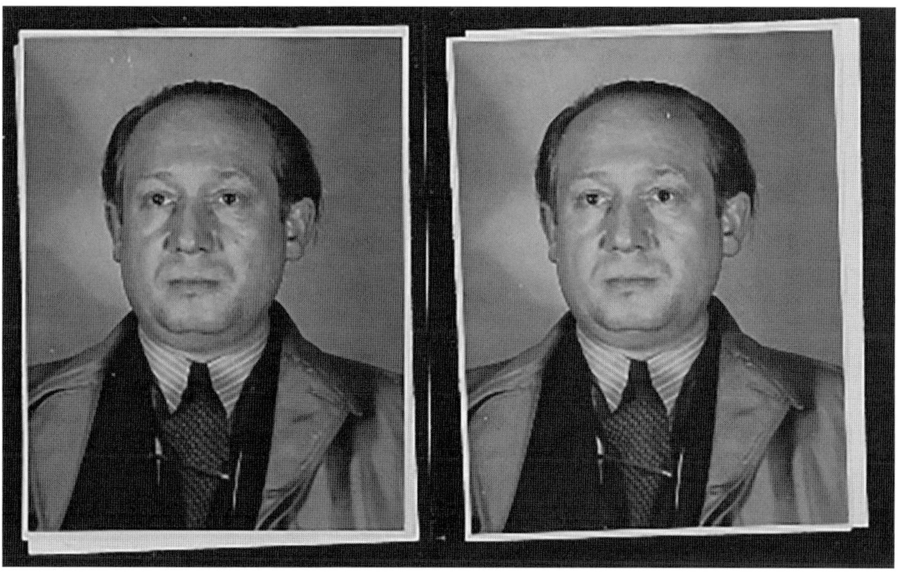

Carl Eitel. Employed as a steward on the pre-war transatlantic liner *Bremen*, Eitel was an experienced Abwehr agent-handler who defected to OSS's Lisbon station. However, when questioned in London, he admitted that he had duped his American sponsors. Accordingly, he was detained for the rest of the war and transferred to the MI19 interrogation centre at Diest.

Kuno Weltzien. A very aggressive Abwehr recruiter in Lisbon, Weltzien operated on the docks under commercial cover and rarely contacted the KOP accommodated in the German legation. Well-connected with the PVDE, he managed numerous seamen agents and mounted several operations intended to penetrate the local SIS station, discredit its staff and disrupt its activities.

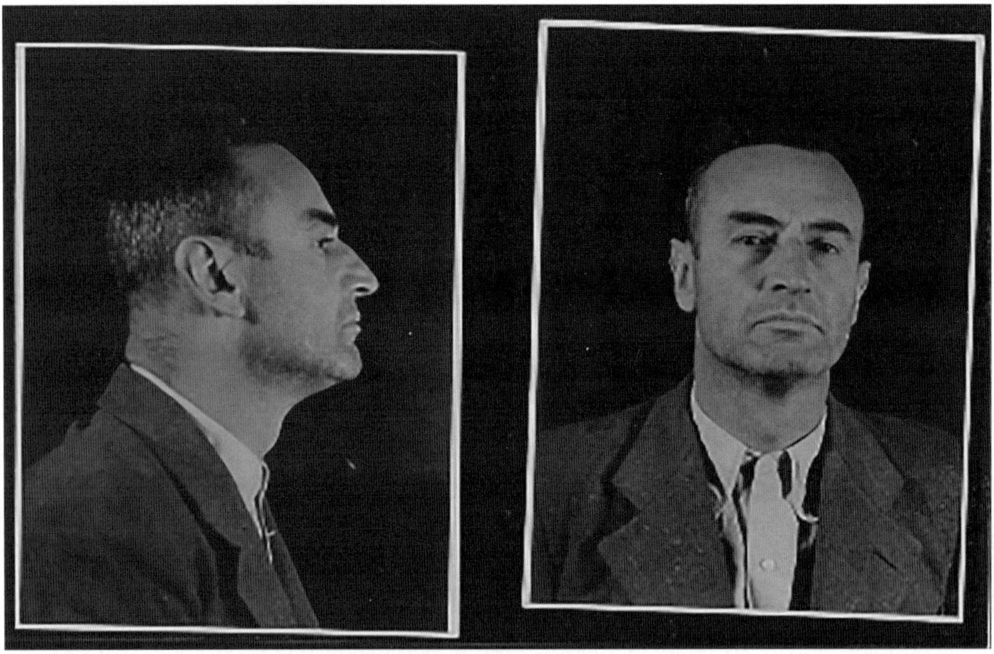

Otto Mayer. An Abwehr officer captured by partisans during an ambush in Dalmatia, Mayer was flown to Brindisi and, fearing he could be sent back to Yugoslavia to face prosecution for unspecified war crimes, agreed to cooperate with the British. He was flown to Scotland via Algiers and revealed that he had served previously in Belgrade and Istanbul.

Paul Fidrmuc. A Czech fabricator based in Lisbon, Fidrmuc sold large quantities of supposedly valuable information to the KO Portugal which relayed it uncritically to Berlin. SIS was suspicious of Fidrmuc, whose apparent guesswork occasionally came uncomfortably close to the truth, but considered him too dangerous to approach or subvert.

Gottfried Paul-Taboschat. The Leiter of the Abwehr Nest in Barcelona, Paul-Taboschat was the senior German intelligence officer in the region and was responsible for supervising a constant stream of enemy agents, often posing as refugees or evading Allied airmen, destined to undertake espionage missions in England.

Nikolaus Ritter. Having run a business in the United States, Ritter posed as 'Dr Rantzau' to deploy agents to England from his base in Hamburg. Following a disastrous attempt to infiltrate agents into Cairo he was transferred to the Luftwaffe to command an anti-aircraft battery.

Emile Kliemann. Although based in Paris, Kliemann often visited Lisbon to rendezvous with his agents, and is pictured here with Lily Sergueiev who went on a mission to London where she was 'turned' by MI5 into a double agent, and was codenamed TREASURE. However, she confessed to the Abwehr which skilfully manipulated her duplicity.

Bertie Koepke. Operating under commercial cover in Barcelona, Koepke was codenamed DON PEDRO and became a familiar figure to MI5 analysts after so many of his agents, usually French or Belgian pilots, travelled to London through Gibraltar or Lisbon.

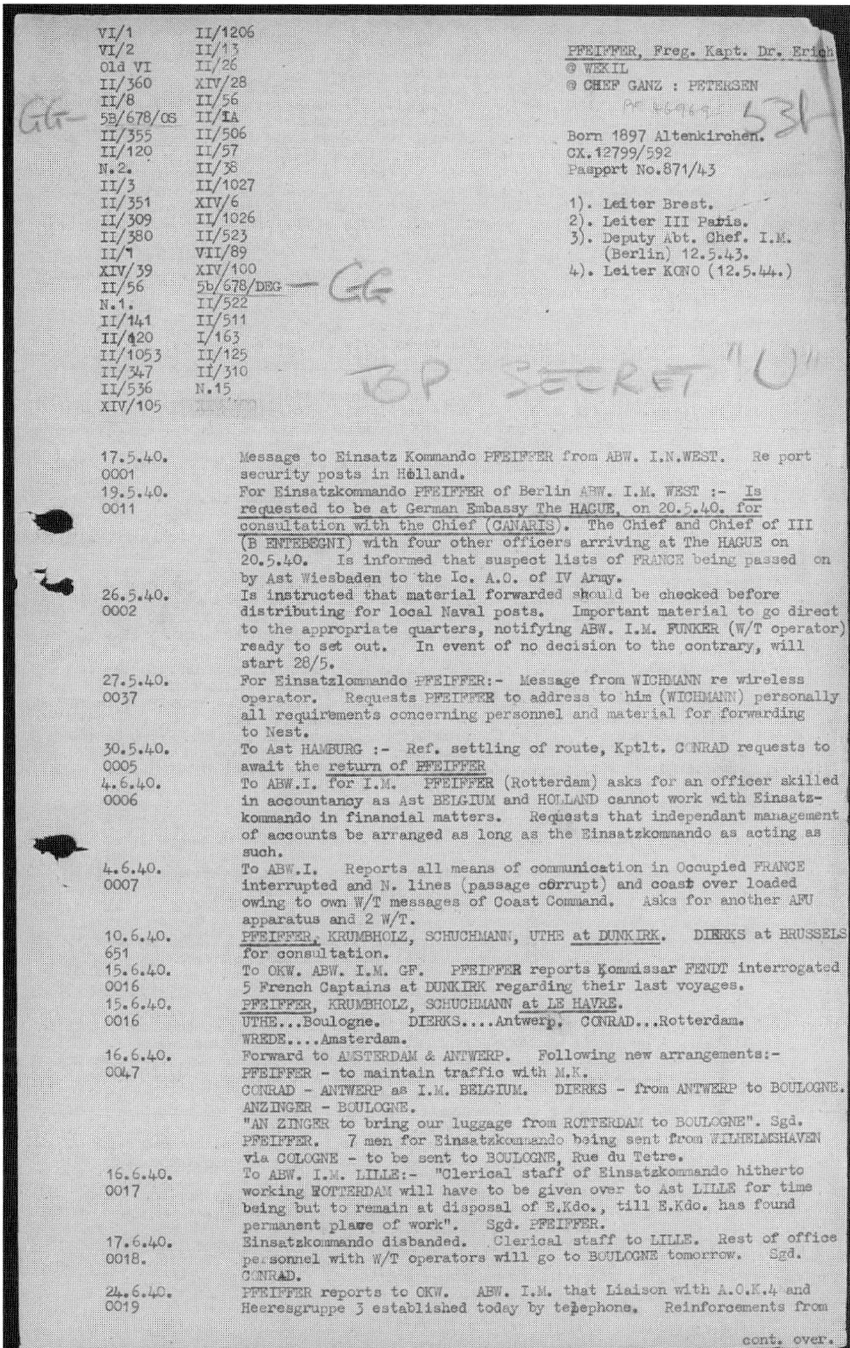

VI/1	II/1206
VI/2	II/13
Old VI	II/26
II/360	XIV/28
II/8	II/56
5B/678/OS	II/IA
II/355	II/506
II/120	II/57
N.2.	II/38
II/3	II/1027
II/351	XIV/6
II/309	II/1026
II/380	II/523
II/1	VII/89
XIV/39	XIV/100
II/56	5b/678/DEG
N.1.	II/522
II/141	II/511
II/120	I/163
II/1053	II/125
II/347	II/310
II/536	N.15
XIV/105	

PFEIFFER, Freg. Kapt. Dr. Erich
@ WEKIL
@ CHEF GANZ : PETERSEN

Born 1897 Altenkirchen.
CX.12799/592
Pasport No.871/43

1). Leiter Brest.
2). Leiter III Paris.
3). Deputy Abt. Chef. I.M. (Berlin) 12.5.43.
4). Leiter KONO (12.5.44.)

TOP SECRET "U"

17.5.40. 0001	Message to Einsatz Kommando PFEIFFER from ABW. I.N.WEST. Re port security posts in Holland.
19.5.40. 0011	For Einsatzkommando PFEIFFER of Berlin ABW. I.M. WEST :- Is requested to be at German Embassy The HAGUE, on 20.5.40. for consultation with the Chief (CANARIS). The Chief and Chief of III (B ENTEBEGNI) with four other officers arriving at The HAGUE on 20.5.40. Is informed that suspect lists of FRANCE being passed on by Ast Wiesbaden to the Ic. A.O. of IV Army.
26.5.40. 0002	Is instructed that material forwarded should be checked before distributing for local Naval posts. Important material to go direct to the appropriate quarters, notifying ABW. I.M. FUNKER (W/T operator) ready to set out. In event of no decision to the contrary, will start 28/5.
27.5.40. 0037	For Einsatzlommando PFEIFFER:- Message from WICHMANN re wireless operator. Requests PFEIFFER to address to him (WICHMANN) personally all requirements concerning personnel and material for forwarding to Nest.
30.5.40. 0005	To Ast HAMBURG :- Ref. settling of route, Kptlt. CONRAD requests to await the return of PFEIFFER
4.6.40. 0006	To ABW.I. for I.M. PFEIFFER (Rotterdam) asks for an officer skilled in accountancy as Ast BELGIUM and HOLLAND cannot work with Einsatz-kommando in financial matters. Requests that independant management of accounts be arranged as long as the Einsatzkommando as acting as such.
4.6.40. 0007	To ABW.I. Reports all means of communication in Occupied FRANCE interrupted and N. lines (passage corrupt) and coast over loaded owing to own W/T messages of Coast Command. Asks for another AFU apparatus and 2 W/T.
10.6.40. 651	PFEIFFER, KRUMBHOLZ, SCHUCHMANN, UTHE at DUNKIRK. DIERKS at BRUSSELS for consultation.
15.6.40. 0016	To OKW. ABW. I.M. GF. PFEIFFER reports Kommissar FENDT interrogated 5 French Captains at DUNKIRK regarding their last voyages.
15.6.40. 0016	PFEIFFER, KRUMBHOLZ, SCHUCHMANN at LE HAVRE. UTHE...Boulogne. DIERKS....Antwerp. CONRAD...Rotterdam. WREDE....Amsterdam.
16.6.40. 0047	Forward to AMSTERDAM & ANTWERP. Following new arrangements:- PFEIFFER - to maintain traffic with M.K. CONRAD - ANTWERP as I.M. BELGIUM. DIERKS - from ANTWERP to BOULOGNE. ANZINGER - BOULOGNE. "AN ZINGER to bring our luggage from ROTTERDAM to BOULOGNE". Sgd. PFEIFFER. 7 men for Einsatzkommando being sent from WILHELMSHAVEN via COLOGNE - to be sent to BOULOGNE, Rue du Tetre.
16.6.40. 0017	To ABW. I.M. LILLE:- "Clerical staff of Einsatzkommando hitherto working ROTTERDAM will have to be given over to Ast LILLE for time being but to remain at disposal of E.Kdo., till E.Kdo. has found permanent place of work". Sgd. PFEIFFER.
17.6.40. 0018.	Einsatzkommando disbanded. Clerical staff to LILLE. Rest of office personnel with W/T operators will go to BOULOGNE tomorrow. Sgd. CONRAD.
24.6.40. 0019	PFEIFFER reports to OKW. ABW. I.M. that Liaison with A.O.K.4 and Heeresgruppe 3 established today by telephone. Reinforcements from

cont. over.

ISOS. Interception and decryption of the Abwehr's radio traffic produced profiles of individual officers and their agents long before they underwent Allied interrogation, giving the Allied counter-intelligence staffs an extraordinary advantage to exploit. Every message was translated, carded on a cross-referenced index, and allocated to a personality profile which, over time, revealed movements, contacts, assignments and aliases.

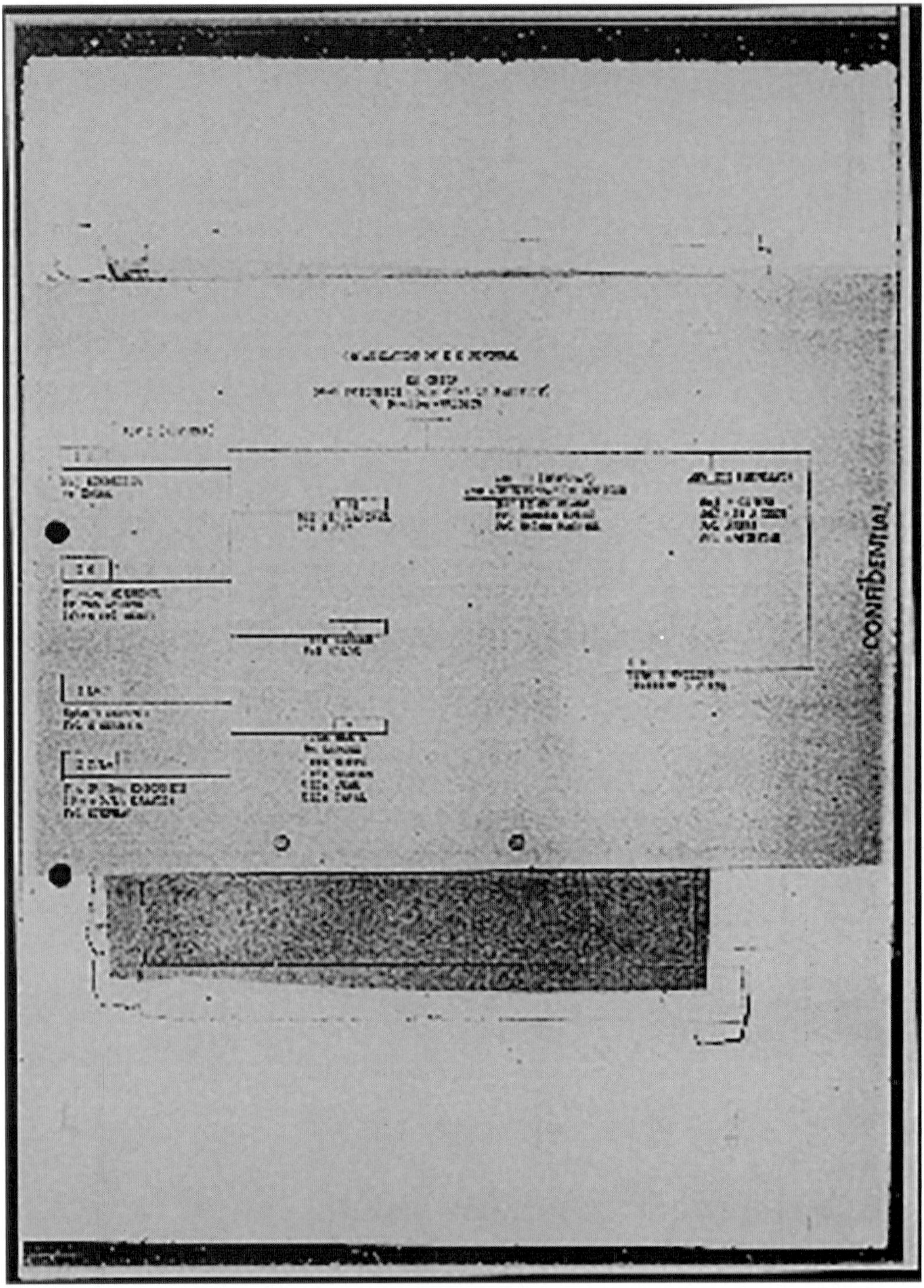

KriegsOrganisation Portugal (KOP). An organisational chart of the Abwehr's network in Lisbon, as supplied by Rudolf Blaum who headed the Abt. II sabotage branch from 1942. He was interrogated in Germany by the US CIC in 1942.

My task in Madrid can therefore be summed up as follows:

Limitation of KO activities to war-essential work; simultaneously reduction of personnel as far as possible.

On the other hand, safeguard of the best possible working condition for the reduced staff of collaborators. That especially included support by the embassy with regard to camouflage and diplomatic protection to a greater degree than before.

The situation I encountered on my arrival at Madrid was as follows:

Position of the KO

The KO did not have a very strong position. It can be assumed that the reason for this is primarily the fact that the Abwehr Department and its superior office, the OKW, had but little power to assert themselves in the Berlin inter-departmental strife against ministries, the SD, etc. Furthermore, the atmosphere in the embassy was somewhat hostile to the military. The KO was often the object of criticism which was not always justified. The military service was treated with materially less consideration than the secretly feared SD. I attempted to strengthen our position as far as possible and in the course of time to remove any tension existing in our relations to other offices, at the same time upholding connections that were running smoothly. On the other hand I endeavoured to avoid a one-sided obligation that might result from too close collaboration with any particular office. It was probably on account of this course that the KO retained an independent factor up to Germany's collapse, although several quarters were working on a proposition to combine the KO with the SD or to subordinate both services to an SD functionary who would have been sent to Madrid.

Question of housing

On my arrival the KO were concentrated in two annexes of the embassy, its public traffic could therefore be easily controlled by the enemy.

Where the KO had formerly occupied half a floor in the main building, it now only retained one room for the officer on duty and the rooms for the wireless operators. The available side-rooms in the building of the Consular Office were occupied by the offices of the police attaché and the Plankort group.

The KO was thus in the most unfavourable position of all. Enemy reconnaissance was made easy as there were no difficulties in watching the 2 annexes in a city area and thereby identifying members and collaborators of the KO. On the other hand the general public traffic in the main building and the Consular Office was so strong that the visitors of the KO would have been absorbed by it.

In the course of this I succeeded in retaining a few rooms in the main building and the Consular Office, so that at least a part of the KO office could again be better camouflaged.

Reduction of Personnel
I came to Madrid with instructions to carry through a limited reduction of personnel by restricting less important part of the KO. That was also intended again to improve our relations with the embassy. However, 10 days later the Spanish Foreign Ministry presented the first list of personnel to be expelled from Spain. This list subsequently overshadowed all former reflections on a reduction of personnel. The question now was to improvise with what was actually on hand. An attempt had to be made to prevent the deportation or internment of more important KO men at the expense of those who could be released. Furthermore, the KO had to insist on the military intelligence service not being the only one to make sacrifices and that the other sectors likewise affected by the deportation action, such as party and SD, took an equal share.

For this reason the reduction in personnel was no longer a matter of objective decision. Its speed and extent were determined by Allied pressure and the resulting Spanish measures in the direction of deportation. The degree of yielding depended upon whatever sector seemed appropriate from time to time.

Organisation and method of work
The list of deportations made it evident that the enemy had been largely successful in disclosing the KO. In the interests of greater secrecy I tried to more strictly seclude the various groups and sub-divisions from one another. Every individual's knowledge of secret affairs was to be limited to what it was absolutely necessary for him to know. For this reason major discussions no longer took place. (Group III, which had been very good at shutting itself off from the outside right from the beginning, was the model for the arrangement.)

In order to prevent outsiders as far as possible from gaining an insight into the KO, intercourse with the other German offices in respect of general matters was limited to the newly-appointed Special Officer (Offizer zbV.) Dr Schoene and myself respectively. The specialised work of the I and especially the III sector naturally remained untouched by the arrangement.

The newly set-up sub-division 'O abV' handled all matters pertaining to the agents of the 'Other Offices' (frend Stellen); viz. the Abwehr office of the Reich and the occupied territories. By concentrating all these things on one responsible man the KO least wanted to assist in clearing up the confusion in this sector of work.

KO Spain R-Network and Capitulation
The conception of an R-network (Retreat network) had been generally introduced by the Abwehr Department since 1943. The R-network was to be established as a precautionary measure in occupied territory in case of a possible retreat. It was only to be made ready for operation

before, in order to be put into action after the evacuation. It was then to provide the military intelligence with information from this territory. The information comprised 2 groups, viz:

1) Information already received in the territory before the evacuation from outside. This had to be passed on in the 'R' category.
2) Procurement of information on the enemy in the evacuated territory.

For this purpose the Abwehr offices in the occupied territories established as a precautionary measure emergency quarters farther back, mostly in the Reich. From here the R-network was to be directed during and after the retreat.

Non-camouflaged preparation for the event of a collapse could have led to dangerous consequences for those involved. (In the inner ring of the KOI called the collapse the 'Z' case.) The formerly planned actual 'R' preparation was therefore cancelled according to the situation.

The Abwehr

The Abwehr Department in Berlin handled the plan to prepare Sigmaringen as emergency quarters but I hardly think that more than the initial stage was reached. At the time it was intended to detail the KO members expelled from Spain to Sigmaringen. In this way men acquainted with Spanish conditions were gradually to rally there and thus establish the necessary platform for upholding the Spanish agents' connections in case the KO should no longer exist.

Events in Spain were as follows:

Preparations for the final remuneration were at an end approximately in March and the funds necessary were available. Payments were effected according to schedule when the embassy was closed.

With regard to unexpected occurrences the gold and foreign currency reserve of the KO were at first removed from the annex to the main building of the embassy and later safely deposited out of town. On account of a denunciation some members of the administration group and myself were arrested by the Spanish police for embezzlement a few days after the embassy was closed down. The gold and foreign currency were handed over to the Spanish police and the Spanish Foreign Ministry respectively. Our release took place about a fortnight later after the matter had been cleared up.

After the capitulation I requested Herr Lindenbarg, whom I knew to be in contact with the head of the American service Colonel Ebright, to inform the colonel as the ranking Allied intelligence officer that I naturally regarded the capitulation of the German Wehrmacht as binding for myself and the KO. I considered that necessary in order to remove any ambiguities, especially in view of those Germans who hoped to be able to hide behind the Spaniards.

In November 1945 the Allied commission which had meanwhile been formed invited me to a discussion at Madrid, The object was to clear up matters regarding the whereabouts and transfer of KO property. For this purpose I again contacted the former group chiefs and major collaborators. The liquidation lasted about a week and was largely completed at the end of December.

When the embassy was closed, I had reserved an emergency fund of 53,000 pesetas for my own disposal. The object was to support KO members who subsequently got into difficulties without any fault of their own. I informed the Allied commission of this in the summer of 1945. A total of about 30,000 pesetas was paid out to small salaried persons, mostly in the case of unexpected doctor's bills, etc. And I myself was arrested by the Spanish police at the end of January 1946 for transport to Germany. I asked my former secretary to hand over the balance as well as the receipts and documents pertaining to these payments to the Allied commission. This is sure to have been done at once.[6]

* * *

In Portugal the KO operated not from the embassy but from an apartment building that was an annexe to the embassy in the rua Buenos Aires, headed by a portly Austrian, Ludwig Kramer-Auenrode, who lived in some style at the Villa Ki-Ana at Estoril. He would be succeeded as KOP's Leiter by Colonel Rolf Friderici, formerly of Abt. III in Berlin, and then by Hans Bendixen. In charge of the KOP's Gruppe III was Fritz Cramer, formerly the manager of the Adlon Hotel in Berlin, who was credited in May 1944 with having broken into the safe of the OSS chief in Lisbon, Robert Solborg. This 'masterstroke' had been accomplished by Cramer's agent Jorge Estranda who, five weeks earlier, had conducted a similar burglary on the safe of a man named Gordier.

Although Lisbon, with a large German legation staffed by nearly a hundred declared officials was effectively the intelligence front line for the Allies, the precise nature and scale of the challenge posed by the Abwehr in Portugal was, until the end of 1941, something of a mystery, as Camp 020's commandant, Robin Stephens, acknowledged in August to his MI5 colleague Dick White:

> Briefly, my attitude is that information on the structure of the German Secret Service in Portugal and Spain should be the result of active SIS espionage in those countries. In point of fact, such information is either non-existent or not available, and I am therefore left, in a counter-espionage centre, to piece together as best I can Intelligence derived

> from certain spies who are with us at the present time. Much of this information is valuable, and much of it is true, but I do not conceal the fact that I have a number of pieces of a jig-saw puzzle without any conception of the size or the puzzle itself.[7]

MI5's discontent with SIS was a reflection of the lack of support felt by the Camp 020 interrogators who were disappointed by the paucity of information available about the German organisation in Lisbon, which amounted to a very misleading brief circulated by Section V's head, Felix Cowgill, in July 1941:

> I Personalities
> 1. The Chief of the Heeresnachrichtendienst, both of the Intelligence and of the Counter-Espionage sections, is, there is little doubt, Albert von Karstorff, assistant Commercial Attaché at the German Embassy in Lisbon. Hans Ruser, who may have been the former chief is now definitely in eclipse, and little is heard of him in the leading German Intelligence Service circle though his advice is still sought on occasion.
>
> 2. Karstoff's principal assistant seems to be Fritz Kramer, an official at the German Legation who lives in Estoril, two doors away from Hans Ruser's house, the Villa Clothilde. Kramer is of Austrian origin, born in 1889, and was at one time secretary of the Adlon Hotel, Berlin. One of his principal preoccupations is the recruitment of agents for the Americas. His secretary is reported to be Ingeborg Evert, described in the Legation list as a typist to the Air Attaché. She hails from Berlin and is thought to be Kramer's mistress.
>
> 3. Other prominent members of the German Intelligence Service are Otto Merkel (Karstoff's secretary), Fred Lang, Dr Oeckel, Julius Joachim Finck (son of Walter Finck and believed to be the local paymaster), Henri Doebler, and Karl Kramer and Schubeius of the German Consulate. The last two are thought to be members of the Counter-Espionage section, but the information about this section is still nebulous. Fred Lang's principal preoccupation has been the illicit conversion of French currency but he has now burnt his fingers and has been summoned to Berlin where it is believed he has to face grave charges of a financial nature. He has now left for the USA via Rome and Pernambuco. Just before he left Lisbon, Lang admitted that he had only acquired German nationality in the name of Lang in the last few years. He is suspected of being Dutch as he speaks the language perfectly. It is believed that one Sichtermann has taken Lang's place.
>
> 4. Henri Doebler, alias Duarte, whose activities have been mainly concerned with shipping intelligence, has recently been expelled from

Portugal but has been given 3 months' grace at the intercession of his mistress, who happens to be the mistress also of an important official in the International Police.

5. Apart from the circle described above, the most important outside agent is Kuno Weltzien, partner in the firm of Cudell and Weltzien of Lisbon. He employs many sub-agents and appears to devote himself mainly to obtaining shipping intelligence, but he is also concerned with espionage and has been responsible for the dispatch of agents to the UK. There is evidence also that he controls in some measure the activities of agents in the Atlantic Islands, or in some of them.

6. Another prominent figure is Theodore Mielitz. He employs several sub-agents and seems mainly concerned with the recruitment of agents for abroad.

II Shipping Intelligence

7. A good deal of information is available as to the collection of information in regard to Allied shipping movements and its subsequent transmission; most of it comes from Oporto, where relations with the international police are better than anywhere else.

8. Three main strands of shipping intelligence collected in Oporto has so far been discovered; two of those have been traced as far as Lisbon; one to Hamburg:

a) Marques d'Agular and Jose Almeida Jr of rua Alves da Vaja 635, Oporto, to Ernst Schmidt in Lisbon, through the cover-address Artur de Carvalho rus do Barao 6-4E and Fernando de Castro, for all information regarding movements of ships not proceeding to a British port. For ships bound to a British port, the reports are sent by telegraph. There is no evidence that the existence of this source is known to the International Police in Oporto, or that it is being tampered with.
b) Customs officers and pilots at Liezoes, through the Edith Tobacco Kiosk at Oporto, where they are picked up by Jose Ribeiro, and passed on.
c) August Beck, Largo 13 do Feveirto, 4, Oporto, through an unidentified relay address in Lisbon to Chemisch-Technisch Gesellschaft Dr Schmitt, Hamburg Esplanade 6, Bock writes direct to Germany, which is interesting.

These three sources are to some extent intermingled, as Marques d'Aguilar appears to have contacted Jose Ribeiro and given his name and photograph to Ernst Schmitt, and also Alemida uses the Edith Kiosk sometimes for his correspondence with Fernando de Castro.

9. Information on the corresponding service in Lisbon is somewhat meagre but it is known that Baptista, a Customs House clerk of the Raul Sampaio da Costa Efrent, hands information presumably relating to cargoes, to Ferreia Borges manager of the tourist agency Sociedade Oceanica do Sul, who in turn hands it to Kuno Weltzien. Ferreia Horges and two other unidentified paid agents also report the movements, name and tonnage of ships. (Note:- Marwues d'Aguilar's brother is the Oporto agent of the Sociedade Oceanica do Sul). An ex-officer of the International Police, Assuncao Aruajo, is also believed to be reporting shipping movements to the Germans.

10. Information is not yet available, but it is suspected that all Portuguese ports are covered by a similar service to the above.

III Propaganda Service

11. The Propaganda Service is a large and diffuse organisation, and is directed by Dr Wilhelm Klein, Chancellor of the German Legation, who has working under him a very large number of journalists and publicity agents of different kinds. The most important of these are von Rheinhaber, Kurt Zehntner, Bermehren, Dr Roth and Richard Gerlach. Zehntner runs the German propaganda paper *Signal* and Gerlach seems to devote himself to acquiring the English newspapers. He has been unable recently to acquire the *Daily Herald* and this failure may cost him his job. Gerlach's chief is Hans Koester who has recently arrived in Portugal, and who is an important representative of the Trans-Ocean and Europa agencies.

IV General

To sum up, the two main purposes of the German Secret Intelligence Service in Portugal would appear to be (1) the obtaining of shipping intelligence and (2) the recruitment and dispatch of agents overseas, to the USA and UK and the Atlantic Islands. It is interesting to note that in the last week or two, Ferdinand Mouths has arrived in Lisbon and announced that he is about to start an entirely new and separate intelligence service in Portugal based on Madrid. It has been said that Mouths is Himmler's representative but this requires confirmation.

12. German influence is very predominant with the International Police (who exercise surveillance over all foreigners in Portugal). In Lisbon, Laurenco, the Chief, is openly and avowedly pro-Nazi, and so are the majority of his officers. One of them, Çumano, is well known to be in touch with Himmler, and to correspond with him. He is expected to become the Chief, if the Germans invade Portugal. In Oporto, however, British influence is much more to the fore, and Romao, the Oporto Chief, is helpful to our interests. He is a possible successor to Laurenco, should the latter retire, as has been mooted.[8]

From a counter-intelligence perspective, after nearly two years of war, this analysis was of almost no value, but may have acted as a prompt because a month later, in August 1941, MI5's John Gwyer drew together all the information that his section, B2(a), had accumulated and produced an eight-page summary:

> The earliest information in our possession dates from July 1940. There is evidence that since then considerable changes and additions have been made to the organisation, as the result, no doubt, of the fluctuations in its objectives. Since the collapse of France Lisbon has been the principal and at times the only place through which the Germans could pass agents into this country or where they could meet them on their return; Lisbon has, of course, also occupied much the same position in relation to the USA. It is naturally this aspect of the German organisation with which this section has come most into touch. Parallel with the work, the Lisbon organisation has presumably continued its espionage activities in Portugal itself – the importance of which has varied as Germany's plans (if any) for the invasion of Spain advanced or were retarded.
>
> 2. Our evidence (which is confirmed from other sources) suggests that the general head of the Lisbon organisation is Albert von Karstoff who maintains an office at the German Legation. It has never been made wholly clear what is the relation of this man with Ernst Schmidt who has also been described to us (and to others) as the head of the German Secret Service in Portugal. On the whole it seems likely that the two are identical, though we have been able to trace no direct connection between them.
>
> 3. Karstoff remains in the first place three assistants or secretaries; a young man, possibly an Air Force officer, who appears to be in his confidence but is not thought to hold a position of any authority; a secretary, and a certain Otto Merckl. Up to 18 December 1940 Merckl was employed (under the name of Jaeger) at the Victoria Insurance Co., Praca Municipol 6, but his present address is unknown. This man, who is almost certainly identical with Marcelle, of whom another of our sources speaks, has been in Lisbon since 1934. Merckl has used as his subordinate a man called Schott, whose address is given as Firma Brinette, Praca Ducue de Terceira 14. Nothing further is known of Schott except his personal description, but a further reference to the firm of Brinette is made below. Merckl has also been in company with a certain Hanke, of whom no description is available, except that he speaks English, French and excellent Russian. Hanke lives in the Palacio Hotel, Estorial, and seems to make it his chief business to make contact with and try to recruit members of the crew of the American Clipper.

4. It is perhaps worth noting that one source who was contacted in Lisbon by Merskl (under the name of Marcelle), had previously received cover-addresses only in Barcelona.

5. Karstoff's second-in-command is thought to be a man named Fritz von Kramer who works in a house directly behind the German Legation, which is reached through the left-hand gate of the Legation garden. He is often to be seen at the Casino and in Lisbon's various restaurants and cabarets; and has been described to us by one source as 'a typical German beer-drinking type' and was not a person of great ability. It appears that his private house is in Estoril, on the way up to the golf-course, two doors away from that of Dr Hans Ruser, to whom reference is made below. We have been warned from outside sources of the danger of confusing this Fritz von Kramer with the Carl Kramer who works in the German Consulate and is also an agent. Unfortunately, as no description of Carl Kramer has been supplied, it is not possible to determine to what extent, if at all, this has been done.

6. The next man in the organisation after Kramer appears to be Hans Doebler, alias Dorner, alias Duarte, alias MADEIRA. This person, among his other activities, shares with Kramer the business of meeting and keeping in touch with visiting members of the German Secret Service, such as those referred to below. We have no evidence that these visitors ever come into direct touch with von Karstoff, though, no doubt if they do, it is unlikely that this fact would have been apparent to any of our sources. Doebler is also reported to have been in touch with a man referred to as 'the Naval Chief' (no description) who seems to have been attached to the Legation, though, since his car did not carry CD number-plates, probably not as an official member of the Corps Diplomatique. It is not known whether this man (who was thought, in July 1940, to be leaving Lisbon shortly) should be identified with the naval officer, reported some months later to have arrived from Madrid to take charge of Secret Service activities. Most likely this was not he but the successor who was expected in July. In either event, the man now discharging the functions of 'Naval Chief' in Lisbon is probably to be identified with the Commander, familiar to students of Dr Rantzau's career; but on this point we have no information from our own sources.

7. A part of Doehler's work is certain connected with sabotage and the dispatch of agents and explosives to the United States. He has been seen in company of a man described as a German agent who had recently arrived in the SS *Siboni* of the United States Export Line and has asked for assistance in contacting members of the crew of the American Clipper and the English ship SS *Cressado.* He is also known to frequent the British, German and American Bar, and the Bar Imperial

in search of British seamen, as well as visiting the other bars and hotels in Lisbon to which English and Americans go. In this side of his work he is thought to have associated with a Spaniard named Don Rigo, of whom only a meagre description is available. It is not known exactly what is the position occupied by this man but he was described by one of our sources as (who is given to exaggeration) as the head of German sabotage activities in Lisbon.

8. Doebler, like most other German agents in Lisbon, is often to be found at the Hotel des Dues Nacoes where he is known to be in touch (officially, so to speak) with the Hall Porter, a Portuguese in whom the Germans place the utmost confidence and the proprietor, Wissmann, a less satisfactory character, almost certainly a crook, who would betray his present employers as cheerfully as he would, subsequently, those who had induced him to do so. Wissmann has been a Party member since 1937 and would seem to have modelled his technique a little too closely on that of his leader. He has three brothers, the cook at the Dues Nacoes, the head-waiter at the Grande Hotel, and the head-waiter at the Hotel Frankfurt, all of whom are equally German agents.

9. We understand that Doehler's present address is the flat in the rua Santa Marte 238 (Tel. 42518), which is probably the same as his mistress, Alice or Alicia de Brito. She is described as a woman of 32, who looks 25 or younger, and is so dark as is reported by one source to be of mixed ancestry, with a high percentage of Moroccan blood. She is said to divide her time between Doebler and Rene Catela, the second-in-command of the International Police in Lisbon, whose mistress she also is. She is likewise reported by one source to be, in addition, a close friend and probably mistress of a Captain Amado, also of the International Police; but a part of this apparent promiscuity is probably to be explained by a confusion of thought between Catela and Amado. She is, in any case, a person of influence with the police, and was able to be of great help to Doebler when he was in difficulties with them in July of this year. It is not known whether these difficulties have been resolved; if not, it is to be expected that Doebler will be leaving Lisbon shortly. For a time at any rate, possibly as a result of these attentions by the police, Doebler is thought to have passed under the name of Antonio Madeira, in connection with which we have been given the address: Sepateiros 35 (Tel. 42518). It is not known if he still uses either this or the other address. Finally, we are informed by an extraneous source that Doebler's salary is in the neighbourhood of £1,500 a year, but that he is nevertheless regarded as an unimportant man. This, if true, suggests an inability of the Germans to distinguish accurately between Eldorado and Estoril, which is remarkable in an otherwise provident nation.

10. The last to be considered of the permanent residents in Lisbon is Dr Hans Ruser of the German Embassy, an equivocal figure whose place in the organisation is hard to define. Towards the end of 1940 he was reported to us as the head of the German Secret Service in Lisbon and we hear from an outside source that he received instructions at about that time to recruit agents for England on a wholesale basis; a business into which he would seem to have thrown himself almost with abandon; and for which he has made much use of the firm of ship's chandlers, Brinette Ltda, (this information is not from our own sources) who are referred to above in connection with Schott. On the other hand, reports that we have of him, dating from February this year, suggest that he was then employed in a capacity not much higher than that of a courier between Lisbon and Madrid. Later reports still state that he is now totally in disfavour. It may be that this is the result of the anti-Nazi opinions which he seems generally to have assumed when contacting agents, being more genuine than was first supposed. A similar doubt obscures Ruser's actual position at the Embassy. We were informed by one source that he was an attaché, and by another that he was a counsellor; in fact he is now officially described as a Diplomatic Courier, but actually works as a Secretary in the Chancellery. The car which he usually drives (like that of the 'Naval Chief') does not carry CD number-plates. Ruser speaks English well with an American accent, and spent nine years of his life as a boy in the United States. He is reported to be a man of good family and a relative of Dr Schacht; he has living with him at the Villa Maire Clothilde, Estoril, a woman, understood to be his mother, who may also be working for the German Secret Service. He has usually been seen by our sources, when business was to be done, in company with Doebler or von Kramer or both. We have also news of the two other men, known to have been associated with Ruser, one Gerschon who is said to have worked as his assistant, and a certain Musik. We cannot certainly identify either of these men with persons otherwise known to us. The description furnished of Gerschon agrees very well with a description, given by one of our sources, of von Kramer, but less well with other descriptions of the same man. We are, therefore, disinclined to accept this identification, although there is nothing in what we know of von Kramer's movements, or what we are told of Gerschon's, which positively contradicts it. In the same way, our Hollerith machine gives, among others, the name of Pankoff as a possible identity to fit Gerschon's description. We have no knowledge of Pankoff from our own sources, but the description given of him tallies to a great extent with that of Doebler. Of Musik we have no description and know nothing further, except that he was often seen in the company of a Hungarian named Agat, whom we believe to be known from other sources as a German agent.

11. It is next necessary to deal with those members of the German Secret Service attached to other centres, who are known to have been in touch with the Lisbon organisation. Of these one of the most interesting, from the point of view of identifying members of the permanent staff, is Dr Kilburg, alias Kliemann, who arrived in Lisbon from Paris on a diplomatic passport in October 1940. He was, and, so far as we know, still is, a member of the Paris-stelle, who was simply visiting Lisbon in order to contact a particular agent. While he was there, he is known to have been in touch with Otto Merskl, and to have employed as a secretary one Fraulein Meinhardt, alias Weingarten, who was at that time described to our source as Ernst Schmidt's secretary. Her address, Avenida Dr Antonio Augustus, Estoril, is owned by Emily Nolte. From the same source that provided this information we also learn that Dr Kilburg carried the following addresses in his note-book:

Arthur von Karstoff, Lisbon
Dr Brandt, embassy, Lisbon
Colea Alcola, 27 Codes Camaze, 10/12

Finally, Dr Kilburg is known to have been in touch while in Lisbon with a man named Fruhling, who arrived from Madrid on 20 October 1940. This was presumably Lenz who has been described by one of our sources as the head of the German Secret Service in Madrid, and one of whose pseudonyms is known to be Fruhling – inevitably Lenz has a personal assistant (who did not accompany him on this trip), a young man of about 25, who speaks English, French and German. He signs letters on behalf of Lenz and is thought to be (from the German point of view) wholly reliable. The only other member of the Madrid organisation of whom we are informed is Ferdinand Mouths, a man of about 53, rather flabby in appearance, who speaks German, Spanish and Portuguese, and is understood before the war to have run a tourist agency. It was reported by one source (who has generally been reliable) that Mouths was employed as an outside man by the Madrid organisation for the purpose of contacting Spanish agents. According to another source, he is a man of vastly greater importance, the head of the Gestapo organisation in Spain, and was recently instructed to create a new espionage service in Portugal, which was to be wholly independent of any existing activities. It is still too early for us to say which of these reports is the more accurate, though we have no reason whatever to disbelieve the latter. We are informed that Mouths visited Lisbon in March of this year, although forbidden by the Portuguese authorities to enter the country. We understand that other sources have also seen him in Lisbon, perhaps at a later date.

12. Another member of the German Secret Service who is known to have visited Lisbon at least twice is the exuberant Dr. Rantzau, alias Richter, alias von Jorgenson, alias Jansen or Hansen, alias Ritter, who may also be identical with a certain Dr Huckreid or Huckreide-Scholz, late of Brussels. He is accustomed to arrive carrying a diplomatic passport, and like other visitors, is usually seen in the company of Doebler or von Kramer, and is also known to be in touch with Ruser. He makes his headquarters when in Lisbon at a house in Estoril, which we have been unable to identify precisely (it is described as being 'two houses up from the top left-hand corner of the Parc de Estoril') but which does not seem to be identical with the Villa Marie Clothilde, He was once accompanied by a young man named Georg Sessler, alias Sinclair, who speaks good English with an American accent, and is understood to have relations living in Milwaukee, USA. Sessler, who is a good shorthand writer, has acted as the Doctor's secretary and also as a courier, but appears to have other avocations, for we received a report early this year that he had lately been wounded in Greece, though whether fighting, and if so in what capacity, is not known. In conclusion it is, perhaps, worth while to record that, according to one source, considerable jealousy and ill-feeling exists between Doebler and Dr. Rantzau, whom the former considers to be a boaster and a liar.[9]

Gwyer's review of British knowledge of the KOP is clearly based on the eyewitness testimony of four double agents who had travelled through Portugal. Firstly, there was DRAGONFLY, who had attended a rendezvous with his Paris I/L handler Emile Kliemann in Lisbon in November 1940. TRICYCLE had been briefed on his mission to London in December 1940 by KOP's leiter, Albrecht von Auenrode, who had adopted the alias von Karstoff. SNOW and CELERY had met Nikolaus Ritter and his subordinate Georg Sessler in Lisbon in January 1941,[10] following which Hans Ruser had driven CELERY across Spain to the French frontier so he could travel to Hamburg for further consultations. Clearly Gwyer's analysis had been based on individual recollections, which had been 'carded' onto a Hollerith punch-card sorting machine, and had not benefited from matches with ISOS, a process that was, at that stage, still in its infancy. Nor, for that matter, had 'Lenz' been linked to the KOS leiter, Wilhelm Leisner, noted only as an important visitor from Madrid.

KOP's unique role within the Abwehr was described in 1942 by Kim Philby who, since September 1941, had been head of Section V's Iberian sub-section, designated V(d):

Lisbon is not only the headquarters of KO Portugal, with an organisation closely resembling KO Spanien, but also a large port which offers by far the best field in Portugal for the recruitment and contacting of agents

> destined for the Americas, Africa, the UK, and shipping between all these places. There is therefore in Lisbon a large field organisation existing side by side with KO Portugal, and it is on that field organisation that our own field organisation naturally and regularly impinges. For this reason, it is misleading to compare Lisbon with Madrid . . .[11]

Much was learned about Cramer through ISOS, and two of his contacts, DARIEN and VIPER, who were both SIS double agents. His SIS dossier revealed that he lived in a house behind the German embassy, and that his secretary, Ingeborg Evert, was also one of his two mistresses.

Cramer had a formidable reputation and employed as his secretary a well-connected socialite, the Baroness Marie von Gronau, whose father was the air attaché in Tokyo, and a veteran spy, Wilhelm Gessmann, who had worked for the French, Italian, Polish and Czech Deuxième Bureaux for more than 20 years. He would become notorious, but with a degree of protection provided by the PVDE's chief, Captain Jose Catela, acted with apparent impunity, travelling on a French passport. Cramer even escaped unscathed when his subordinate, George Hoffmann, and his French mistress Jacqueline Taylor, were caught red-handed as he attempted to install a tap on the PCO's telephone cable.

Among Cramer's coups was the acquisition from the senior Czech intelligence officer in Lisbon, Colonel Vaclav Pan, of two British SIS transmitters, fully equipped with their book-codes, supposedly for onward delivery to what turned out to be a pair of non-existent resistance networks in Marseilles and Paris. Both entrapment operations, codenamed PORTO and PORTO II, resulted in many arrests in France, over Christmas 1941, and accolades for Gessmann and Cramer. In July 1947 Gessmann's interrogator at Oberursel, Arnold Silver, described him as 'absolutely unscrupulous and without moral integrity'. Although he was hard to pin down, Silver and Klop Ustinov agreed that Gessmann's espionage career had started in Austria, many years earlier, when in 1936 he had acted as a liaison intermediary with the French Deuxième Bureau for Colonel Lahousen when he headed the pre-Anschluss Austrian intelligence service. Gessmann also claimed that in 1929 he had betrayed a German spy in Belfort, Captain Georges Foge, to the French.

Gessmann, who often adopted the alias Alexander, was also in touch with the Americans, whom he originally contacted in March 1941, and the British, but he was compromised by ISOS in September 1942 before he could do lasting damage. Nevertheless, when Cramer was repatriated to Germany and interrogated in September 1946, he detailed the information about Allied intelligence agencies supplied by Gessmann, who denied the allegations and was described by his CIC interrogator at Ludwigsberg as 'wholly unreliable'.

> I/H was not established at KOP until September 1943, with the appointment of Dr Aloys Schreiber to replace Otto Kurrer, alias Kamler, a pre-war businessman and chemist who had lived in Wimbledon with his Swiss wife, Natasha. Schreiber's role was to manage and relay intelligence reports, without any analysis.
>
> Schreiber's only contact with Berlin was through the diplomatic courier service, or in urgent cases, the KO radio. He had nothing to do with the operation of either, but turned his reports over to whichever facility he deemed appropriate for the transmittal of a particular report. Orders from Berlin stated that there was to be no evaluation made at Schreiber's end of any information received from his sources, but that all the evaluations would be made in Berlin. From the heterogeneous conglomeration of opinions, facts and fantasies the agents turned in, Schreiber's only task was to sift out that which did not pertain directly to the military and pass this on to the Referat concerned, either air or naval intelligence. Schreiber, however, did not always conform to these instructions from Berlin, in many instances throwing out entire reports from agents because they were obvious figments of the imagination.[12]

According to his post-war interrogation, Schreiber said that in his two years as I/H chief in Portugal Schreiber acquired the services of seven Portuguese who were either Germanophiles or strongly influenced by pecuniary incentives.

> Some of these agents also had sub-agents working for them, with whom Schreiber never came in contact and whose names he never knew. Schreiber also gleaned occasional bits of information through purely social contacts in business or diplomatic circles, but these sources cannot be considered as agents.
>
> The following is a list of the names and a brief outline of the activities of each of his agents:
>
> (1) COSTA SILVA, Maximo had the cover name RADIO, was an ex-sailor and radio operator, worked for a radio firm near Rossio, was a member of the Portuguese Legion and quite in accord with the Axis aims. He organised 4 or 5 sub-agents who in the event of an Allied invasion of Portugal, were to remain with him as a stay behind organisation and report by radio on Allied activities, ie, ship movements, loading and unloading of supplies, troop locations and concentrations, weapons and other activities. The organisation was not expected to function for much more than two or three months, because of the uncertainty and

undependability of Portuguese agents. The organisation was finally dissolved in February 1945 because the Allies invaded France.

(2) NASCOUCSLHOS, Antonio had the cover name FRUTA and was employed by a coal mining concern in Ponta Delgada on the island of Santa Maria in the Azores. Since the islands were being used by the Allies as an air and naval base, activities there were of extreme interest to the German Intelligence Service. Foreigners were not permitted on the island and even natives had difficulty observing anything because of effective Allied security measures. The main difficulty encountered by Nascoucslhos was the lack of radio communication, so that by the time the information arrived by ship it was often out of date and useless. His activities ceased when the firm for which he worked transferred him to the Lisbon branch.

(3) MACHAEO, Jose Carlos had the cover name JOCCA, and was a fairly good linguist. He was rather down and out, however, and peddled newspapers, magazines and pornographic pictures. In this capacity he was an ideal contact man and also excellent for picking up bits of information in hotels and cafes, particularly from crews of Allied planes which had made forced landings, etc. Quite often his information was obtained while his unsuspecting informants were under the influence of alcohol. He was quite a capable agent and furnished a fair amount of valuable information. At the beginning of 1945 Machado went to Lourenco Marques, Mozambique, ostensibly to go into business with his brother.

(4) NOG UEIRA, Eduardo was employed in the Ministry of Public Works, was an extreme Germanophile and expected to obtain a job in a German firm after the war. Occasionally he supplied valuable information concerning the arrival of war materials in Portugal. Most of his information was not obtained through his own observation and efforts, but gleaned from friends of his who worked on dock installations, warehouses, transports, etc. His services ceased abruptly toward the end of 1944 for unknown reasons.

(5) PERUGI, Carlos was referred to as MOEOKKANER, and was a capable and versatile person, but of somewhat dubious character. He had served for several years in the Spanish Foreign Legion and maintained many connections in Morocco. His reports were mostly concerned with troop movements in the posts along the coast of Portugal. After several obvious errors and exaggerations were noticed in his reports, he was dismissed in the early part of 1945.

(6) de BREUILLE, Alice, was a French emigrant and her cover name was BLANCHE. She was acquainted with a number of persons in Allied diplomatic circles, and besides reporting on general Allied attitudes and opinions, she also gleaned occasional bits of information which were of military interest. She was also in frequent contact with Allied air and military personnel passing through Lisbon and obtained information from them which proved of interest to Referat I-H. Her activities ceased in March 1945 when she allegedly married a Brazilian.

(7) PEREIRO, Alberto had the cover name MAGISTER. He was supposedly a distant relative of the Portuguese politician Dr Armindo Monteiro and consequently had access to Portuguese political circles and their discussions of foreign opinions and activities. Their discussions also touched upon military matters, and since Monteiro was oblivious of the fact that much of the subject matter of these discussions was falling into German hands, it was valued all the more highly. Schreiber was never quite sure of Pereiro's trustworthiness, however. He became ill in late 1944 but Schreiber thinks that his activities ceased because the situation was becoming a little too risky for him.

(8) In the case of Paul Fidrmuc, Schreiber received orders from Berlin to contact Fidrmuc and give him a sealed envelope, and was told that he was to receive similar sealed envelopes from Fidrmuc at intervals. These were to be labelled by a certain code designation and sent by courier to Berlin. This code designation changed occasionally; the one which was used for the longest period was probably OSTRO, while others used were MAX and ERNST. Schreiber claims that he was told that these letters pertained only to business and economic situations and were out of his field. Consequently, his position was simply that of a middleman with no interest in the subject matter at all.

Schreiber did not consider Fidrmuc as one of his agents, but only as an added duty which might just as easily have been given to any of the other Referat of the KO. Schreiber believes that for some time prior to his arrival in Portugal, Fidrmuc turned in similar reports directly to the embassy in Lisbon which were then sent by diplomatic courier to Berlin.[13]

Although Fidrmuc was an important I/H source, his principal handler was Otto Kamler, head of the KOP's Abt. I, who employed his secretary, Lillie Kraatz, as an intermediary.

What made KOP unique was the extent to which it had been penetrated by the British, and the fact that Berlin understood at least some of the compromise because of the defection of Hans Ruser from Madrid in November 1943. This event, followed by the Vermehrens' defection in January from Istanbul, triggered an internal security review conducted by III/F's Fritz Cramer who evidently exaggerated the crisis and reported to Berlin in March 1944 that 'Brandes and Deussen are probably British agents, that Werner Stubbs is almost certainly a British agent' and that Johannes Jebsen possibly was too.

Ironically, Cramer would defect to the Americans in March 1945, but when he was repatriated from Lisbon in March 1946 on the *Highland Monarch* he was interrogated as a prisoner. A larger picture emerged, with OSS acknowledging to MI5 that Cramer 'was at that time doing certain work for us, having "come over" to us shortly before the German surrender. Prior to Cramer's repatriation he furnished us with one or two reports a week, some of which were alleged to have been received by him in secret ink, all of which he claimed had come from an agent who was working for him in Barcelona . . .'.[14]

Berlin feared that KOP was vulnerable after Ruser's defection, but never guessed the scale of the penetration that was already underway when he switched sides. In July 1943 a Yugoslav double agent controlled by MI5 reported while on an extended three-month visit to Lisbon, that his KOP handler and original recruiter, Johnny Jebsen, was himself ready to switch sides and was apparently convinced that his university friend Dusan Popov was playing a double game. Popov duly reported Jebsen's sympathies for the Allies to SIS which conferred with MI5 because at risk was Popov's network of sub-agents in London, among them his friends METEOR[15] and FREAK,[16] his brother DREADNOUGHT,[17] his girlfriend GELATINE,[18] and an MI5 nominee, BALLOON.[19] All were engaged in a complex deception campaign and the entire project could be jeopardised if Popov confided in Jebsen, now codenamed ARTIST, changed his mind, or was himself acting in a Machiavellian counter-intelligence role.[20]

Curiously, Cramer, who had been in his post continuously since October 1940, had voiced his suspicions about two of his colleagues, Juan Brandes and Werner Deussen, but he was wrong about both. Brandes, a 24-year-old adventurer who was under the personal protection of his family's friend Admiral Canaris, had been employed to handle VIPER, a double agent run by the British, and employed as a receptionist at the Aviz, arguably Lisbon's most luxurious hotel. SIS later learned that VIPER had been recruited by Cramer early in 1941 on the promise of a job at the Adlon, as a triple agent, 'to send true information too late for action, in the hope that VIPER would be put in touch with British w/t sets in Germany'.[21]

An Austrian from Mulhausen, Cramer had been identified by Ruser, his neighbour in the rua Timor, Estoril, who described him as a venal opportunist, 'highly intelligent, sly and probably just the man for his present job' but also 'completely without morals', as another potential defector, and in early 1944 he approached the Americans with an offer to work for them, which was accepted. Cramer supplied an unspecified quantity of information to the Americans, and introduced them to his principal agent, codenamed ORLOFF, who turned out to be Gessmann, who had acquired a Portuguese passport in the name of Guilherne da Silva Martin.

> At that time he furnished us with quite a large volume of material concerning political activity in Spain and especially concerning the separatist movement in Catalonia, in which he claimed to be very interested. Later, his reports embraced political activity in Portugal as well as Spain, and he gave us many reports which he claimed to have obtained from a source high up in the Portuguese 'International' Police (PVDE). To the best of my knowledge, most of the reports furnished by him were accurate, although many were, of course, coloured by the extreme bias of the local police to whom every opponent of Salazar is a communist. When we discovered, through R/BD, that Martin was in fact identical with subject, he was arrested and held by the Portuguese police until repatriated. As a result of his arrest, and of documents found in his possession at the time, at least three contacts in the international police were arrested and confined.[22]

While this episode demonstrated, once again, that Gessmann was completely unscrupulous, it also suggested that he and Cramer had enjoyed a very close relationship with the PVDE, having cultivated Captain Catela and at least four of his subordinates.

When Ruser defected, and provided his interrogators with a detailed profile of Cramer, he revealed that Cramer had sources inside 'the British Secret Service'. He explained that he had arranged his defection through a Polish diplomat whom he had known in Madrid during the Spanish Civil War who had moved to Lisbon. They had remained on good terms and the envoy had agreed to negotiate with the British authorities through the Polish government-in-exile in London. According to Ruser, Cramer had discovered his plan. Ruser, who worked under Reich Economics Ministry cover at the embassy and also acted as a journalist for the Europa Press news agency, stated that

> most important of all, I do think to have sufficient evidence to assert that he has got someone within the British Secret Service, or at least very near it, for quite some things, as you will presently see, are getting through to him from there. And I also here reassured myself that he has

> a direct way of getting news and evidence passed on to your Lisbon Service of the kind he just wants to get there. Whether he does that by the same source which brings him information from there or in some other way I do not know. Kamler told me that Cramer once boasted that some information I/M had sent through to the British Service had come back to him by another way.

Ruser cited two pieces of evidence to support his claim that SIS had been penetrated by Cramer. One was a letter of introduction he had written for a Hungarian journalist in which he had unwisely put in a few decidedly anti-Nazi phrases not knowing that the recipient 'would misuse the letter and abuse my confidence. As a matter of fact he must have handed it to the British Secret service . . . Only a very few days later Cramer was in possession of a full copy of the letter. This I knew as Kamler, head of the military intelligence department of the SD, had come to tell me and warn me.'

Ruser elaborated: 'Another example of the leakage of certain things from your Lisbon Service to Cramer afterwards almost proved catastrophic for me.' He had negotiated with his Polish friend

> and had a reply to the effect that, in cooperation with the British I could be taken out secretly to England where I would have to stay some 6 months in a specified area. After this time, however, I would be free to go wherever I wanted to and could also continue to South America. All this had immediately come to the knowledge of Cramer together with certain other things about me, known only to the British Secret Service. It was only by a rather lucky chance that I got to know this. Anyway, knowing this I was never able to accept that offer of my friend [XXXXXXXXXXXXXXX] or maybe rather that first British invitation extended to me.[23]

The Lisbon KO suffered yet another breach of security in September 1943 when I/M's Carl Eitel approached a German refugee, Jacob Silverberg, through an intermediary, a member of the Portuguese International Police, José Mesquita, and a notional Pan-Am source, Jose Maria San Bernardo, and became an OSS asset for Colonel Robert Solborg's subordinate Charlie Grey. When he first arrived in Lisbon, Eitel shared a flat with the Spaniard San Bernardo in the rua de Berne, and he had introduced him to Inspector Mesquita. Meanwhile, it would later emerge that Eitel had also recruited San Bernardo for his I/M superior, Erich Buecking. 'San Bernardo was approved, told to obtain information about the Azores and make contact among Pan American Clipper crews; he was to be paid 2,000 Escudos monthly.'[24]

Naturally, OSS was eager to cultivate Eitel, who was described as being in possession of 'unlimited information of infinite value to the United States Government'. Apparently motivated by self-preservation and a desire not to transferred in an impending cut in personnel, an economy measure which would affect six or seven KOP staff, 'Eitel supplied information on the Abwehr in general, and its Lisbon personalities in particular; and he was used by his new contacts to "feed" false information, directly or indirectly, to his full-time masters'.[25]

Eitel had no wish to be moved to Zossen or, worse, be dismissed from the Abwehr and returned to the Wehrmacht, and so 'offered his services in any capacity in Europe or North Africa' but he was informed that 'in reply to this offer, that he would be of doubtful use to us if he does not remain in the Abwehr and get reassignment'.

In his initial report Solborg noted 'I have the impression that Eitel is a sharp trader. On the one hand, he does not want to sacrifice himself for Hitler, on the other he would like to make a little profit on the side.' Eitel readily admitted that he had been unsuccessful in speculating in platinum buying at $105 a gram, but had made a profit by dealing in black market American cigarettes.

Eitel was, of course, well-known to the FBI as his name had featured in the 1938 espionage prosecutions involving his role as a courier and recruiter on the transatlantic liners, so his credentials as an enemy master spy were accepted immediately. When asked why had gone to the US embassy, instead of the British, he explained that he had previously dealt with Americans when he had served on the SS *Bremen*, and because 'in Germany he had heard of British Intelligence killing persons and had been told that they were in the habit of dropping of agents'.[26]

In a bid to ingratiate himself with the Allies, Eitel claimed that a few days earlier he had been left alone briefly in Buecking's office and had seen a file lying open on his desk. Seizing the opportunity, Eitel had read a document indicating that another KOP officer, Abt. II's Dr Rudolph Baumann, had received an urgent message from 'Source SILVIE' which had been passed instantly to Berlin: 'The Portuguese consul at Dakar declares that in the coming days a large convoy consisting of troops and war materials is to sail from Dakar. It will meet a convoy at Casablanca. The convoy is to be accompanied by warships lying at Dakar and warships of similar tonnage which arrived in Dakar.'[27]

In a second report in the same file, Eitel glimpsed a message from the same SILVIE who had reported on 16 April that 'a plane 18609 had arrived carrying passenger Augusto de Oracao e Brito who reported that American motorised troops consisting of about 50,000 men had been concentrating in Dakar. These troops are to go back on warships within the next few days.'

Eitel also claimed, presumably in an attempt to gain attention, that the same file contained handwritten letters which had been marked 'From Mr Michael Stuart and Mr David Walter, Press Department, British Embassy'. 'In two of these letters localities were mentioned where eventual landings might take place. The third letter referred to political questions between England and America for one part, and Portugal and the Allies for the other.'

This sort of information could not be ignored, and terms were reached about his role under OSS's control, codenamed ELLERMAN. Meanwhile, Eitel undertook his Abwehr mission, to negotiate the purchase of wolfram as a strategic commodity for the manufacture of munitions, and also concentrated on the recruitment of foreign seamen along the waterfront, thereby developing a good understanding of the KOP's personnel and their activities. Specifically, Eitel provided personality profiles of his colleagues, and handed over copies of questionnaires from Berlin, or at least the KOP replies to them. These documents possessed an added value because, as well as betraying strengths and weaknesses, they were often circulated regionally by pouch, and therefore were immune from wireless interception. One such, dated May 1944, concerned the Azores and, like all such documents, revealed the Abwehr's areas of current interest:

> There are 4,000 American troops in the vicinity of Horta. In the vicinity of Castello there is an American Metrological station with a WT station annexed. United States engineers have constructed a subterranean gasoline storage with a 30,000 litre capacity. The material for these tanks was sent from England. There are 12 Catalina amphibian aircraft stationed at Horta. They patrol daily in the vicinity of Terceira from an airport there. San Miguel is not occupied. British HQ is located on Terceira. There are four well-equipped airfields at Fayal.[28]

Before his arrival in Lisbon, Eitel had spent three years at I/M Brest under a commercial cover organising five local French fishing boats to patrol the coast off Lorient. During that period he had also bought a bar in the rue Quartier Maitre Bondon with his mistress, Marie Cann, a widow. His transfer to KOP under the cover of a diplomatic courier had been unexpected, and had been triggered by the expulsion of Hans Grimm from Portugal.

In anticipation of his new assignment Eitel had been posted to Zossen, and was able to describe the site after the Abwehr headquarters on the Tirpitzufer had suffered bomb damage in an RAF air-raid:

> The entire plant consists of 14 buildings, well camouflaged, the roofs being painted so as to resemble the nearby pine forest. They are ordinary houses with peaked roofs, having only one floor above the ground but two below ground where the gas-proof chambers and sanitary quarters are installed. Eitel says that he can make an exact plan of the various buildings if a map of Zossen is put at his disposal, as he visited these buildings daily.
>
> Among these 14 buildings is the administrative office of Canaris, and there is always a lot of activity here among the higher officers. Eitel was assigned to the office of the I/M leader. There an officer gave him all the reports which came from section I/M Lisbon and Madrid, to study. The files contained reports covering a period of over six months, and referred to shipping traffic in various ports, American, British and African. Three weeks were required for these studies. A Captain of the Luftwaffe named Sprecht instructed him concerning the Abwehr Dienst, and especially concerning all the possible radio apparatus which the Allies have on ships or airplanes to locate the exact position of U-boats. Since this apparatus has been in use, submarines have not been able to leave port, without being immediately detected. A good many U-boats damaged by deep-water bombs return a few days after their departure, having been located by these devices. It is said that this apparatus consists of a hollow mirror which is equipped with an antenna measuring from sixty to one hundred and twenty centimetres. German circles believe that if the length of the antenna were known, a neutralising mechanism could be found. Everything is being done, large premiums are being offered, to anyone who will discover this. German agents have instructions to watch for emergency landings of the RAF on airfields and try to observe the device and possibly to secure one There is such an agent at the Portals Airfield.
>
> In April, the Germans put some submarines in dry-dock in Brest and Lorient and sprayed them with liquid rubber which hardened and was said to become salt-water resistant. Nevertheless, the U-boats were found by the airplanes and the procedure was given up as unsuccessful.[29]

Having described Zossen and the priority attached by I/M to anti-submarine countermeasures such as radar, Eitel disclosed the identity of Jean Frutos, a stay-behind agent in Cherbourg who consequently was arrested by OSS's X-2 in July 1944 and 'turned' into a double agent codenamed DRAGOMAN. A Portuguese employed by the American Express travel agency as a baggage-master, Frutos had first appeared in ISOS in August 1940 and would prove to be an important double agent controlled by the Allies who, by the end of the war, would exchange some 200 messages with the Abwehr.

When he arrived at KOP Eitel was introduced to his colleagues, and learned of a 'shadow' organisation, based on sixteen Portuguese wireless operators, who would run the organisation if the diplomatic premises in Lisbon and Oporto had to be evacuated. This sophisticated stay-behind group transmitted twice a month to practise their technique and confirm their existence. In addition, KOP ran six German-manned stations, including one in Cascais handling I/M traffic, and a clandestine unit in Casablanca. One of Eitel's offers to his OSS contact was to introduce a Portuguese nominee who could infiltrate the organisation to acquire its ciphers.

Fluent in Spanish and Portuguese, Eitel's assignment was to procure the wolfram and smuggle it in small boats to Spanish ports whence it could be sent by rail to Germany. However, from November 1943 he was meeting Solborg twice a week at the latter's villa in Estoril to give him 'information on the Abwehr organisation and personnel, German purchases of raw materials' and three specific items: the identification of the Portuguese consul in Dakar as a German spy; details of a Russian woman, Lily Sergueiev, run by the British as a double agent who was flown to England in April 1944 after she had confessed her role to Buecking and agreed a method of communicating with him;[30] and the creation of WINCHESTER, a notional Portuguese employee of Imperial Airways with a wide circle of well-informed friends who supposedly had been recruited as a mercenary source by Eitel. In reality, Tarleton Winchester did work for US Lines and Pan American, but was not a spy. This informant was later assigned a handler, Theodor Schmoele, from KOS, and his twice-weekly letters, written in an alum secret ink, were actually composed by Silverberg's wife, signing herself GEORGE. Hitherto, Schmoele had been operating in Madrid under a commercial cover provided by his father's cotton trading business in Bremen. According to Eitel, who was regularly interviewed by staff from the local SIS station led by Rita Winsor, Schmoele's principal preoccupation had been the collection of Spanish political intelligence from a source named Pelizaeus. At his final rendezvous with Winsor, held on 14 May, a few days before his departure for Brest, he named von Auenrode's replacement as KOP's leiter as Colonel Friederichi, a SD officer and formerly employed as a manager by I.G. Farben at Frankfurt who had lived in Brazil and therefore spoke good Portuguese. Eitel also identified Schmoele's chief agent as a Portuguese naval officer, Lieutenant Garvaho Andrade, who was presently serving on the SS *Douro*, and asserted that another officer, on the SS *Lima*, reported regularly from the Azores, as did the commandant of the port of Horta. Obligingly, Eitel gave Winsor a copy of the information received on 11 May from Schmoele's sources in Ponta Delgada, which he had promptly relayed to Bremen:

1. The field of mines barring entrance to Horta has been removed.
2. A submarine net has been placed across the entrance to the port. This can be passed by ships through a passageway which is closed from 9.00pm to 8.00am. During this night interval all ships reaching the island are obliged to remain at sea in the vicinity.
3. There are no Allied troops occupying Horta.
4. The port has a daily turnover in shipping of 10 to 15 merchant vessels and naval ships.
5. A recent convoy has brought 5,000 troops, representing various services, to Terceira, which brings the occupying forces on that island to a total of approximately 15,000.
6. Four airports on the island of Terceira are being extensively improved and enlarged.
7. Aircraft approaching the island to land on any of those fields are required to arrive from the north and circle the island to the right, otherwise the anti-aircraft defence, with which the island is heavily equipped, will open fire.[31]

Finally, Eitel revealed that his replacement was to be Johannes Bischoff, who was reputed to have managed networks in Switzerland, Spain and Sweden.

Under Winsor's supervision, WINCHESTER was approved for high quality 'chicken-feed' and quickly established a reputation as an important conduit for conveying deception. From the KOP's viewpoint, the source was deemed reliable as some of the information had been verified from other sources. For instance, at a rendezvous on 16 May Winsor provided Eitel with a tempting morsel:

1. The true position in the port of Casablanca on May 2nd was as follows; 20 warships, including the French battleship *Jean Bart* and 18 merchant vessels.
2. On May 4th two American aircraft carriers arrived at Casablanca. They discharged an important number of aircraft including 'Lightening' fighters. These aircraft were already assembled except for wings and propellers and were driven through the streets of the city to the airfield.[32]

Subsequently, at their next meeting, as Winsor reported to London, Eitel

> stated that the chicken-feed given to him May 16th . . . was passed to Buecking and Bendixen on May 17. Both were impressed when informed as to the 'source'. Bendixen stated that the report of the aircraft carrier at Casablanca had already been reported and it is Eikel's impression that the secret W/T station at Casablanca may have been responsible for this. Bendixen's comment on the information regarding the true position in the port of Casablanca on May 2 was that it was without value unless names of ships concerned could be furnished. Both Bendixen and Bueckling appeared extremely interested in the fact that the information comes from WINCHESTER and has asked Eitel to arrange for this contact to be passed on directly to themselves.[33]

After this meeting Winsor, designated BD001 at the Lisbon station, known itself as 24000, informed London:

> Eitel was given the following chicken-feed which 24000 requested as to have him pass:
> Two transport ships are presently in the port of New York preparing to sail early in June for the Mediterranean, namely: The *Ile de France* and the *Nieuw Amsterdam*. The number of troops aboard both ships is approximately the equivalent of one division.

The notional source was to be the WINCHESTER contact, who received the information from recent Clipper arrivals and told Eitel that some of his own friends were included among the troops. He said that he would inform Bendixen personally of the foregoing on the evening of 17 May.

At the end of May 1944 Eitel had been transferred from Lisbon to Berlin, and then posted to Nest Bremen where he was able to send four letters written in secret ink to OSS cover-addresses in Lisbon, undetected. One of them contained an Abwehr report on V-1 bomb damage in London. In August 1944 he was sent on a mission to St Jean de Luz but could only reach Nancy, where he was captured by Free French soldiers who handed him over to the US Third Army. Having been employed again briefly by OSS, he subsequently underwent interrogation at Camp 020 in October 1944. Eitel's experience at the hands of the British was not entirely comfortable as his ISOS traces had revealed his alias as 'Conrad Eberle', codenamed CARLOS, and proved that he had misled OSS on numerous issues, including his recruitment operations in the Lisbon docks.

By August 1944, despite the departure of Eitel, Portugal had developed into a centre of global espionage, even if KOP itself was becoming increasingly isolated because of the battle for Normandy, which had cut lines of communication across France. To address the escalating counter-intelligence pressures, MI5 transferred Richmond Stopford to SIS for him to be appointed to the Lisbon station which was becoming increasingly preoccupied with the need to provide its growing number of penetrations with sufficient chicken-feed to retain their interest. Among the active operations was ECCLESIASTIC, a 22-year-old Czech, Olga Zamanova, who had become the mistress of KOP's I/TLW expert, Franz Kosnchik; DARIEN, who passed III/F counter-intelligence material to the assistant air attaché, Fritz Cramer; Flight Lieutenant G.M.F. Stow, who was in contact with Amt VI's Hans Vollbrecht; and PIGEON, an Austrian SD agent supposedly in contact with the US assistant naval attaché, Commander Theodore Rousseau.

It was not until Eitel was interrogated at Camp 020 for a week in October 1944 that various contradictions emerged in his narrative, and it became clear that he had duped OSS from the outset. For example, having originally asserted that he had joined the Abwehr in 1939, he confessed that he had been recruited by Erich Pfeiffer while working aboard the *Bremen* in 1934. He had also lied about an intelligence questionnaire which had been found in his possession when he had been captured in Nancy. At the time, he had claimed he had stolen it in his role as an American agent, whereas it had actually been given to him by Bischoff for delivery to St Jean de Luz. Greatly embarrassed, OSS's Norman Holmes Pearson conceded that his organisation had been manipulated by Eitel for his own ends.

Initially, Eitel had been accommodated at an MI5 safe-house in Rugby Mansions, Hammersmith, and driven daily to Ham for his interviews, but when it was realised that there were strong suspicions about his veracity, he was incarcerated until July 1945 when he was moved to Diest.

The complexities of the Eitel case illustrated the hazards of managing agents, double agents and even triple agents in such a febrile environment, as his handlers would have had to take great care not to compromise sources which questioning him while he was still at liberty in Lisbon. Indeed, the KO had acquired quite a reputation for mounting aggressive operations, at least some of which were clearly intended to interfere with SIS's activities which had been headed by Ralph Jarvis and his colleague Charles de Silva.

The SIS station, masquerading at the British Passport Control Office, was plainly a KOP target, although opinions varied in Section V and MI5 about the precise roles of the various Abteilung. Were the numerous efforts to penetrate the PCO Abt. III operations or sponsored by I/M in support of its other activities? As early as September 1940 Costa Silva had offered himself as an agent, but the then station commander (on loan from MI5) Richmond Stopford had vetoed his recruitment: 'I turned it down emphatically as an obvious double-cross. I am at a loss to understand how Costa could subsequently have been taken on and regarded seriously.'

Long before the appearance in late 1943 of Hans Ruser and Carl Eitel, the SIS station had been very conscious of the energy devoted by Hans Bendixen and his I/M subordinate Schubert to running agents destined for England. Initially, information about KOP's personalities had been gleaned from various double agents, such as SNOW and CELERY in 1940, and TRICYCLE in 1941, who had encountered KOP personnel. Section V had used their testimony to find the relevant traces in the ISOS traffic, analysis of which had led to the interdiction of certain espionage cases, such as Ernesto Simoes.

The officer who exemplified the KOP's aggression was Kuno Weltzien, the Krupp representative in Lisbon for the past ten years. Fluent in Portuguese, he was well-known as an important figure in the German colony whose wounds in the First World War, in which he had served as an infantryman, had left him with a permanent limp. His family secret was that grandmother was a member of the Ringhoffers, the well-known Jewish owners of the Ringhoffer train carriage manufacturers of Prague. The connection was not known to the Allies because he was never underwent interrogation post-war, when he was in French custody.

In 1940 the SIS station had been approached by a Portuguese named Campos who offered to travel to England as a double agent, having been recruited by Weltzien. This episode was interpreted as a rather crude attempt to penetrate SIS, and Campos was rebuffed. Having been identified as a very active Abwehr spy, the SIS station in January 1942 was persuaded by a source, Frank Verscheuren, that Weltzien's office in the rua Sạo Paolo 121 contained a card index listing all his sub-agents. As proof, he had provided three which purported to identify three British sources, all resident in Lisbon whose name were passed to MI5, as Guy Liddell recorded in his diary:

> A Mr Stillwell, a local business agent for various firms and an honoured member of the British community, whose son Francis is the assistant naval attaché in Lisbon. It is thought that the son may be quite innocent but that the father may be extracting information from him without his knowledge.

> The son has been recalled to this country to undergo a naval course.
>
> A Mrs M. Lawrence, who is No.4 in the UK Contraband Control office in Lisbon.
>
> A Mr W. Haeburn Little, an Irish artist now employed in our naval shipping office in Lisbon. He has been in close touch with Section V officers and knows a great deal about the SIS organisation in Lisbon.
>
> There have also been obtained the names of two ships' captains, concerning whom it is said we have already received notification. One of them is named Peck or Beck and serves on the *Sylvan Arrow*, a tanker flying the Panamanian flag.
>
> We are at the moment principally concerned with W. Haeburn Little, Lieutenant RNVR, who is the confidential assistant to the NCGC Lisbon, and is proceeding on the yacht *Venus*, due to arrive at Gibraltar from Lisbon at noon on Monday, 12 January. The yacht is going to pick up certain wireless equipment at Gibraltar and return almost immediately to Lisbon.
>
> The card about Little which is alleged to have been taken from Weltzien's index gives certain particulars and the numbers of the German agents who are in touch with him. It also has entered upon it in ink the dates and the amounts of payments which Little has received from Weltzien.[34]

A burglary was arranged, and elaborate arrangements were made for a duplicate key to be cut in London and flown out to Lisbon on 19 January 1942 so a pair of photographers, an Austrian and his Swiss wife, could make a surreptitious entry and copy all the cards. In the event, Captain Lourenco of the PVDE had hidden some of his men on the premises and arrested the intruders, causing much embarrassment for the embassy and the SIS station, then headed by Philip Johns.

As if confirmation was needed, this debacle demonstrated that Weltzien exercised considerable influence in Portuguese circles, and enjoyed the protection of Joaquin Ferreira Borges and Carlos Santos of the Portuguese Legion. The sensitive relationship that existed between the Legion's own intelligence organisation, headed by Cazais, and the PVDE was explained to SIS's Gene Risso-Gill by Captain Catela who, in May 1943, arrested Borges and Santos on what turned out to be a forgery suggesting they had conspired to penetrate the War Ministry. Although the evidence was tainted, a search of the home of the mother of one of the suspected conspirators, Machado, revealed an illicit transmitter concealed under her dog kennel.

More than a year later, in February 1943, MI5's Dick White cited Weltzien as an example of an Abwehr exercise intended to inflict reputational damage on its British adversaries. Addressing an intelligence conference in Beirut in February 1943 he declared that

> The nuisance value of such tactics could be considerable and he mentioned a case in which the Germans had successfully planted some evidence upon the British Intelligence Service indicating espionage on the part of two British subjects in Lisbon. Only after prolonged investigation involving the arrest of one of these persons was the ruse discovered. It had caused considerable embarrassment to MI5 and he could therefore testify that the limited use of the technique suggested might likewise have damaging results upon the Abwehr.[35]

An opportunity to learn more about Weltzien's activities occurred in November 1942 when SIS learned that he was anxious to recruit a source aboard the SS *Amarante*. Accordingly, a nominee codenamed PUMPKIN was deployed and instructed by Weltzien 'to keep a diary of all he saw and to note particularly number, tonnage and type of all ships under construction in American ports'.

By this time Weltzein had been implicated in three other cases of espionage. The first involved an Anglo-Portuguese, John H. Price, whose father was employed as night-watchman at the British embassy. A former member of the Portuguese Foreign Legion, Price became a seaman and in April 1943 was approached by Weltzien who suggested he travel to England as a spy. SIS learned of the recruitment from his father, and he was codenamed WASHOUT. When his ship, the Panamanian-registered SS *Inaki*, docked at Cardiff in June, Price was arrested and interrogated at Camp 020, where he implicated Weltzien.[36]

Soon afterwards there was another similar case when an impressionable young seaman, Duncan Scott-Ford, was recruited on the waterfront while his ship, the SS *Finland*, was docked in Lisbon. Short of money, Scott-Ford was introduced to Weltzien who, during a four-hour interview in his Cudell & Weltzein offices, successfully recruited him. Scott Ford then sailed to Liverpool, and reported back to Weltzien on his next voyage, in June. His ship then steamed to Salford where he was arrested, MI5 having linked him to an ISOS personality codenamed RUTHERFORD. Under interrogation Scott-Ford confessed to having been instructed by Weltzien, and he would die on the scaffold at Wandsworth in November 1942.[37]

In July 1943 Weltzien was incriminated in yet another operation, this time involving an unemployed Portuguese aircraft mechanic, Ernest Simoes, whose mission to England had been compromised by ISOS before he even landed at Poole. He had been introduced to Weltzien by a mutual friend, Armando Annes, and after two meetings, one at the office in the presence of Weltzien's secretary Lotte Pohl, and the other at a private home of KOP's Ernst Schmidt in the Jardim do Rigador, where he had been given a questionnaire setting out his task to report on:

(1) Construction and movement of warships.
(2) Movement of troops.
(3) Anything of interest regarding aircraft.
(4) Arrival of American troops.
(5) Economic conditions in England.[38]

Simoes came to England to take up a position at Percival Aircraft in Luton, and was under continuous MI5 observation for nearly four months, but made no attempt to engage in espionage, apart from corresponding with a KOP cover-address in Lisbon. The comprehensive surveillance included his landlady, Mrs Mary Gibbs, at 27 Alton Road, Luton, who was recommended by the local police, and a Spanish-speaking girlfriend, codenamed EGGS, supplied by MI5's Bi(g) Spanish section from September 1943.

In November Simoes was questioned by the police in Luton, detained overnight and sent to Camp 020, having made a full confession. He was eventually released and deported in September 1945. In his confession Simoes had mentioned Armando Annes, who was already known to SIS because back in June 1942 another of his acquaintances, Mario Ferreira, a 26-year-old clerk employed by the Port of Lisbon Authority, had offered himself as a double agent. He claimed to have been selling British shipping information to the Germans for the past year, at a rate of between 4,000 to 5,000 escudos. The invitation had been declined, but Annes had been logged as a recruiter for Weltzien's network.

The issue of addressing the espionage threat from the Abwehr would divide MI5, where John Gwyer saw a distinction to be drawn between Weltzien's organisation and von Auenrode's KOP. Gwyer noted that Section V's Ralph Jarvis had complained about local conditions which meant he was 'accustomed to work through Portuguese informants whose movements cannot be controlled and who more often than not avaricious, dishonest and without loyalty to any cause'.[39] Furthermore, Richmond Stopford expressed his opinion on 'Weltzien's purpose in life':

> I always felt he was mainly engaged of pulling the leg of SIS in Lisbon. I certainly would not trust any agent who came to this country and said that he had been recruited by Weltzien as a straight German espionage man, because in my opinion he is almost sure to be another of Weltzien's efforts to waste our time and plant somebody on us.[40]

MI5 and SIS disagreed on how to view Weltzien, with Section V's Kim Philby describing him as 'one of the leading figures, if not <u>the</u>

German field organisation in Lisbon'. In May 1942 Gwyer took a very different position:

> Since he distinguishes this organisation from KO Portugal I presume he means that Weltzien is a recruiter and outside worker rather than one of the controlling officers of the Stelle. This may be so, but it seems to me wholly inconsistent with SIS's previous reports that Weltzien was (1) responsible for soliciting shipping intelligence in Lisbon; (2) responsible for the despatch of agents to England; (3) the controlling officer of certain agents in the Atlantic Islands; (4) the controlling officer of a group of agents working in Portuguese West Africa; (5) responsible for the despatch of agents to the USA. Almost all of these activities are those of what I presume that SIS in their own organisation would call a representative as opposed to an agent or outside worker. It seems to me perfectly clear that the control of agents in the Atlantic Islands must be a function of KO Portugal, not of any field organisation it maintains in Lisbon. Similarly, we know from our own experience that undoubted members of KO Portugal such as Cramer of even [von Auenrode] himself, are actively concerned with the despatch of agents to England and America. There is no question of them staying in the background and leaving the actual handling of agents' cases to outside workers. On the contrary, [von Auenrode] for example, has throughout participated actively and personally in all the details of TRICYCLE's case. His status in this affair was in no sense different from the status which Weltzien is alleged to have had in the cases of SISYPHUS, Roqe Laia or Calca.[41]

Gwyer's critique centred on the admission that Section V's Ralph 'Jarvis is compelled to work above all with men who cannot reasonably be expected to know very much about the enemy's organisation'. This assertion prompted Philby to claim that by exploiting the ISOS material, SIS had begun to penetrate Otto Hinrischen's Nest in Bilbao, remarking, 'Have no fear. If our CE work in Bilbao develops as quickly as it is doing at the present moment, there are good prospects of being faced at no very distant date with cards from "Hinrischen's Index"'.[42] Not surprisingly, Gwyer expressed himself as 'horrified at the suggestion casually rejected by Philby' about the imminent prospect of access to Hinrischen's index.

> As we know to our cost, the information which the informants in touch with Weltzien provide is more often than not inaccurate where it refers to the activities of alleged German agents. Philby's statements about the inherent unreliability of these sources does not suggest that there is likely to be much improvement in this respect in the future.[43]

Philby, on the other hand, was quick to insist that Section V was not entirely reliant on ISOS:

> It is by no means true to say that we receive 'no casual reports but only information from most secret sources' about the real leaders of the Abwehr organisation in Portugal like [von Auenrode], Cramer, Merckl, Finck and Ruser have been the subject of quite a number of reports from Lisbon; to these we may add the names of important figures outside the Holy of Holies who appear regularly in our special sources, e.g. Fidrmuc, Alexander, Knigge, who frequently figure in Lisbon messages.[44]

While admitting that Section V inevitably dealt with 'corrupt channels', Philby explained that

> It is of course quite true that our channels are often corrupt. Leaving aside our own shortcomings, which I need not discuss here, this is attributable partly to the difficulties inherent in work in a place like Lisbon and partly to the necessity, in all matters of penetration, of playing to a certain extent to the German tune.

In acknowledging the hazards of Section V's work, Philby also provided a reason why Weltzien's network was so unusual as a counter-intelligence target: 'The fact that the field organisation and KO Portugal are located in the same city has robbed us of our most important source of exact information – the traffic between headquarters and the field – and therefore also of the well rounded contours characteristic of our picture of the German organisation in Spain.'[45]

MI5 came to suspect that the Abwehr had completely outmanoeuvred SIS and, worse, that Weltzien's entire organisation had been largely subsidised by the Lisbon station which had rewarded his agents so well. The whole sorry story was set out in July 1942 by Gwyer, which made uncomfortable reading for Section V.

> At various times since the end of 1940 and the present day Weltzien has been reported to us, both by SIS and the Poles, as one of the leading German agents in Lisbon. According to SIS reports Weltzien is responsible for the collection of shipping intelligence, the despatch of agents to England and the control of certain agents in the Atlantic Islands. It would also appear from certain letters which were intercepted in May of this year on the Portuguese SS *Quanza* and were addressed to Genalho Raposo, who is said by SIS to be a contact of Weltzien's, and to Henriques Santos, who appears to be Weltzien's store-keeper, that Weltzien is also concerned with espionage activities in Portuguese

West Africa. Moreover, according to an SIS report of 29 January 1941, Weltzien was involved in an act of sabotage by which the munition factory Braco de Brata in Lisbon was fired on the morning of 21 January 1941. It would appear, therefore, that Weltzien's activities are widespread and embrace more than one branch of Abwehr activity. According to SIS Weltzien is assisted in his work by a certain Baptista, a Customs House clerk in the firm of Raul Sampaio da Costa Effrend, Ferreira Borges, the manager of the tourist agency Sociedade Oceanica do Sul, and Theodore Mielitze, a Trans-Ocean correspondent in Lisbon, who is said to visit him frequently. Weltzien is also reported to be associated with a certain Ernst Schmidt who has been described to us by SIS as the head of the German Intelligence Service in Oporto, where he receives shipping reports from the Marques d'Aguiar (who is also associated with the Sociedado Oceanica do Sul) and Jose Almeida Jnr through a cover-address in Lisbon. Later information appears to suggest that Ernst Schmidt, of what at any rate we know very little, is also connected in some way to the firm of Brihette Ltda, the ships' chandlers familiar to us from more than one case. There seems to have been in the past some doubt about the relative stature of Weltzien and Schmidt, but it is now apparently agreed that the latter acts as a recruiting sergeant for the former. In addition to these general reports Weltzien has been brought to our notice in the following specific cases.

1. In October 1940 SISYPHUS, a Portuguese who had been supplying SIS with economic information in Lisbon, was approached by Weltzien and Schmidt who proposed to him that he should work as a German agent in England. SISYPHUS accepted this proposal in principle and kept SIS informed of subsequent negotiations as they proceeded. He was provided by Weltzien with secret ink and a comprehensive questionnaire, the greater part of which relating to shipping and naval matters. It also contained some questions relating to troop movements, coastal defences, air-raid damage, and industrial production. In addition he was asked to report upon the position of aerodromes and the type and number of aeroplanes upon them. In the course of a conversation with Weltzien in December 1040 SISYPHUS was informed that one of Weltzien's agents had reported that on 28 November 1940 a convoy had left Poole escorted by three cruisers and a number of destroyers. The convoy was composed of troop ships and a large number of cargo vessels loaded with war material, including a number of rafts and flat-bottomed landing-craft. Weltzien also informed SISYPHUS that he had succeeded in buying for 2,000 escudos from the second officer of a neutral ship the plans of the buoy markings at the entrance to Gibraltar harbour. The first of these two pieces of information was certainly untrue, nor have our enquiries discovered any factual basis for the second. In the end, SISYPHUS's case came to nothing for in January 1941 he was informed by Weltzien

that he would not after all be sent to England, though no reason was given for this decision. SISYPHUS remained, however, at any rate until January, and possibly later, in touch with SIS's representatives in Lisbon.

2. On 27 September 1940 a Portuguese structural engineer named Renato dos Santos Roque Laia arrived at Whitchurch aerodrome from Lisbon. He claimed to be travelling upon business connected with the purchase of aniline dyes but does not in fact appear to have transacted any business at all. Nothing, however, was discovered to his detriment during his visit. Although he had arrived in the same plane as the German agent POGO and had subsequently stayed at the same hotel, as far as can be discovered they were not acquainted with each other. On 6 November 1940 Roque Laia returned to Lisbon. Two days later Most Secret Sources revealed that an anonymous V-mann recently returned from England had made a report in the following sense: that bombs produced by the Skoda works contained a high percentage of duds as the result of the spring in the detonator having been affected by damp or cold, that in Clapham Park, north of Queen's Station, a large motor showroom and garage had been turned over to the assembly of aircraft from America; that aircraft coming from America were flown to Northern Ireland by Canadian airmen and delivered to Glasgow, where they were tested in the Rolls-Royce works before being put into service, that that the Rolls-Royce works at Derby no longer manufactured aircraft engines and that the Royal Family, although in Buckingham Palace in the daytime, slept each night at Windsor Castle. This information was not checked at the time but current enquiries, though necessarily inconclusive, tend to show that it contained not a word of truth. In December 1940 SISYPHUS informed SIS that Roque Laia had been acting as a German agent during his recent visit to England, that he had signed his reports AUGUSTO and that he had provided Keltzien with information with which the latter was very pleased and which had included the statement that Rolls-Royce engines were no longer manufactured at Derby. This appeared to link Roque Laia conclusively with the messages upon Most Secret Sources referred to above. The situation was, however, slightly complicated by the fact that whereas these messages had no name attached to them, other messages were passing at the same time which referred to a V-mann AUGUSTO but in a context which made it improbable, if not actually impossible that this man should be identical with Roque Laia. SISYPHUS also informed SIS that Roque Laia was about to make a second journey to England, again in the capacity of an agent, for which purpose he had been provided with a detailed questionnaire about the British railway system which asked, inter alia, for information about the loading and switching facilities existing at various stations. Arrangements were made to facilitate this journey but on 6 January 1941 SIS informed us that Roque Laia had been arrested by the Portuguese

police when about to board the aeroplane for England, on the grounds that he was a member of a foreign group plotting against the security of Portugal. On 27 April 1941 we heard again from SIS to the effect that Roque Laia (now apparently at large again) had abandoned his intention of coming to England and had also quarrelled with Weltzien as the result of his having failed to return to him the money which had been advanced for his air passage to England and his expenses here. On 7 July 1941 SIS informed us that as a result of his quarrel with Weltzien, Roque Laia had made a voluntary statement to their representative in Lisbon. The substance of this statement was as following:- He had come to England on 27 September 1940 in the capacity of a German agent. He did not explain in any detail what his instructions had been, but did say that he had been told by Weltzien to observe the source of the aeroplane on his flight to England and to give any possible information that he could with regard to anti-aircraft defences. In these respects his instructions were evidently similar to those given to SISYPHUS. Roque Laia said that he had written from England one letter to a cover-address in Portugal. This had been ostensibly a business letter to a man known to him as Mendes, whom he had met by appointment outside the tourist office Casa di Portugal, 20 Regent Street. Mendes had written a message in secret ink upon this letter and had then posted it. Roque Laia also said that while in England he had been instructed to keep in touch with a certain Lieutenant Joachim de Brito Subtil, a member of the Portuguese military mission, He had not supposed this man to be concerned with espionage himself but had been instructed to pick his brains in the course of ordinary conversation. In addition to these particulars about himself, Roque Laia produced certain miscellaneous items of information. He alleged that a hairdresser named PAULO at the bottom of Shaftesbury Avenue was used by the Germans as a postbox and that two other Portuguese, whom he described, had arrived in England during the course of November 1940 in the capacity of German agents.

Roque Laia's information has since been carefully examined with very little result. Lt Subtil certainly existed and was a member of the Portuguese military mission who had subsequently remained behind in order to undergo a course first in an OTU at Kinloss and subsequently in the Rolls-Royce works at Derby. He has since returned to Portugal. As far as can be discovered, he is a man of pro-British sympathies and there is no reason to suppose that he was ever engaged in espionage.

The German agent Mendes was never identified unless indeed he is a certain Antonio Bento Mendes, a Portuguese resident in London who fits fairly closely the physical description given by Roque Laia but against whom nothing is known. Similarly, enquiries have shown that there are no Portuguese fruit merchants in London, the entire trade being in the hands of English and Spanish firms, and there is no barber named PAULO in Shaftesbury Avenue, although there is a barber there trading under the name PAUL whom we have no reason to suspect of illicit activities. The two other Portuguese agents referred to by Roque Laia have never been identified, and as far as we have been able to discover no Portuguese fitting the descriptions given by him arrived in England upon the dates in question. From this it would appear that the information given by Roque Laia to SIS was in point of veracity upon a par with the information about England which he had previously given to the Germans.

3. On 14 February 1941 the double agent SNOW arrived in Lisbon by air in order to confer with Major Ritter @ Dr Rantzau. SNOW's sub-agent CELERY, who was also due to be present at this meeting, had left by boat some days earlier on the SS *Cressado*. Exactly what happened after SNOW's arrival in Lisbon we do not know since we are dependent on his own account of the affair, which may or may not be truthful. He has said, however, that he saw Dr Rantzau on the evening of the day on which he arrived in Lisbon and was then taxed by him with working as a double agent under British control. He says that he admitted this charge to the extent of saying that he had been so working for a period of three months. This statement presumably implicated CELERY since the latter had only recently been recruited by SNOW, so if SNOW had been known to us for three months CELERY must necessarily also have been under our control. On 8 March 1941 we received a report from SIS to the effect that on or about 16 February 1941 (that is to say immediately after SNOW's arrival in Lisbon and just before that of CELERY) Kuno Weltzien had told one of his agents, who was in touch with him, that he was anxious to discover what had happened to the *Cressado*, as he believed that she had been torpedoed while in convoy, which was particularly annoying since he had on board one of his best agents, whose duty it was to communicate by wireless the position of ships in convoy. It seems excessively improbable that this statement could have referred to CELERY, who possessed no wireless set and had not been instructed to make any report about his voyage to Lisbon. In the following July, however, Mr [Cyril] Mills went from this office to Lisbon in order to consult with SIS's representative there, and brought back with him an alternative and far more probable account of what Kuno Weltzien was alleged to have said upon this same occasion. According to this version of the story, which was taken verbatim from the records of SIS's Lisbon representative, Weltzien said that he had on board the *Cressado* a reliable agent who had at one time been in the RAF and was now a valuable medium for planting false information on the British. If this was the true version of the story (and, if so, it is impossible to understand how SIS's letter should have reached us in the form in which it did) then Weltzien was undoubtedly referring to CELERY who had served in the RAF and, moreover, since he and SNOW were

then compromised, was only valuable to the Germans as a medium for planting false information. It is worthwhile to observe that whereas the first version of the story seemed to show that Weltzien was ill-informed, the second version show him to be both well and promptly informed, since his conversation with SIS's agent took place within about two days of SNOW's arrival in Lisbon and evidently referred to the situation which had been created by SNOW's admission to Dr Rantzau that he was a British double agent.

Mr Mills' report also contained the statement that on 26 February 1941 Weltzien had alleged to an SIS contact that there were at that time three German agents operating wireless transmitters in England. One of them had been silent for some while but recently come on the air again with the explanation that he had been in need of a new valve which he had purchased in Birmingham. Up to a point this statement was undoubtedly correct, since there were to our knowledge precisely three German agents then operating wireless sets in England, viz. TATE, DRAGONFLY and SNOW, the last-named having made arrangements for his transmitter to continue to operate during his own absence in Lisbon. On the other hand, none of these agents had been silent for any abnormal time with the possible exception of DRAGONFLY, in whose traffic, however, there had been no mention of a new wireless valve or a visit to Birmingham.

4. Early in 1941 a certain Jose Lucio Atayde Costa, a Portuguese, was taken on at the British Consulate as an assistant to a certain Dante Mario de Müller e Souza, a British-protected person born in Zanzibar who has been employed at the Consulate as a clerk for at least 15 years. To all appearances both Costa and Souza were reliable persons and strongly pro-British in their sentiments. Besides their work in the Consulate both assisted from time to time in minor ways both SIS's representative in Lisbon and Captain [Arthur] Benson, the NCSO. In the autumn of 1941, however, when Costa was acting as an intermediary in some delicate negotiations which Captain Benson was then conducting, his conduct was such as to raise some doubts as to his loyalty, but on account of the delicacy of the affair no action was taken against him. In December 1941 Costa and Souza through the intermediary of a certain Alfredo Arujo, an undesirable character who had previously acted as an agent of the International Police, put themselves into contact with a taxi-driver named Julio Garcia, who was frequently employed by Kuno Weltzien and is alleged not only to have his confidence but also to have some hold over him which he uses apparently for the purpose of blackmail. Garcia alleged that Weltzien had in his office two card-indices, one containing the names of his own agents in British circles in Lisbon, and one containing the names of British agents, and that he was in a position to abstract some of these cards and, as he was in need of money, would offer them for sale to the

British. It is unnecessary to enter into the details of the negotiations which followed which were both complicated and protracted. It is sufficient to say that one of the intermediaries upon the British side was a certain William Hawburn Little, an Englishman resident in Portugal for some years who was then employed in the NCSO's office. Little had before the war a number of contacts in German circles in Lisbon among which had been included at least three persons whom we have since come to know as German agents – Wolfgang Schott, Ernst Schmidt, and Ferdinand Mouths. It was indeed on account of his knowledge of these people that Little had originally been employed and it was generally agreed that, even before the war, he had been at pains to drop these undesirable acquaintances. The final upshot of the matter was that Garcia sold in all five of Weltzien's cards, all of which allegedly referred to Weltzien's agents in British circles in Lisbon. Among these cards was one relating to Little himself, which purported to show that he was in touch with Weltzien himself through an intermediary known as C-54, and that he had received sums of money from Weltzien totalling in all $84,500. After these cards had been examined, an attempt was made on 19 January 1942 to burgle Weltzien's office in Lisbon and obtain possession of the remainder of the cards. The attempt came to nothing for Weltzien, who had evidently been warned beforehand, had told the police of what was impending with the result that on the night in question the police were already waiting in Weltzien's office to receive the burglars. The question naturally arose whether in fact the whole business of selling those cards had not been a plant on Weltzien's part from the start. There is ample evidence for supposing that this was in fact the case. In the first place, it seems incredible that Little, who knew at an early stage in the proceedings what was the nature of the cards which were being offered for sale, should not, had he in fact been one of Weltzien's agents, have informed Weltzien of what the taxi-driver was doing so as to guard against the possibility that his own card, which he must have known would be there, should fall into the hands of the British. Indeed, it would seem that for his own protection Little could scarcely have believed otherwise. Equally, it seems clear that if he did inform Weltzien he must have done so at some date before any of the cards were handed over, since he himself only acted as an intermediary during an early stage in the negotiations. Consequently, we are obliged to assume that, if Little had been an agent of Weltzien's, Weltzien would have been informed of what was happening before the actual sale took place and therefore in a position to have prevented the sale had he wished to do so. Similarly, the taxi-driver Garcia has stated that, apart altogether from the cards, he knew by his own personal knowledge that Little was one of Weltzien's agents as he had frequently driven him in his taxi to Weltzien's house. He has also stated that he recognised Little at the first meeting which took place between them while negotiations for the sale of the cards were proceeding. If this were true it seems abundantly clear that Garcia would never dared in the circumstances to proceed with the negotiations after he had discovered that one of the negotiators was a man whom he knew to be in Weltzien's pay. He could have had no guarantee that Little was not acting in the matter as a provocateur on behalf of Weltzien with the object of seeing how far Garcia was willing to go in double-crossing his employer.

For these reasons we have been driven to the conclusion that the sale of the cards was a plant on Weltzien's part, and that the cards themselves were fabricated by him with the object of throwing suspicion upon innocent people and causing us to embark upon a number of profitless enquiries. If this was Weltzien's object, he succeeded very well, since the immediate results of his manoeuvres were first the attempted burglary of his office, which he was able to reveal to the police, secondly the removal of Little to England under arrest and thirdly the bringing over to England, under deep suspicion, though not actual arrest, of a third person, [Victor] Stillwell, who had been named upon another of the cards.

5. In February 1942 Joaquin Calca, a Portuguese national who had lived for some years in the United States, where he has relatives, was approached by Kuno Weltzien or his agent and asked whether he would be willing to go to America and act there as a German agent. He was told that a week after his arrival in America he would be contacted by another German agent and would be given a cover-address in Lisbon. He was also given in Lisbon a certain amount of instruction (we do not know how much as SIS have not rendered a full report upon the case) in secret ink and codes. In the end, however, Calca's case, like that of SISYPHUS earlier, came to nothing, apparently, to judge from Most Secret Sources, because the Germans, after making enquiries about him in Berlin, had learned that he was suspected of being an agent of the American Secret Service. In the absence of any full report from SIS it is impossible to make a final judgment upon his case. We are, however, informed by them that Calca, who has already been deported once, if not twice, from the United States, would use any means that he could to gain entry there again. It is therefore not impossible, since Most Secret Sources, although they show that the Germans were interested in Calca, do not show that they ever employed, or contemplated employing him as an agent, that himself may have embroidered the story of his approach very considerably in an attempt to get his visa for the United States under the aegis of SIS by offering as he did to act for them in the capacity of a double agent.

6. In March 1942 SIS reported that one of their contacts had learned from Weltzien that the latter had obtained information from a member of the crew of the British ship *Empire Gale* who was alleged to be a communist,

and that this man had sold to Weltzien a quantity of gas-masks from the ship's store at the price of 600 escudos apiece. So far as we can discover, this story was without foundation, in as much as no member of the crew of the ship in question is known to have communist leanings and no gas-masks were missing from the ship's store on her return to England. On 22 April 1942 we received a further and not dissimilar report from SIS to the effect that Weltzien had succeeded some months before in obtaining information about Spanish Morocco from an officer of a British merchant ship then lying in Lisbon. For a payment of 2,000 escudos this officer had obtained or had compiled a document about Spanish Morocco, which he had handed to Weltzien who had photographed it and returned it to him. When he did so the officer seized the photograph from Weltzien's hand as well as the original copy, and demanded a further payment of 5,000 escudos. Weltzien, however, called his bluff and pointed out to him that he had had several photographs made. According to the report the officer in question continued in Weltzien's employ thereafter. So far our enquiries have not established the identity of this officer, and it appears possible that the story has no more substance at it that the one which related to the *Empire Gale*.

7. At the end of May 1942 a double agent employed in Lisbon both by SIS and Kuno Weltzien introduced to Weltzien a certain John Henry Price, a man Portuguese by birth but ultimately of British origin. Price had fought with Franco's army during the Civil War in Spain and had twice been wounded. He had been heard on more than one occasion to express anti-British sentiments. He is also suspected of having been the medium through which certain minor leakages have taken place from the British Embassy. He is not himself employed at the Embassy but his father has been a night-watchman there for a considerable period and he is therefore often in the Embassy and is acquainted with members of the staff. It appears that Price had in all three interviews with Weltzien, one on 19 May, when he was introduced to him by SIS's contact, the second on 26 May when he received about an hour's instruction in the use of elementary secret ink, and one some days later when he was taken by Weltzien to a villa in Estoril and there interviewed by another German whose name he did not know, but whom he supposed to be Weltzien's superior. Price was instructed by Weltzien to go to England and obtain work there in a munitions or aircraft factory. He was given no regular questionnaire but was told to discover all that he could about troop dispositions in England, with particular reference to American, Canadian, and New Zealand troops. He was also told to seek for information about prospective British landings on the Continent, to discover what he could about the arrival and departure of ships from English ports and to obtain information about British aircraft production. He was also instructed to seek any opportunity that he could to steal

confidential papers from the factory where it was hoped that he would be employed. At first Weltzien appears to have proposed to give him the names of five German agents whom he alleged to be working in England. Later, however, he restricted this offer and said that he would only reveal the names after Price had served an apprenticeship of some months and if he had in his possession any documents or other material which it was impossible for him to transmit himself. It was apparently agreed that Price himself should travel to England by obtaining work on some ship sailing here but the arrangements finally enabled him to do so were entirely the work of SIS and not either of Price or the Germans.

Price finally arrived here on 19 June 1942, that is to say within a month of his first meeting with Weltzien and has since created the impression of a densely stupid man who is for this reason entirely unfitted to work as an agent. Before leaving Lisbon Price had rendered a full account of his dealings with Weltzien to a member of the British Embassy there; it would appear that this statement was entirely voluntary but some ambiguity on this point still remains.

There are several things which strike one forcibly about Kuno Weltzien's story as set out above. In the first place it is apparent that Weltzien has been reported as a German agent too often for it to be likely that he has no connection with the Abwehr, and equally too often to make it probable that he is in some sense a leading figure in the Abwehr. It is unlikely that a genuine businessman, trading as Weltzien does in a neutral country, would foster the idea that he was a secret agent if in fact he was not. At the same time it is also obvious that the real leaders of the Abwehr organisation in Portugal are persons like [von Auenrode] about whom we receive no casual reports but only information from Most Secret Sources, or from the reports of a particularly successful and trusted double agent. For these reasons it is permissible to assume that Weltzien's true place in the organisation is somewhere upon its fringe. Secondly, if we are to believe all the reports which we have received, it is clear that Weltzien's activities on behalf of the Abwehr cover almost the whole range of the organisation's activities. SIS say that he is primarily concerned with shipping intelligence, and this may well be so. It certainly agrees with the nature of the questionnaire which he is said to have given to SISYPHUS. On the other hand it would seem from Most Secret Sources that Roque Laia, during the time that he was in England, was reporting largely or wholly upon matters of interest not to Eins Marine, but to Eins Luft, to whom, indeed, his reports were forwarded. For his projected second visit to England he was given a questionnaire referring in great detail to the organisation of British railways, his answers to which would have been presumably of interest either to either Eins Heer or to Eins Wirtschaft, or possibly to both. Lastly, we have the report from SIS, referred to above, which alleges that Weltzien was concerned in an act of sabotage in Portugal, which would fall presumably within the scope of Abteilung II, and the statement of Garcia that he maintained a card-index of British agents in Lisbon, which would appear to be a function of Abteilung III. Similarly, we are offered evidence that he is concerned with the running of agents in England, in Portugal, in the United States, in the Atlantic Islands and Portuguese West Africa. This catholic activity certainly does not agree very well with what we know about the general organisation of the Abwehr, which reveals it as a departmentalized body the individual members of which are usually concerned only with work within a single and well-defined sphere. This should be particularly true of a well-developed and highly organised Stelle such as that which undoubtedly exists in Lisbon. Thirdly, one cannot help but observe in how many cases information emanating from Weltzien has been revealed upon enquiry to have little or no basis in fact. Indeed, upon at least one occasion (the episode of Little and the card-index) he appears to have been concerned in a deliberate attempt to plant information upon SIS. It is by no means impossible that much of the rest of the information which has come from him and is related to ships' officers from whom he is alleged to have obtained information or agents who he is alleged to maintain in this country, was similarly false and designed wholly to spread confusion and to involve ourselves or SIS in laborious and vain enquiries. On the other hand, on at least two occasions Weltzien has shown himself to be well informed about the Abwehr's activities. His statement that there were three German agents using transmitters in England was true in the main, though open to question in its details. Similarly, the second of his two recorded statements about the SS *Cressado* was not only true but argued that he was wholly in the confidence of Dr Rantzau or his associates, since he had apparently learnt CELERY's true status within two days of SNOW's arrival in Lisbon. It is important to emphasise this point, for the statement that CELERY was a valuable means of planting false information upon the British was only true upon the assumption that the Germans believed him to be either a British agent or a double agent working in the British interest. However much they may have suspected previously that this was the case they could not have satisfied themselves upon that point until after SNOW had made his confession to Rantzau on the evening of the 14 February. Yet within two days of this occurrence Weltzien was able to give what was substantially a true picture of the situation. It is, however, most unsatisfactory that this information should not have reached us until the following July and that SIS's original letter should have given no hint of it, for this to some extent vitiates the value of Weltzien's alleged statement, since it introduced an element of doubt whether he did in fact make the statement at the time stated or whether perhaps he said it on some later occasion when it would have been less remarkable. Lastly, one is very forcibly struck throughout with the unsatisfactory status of the intermediary between SIS and Weltzien wherever this person is named or described. In the beginning it would appear that SIS derived their information about Weltzien from SISYPHUS, a man who, according to one of their own letters, 'undoubtedly was in the service of the Germans before approaching us'. This presumably means that although SISYPHUS had been an informant of SIS before he was approached by Weltzien he had at some earlier date still been in the service of the Germans. It is certainly true that he had known Ernst Schmidt for a period of some eight years. It therefore seems that his bona-fides as an informant was to some extent at least open to question from the start. SIS's next informant was apparently Roque Laia, in every way an unsatisfactory character and, as later enquiries showed, a financial crook and a suspected smuggler of drugs. It was, in fact, upon that account and because the Portuguese Police were suspicious of the true contents of a bag of coffee beans that he had with him that Roque Laia was detained by them on his second attempt to come to England. It appears that he was not actually arrested on this occasion but only detained pending enquiries for long enough to ensure that he missed the aeroplane. The discrepancy between this story and that contained in SIS's original letter seems to demonstrate clearly through what a faulty channel they are apt to obtain their information. Similarly, nothing could have been less satisfactory than the various intermediaries that were employed by SIS in the case of Little and the negotiations with regard to Kuno Weltzien's card-index. As has been pointed out above, Costa had already come under suspicion and was a close friend of Souza who was in fact the man who had introduced him to the Consulate originally. The taxi-driver Garcia was, to judge from his incredible statements about Little, a most unsatisfactory witness and one who at the best had none but a financial interest in the affair. Moreover, it remains entirely obscure why, if he had the blackmailing hold that he is alleged to have had over Weltzien, he could not have obtained what money he wanted from him without placing himself in the dangerous and awkward position of opening negotiations with the opposite side for the purpose of betraying Weltzien. The fourth party to these negotiations, Araujo, would seem to have a reputation for reliability even lower than that of the preceding three. Since in these cases where SIS has informed us of the identity of the intermediaries, this intermediary has always proved to be a person of questionable reliability it is at least pertinent to enquire whether the other unnamed ones who were responsible for the balance of information which had come from Weltzien, were themselves of any higher standing. Indeed, the likeliest explanation for the whole Weltzien story seems to be that he is himself a member of the Abwehr, though not perhaps a person holding a very high position, who is more or less continuously in receipt of information about Abwehr activities of varying importance, but that the channel of communication by which this information

> reaches SIS's Lisbon representative is corrupt, either in the sense of the intermediary is an inaccurate reporter of information which he has picked up himself, or in the sense that the intermediary is known to Kuno Weltzien for what he is, and is therefore deliberately fed with tendentious information. It is not possible upon any other basis to explain the flood of inaccurate information which has had its origin in Weltzien and to explain at the same time those admittedly few incidents in which the information has proved to be accurate. It is extremely difficult to form any judgments with respect to the agents whom Weltzien has attempted to send abroad. Two of them, SISYPHUS and Calca, failed to reach their destination, for reasons which in neither case are wholly clear, but which appear to have resulted from Weltzien's having recruited an agent over-hastily without first enquiring whether or not he was suitable for the work intended. Similar criticism might be made of the agent Price who is not only constitutionally unsuited to be anyone's agent, but was only provided by Weltzien with training of the most inept and rudimentary type. The remaining agent Roque Laia, if we are to accept the apparent references in Most Secret Sources, was entirely unsatisfactory and composed his reports largely upon a basis of imagination. From this one might legitimately deduce that the running of agents is not a part of Weltzien's regular business but is nevertheless a thing in which he is anxious to engage, perhaps because of the financial profits which we know that it is possible for an Abwehr official to make thereby. Alternatively, it would be possible to argue that in such cases the alleged agent was simply the instrument of what was intended by Weltzien to be a plant at the expense of SIS's Lisbon representative. This would explain why SISYPHUS failed to reach England and Calca failed to reach the United States. It would also explain why Roque Laia's attempt to come to this country lapsed after what was apparently a trivial brush with the police of a kind with which he must have been very familiar. Indeed, the evidence in Most Secret Sources is by no means inconsistent with the view that Roque Laia, on his first visit to England, was not a German agent, but simply rendered a report to the Germans upon his return to Portugal. On this footing it is not hard to explain why the statement made by Roque Laia about his career as an agent in England stands the test of enquiry so ill. With regard to the last agent Price it is arguable that the impetus which impelled him to these shores came not from Weltzien at all but from SIS. Upon this footing one might say that Weltzien had intended Price simply to be used in order to sow doubts in the mind of SIS about the security of the British Embassy in Lisbon, and that Weltzien himself was taken by surprise when the affair developed so rapidly as to ensure that Price actually came to England.[46]

Although Gwyer could not be certain of Weltzien's precise role in KOP, he knew that he had masterminded a series of operations, some intended to send agents to England, the others to penetrate and maybe disrupt his local adversaries, the PCO in the rua da Emenda. Gwyer and Philby disagreed on how to interpret the evidence to determine Weltzien's exact status, but the issue became somewhat moot in June 1943 when he was detained at the Alcantara police station and then entirely redundant in October 1943 when he was expelled from Portugal permanently and withdrawn to Paris, accompanied by his wife and Portuguese-born son.

The background to Weltzien's detention by the PVDE was a determined effort to embarrass him, while simultaneously applying political pressure on the Portuguese government. Weltzien was persuaded to accept an agent, codenamed PUMPKIN by SIS, a seaman off the SS *Amirante*, and another asset, codenamed COLACO, became a valued inside source. Possibly the final straw was the SD's recruitment of Rogeiro de Menezes, a junior clerk posted to the London embassy in July 1942. His cultivation by Amady Kaes and Kurt Foester was documented contemporaneously by ISOS and de Menezes was kept under surveillance until February 1943 when the Portuguese ambassador, outraged by evidence that his young subordinate had been abusing the pouch to send correspondence in secret ink to Lisbon describing London's air defences, removed his immunity. Under interrogation at Camp 020, de Menezes quickly confessed, and was sentenced to death at his trial in April 1943. He was reprieved the following month, following representations from the Salazar regime.[47] Within months, the diplomatic and strategic landscape would change in the Allies' favour, and the outstanding issue of aviation facilities in the Azores was granted in October 1943.

* * *

The relative importance of KriegsOrganisation Spanien in Madrid, without sea and air links to Great Britain and the United States, was initially at least something of a puzzle to British intelligence analysts who had come to rely on two principal sources, ISOS and Camp 020. Of the two, ISOS was the less useful because the traffic was quite difficult to interpret unless the Abwehr's cover-names could be properly identified. Very often that information came from interrogations conducted at Ham.

Apart from the individual personalities, it seemed obvious that the KOS's principal objectives would be directly related to Spain's geopolitical position, in terms of being a supposedly neutral country bordering occupied France; its historic claim to Gibraltar; the pro-

German alignment of the Falange; and the country's position as a transit route to Portugal. These realities militated towards a major role for Abt. II and, given the strong historical links between the Luftwaffe and Franco with their origins in the Civil War, and the exercise of political influence for the regime to support, if not actually join, the Axis. Additionally, the Spanish Seguridad turned a blind eye to I/M shipping intelligence collection activities in the ports, cooperated with monitoring transits through the Straits of Gibraltar, and were suspected (wrongly, as it turned out) of providing refuelling facilities for U-boats.

There were two other considerations that stemmed from the above. Firstly, the British embassy staff in Madrid was greatly circumscribed by the ambassador concerning any potentially embarrassing clandestine activity, and this was enforced by the ambassador, Sir Sam Hoare, himself a former SIS officer, who did not hesitate to remove the pre-war PCO, Edward de Renzy-Martin. The tiny SIS representation in Madrid worked under severe restrictions, only too well aware of Hoare's status as the prime minister's personal envoy.

In contrast to Hoare's prohibition on covert entanglements, the KOS received much support from the ambassador, Baron Eberhard von Stohrer, who had served in the embassy during the First World War when he had been heavily involved in subversion, to the point that he had been withdrawn when exposed as funding the Catalan separatist movement.

Secondly, there was, from a counter-espionage perspective, an acknowledgment that the Spanish embassy in London acted akin to a Nest, overseen by the press attaché Angel Alcazar de Velascio[48] and his subordinate, Miguel del Pozo.[49] In consequence, the embassy was a target for MI5 surveillance and penetration, and was the backdrop to several investigations, including that of Luis Calvo, who was arrested in February 1942.[50] Embarrassingly, upon his return to Madrid in 1941, Alcazar de Velasco published his memoirs in which he boasted of his German espionage in London.

In August 1941 Captain Pank circulated this assessment of the Abwehr's presence in the Peninsula, and in retrospect his review marks a watershed moment, illustrating the limits of British knowledge of the enemy. Here is no mention of ISOS, then in its infancy, and he was heavily reliant on the recollection of individual agents, most of whom were still languishing in Camp 020.

> With all the information at our disposal regarding German espionage activity in Spain and Portugal, the actual build-up of the organisation remains, to say the least of it, obscure. The purpose of this memorandum,

therefore, is to advance a reasonable hypothesis based on certain facts in our possession, with a view to obtaining a clearer insight into the tremendously powerful opposition with which we have to contend.

It is plain that the centre of German espionage in Spain is in Madrid, from which city, smaller centres such as Barcelona and perhaps other at present unknown to us (if not to SIS) are controlled.

There are strong grounds for the belief that the key point of German activities in the whole of the Peninsula is in Lisbon and that whilst agents contacted in Spain are recruited, trained and groomed in Spain, the final instructions, interviews and payments are given in Lisbon, prior to departure from that port.

The cases of [Jose Antonio] del Campo and [Edward] Ejsymont clearly show that preliminaries took place in Madrid for the former, and Barcelona and Madrid for the latter. Lisbon was chosen for the final instruction and payment of Ejsymont. Ejsymont gave it as his opinion that Lisbon was the centre of outstanding importance, as this was the impression he had gained from his considerable contacts with the German Secret Service in the Peninsula. It is in Lisbon that all papers and passports are put in order, and it is interesting to note that all the agents in our hands ([Albert] de Jareger, [Karel] Van Gils, [Joseph] Laureyssens, Willem, Gerth van Wijk, Ejsymont and FATHER) have arrived in this country, via Lisbon, quite legitimately and with all their papers in order.

The actual espionage of agents from the Peninsula differs quiet plainly from others who graduate from various other 'Stellen', of which we know in Northern Europe. There has been no trace of anybody being sent for what might be called 'shock espionage', or for the purposes of obtaining important information quickly. Either it would appear that those agents who are sent from Spain and Portugal are protected by their particular calling, enter England quite legitimately and that there is no great urgency for their reports.

Cover addresses and secret inks are the medium for the conveyance of all information sent to England: in not one case had the use of radio transmission even been contemplated. This raises the point that either the technical difficulties of transmission from this country to the Peninsula are too great, or that espionage reports to Spain and Portugal are dealt with exclusively in those two countries. This has not been the case in 'shock' espionage attempted by recruits from the Belgian and Dutch Stellen, where radio messages, at times, were to be received in France.

The Peninsula is therefore presumably a self-contained entity with the chief of the Secret Service making periodical reports to Berlin and where the decentralisation practised in other countries is not observed.

Whilst the following speculation as to the German organisation is problematical and therefore open to considerable critic, information in our possession does to a certain extent support the hypothesis which is the subject of this memorandum.

With a view to gaining a clearer insight into the organisation it would be well to review the personalities of whom we know and speculate as to the various parts they play in their espionage activities, against this country.

The German Secret Service in Spain and Portugal appears to be run on semi-military lines and departmental lines, with certain section chiefs dealing with certain types of espionage missions. There is strong evidence to support the theory also that the better class of agent and those who are well-connected, are looked after by more senior officials of the German hierarchy, than those who are seafaring men of a lower strata of society. Before offering to substantiate this premise however, it is better to discuss the various Secret Service personalities in Spain and Portugal, and the picture thus gained, should render the suggestion eminently plausible.

On the sheet attached is a plan drawn up on somewhat genealogical lines to illustrate the probable organisation responsible for the recruitment and management of agents in Spain and Portugal, for duties directed against this country.

There can be little doubt that PABLO is the chief of the German Secret Service in the Peninsula and although there is no actual proof that the DON PABLO of Barcelona is the same person, there is little doubt that his is indeed the case, to judge from the personal descriptions that we have in our possession.

It was he would dealt personally with the training and grooming of van Wijk who is the best born and connected of any agents who have passed through our hands. Lesser fry have in only one instance come into contact with PABLO and that was in the case of Del Campo, who only talked with him for half an hour.

The next person of importance in Spain is PABLO's assistant EMILIO, who is reported in charge of German espionage in Spain. EMILIO was in charge of Del Campo (recruited by his assistant HERMANN) and was used as a messenger by PABLO on one occasion, in dealing with Van Wijk. EMILIO seems to act as general supervisor of Secret Service officers and is probably in close touch with Lisbon, as it is known that he pays periodic visits to that city.

Ramon Hermann is probably in charge of German Secret Service activities in Madrid, under supervisor EMILIO, but his particular function appears to be German espionage contacts and recruitment vis-à-vis the Spanish Falange. He is in close touch with Colmenares, Carbinares Garcia, de Frances and other Falangists, and was responsible for the selection and recruitment of del Campo and his abortive mission to Punta Delgada in the Azores.

It has not been established that HERMANN has been connected with the activities of any agent but Del Campo, and as all his reported contacts have been with Falangists, it is reasonable to suppose that his activities are confined to Falangist/German espionage.

FEDERICO has only appeared in the case of Ejsymont, and as this latter was a cadet pilot, it is possible that his activities extend to espionage by members of the forces.

Drs Hacke and Rademacher are from the Brussels Stelle and are only attached temporarily to PABLO's staff when in the Peninsula. Hacke is an ex-Condor captain and Rademacher an ex-engineer and it is likely that they hold a somewhat more technical position than others that we know.

JULIA does not appear to be of very much importance and acts as a sort of 'letter-box' and 'dogsbody' to PABLO.

DON PEDRO is probably in charge of the Barcelona zone of influence. He is junior to HERMANN who makes periodic trips there. Mohre CARLOS is his assistant with PAPS as a sort of office boy/manager.

The activities of REIG and the Russian are obscure, but it is almost certain that they are on PABLO's staff.

GARBO is established as PABLO's messenger and presumably employed on other but so far obscure duties. Her real name is probably Anna, an ex-communist agent from San Sebastian. She is a friend of Colmenares and possibly used by HERMANN in Falangist matters.

ENRICO is a concierge who keeps his ears open, and possibly reports to REIG, the Russian, or perhaps EMILIO.

It will be seen that an important agent like Van Wijk was dealt with only by PABLO and his staff, whilst del Campo on a mission of possibly less importance was looked after by EMILIO's assistant HERMANN, and then passed on to PANKOFF of the German Consulate in Lisbon. Ejsymont the Pole was recruited by FEDERICO and then instructed to approach Merckel of the German legation in Lisbon.

In Spain the departmental differences of the organisation are not very apparent, but an examination of the plan of the workings in Lisbon does seem clearly to indicate that special sections look after special types of espionage activity.[51]

Pank's memorandum illustrates how, by August 1941, with ISOS in its relative infancy and just a limited number of interrogation reports available to synthesise with inadequate SIS field support, only a fraction of the jigsaw puzzle had begun to emerge, and many of the assumptions would turn out to be plain wrong. PABLO was Gottfried Paul-Taboschat, head of Nest Barcelona;[52] and DON PEDRO was Bertie Koepke,[53] who emphatically was not the senior Abwehr officer in the region, and the Russian was Boris Lowschin, the Nest's principal agent-runner. German use of cover-names in their radio messages would prove quite a challenge to the RSS and Section V analysts who would learn that the KOS's Karl-Erich Kuhlenthal had also been assigned the codename PABLO.

The RSS and Section V analysts got to know these ISOS personalities as old friends, and became familiar with their patterns of travel, the senior officers often making tours of inspection or attending special conferences which were convened in congenial locations safe from Allied air-raids, such as Salzburg or Budapest. The Holy Grail itself would be variously referred to variously as 'Mr Hart's material', ISOS, PAIR, TRIANGLE or ICICLE, and was always subject to handling and circulation restrictions. All the documents bore severe injunctions to remind the indoctrinated recipients. Absolutely no action could be taken as a consequence of the messages without the originator's specific consent. Having connected individual KOS personalities to their cover-names, Section V set out to find their home addresses, telephone numbers, car registration plates and even the names of their mistresses. Thus the card on the KOS's chief, Kapitan Wilhelm Leisner, alias Colonel Gustav Lenz and codenamed PEDRO, recorded that he had served in the Kaisermarine during the First World War, and afterwards had emigrated to Nicaragua. He was listed at the embassy as an honorary attaché, and it was noted that his mistress was a manicurist, Matilda Ruiz.

The summer of 1942 proved to be something of a turning-point in the Peninsula, for in June SIS compiled a list of 110 members of the German embassy staff in Madrid, and assembled a continuously-updated and increasingly accurate roster of the diplomatic, consular and KO personnel. As access to ISOS escalated, and more prisoners passed through Camp 020, the accuracy of identifications became more acute with, for example, FEDERICO confirmed by the double agents as Friederich Knappe-Ratey, a senior case officer and long-time Madrid resident married to a Spanish wife.[54] He had handled both CARELESS, the Polish pilot, Edward Ejsymont, and John Price, codenamed WASHOUT, as they had passed through Madrid, and would also be responsible for the Spanish volunteer Juan Pujol.

Cover-addresses for mail and safe-houses used to accommodate training facilities, all added to the developing picture. As early as March 1940 Hans George, known to MI5 as DRAGONFLY, had been given a cover-address in Lisbon, while Maria Marek, a Yugoslav domestic servant known as THE SNARK located sites in Madrid where she had received instruction in secret writing. An MI5 analysis of the cover-addresses in Spain and Portugal supplied to eleven agents

(Goesta Caroli; Wolf Schmidt; Albert de Jaeger; Joseph Laureyssens; DRAGONFLY; FATHER; Joseph Lenihan; Gerth Van Wijk; Edward Ejsymont; THE SNARK; and Alphonse Timmerman) showed that there were nine in Lisbon, five in Madrid, two in Barcelona and one in San Sebastian.

In November 1941 MI5, SIS's Section V and Camp 020 combined together to complete a comprehensive analysis of what was then known about German espionage in the Iberian Peninsula, drawn from nine interrogations, plus additional contributions from THE SNARK, DRAGONFLY and the Belgian pilot FATHER (see Appendix II). At that stage there was little understanding of the system of Nests, nor of the existence of the many commercial covers exploited by the Abwehr, such as Kuno Weltzien's office in Lisbon. Indeed, the document demonstrates the complimentary nature of the various components of intelligence, and the disadvantages of reliance on a single source. However, through comprehensive study of the Abwehr's radio communications, a picture began to emerge in 1941 which, when overlaid with Camp 020 interrogations and eventually information from defectors and penetration agents, the scale of the Abwehr's investment in the Peninsula became evident, and in October 1941 Section V circulated a paper entitled *Organisation of German Secret Service in Spain and the Spanish Dominions* which set out the dependency on wireless;

> Wireless communications in Spain centre on two stations in Madrid, The first of these (SABINE) sends to and receives from Berlin, Paris, Bordeaux, the Bordeaux area and Spanish Guinea directly, but deals with the more local stations in Spain and Spanish Africa through the second station (E) which is subsidiary to it. The two stations are linked by a relay service known as 2/135. The second station (E) sends to and receives from a series of out-stations which, apparently at Marseilles, are all in Spanish territory. They are situated at Barcelona, San Sebastian, Bilbao, Vigo, Algeciras, Tangier, Tetuan, Las Palmas and Teneriffe.
>
> These out-stations in their turn have their satellite stations. Bilbao is in communication with an unknown station, as is Algeciras; Tetuan has a link with Mellila and Las Palmas collects information by wireless from Ifni, Cape Juby and Cieneros. Some out-stations are in communication with one another, independently of the 'E' centre. Tangier has links with Tetuan and Algeciras which appear to have been linked themselves for some time. Finally, there are isolated wireless links between Madrid (?) and Algeciras (?) and Madrid (?) and an unknown station. Intelligence material also indicates a probable W/T services between Tetuan and Casablanca.

> Mention must also be made of Lisbon and Corruna. Lisbon, like Madrid, has two W/T centres. One of these is situated in the German Embassy and makes contact with Berlin on the Nauen schedule, using machine-cypher. It has no direct contact with Madrid and the link between those places is through this Berlin route. This route is also used by the Spanish out-stations when they wish to make contact with Lisbon, as is clear from a message sent by CRUSE at Tangier to Madrid on 30 September 1941, seeking that a message of 355 letters should be forwarded through SABINE and Berlin for LINA (= Lisbon). Intelligence material, however, suggests that a direct link between Lisbon and Tangier may soon be in operation.
>
> The other W/T Centre in Lisbon is situated outside the Embassy and works to the Azores. Corunna is known from intelligence and interception evidence to have had a W/T station in contact with Madrid until the end of April this year, Thus, on 5 April 1941 Madrid was able to inform Vigo of conditions at Corunna, though since then information from Corunna has had to go through Vigo. Interception evidence confirms this picture and, and the last message picked up between Madrid and the station, believed from D/F evidence to be Corunna, was on 16 April 1941.[55]

The KOS was heavily, but not entirely reliant on its radio network, and occasionally used the regular mail service and diplomatic couriers who either flew by domestic airlines around the region or, in the absence of trains, used motor vehicles. This was evident from messages exchanged with the Vigo satellite which, devoid of a local airport or train service, had a heavy proportion of 'requests for petrol coupons and second-hand motor-car tyres'.

ISOS analysis gave Section V a fascinating insight into KOS's collection capabilities and priorities, with an evident emphasis on I/M material:

> The main source of information is its own organisation of V-men. The statistics of the network controlled by Müller of Tetuan given in a message of 5 September 1941 . . . illustrates how far-reaching these organisations have become. Müller reports no less than 60 V-men in his employ operating between Cape Blanco (south-west of Casablanca) and Oran, and over half of these are concentrated in the Tangier-Tetuan area, 17 V-men being in Tangier alone. The other out-stations have similar organisations, with permanent V-men placed in nearby posts. Thus Barcelona is known to have placed a V-mann at Palamos, and Vigo has controlled the agent (JIMENEZ) at Corunna since the w/t station at that place was dismantled. V-men are also used to go on journeys through areas not otherwise covered; there has been a recent report sent in by Vigo to Madrid on V-mann MIGUEL's 'last Portugal journey'.

> Such information as is not collected by definite V-men is obtained through connections with Spanish officials. In certain cases these officials are enlisted outright as V-men or for example the officer or the Spanish General whose far-fetched reports are sent to Madrid by Vigo. But on the whole the connections with Spanish officials are not as clear-cut as this. Müller, who relays from Tetuan a stream of information sent in by the Spanish coastguards (SIRENE), speaks of nothing more than 'very close cooperations with SIRENE'. SIRENE observers are known to exist at Ceuta, Tangier, Tetuan (Temeraria), Larache, Infi, etc., while the Barcelona station has links with the SIRENE frontier-guards. In the same way the Vigo station has contacts with lighthouse-keepers at Capes Finistere and Silleiro, and with the Spanish police in the district.[56]

As well as this sophisticated coast-watching coverage at the strategically important western end of the Mediterranean, the KOS out-stations had developed sources at sea, a project pioneered in Bilbao where

> agents are for the main part originally planted on ships by that station. Barcelona, San Sebastian and Vigo are also concerned in this work, though to a small extent in proportion with their slighter importance as ports. The agents employed in this way are used for gathering information on the main Atlantic shipping routes. Local information is collected either by placing V-men on the coastal shipping routes or, as is more usually the case, by gaining control of the fishing fleets. The latter method has been adopted on a large scale by the Las Palmas station. Reports from fishermen on the movements of Allied shipping in the vicinity of the Canary Islands form the greater part of the content of the messages sent by Las Palmas to Madrid. The organisation used to collate the information supplied by the fishing trawlers is simple, and in one case is known to consist of nothing more elaborate than an ambulatory middleman. The number of ships concerned is considerable, *Canarias III, Sil, Abaire, Los Solos, Oscar* and *Visparia.*
>
> Vigo has a similar organisation of fishing trawlers, though on a smaller scale; this is worked from Coruna by a V-mann known as V-5007, who is in charge of the steam trawler report department of the local wireless station. Evidence from other sources confirms and adds to this picture; the number of trawlers concerned is four – *Salman, Santa Rosa, Tiburon* and *Fernando* – and they work in conjunction with Richard Junkers of Coruna (T = JIMENEZ) through the agency of Francisco Dalgado Sorzano.[57]

Although there is an evident bias towards I/M collection, KOS's responsibilities went far wider:

The information required by Madrid is mainly naval; this is in keeping with the position of the outstations which are all on the coast except Tetuan, and with the organisations at their disposal. Political information is the work of the Ribbentrop Bureau, except the everyday details of occupation, which form part of the content of the French and Norwegian services, are not yet required in Spain.

The kinds of naval information wanted by Madrid are numerous, but particular interest is shown in the movements of convoys . . . where the distance from Cape Spartel of outward bound convoys is the subject for enquiry – in the details of shipping at Freetown., and in the passage of ships between Spain and Ireland. Reports on warships, provided they are sent promptly, are always welcome . . . as are reports on all suspicious ships. The highest interest is shown in all naval information sent in from North African ports organised from Tetuan, and a recent message from Madrid asked for a special watch between 12 and 15 October for an important Allied convoy which Tetuan has passed on to Tangier and to Melilla for the observers at Cape Tres Flores and on the island of Alboran. Sometimes there are particular cases for enquiry, as with the sinking of the SS *Ida Knudsen* which may arise from original interest on the part of Madrid, or which may be occasioned by preliminary and unsolicited reports from the outstations, as with the fishermen's observations of warships in the Bay of Biscay.

The naval information is not the only kind required. Madrid is particularly concerned with any possible Allied military action against Africa or Spanish Atlantic islands. In messages of 15 July 1941 already quoted, the stations at Las Palmas and Tenerife were instructed to report immediately on possible Allied intentions against the Canaries. Previous to this Las Palmas had been asked to supply details of the garrison strength of the islands in peace and war.

Finally, Madrid uses the outstations to supply personal data on suspicious persons or on potential V-men. The example of MONTAG is a case in point. Vigo reported his claims to be in touch with an Abwehr representative on the French frontier to Madrid; Madrid promptly referred the point to San Sebastian and received in return a full report on MONTAG's position.

A regular aspect of this side of Madrid's work is the organised transport of Scandinavian seamen from Spain into Germany, possibly with the object of using them as V-men against England. This practice was particularly noticeable during April and May this year in the content of the Barcelona messages which indicated that the seamen were thought to desert their ships at Barcelona or Lisbon and flown from those places to Stuttgart. More recently Tangier has been in long communication with Madrid and Tetuan concerning the securing from the Spanish authorities of 3 or 4 shipwrecked Danish seamen whom the English and Danish consuls had tried to have released for transport to England.[58]

Study of the ISOS intercepts gave the Section V analysts an understanding of the independence exercised by the KOS outstation in the field of intelligence collection in all areas except I/M reporting: The Nests

> send in material according to their inclinations and sources along these lines. Only in shipping reports is there a consistent and regular flow from all stations. This information is sent into Madrid in far greater volume than is definitely requested, which indicates that the requests made by Madrid are in addition to the everyday information that is accepted as a matter of course, The sum of this information is collected for the 'Marine Attaché' at Madrid and may possibly be sent on from there to Berlin on the machine-cypher services. The old Lisbon shipping reports were known to go to 'MARTIN and MEHMERT' in Berlin, and as the same Lisbon station is now working with the Spanish coastal stations, it may be that all the shipping reports were sent on from Madrid, not only to Berlin, but also possibly to Bordeaux and Paris with which Madrid had similar machine-cypher services, and to all three of which identical messages are regularly being sent.[59]

Although the Section V authors of this paper did not spell out the implications of this narrative, the cryptological implications of the Abwehr's repetition of identical messages in hand and machine ciphers represented a huge Achilles' heel in the German procedures, and of course it is now well recognised that this opportunity to exploit Enigma was not overlooked.

As the Section V analysts scrutinised KOS and its subsidiary satellites they discovered that the Abwehr officers

> at Biarritz are in direct contact with Madrid and seem to work as an appendage of the Bilbao and San Sebastian stations. Curiously enough, it seems to run fairly important agents in the USA, e.g. one CHARLY and also one LANG. In August 1940 AUGUSTO, then in Lisbon, was instructed to transmit money to CHARLY, then in New York, and in November it appeared that AUGUSTO was to travel to New York, but his journey was postponed after consultation with LANG. Money required for CHARLY was sent to him through a certain Carlos Vejarano who travelled in November of the *Marques des Commillas,* with $1,000 to facilitate CHARLY's entrance to, and remaining in, the USA.
>
> The officer in charge of the German Secret Service activities in Biarritz is Hauptman Weiss. He is much concerned with the Sofindus ships running the British blockade. In September a certain Hauptman Heidschuck was also working for the German organisation in Biarritz and taking part in interrogations.[60]

The Section V review of the KOS's component parts began with the largest sun-station or dienstelle, in Bilbao:

> Bilbao has been from early days in the present war an important centre for German naval espionage. It is not known when the Dienststelle was first established, but wireless communication with Madrid was in existence early in 1940.
>
> Three main functions can be distinguished by the work of the Dienstelle:
>
> 1. The reporting to Madrid of all sailings from and arrival in the port, of shipping of all countries.
> 2. The recruiting of agents among the crews of vessels leaving the port for purposes of espionage.
> 3. The insertion of a higher class of agent among ships' officers or as W/T operators in Spanish vessels sailing especially between the Americas and North Spanish ports.
>
> Sailings of Spanish vessels are reported with particular care, but attempts are apparently made by Bilbao to supply Madrid with a complete list of all sailings and arrivals, and besides Spanish, Swedish, French, Belgian, Icelandic, American, Portuguese, Italian, Japanese and even German vessels are included in the almost daily lists which are passed by Bilbao to Madrid. Occasionally Madrid requires and obtains from Bilbao particulars of passenger ships sailing for specified destinations, e.g. between Bilbao and Lisbon, in April, May and June 1941, and to the Canaries, Cuba, New York, Buenos Aires and Spanish Guinea.
>
> The sources of information, apart from direct observation, on which Bilbao draws for the purpose of making these reports, include contacts in the local Shipping Offices, especially the Campsa Agency. These sources apparently supply the Dienstelle with very detailed information, since it exhibits familiarity with the details of ships' Orders, etc. In some cases too, these shipping circles are able to supply information about previous sailings, e.g. from the UK to ports in Spain.
>
> The Dienstelle keeps an eye open for vacancies in crew of foreign vessels in the hope of filling them with seamen working as agents. The *Agia Varvara,* off Bilbao in November 1940, which arrived in the UK in January 1941, is an instance of this. A Spanish fireman was recruited by the Bilbao Dienstelle and signed on, but the ship was compelled to return to port, and the agent did not succeed on this voyage at any rate of getting to England. The Spanish ship *Embla* was considered by the Dienstelle Bilbao for similar purposes and a sailor Muner Castrillion was sent by Bilbao to Madrid as a possible recruit in February 1941, There is apparently a fairly close liaison between Bilbao and the port of

Huelva for working this class of agent, and recruits suggested by Bilbao are sometimes sent on to join a ship on which they intended to work to Huelva via Madrid.[61]

A major focus of Bilbao's activities was on the recruitment of ships' officers, and considerable success had been achieved 'in inserting such agents among the wireless operators and other officers of a large number of Spanish ships'.

Most of these vessels sail between Bilbao and such ports as New York, Buenos Aires, Valparaiso and elsewhere in the Americas, and their functions are to observe and report upon the shipping traffic in American ports, details of convoys, and all British naval units, observed on route across the Atlantic. Further, such agents are contacted by German Secret Service personnel abroad, e.g. in Buenos Aires, and are given secret mail to take home to Spain. Apart from American ports, agents of this class have been put on ships, e.g. *Cabo Buena Esperanza,* Freetown, and have to report through intermediary agents about the state of shipping in that port. Similar agents have been placed also on ships going down the West African coast, to Spanish Guinea. The reports brought back by such agents on vessels visiting New York have in recent months been extremely detailed and extended to particulars of gun emplacements on the coast, troops in training and aircraft construction and numbers, as well as ordinary shipping reports. Recently Cuba has become an object of interest to the Bilbao Dienstelle and attempts have been made to establish connection between a wireless operator, UGUATE, sailing on the *Magallanes,* who has been recruited by the Bilbao Dienstelle, and a radio amateur in Cuba. In June 1941 a new agent was recruited, an ex-officer of the Spanish Secret police, who was instructed to get off at Cuba and miss the ship on its departure.[62]

Section V identified thirty-eight Spanish ships accommodating Abwehr agents, and circulated a list oi their V-mann numbers, their true names, and their ranks, all linked to their first appearance in ISOS, followed by the date of their most recent reference. In counter-intelligence terms, it is hard to imagine a more comprehensive coverage of an adversary's espionage system.

Closely associated with Bilbao was the dienstelle at San Sebastian, although in October 1941 relatively little was known about it in London:

It is in close connection with the dienstelle in Bilbao and assists in the latter's work, e.g. Bilbao having to supply an officer for the Swedish ships *Emba* and *Vega,* informs San Sebastian of this. San Sebastian was also instructed to acquire Lloyds Register.

It appears however that San Sebastian runs an occasional agent in a Spanish ship sailing in the Americas, e.g. one ROMERO sailed in November on the *Monte Albertia* for Pernambuco and Buenos Aires. Apart from these activities San Sebastian is important for the purpose of facilitating the journeys of German Secret Service personnel across the frontier and for reserving sleeping-cars, etc. for the higher grade officials. Occasionally these journeys are sufficiently secret to mean the smuggling through of the persons concerned.[63]

After Bilbao, the KOS's next most important subordinate satellite in Northern Spain was Vigo which 'works in close touch with the German Consulate through whom the salaries of the members of the Dienstelle are paid':

In some cases the Consul cooperates in Secret Service business. The Dienstelle is also in touch with the local Spanish police and on occasion draws its agents from the Guardia Civil. The monies of the Dienstelle are banked in the name of C F Meyer at the Banco Hispano Americano in Vigo.

Vigo controls Secret Service activities in both Corunna and at Cape Sillerio where there is at least one V-mann in W/T connection with Vigo. There is also obscure reference to a place called Santa Tecla. For the purposes of its work Vigo uses a Mercedes touring car, purchase No. 303339, year 1938, factory No. 409573, model 250, and also a motorbicycle W. 1309/41

The main business of the Secret Service station at Vigo may be classed under the following headings:

1. Observation of movements of shipping. Regular messages are sent to Madrid reporting the passage or movements of shipping and various sea positions off the North-Western coast of Spain. The ordinary references of latitude and longitude are not used, sea positions being distinguished by references to map squares – thus – 211L, 180, 22E.

Great importance is placed on these reports and Vigo now makes use of four steam trawlers who report by W/T and in cipher to Vigo their observations. It seems likely that these steam trawlers belong to the official Spanish Coastal Service which the German Secret Service has successfully penetrated. Their reports are very frequent and fairly regular and on occasion the Secret Service authorities in Madrid attempt to check or corroborate them by reference to a similar Observer Post at Finisterre. To supplement this service Vigo employs at least one agent at Cape Sillerio with whom Vigo is in W/T connection.

The Secret Service activities at Corunna may be similar and at any rate were important enough in March to merit a visit from SOMER from Madrid.

Ships sailing between Eire and Vigo: Since July 1941 the Secret Service station at Vigo has concentrated on the task of planting an agent on ships sailing between Vigo and Eire. Two ships, the *City of Bremen* and the *City of Antwerp,* have already visited the port since July but until October 1941 the Secret Service had failed to get an agent on board. On 9 October 1941, however, the *City of Antwerp* arrived in Vigo and all preparations for placing an agent on board had been made. It included the provision of a reliable postbox in Vigo to which the agent would take mail from Eire and photographic material. This postbox is:-

Antonio Aruna Pereira, Privaia Moderna 5, Ground Floor, Vigo

The Secret Service station at Vigo also maintains a fairly close contact with the local fishing fleets and is extremely nervous lest anti-German feeling should arise among them as a result of sinkings of these craft while out fishing. These craft fish in the Gran Sol and it is clear that they male contact with Irish fishing fleets or even visit Eire in the course of fishing expeditions.

The Section V analysis of the Vigo dienstelle concluded with a summary of its collection priorities:-

(a) Weather and visibility reports from Madrid which are not apparently demanded very often.
(b) Acquisition of British Admiralty charts. Madrid has given instructions that these are only to be acquired if used and marked by course steered, minefields, fortifications, etc.
(c) Report on the fortifications, batteries and guns at Cape Sillerio and Porteveedro Bay.
(d) Contact with an agent, one Paul Alvarez, who in August was on the Magallanes in Vigo and visited the Secret Service station. At this time there was a prospect of his receiving instructions to work in England but this was later abandoned.
(e) In July a special enterprise whose object is uncertain involving the use of a motorboat and a Leica camera with a special exposure matured and a request was made to Madrid for a 'specialist'.[64]

The other major Abwehr centre in the KOS's orbit was Barcelona where

its activities extend to French possessions in Africa, Spanish Guinea, Occupied and Unoccupied France, England and the USA and at least 56 agents are known to be connected to this stele.

The Stelle is in close contact with the Spanish Police, the Seguridad, and the local chief of the Military Police (Jefe of Sector Norte Servicio Informacion Policia Milita), and the relationship is such that the German Secret service are supplied with documents by the Military Police and given detailed information about such matters as attempts to slip illegally across the frontier from France into Spain. It is also probable that the German Secret Service has a close relationship with the local Post Office in Barcelona, and with the Censorship. The following paragraphs contain an account of the various spheres of Barcelona's activities, and such particulars as are known concerning the Barcelona agents operative there.

1. Africa

Barcelona is much concerned with French Morocco and with the insertion of agents into Oran and Algiers is one of its main activities. One method of inserting agents consists in illicit landings by fishing smacks, and the point of departure is sometimes Malaga and sometimes Majorca. Other agents appear to pass through the ordinary travel controls, sometimes making their way round from Spanish Morocco. On several occasions Barcelona agents have been arrested by the Spanish Police and representations have been made in Madrid on their behalf.

One fishing smack expedition left Majorca in May with two agents, MAX and MAURITZ. The expedition was an expensive one, finally involving an expenditure of as much as 67,000 pesetas.

A second expedition left Malaga early in June with four agents, 674 = SIDI, 677 = RAMESES, 679 = ASTRAY and 684 = HANSEN. All arrived safely in Oran and in due course sent back reports through the post to their controls at Barcelona. Such reports included descriptions of the nature of police control in Algiers and Oran, and [corrupt] that for the purposes of communicating such agents Barcelona has a number of cover-addresses in French Morocco.

Another type of agent operative in French Morocco is concerned with obtaining information e.g. from Tunisia, about the French military forces established there, and in June 1941 an agent MOLA, and also an agent V-682 DIEGO alias Miguel Lopez, sent back reports on this.

These agents are kept supplied with money by remittances to special cover-addresses in Oran and Algiers, the sums being generally sent from Madrid.

2. Spanish Morocco

Barcelona is active in building up a connection with Spanish Morocco and also sends agents down the West African coast to Spanish Guinea and Freetown. In February 1941 some enterprise was contemplated in Fernando Po and in July 1941 W/T connection was on the point of being established between Spanish Guinea and Madrid, the Barcelona station being particularly interested in this.[65]

Section V's survey of the Barcelona dienstelle covered the infiltration of agents into France by 'slipping them over the frontier between Cerbere and Perpignan' to operate as far away as Paris, with others 'function as near home as Port Bou where, among other matters they report aircraft sighted there'. Of particular interest to MI5 was the section describing Barcelona's role in infiltrating spies into Britain:

> Barcelona attempted to recruit agents for work against the UK and on one occasion in January 1941 drew Madrid's attention to the presence there of a certain Pal Olchansky who had been trying to get into the British Army and suggested that connection should be taken up with him by the Madrid Secret Service authorities.
>
> Another potential agent of this character is a British subject, Major Thomas Knapman, who had been in Barcelona prior to January 1941 when he went to Lisbon. After months of trying he failed to get a visa, in April 1941, and the Lisbon Secret Service authorities were then contemplating taking him over from Barcelona as their agent. In July, however, it appears that Barcelona was still interested in this man.[66]

This type of ISOS advance warning of an attempt to insert agents into Britain would form the basis of refugee screening conducted in London, and would give MI5 an invaluable advantage in the counter-espionage field. Evidently the Barcelona dienstelle appreciated the need to penetrate its local adversary:

> In September 1941 THEO, official or agent of the Barcelona Station, was planning to set up an energetic organisation against the British Secret Service at a cost of 20,000 pesetas a month. It had been proposed that this organisation should be independent to a large extent of the regular Secret Service work in Spain, but objections were raised to this suggestion.[67]

Barcelona's network also extended to the United States, and ISOS revealed an early success:

> Barcelona runs at least one important agent in North America. This is Pedro Rodriguez Valiente, alias REMUS, V-611. He travels apparently on a Costa Rica passport and until March 1941 was in Rio. On 14 March he left Rio and arrived in New York on 7 June via London. Large sums are remitted to him from Lisbon to the Central Hanover Bank, New York City, or PO Box 766 Grand Central Annex, New York City. In August 1941

> the address for payment was moved to the Banco Nactional, Mexico City. At the end of that month REMUS's callsigns were heard at Barcelona on two wavelengths from New York, and he was then requiring further money for the construction of a transmitter and for general expenses. In September 1941 he was staying at an address, Hotel Mina, Mexico City. He passed as a businessman and old USA soldier.[68]

Barcelona's Central American organisation was headed by an agent codenamed DINTER and by May 1941 was especially well equipped with false passports, many of them from Uruguay. In addition, Barcelona maintained a network of wireless-equipped agents in the Canary Islands originally sponsored by Madrid, and had responsibility for the management of agents on four Spanish ships on the Tenerife route. They were the *Villa de Madrid*, the *Ramon Alonso Ramos*, the *Domine* and the *Taria*, and Section V accumulated a list of twenty-two seamen of various nationalities that were known recruits. A further three, the *Novimar*, the *Cuidad Sevilla* and the *Marnegro*, were part of a network codenamed QUEROL, run by Angel Urzaiz, the managing clerk of Mediterranea Cia, based in Barcelona.

* * *

Although Section V and MI5 came to depend on ISOS, the source was of little help in two areas of great importance to British interests in the Peninsula, and specifically Gibraltar, which was a constant target for espionage and sabotage. However, although some of these operations were sponsored by the Abwehr, the attacks on shipping conducted by frogmen from Spanish waters were planned and executed by Italians who operated entirely independently, and therefore escaped compromise by ISOS. Similarly, Abt. II sub-contracted the infiltration of agents onto the Rock to the Falange, which had its own motives for undermining the British presence. Once again, there was little on ISOS to assist in the interdiction of Spanish spies and saboteurs seeking to damage the Dockyard, apart from the identification of individual Abt. II personalities at KOS who liaised with their Spanish colleagues.

As the Allies learned through their various sources, Abwehr headquarters in Berlin perceived the Peninsula as probably the most productive territory in which to operate with relative freedom, and to infiltrate agents into target Allied countries. As has been seen, both KOs were well staffed, mostly with intelligence professionals with a background that gave them the appropriate language skills. By any measure, the Abwehr represented a formidable, well-resourced opponent.

Chapter VI

GERMAN INTELLIGENCE IN THE MIDDLE EAST

I did not take detective stories or the films as an example for my work. But rather tried to master this trade with sound, serious and diligent work.

Thomas Ludwig, June 1945[1]

One of the Abwehr's greatest challenges was in the Middle East where its activities were undertaken at a severe disadvantage because of the lack of neutral bases from which to run operations, combined with the obvious vital need to collect intelligence in the region, and the ubiquitous nature of the Allies in the form of a large and effective security apparatus, Security Intelligence Middle East (SIME), and the aggressive counter-espionage strategy adopted by the theatre's SIS surrogate, the Inter-Services Liaison Department (ISLD) and latterly by X-2, OSS's counter-intelligence branch.

The only Abstelle in the area was accommodated at the consulate-general in Istanbul, a city teeming with intrigue to create an environment in which the Axis, represented by the Japanese, Hungarians, Romanians, Italians and Bulgarians, schemed to recruit useful sources, winkle out double agents, and frustrate the adversary. Not surprisingly, sharing borders with the Soviet Union, Iran, Iraq and Syria, neutral Turkey was a hotbed of espionage, with the British, in an occupation role across much of the region, adopting an aggressively defensive role against a very considerable Axis threat. However, conditions would change dramatically in February 1944 when the Abstelle, designated a KriegsOrganisation since July 1942, suffered a catastrophic series of defections. Known as KONO (KriegsOrganisation Nehe Orient) the Ast, with a staff of twenty-two, was quite unusual in that its geographic position made it a clearing-house for information across the region, a centre for counter-sabotage, with elaborate plans for Abt. II personnel to prevent the Soviets from destroying Romanian oilfields, and a requirement for an enhanced III/F capability to monitor Allied intelligence operations. Additionally, KONO ran an Abstelle in Ankara, headed by Major Rudolf Roser, and Nests at Izmit, Adana, Alexandretta and Mersin.

The best knowledge of German activities in Turkey, apart from the invaluable ISOS material, came from the defection in January 1944 of a senior I/H officer Erich Vermehren, who was the first to put flesh on the COMINT bones by submitting source PRECIOUS to lengthy 'conversations' and interrogations as indicated by a summary drafted in May 1944 by Gilbert Ryle of SIS's Radio Intelligence Service:

> Source explained that the Abwehr in Berlin relies on KONO Istanbul and its dependencies in the Hatay for the majority of its information on the Middle East. However he is sure that Berlin also have several valuable sources which he thinks reports to Athens or Sofia. His reasons for believing this are as follows:-
>
> In Istanbul KONO used to receive a regular report from Berlin giving Allied Order of Battle in the Middle East. KONO could see from this just what they themselves had passed to Berlin, and it was clear from the balance of the information that there must be a number of additional sources unknown to Istanbul. Judging from dates he had concluded that some good W/T agents must be involved in this number, as well as other sources such as Prisoners of War.
>
> As regards KONO itself, informant explained that their sources of information were nearly all of the 'visiting' agent variety and included no fixed cells at all. The only really regular and sound information they received was from wagon-lits attendants and it followed from this that the only areas on which KONO were kept directly informed were northern Iraq and Syria.
>
> Source claimed that although the reports from these were by no means good, they had enabled the order of battle in northern Iraq and northern Syria to be pretty well established. In consequence they were able to get several cross-checks and had little difficulty in discovering which agents were giving them information planted by ourselves.
>
> Source wished to warn us that it would be most difficult for us to deceive KONO successfully in Baghdad, Aleppo, Beirut or Damascus, since these areas were too well covered. In Egypt, southern Iraq and Persia we could tell what lies we pleased and KONO would be none the wiser.

> In Palestine we would be on thin ice too because just recently a new agent, with the cover-name HELMUTH, had started there who was giving good information. He reported by secret ink letters collected by a wagon-lits conductor in Tripoli. He thought this conductor was probably an agent with the cover-name ARTHUR whom PRECIOUS describes as the best of this type of source.
>
> HELMUTH's reports consisted of eye-witness facts, divisional numbers, etc. and had been very well received. He would be a great danger to any attempts by us at deception in Palestine.[2]

This item, in particular, must have come as a great comfort to the Allied deception planners in Cairo, for they recognised from Vermehren's description that his ARTHUR was actually their asset Ahmed Bey, codenamed DOLEFUL, and that HELMUTH was DOLEFUL's entirely notional sub-source SCEPTIC. The news that the Abwehr felt confident about its assessment of the Allied order of battle was also a relief as the original information on which it was built had been carefully crafted, in exaggerated terms, by another controlled agent, CHEESE. In other words, the Abwehr edifice had been constructed on the most unreliable of shifting sands.

'Turning to W/T agents, source stated that KONO up to the present has no sets working in the Middle East. However, two had recently been dispatched, one by I/Luft and the other by I/Marine.'[3] In assessing this claim, SIS concluded that the I/L transmitter most likely was one of those that had been delivered to a controlled double agent, BLACKGUARD.

> Of W/T sets run from stations other than Istanbul, Source had no detailed information, but thought that they were probably situated in Cairo or Alexandria, and some Syrian town. From Sofia he thought three groups of agents were operating in the Middle East, of which two were good and one bad. Athens also had some W/T agents working. Source knew this because Rossetti, when in Istanbul, had told him that he had sent two successful parties to the Levant.
>
> Of the W/T agents source knew specifically of only one, called COSTA, copies of whose reports had been forwarded to Leverkuehn in Istanbul. He was a good agent, covering several localities and reporting eye-witness facts such as divisional signs, units, etc. which were well looked upon at KONO.[4]

Once again, Vermehren's comments were very reassuring to the SIS analyst who recognised COSTA as a controlled agent, and a member of a wider group codenamed PESSIMISTS.

> Source then spoke of the technique of framing deceptive reports. He insisted that to be convincing, reports must be based on a solid background of eye-witness facts, divisional signs, badges, etc. He himself had sent many reports framed by the Germans for issue to their double agents, and had been much struck by their compelling nature. Continuing on the subject of badges and divisional signs, source claimed that the Germans knew by now knew all the signs and badges which are present in the Middle East, and that deception would have to be especially subtly carried out.
>
> As a matter of general interest, though unconnected with the Middle East, source then spoke of the Allied Order of Battle in England. From reports sent from Berlin to Istanbul he had observed that we had some 60 divisions in England. It was clear, he thought, that this did not represent a sufficient force for the projected invasion of the Continent. However, while it was no doubt possible for us to conceal a few extra divisions here and there, he could hardly suppose that any large additional force could be hidden from German agents in England, and he had been much puzzled as to the truth of the matter.

At this stage, in May 1944, the FORTITUDE deception campaign had been in full swing for several months, so Vermehren's welcome comments amounted to further proof that the cover-plan for OVERLORD, the landings set for Normandy in early June, was having the desired effect on the enemy. It must have been quite an irony for those engaged in preparing and delivering the scheme to receive advice from an I/H officer, albeit one having been based in Istanbul until recently. Doubtless there was also some mirth at Vermehren's claim that the Abwehr in Turkey is 'ludicrously understaffed and cannot hope to compete with the British and American I.S. whose members outnumber the Abwehr by nearly 10–1'.

> Vermehren stated that when he first arrived in Turkey the KO relied for its estimations of the worth of its sources entirely upon the comments passed by Fremde Heere West upon the veracity and importance of the reports submitted to the Abwehr HQ. These appreciations were not very satisfactory since they depended upon Fremde Heere West processing independent evidence by which to check the veracity of the reports of the KO's agents. Later on KO was put on the distribution list with the Service Attachés, for OKW Situation Reports and order-of-battle charts. In many cases [Erich] Lochner was able to show that the information available to the OKW was inferior to that got from some of the KO's sources. Vermehren gave the impression that there was no centralised grading-office responsible for assessing the bona-fides or the acumen of agents. Though Vermehren was not interrogated upon the point, he did

> not seem to be aware of the existence of any machinery for scrutinizing the long-term record of an agent for symptoms of control or indirect chicken-feeding.[5]

When Vermehren arrived at KONO there were already three missions operating in Persia, originally established as stay-behind organisations intended to operate after the Anglo-Soviet occupation of the country, which happened in August 1941. One was headed by the SD's Fritz Mayr, the second by his friend, I/L's Ramon Gamotha, and the third by the German vice consul in Tabriz, Berthold Schultze-Holthus. This was the foundation upon which KONO sought to develop a network to engage in sabotage, foment rebellion and collect intelligence, but the unexpected Allied invasion disconnected Mayr and Gamotha, working since November 1940 under commercial cover, from the legation on which they had relied to communicate with Berlin via the pouch. However, within a month of the arrival of the Allies in Tehran, Gamotha, a 23-year-old former Vienna University medical student, was arrested by the NKVD, and would eventually be interned in December 1942 as he crossed the border into Turkey, having apparently escaped from Soviet captivity.

At the end of July 1942 three SD agents accompanied by a Farsi interpreter were dropped in support of Schultze-Holthus. Codenamed ANTON, the group led by Martin Kurmes consisted of two young Waffen-SS radio operators, 23-year-old Kurt Piwonka from Vienna and 19-year-old Kurt Harbers from Oldenburg, and a translator, Homayoun Farzad. The team had been flown from the Simferopol airbase in the Crimea and was captured eight months later, in March 1944. A few days later Kurmes, a fanatical Nazi, committed suicide before he could be interrogated by throwing himself out of a Tehran hospital window, simultaneously killing his SIME guard. The others proved cooperative, and although Piwonka and Harbers were detained, Farzad proved to be as pro-British as his brother Massud, who was employed as a BBC radio announcer in London, and was released following five days of intensive interrogation at SIME's Palestine facility, the former Cistercian monastery at Imas in the village of Latrun.

Aged 25, Mayr narrowly escaped a trap in November 1942 when he was betrayed to SIME by an associate. However, some of his documents were recovered, and these compromised much of his network, leading to the arrest of 150 suspects, He was finally arrested at gunpoint in August 1943 by SIME's Defence Security Officer, Joe Spencer, a pre-war petroleum engineer who knew the country well. Under interrogation Mayr, described as a 'master of subterfuge' with a 'strange personality', revealed how he had fought in Poland with the 1st Prussian Armoured Division before working in Moscow for a German economic mission between December 1939 and February 1940. Upon his return to Berlin he had joined the SD, and in October that year travelled to Pavlevi with Gamotha, under Nouvelle Iran Express Company cover. When questioned, Mayr was at a considerable disadvantage as SIME had the benefit of his diary that had been captured in Isfahan in November 1942, when he had been forced into hiding.[6] Whilst a fugitive, he had been joined at the end of March 1943 by six more agents who landed by parachute at Siyah Kuh on a mission codenamed FRANZ, consisting of Karl Korel, a 38-year-old Persian interpreter who would succumb to illness soon afterwards, and radio operators Georg Grille, Hans Holzapel, Werner Rockstroh, Hans Graepe and Otto Schwerdt.

The first of the FRANZ team to be captured was Rockstroh, caught with his transmitter in a house in Tehran owned by a dentist, Dr Qudsi. The raid also yielded Holzapel and his radio, and led SIME to Grille's hideout, where his wireless was also seized. Finally, Mayr too was betrayed, and he was taken into custody. Information extracted from the prisoners then resulted in an ambush in which two more Abt. II saboteurs, members of the ANTON mission, Günther Blume and 22-year-old radio operator Ernst Kondgen, were caught.

In October 1943 Mayr was flown to Cairo for further interrogation, and would remain a detainee until his escape in August 1946. The only other agent to return to Germany during wartime was Schultze-Holthus who, uniquely, would be freed in January 1945 through a prisoner exchange negotiated through the Red Cross in Switzerland in return for Ferdinand Rodriguez-Reddington, an SIS wireless operator who had been arrested in France as part of the ALLIANCE network and condemned to death. Codenamed PIE, Rodriguez-Reddington had been exfiltrated from France at the end of his first mission in October 1942, but had been captured on his second in Aulnay sur Bois in September 1943, together with Jean-Pierre Sneyers, who was executed in August 1942 in Heilbronn.

Despite the efforts made to build up the networks in Persia, all three missions failed, largely because of SIME's skilful exploitation of ISOS. In retrospect it becomes obvious that the missions to Iraq and Persia were doomed to fail. The teams were operating at the limits, with little chance of resupply from the Luftwaffe which suffered a shortage of the Fw 200 Condor and the Junkers Ju 290, the only two aircraft with the necessary range. The nature of their missions was ill-defined, conditions for radio communications with Berlin poor, and the opportunity of exfiltration overland through enemy-occupied Syria to neutral Turkey very uncertain. Finally, the participants themselves, all volunteers, had been briefed that they would be executed if captured by the Allies, but almost all agreed to cooperate with their interrogators at Maadi in the hope of surviving the war, which they did in internment camps in Australia.

* * *

As a reflection of the need for vigilance, KONO possessed an unusually large III/F staff, led by an exceptionally able officer, Thomas Ludwig, who was described by SIS as highly competent. 'Certain of the junior members of the German embassy staff in Istanbul were undoubtedly scared of Ludwig who posed as a mystery man, and he was believed always to have attempted to dissuade his colleagues from greeting him in the street in order no doubt to foster that impression.'[7]

A 46-year-old painter, Ludwig had joined the Abwehr in Munich as an office clerk in 1933 but, after having served in Salzburg and Vienna, in 1939 was promoted to III/F. Soon after the outbreak of war he was posted temporarily to the Belgrade embassy, where he met and married a typist, Ilse Martens, who would become his assistant. In 1936 she had lived in London and Chester with an English family as an *au pair.* Ludwig was then sent on a short assignment to Otto Wacher's III/F office at headquarters in Berlin, and in May 1941 was appointed by III/F's chief Colonel von Egbert Bentivegni to Istanbul where he was subordinate to Walter Schulze-Bernett until May 1943 when he was replaced by Paul Leverkuehn, acting as assistant military attaché.

Descended from an old Hanseatic trading family in Lubeck, where his father had been a judge, Dr Leverkuehn had worked pre-war in Bremen as a lawyer. Having spent much time in Scotland in his youth, he was fond of quoting Scottish poets. According to his MI5 file he had 'remarkable connections in USA as firm had very good reputation in America as one of the most expert in international corporation laws'. He lived in Istanbul's Park Hotel and his office was on the first floor of the consulate in Beyoglu.[8]

Much of MI5's information about KONO originated from Eberhard Momm who had been appointed to a commercial post, as a mohair buyer, in Istanbul in November 1940. Although he never enjoyed the access or status of Ludwig, Momm had a very different perspective and, as he explained during his interrogation in Salzburg in October 1945, was recruited into KONO by Leverkuehn in July 1942

While under interrogation at Camp 020 in May 1945, having been detained in Liverpool aboard the *Drottingholm,* Ludwig undertook to tell the truth because, as he saw it, there was 'no longer any point in concealment'. He then proceeded to explain how the KO personnel were accommodated across the city under a variety of consular, diplomatic and commercial covers, ranging from the naval attaché's office to private firms, such as Schneider. The organisation included representatives from the SD, the Gestapo, the Nazi Party, the Reich Foreign Ministry's own intelligence agency and the KO Bulgaria, which delegated responsibility for operations aimed against the Turks to Dr Schubert. His assistant, Herbert Rittlinger, ran the agents in Istanbul with Rittmeister Oppenborn based in Ankara. In addition, Ast Vienna had yet another organisation, headed in Sofia by a former tobacco importer, Hektor Ducidma. For each overlapping organisation Ludwig provided a comprehensive breakdown of the staff, their assignments and a brief profile of the personalities. For the Nazis, Ludwig identified Liebl as head of the adesgruppe, who had introduced him to the man who would become his chief agent, Alexander Nikolovic, in 1942, the year that Liebl was succeeded by Mani Lippold.

Finally, Ludwig explained KONO's relationship with the other Axis powers, with Italian liaison handled by Clemens Rossetti, who spoke the language fluently, although Ludwig described his reports as 'almost worthless', with the exception of the material relating to Turkey, which he judged 'very good'. Additionally, Walther Hinz, the I/H deputy leiter, held regular meetings with the SIM representative, Lieutenant Andora. The Hungarians were represented by the military attaché, Colonel Haatz, who would be replaced after he was implicated in illegal currency dealing by Colonel Bartalsi who was 'not very pro-German'. Liaison with the Bulgarians took place largely in Sofia through the local KO where Colonel Wagner had developed a close relationship with his opposite number, Colonel Kostov. Just as Ciki, the trade attaché of the Hungarian Consulate, had been run by Ast Vienna, the Romanian vice-consul, Uhrlatzlanu, was also on the SD's payroll. Links with the Japanese intelligence service were also good, channelled through the military attaché Colonel Yatamati, and the press attaché Mori Aoki. The Spanish service was headed by a Russian émigré, Vladimir Velikovsky, who appeared to be a mercenary, relying on leaks from the Soviet embassy and selling information to no less than seventeen other agencies. To complicate matters further, Velikovsky also worked in Sofia for Hauptman Koller of Ast Vienna. Finally, Ludwig disclosed that the Afghan minister in Ankara was also an SD asset.

As for German relations with the Turks, Ludwig described them as a two-tier arrangement, with a secret, semi-official link between Colonel Celal with Leverkuehn and then his successor Colonel

Walther Hinz; and a more formal contact between Kamal Zaya and Hinz. The latter was exceptionally qualified to cultivate the MIT leadership, having been pre-war a Professor of Oriental Languages at Gottingen University, and fluent in Persian, Arabic, Turkish and classical Greek.

> To sum up, the Turkish Intelligence service was very adept at exploiting for its own ends all the powerful intelligence services available in the country. It accepted money from all of them, except the Russians, to swell its funds and carry out the most intensive intelligence activity against Russia with those funds.[9]

Long before his arrival in Liverpool, Ludwig was well-known to MI5 and SIS, and the latter reported that 'according to Vermehren and others he had thoroughly penetrated the British Intelligence Service in Turkey and the office of the Ministry of War Transport'. Nicholas Elliott of SIS's Section V referred to Ludwig as 'a somewhat Phillips Oppenheim character' and observed that

> Although probably the most able Abwehr officer in Istanbul, Ludwig was regarded as somewhat of a joke by certain of his colleagues on account of the hypersecretiveness of his behaviour. He kept his work very much apart front that of his Abwehr colleagues and, with the possible exception of in the first place Leverkuehn, and later Pfeiffer, it is unlikely that any of them were allowed access to his records.[10]

Upon arrival in Istanbul he had been billeted at the Pera Palace Hotel and allocated a green Fiat for his transport. Ludwig reported directly to the Berlin referent for Turkey, Hans Milo Freund, and that when he arrived in Istanbul he had little experience and nothing more than 'an empty desk'. His task was to collect intelligence, principally against the Allies (rather than the Turks) and it was similar to the challenge faced by his colleagues in, for example, Spain and Portugal, who were seeking to send agents to England and the United States. Retrospectively, Ludwig described how he had made a distinction between various types of agent, and double agent:

> From the outset I adopted the principle of:-
>
> (1) Having only a few agents, trustworthy and well-trained ones;
> (2) Sending as few individual reports to HQ as possible, but rather intelligence material which was essentially complete.

In III/F we differentiate between:-

'E' (Erkunder) agents and
'GV-Leute' (V-Leute being Gegner) i.e. 'double-agents'.

'E' agents are those who are in a good position to provide information, for example, independent agents or agents who are attached to Intelligence services in the country from which information is required. Or who have connections with such persons. Under this category I have the following agents:-

ROZNICUK
HENDLE, the link with-
DURANT
FEILAND
MISSIR
STREITER, the link with –
OPIENSKY

I started by giving [Alexander] Nikolovic, who was by no means well-trained, an idea of the type of thing he would be expected to do by allotting him troublesome old jobs and after about six months – so far asI remember this must have been the end of 1942 – I had my first success.

Nikolovic became acquainted with Lieutenant-Colonel Penic, Head of the Yugoslav Intelligence Service, and shortly afterwards with Edouard Moussat who was at that time working in the French Intelligence Service. Some time later he became acquainted with the British Intelligence officers Archibald Gibson and Roman Sulakov. Soon afterwards he went on an espionage mission on behalf of the three above-mentioned Intelligence services to Germany and the Balkan States, the results of which were regarded as 'useful'. It was soon apparent that the false intelligence supplied by the Berlin HQ was usually examined very critically by the British Secret Service and stood the test only with great difficulty, whereas it was comparatively easy to satisfy the other intelligence services.

Nikolovic adapted himself extremely well to III/F work once he had managed to bring about his first success. During the course of the next two years he succeeded in gaining an entrance into almost all the Intelligence services working in Istanbul, and thus came to know, either personally or at least by name, the majority of the most important Intelligence officers.

Contact was also established with the Russian Intelligence service which, on my instructions, was not pursued further, for interference on the part of the Turks had to be avoided as far as possible, for they regarded all persons who had anything to do with Russian agents or intelligence officers with great interest and kept a very strict watch on them.

Finally, a contact was also established with the British Security Service, namely with the equivalent of the III/F Referent in the British Secret Service, a man who called himself 'Mr Roberts'. His real name was also soon reported, for enquiries were made at his home and the landlady told Nicolovic his real name. I have forgotten what it was.

In addition to learning the names and type of work of the majority of the Intelligence officers, the addresses were also known where they were in the habit of meeting agents. If I had possessed a suitable means of surveillance – unfortunately I did not – it would then have been an easy matter for me to identify many other agents. During these three years I was unable to set up even a moderately useful control service capable of working in the town. The Turkish police very quickly got on to the track of all persons thus employed, and made it impossible for them to continue. I then tried to come to an agreement with any of the Turkish police, in which event I was unsuccessful. With this deficit, unfortunately, the results obtained by the III/F Intelligence service, which in themselves were good, could not be adequately exploited.

Finally there followed the last espionage mission to Germany, from which Nicolovic never returned. After his departureI never heard from him again. For this journey he was given missions by the following intelligence services: British, American, Yugoslav and French. He was supplied with a w/t apparatus and received from each of the four services a code for his reporting. He also had a number of addresses which, apparently were not clues to agent-outposts (Agentstellen). I never learned what action Berlin had taken in this matter.[11]

Another of Ludwig's original agents was Paul Glueck, who

was until 1943 an agent of Major Fabian (deceased), at that time III/F Referent of KO Bulgaria. On orders from Berlin (Oberstleutnant Freund) Glueck was sent to me on trial, after Sofia had finished with him. I soon realised that up till then Glueck had had hardly any experience of III/F work, but had mainly supplied Major Fabian (cover-name Dr Maier) with reports on Syria and Palestine from the Turkish Foreign Office. These were mostly of military or economic interest, and he obtained them from Ali Miti Odami, who had been his company commander in the 1914/16 war and eventually became consul for Turkey in Vienna. Glueck also had an even closer connection with Ali Miri's wife which enabled him to pass money to the family in a discreet fashion. With Ali Miri's transfer to Vienna information nevertheless ceased to come in from this source and Glueck had to look around for new sources of information.

At that time Glueck started to have difficulties on account of his Jewish business partner, Weinberger; these were obviously brought about by his competition. He was ordered by the Trade Department of the Consulate, as well as by other German departments, to separate from this partner if he did not want to lose his export license. Glueck, a crafty businessman, calculated as follows: 'I will so contrive that Weinberger supplies me with a source of information, then he will be sheltered by the Abwehr service and that will enable me to continue to maintain my connection with him unofficially'. Thus it happened and Weinberger promptly supplied a contact with the Polish Intelligence Service which later led to the British I.S. I strongly suspect that Glueck discussed these things openly with Weinberger. He was by no means an idealist, but on the contrary put his own interests first. No doubt he had already toyed with the idea that 'if Germany lost the war he, Paul Glueck, would appear on the British side, whereas, if Germany were successful, he would have the favour of the Abwehr on his side'. Glueck named as his spy-master Colonel Edouards, and his assistant, a Mr Browning.

As regards 'information', I handed him for transmission to his British spy-master details of the persons in Istanbul who were working for the NSDAP. The information I gave him was entirely correct, and I gave it to him in this form purposely, in order to give the British service material which they could use against these so-called officials. Naturally, Glueck was unaware of this, but nevertheless in order that I should not be guilty of any indiscretion I subsequently submitted the information provided to my Berlin office for their consent to passing it on.

With regard to the connection established by Glueck with the Russian Intelligence Service, I will deal with this under the heading 'Espionage against Russia'.

Glueck informed me that he had actually told his British spy-masters of his Russian contacts, and the results of conversations with them. It was chiefly a matter of the Russian attempt to bring leading military persons – such as General Rohde, Admiral von der Marwitz – over to the Russian line, General Seydlitz and the German Officers League.

To sum up, it must be stated that Glueck's contacts for III/F were not so productive as they should have been in proportion to the information provided. It was not possible to proceed further as Glueck was expelled from Turkey with the German colony. Since then I have heard nothing further regarding his fate.[12]

Ludwig also described another of his early sources, an individual named Hochleitner who

was a German married to a Turk. He himself was called up for military service in Germany; his wife lives in Istanbul. At the end of 1943 Hochleitner presented himself to the Landesgruppe of the NSDAP and stated that he had been approached by what appeared to be a Czech group requesting him to conceal certain espionage material in trunks, tins of preserves, ladies' handbags and leather cigarette-cases. These obviously were to be given to travellers who were probably unaware of the contents, for delivery to a certain address in Vienna.

I informed Hochleitner – through the offices of the Party – he himself had never seen me – that he must accept the mission and report what it was he was given to conceal and find out if possible when the object was to be sent to Germany and to what address it was to go. Hochleitner reported frequently on what he was given to hide and gave sketches thereof, but was unable to report on any further progress in the matter, so all enquiries led to nothing. At any rate, I did not receive any report of success in this matter.

At the time when relations were broken off Hochleitner was given by his pay-masters a W/T apparatus built into an ordinary wireless set and told to send it to Vienna via the diplomatic courier where it would be taken over.

Hochleitner delivered the set to the Landesgruppe of the NSDAP. It could not be delivered because travelling on the railway was no longer possible in August. It is still in the Consulate in Istanbul, among the packages left behind.

Another of Ludwig's well-placed contacts was Dr Burman:

He was an agent of Ast Romania. I became acquainted with him through Oberstleutnant Freund. After that he paid me two brief visits in Istanbul. I myself did not employ him as an Intelligence agent. All I know of his activities is that he had dealings with the [US] Office of War Information in Istanbul and paid frequent visits to the Ambassador, [Lawrence] Steinhurd, on his trips to Istanbul. His reports must have been chiefly of a political nature.

He worked in close collaboration with Dr Arthur Tester who was resident in [corrupt] and produced a British passport. I met him on the rare occasionI thatI met Dr Burman and after that did not see him again.

Another agent known to Ludwig was Urlatzlanu, 'the Romanian Vice-Consul':

He was a double agent of [Bruno] Wolf's SD office. I do not know him personally. But I once heard from Wolf that Urlatzlanu had performed very good work for him. In particular he brought a W/T apparatus to Bulgaria on the orders of the American Intelligence Service which gave Wolf the opportunity to send out false information by that means. I heard later that, after some time, the Americans began to doubt

> his genuineness in this matter. I do not have anything more detailed about him.

Ludwig also listed Heinrich Ritzer, described as a

> confidential clerk to the firm Schierger of Istanbul. A double agent of Major Fabian (KO Bulgaria). He was given missions by the British intelligence officer [Arthur Ellington] of Istanbul, and was also in contact with the American and Russian Intelligence services. I do not know Ritzer personally and cannot go into details regarding his activities.
>
> At the beginning of 1944 Ritzer was transferred to Sofia, and, according to whatI heard, employed in Hungary by Major Fabian.

Ludwig also described 'the cat-gut merchant from Sofia whose nameI no longer recall'.

> He was one of Major Fabian's good double agents and travelled fairly frequently to Turkey. As far as I know, his activities were chiefly concerned with the American Intelligence service and he had already been working in this capacity, undetected, for a number of years. At any rate, Fabian always had a high opinion of him. I do not know any details of his activities.[13]

Another of Fabian's double agents was Heinrich Rauh, allegedly

> a representative of the Hamburg firm Eleka. A double agent of Major Fabian, he travelled frequently to Istanbul and came into contact there with British and American Intelligence centres. In 1943 he received from British circles some quartzes which were intended for a w/t apparatus which was to be set up in Hamburg. I do not know to what extent this undertaking was carried out.

Ludwig also described Halidun Vhibi,

> a Turkish citizen, possibly a double agent of the Turkish Intelligence service, worked in Istanbul. The predecessor of Herbert Ritzinger in Istanbul was a certain Thanen who had been sent by Dr Delius of Sofia in order to run a military intelligence service to work against Turkey. This Halidun Vhibi who simultaneously was in close connection with Oberst Celal continually offered to help Trauten by supplying him with information of a military nature. It is quite obvious that he had done this in collaboration with Celal. Subsequently Halidun promised to provide important reports which, however, never appeared; and, from what

I heard, he was still in contact with German espionage services right up till the time of the breaking off of (diplomatic) relations. He demanded large sums of money, promised much but in the end produced little or nothing. I do not know him personally, and never worked with him, not even indirectly.

Ludwig also knew of Sefik Yasa,

a Turkish citizen, a barrister in Istanbul, possibly a double agent of the Turkish Intelligence Service. He had connections with Dr Delius (1940 in Bucharest), Trues (head of the Freight Control Office (Frachtonicleitstelle) in Istanbul, 1942) and Zaehringer (office of the naval attaché, Istanbul, 1944). He tried to interest the German Stellen in attempts against Allied embassies and leading Turkish personages. He stated that he was acting on behalf of a group of influential Turkish generals who were dissatisfied with Izmet Inonu's government and wanted to have dealings with German circles. This also was obviously a case of a double agent of the Turkish Intelligence Service who in this instance was acting more in the nature of an agent-provocateur.[14]

Ludwig's position with KONO gave him a supervisory role over the range of its operations which was almost entirely dependent on agents. In summary, KONO ran four main categories of networks, the first of which was a railway reporting group based on the Istanbul-Baghdad line which gave its staff opportunities to make observations while travelling through British-held territory, and to act as couriers. Among the sleeping-car attendants identified by Ludwig were Bahri Karth and by least four others, codenamed BLIST, GOLD, KUPPER and SILBER.

This network was headed by the redoubtable Paula Koch who was based in Adana, having been employed as a midwife in Beirut for many years. She had also worked as a nurse in China and Brazil, and was well-known for offering support to Syrian deserters. Her principal aide was Michael Mikojan, who operated under journalistic cover as the Levant correspondent for the German TransOcean News Agency. Described by Georg Hansen as 'worth any ten Abwehr officers', Koch was 'rebellious and difficult to handle, refusing to take orders from anyone younger than herself'.

Her principal agent was one Josef Ayvazyan to who she referred always as her 'Milchbruder' (half-brother), for Ayvazyan, an Armenian, had been adopted as a baby by her parents and brought up with her at the time when the Turks were persecuting the Armenians. Between them, the woman and Ayvazyan, aided by a few Italians who may also have been on her strings, obtained reports out of Syria of reasonably good value.[15]

Koch's other sources included Arab deserters and Syrian nationalists, and assistance from the Turkish Intelligence Service (MIT) on matters relating to the Soviets. As Ludwig explained,

> in the opinion of the German Intelligence who were most deeply involved, intelligence work against Russia was only possible with the knowledge and the open assistance of the Turks. In this respect the Turkish Intelligence service, as far as the German experience goes, is so alert that scarcely one undertaking in this sphere remained unknown to them.
>
> For example, a reconnaissance expedition to the Caucasus prepared by Zaehringer in 1942 failed completely because the members were quietly arrested by the Turks in Jars and Ezrun. The expedition consisted of three groups, each of seven men, one of whom was a radio-operator with a set, weapons, code, etc. Zaehringer waited for months for news that one group, at any rate, had arrived. It finally transpired that the Turkish counter-espionage service had insinuated a certain Kazim into the scheme from the very beginning and was consequently precisely informed from the first of all preparations for the journey.
>
> Widmann initiated a similar undertaking for the SD. Said Dalil and Befesuklu took part in this venture which consequently had Turkish approval and was apparently, as far as I learned at the time, successful.
>
> The disadvantage of this procedure was that though the German Intelligence service paid the costs, the Turks received any intelligence acquired first, and passed it on second-hand and appropriately abbreviated, without doubt, to the financier, the German Intelligence service. The SD availed itself again of that procedure, despite its disadvantages.
>
> A further source of intelligence about the Russian armed forces was the contact between Dr Leverkeuhn and Colonel Celal. I do not know how this contact was originally made. It took place in the following way; a man, whose cover-name was AUEST and who was in fact called Fauii Serhatli, and a member of the Celal Bureau, rang up Dr Leverkuehn and announced that he would call on behalf of Colonel Celal.
>
> In practice the result of the contact was that Celal supplied information about Russia for which Dr Leverkuehn paid relatively dearly, and received in exchange German information about the British forces in the Near East.
>
> A further contact with the Turkish Intelligence service, Kemal Ziya, likewise a member of the Celal Bureau. This operation was through Oberstleutnant Hinz. Kemal Ziya never revealed that he belonged to

a Turkish Intelligence department. I am nevertheless convinced that he had this contact with Hinz with the knowledge of Celal. Ziya supplied chiefly the results of interrogation of Russian deserters who had crossed the Turkish frontier to Haru and Hrzorun.

A very productive – and yet according to reports – unreliable source of military information against Russia was directed by Vladimir Velicovic, intelligence member of the Spanish embassy in Istanbul. After his expulsion from Istanbul he continued to work in Sofia with almost the same connections for Hauptmann Koller (Ast Vienna). I do not know his sources. I am however of the opinion that they were based on Turkish informers, namely Sayed Samil, Hamal Matschili, Heresvili.

In 1942 the Foreign Office sent several specialists on Russia and the Caucuses to Istanbul, of whom only Vice Consul de Haas remained at the Consulate-General until the end. All the others returned at the end of a few months. De Haas probably had a small intelligence service against Russia, depending on chance items of information.

Boris Horn, Turkish citizen, of Istanbul, agent of Hauptmann Koller, Ast Vienna, was a former collaborator of Velikotni. He supplied good information about Russian personalities in Istanbul embassy and Intelligence staff. I do not know his subordinate sources. Horn is a Russian émigré.

Boris Archipov, Czech citizen, agent of Zaehringer, from whom I too obtained occasional information, drew up lists of all Russian with notes about their political opinions. He was imprisoned for about a year in Ankara because he was erroneously implicated in an affair of Turkish military espionage by Velikotni and Sarafanov. I believe he was eventually exonerated.

Paul Glueck is the only political intelligence link I could make with the Russians. He was commissioned by me to report to the British Intelligence officers in Istanbul his conversations with the Russians in the Summer Embassy at Buyukdere. Apart from some personal information about the German colony in Istanbul it was mainly a question of directing leading German soldiers and politicians to the line taken by General Seydlitz – Free Germany – German Officers' League. As a result of my internment, the contact had not developed further.

Through Dr Leverkuehn I tried once or twice to exploit the link with Colonel Celal for Abwehr III/F work. Unfortunately I had no success, although Celal did not decline.

To sum up, it was difficult for all of us to develop against Russia contacts which were really durable and supplied more than chance items of Intelligence.[16]

* * *

During his interrogation, which lasted for five months until October 1945, Ludwig was cross-examined on the seven main sources he had listed, beginning with Lieutenant Roznicuk, a Czech codenamed FRANZ who had been recruited originally by the naval attaché's office.

> He became my first agent and up to mid-1942 the whole of my information was obtained from him. His reports were completely reliable for he had had practical experience in his work. He reported on the following subjects:-
>
> 1. Organisation of the British Intelligence Service in Turkey.
> 2. Organisation of the Czech Intelligence Service in Turkey.
> 3. Organisation of the Polish Intelligence Service in Turkey. (He supplied photographs and personal particulars of the intelligence officers concerned.)
> 4. Organisation of the espionage school in Jerusalem in which he himself had taken part.
>
> He further gave information regarding a very important English/Czech agent who was working for the British and Czech Secret Service in Belgrade. Besides supplying military information, he had betrayed the knowledge which the German Intelligence Service personnel had concerning British Intelligence officers. The agent used the cover-name FRANZ JOSEF for his Czech Intelligence work. Roznicuk did not know his real name; all he could say was that FRANZ JOSEF must be 'a senior figure in the Gestapo in Vienna or Prague'. I sent this report on to Berlin and received a reply to the effect that they had similar reports from other quarters and that all details would be of value. Eighteen months later I learned that it had concerned an official of Ast Prague, named Holm.
>
> At the end of 1941 Roznicuk was recognised by his superiors as a German agent, and was to be transferred to Jerusalem. In view of this state of affairs he took refuge in the German Consulate and remained hidden there for three months. With the aid of Zaehringer (of the Naval Office) we were able in the spring of 1942 to smuggle Roznicuk into Bulgaria in a sailing-boat. Here he was taken over by Major Fabian, the III/F Referent of KO Bulgaria.[17]

Helpfully, Ludwig gave a detailed accounting of his principal agents, identifying Friedrich Hendle as

> a German citizen, born in Istanbul. Had been an agent of the naval attaché since 1933, I took him over in 1942. He had two connections which were valuable:-

a) Mrs [Mariana] Dumont, employed by Mr Walton in the office of the Shipping Department in Istanbul. She passed to Hendle all correspondence which was of interest to the German Service, For instance, they wanted to know about the SFND lawsuit (and in particular the date of the coming trial). The material that I obtained from this source I passed on to Dr Leverkuehn without any comment since it as not within the scope of my work.

b) This connection was betrayed to the British Secret Service by Vermehren. Mrs Dumont was arrested, and Hendle obtained a personal report from her in this respect. Mrs Dumont neither asked for nor received any compensation for her services. I do not know her personally; according to Hendle she did it out of admiration for Adolf Hitler.[18]

Next on Ludwig's list was Resid Yumnu, 'a Turkish citizen employed in the Office of War Information (OWI), Istanbul. Through him Hendle obtained information regarding changes in personnel in the OWI. These reports were not exactly valuable but were useful in answering individual questions. Yumnu also did not receive any remuneration.'

Rolf Freiland was described as

> a German citizen, representative of business firms. Up till 1943 Freiland had been working as an agent of the I-Luft office, and was then transferred to me. He had three useful connections:-

a) A woman (whose name I do not know) with the cover-name ELLI. She had contacts in OWI through which she was able to report on matters of personnel. These provided a valuable background for piecing together the reports sent by Yumnu.

b) A contact in the office of the Italian Oberstleutnant Levesi which produced copies of reports on the German Intelligence Service which Levesi was giving to the Allies. On one occasion this contact produced valuable information from these reports for two persons were mentioned therein when Meringer was intending to send in w/t operators to Persia. Their dispatch was thereupon controlled. In general, however, the reports were very bad and full of inaccuracies and downright fabrications; the source was not to blame for this, but the Italian informant.[19]

Ludwig then mentioned two Italians, Skembry and D'Andria, 'who had been working for the British Service, put themselves at the disposal of the Germans. Nothing came of this however, as the breaking off of [diplomatic] relations occurred before things got beyond the initial stage.'

Next was Emil Missir,

> a German citizen in Izmir. From the beginning of the war until mid-1943 Missir was an agent of KO Bulgaria. He was then given to me. He had had to procure information of a purely military character for Bulgaria, so I had to train him in III/F work.
>
> We never found any GV (double agent) connection, but on the other hand created a number of useful E connections with among his Italian friends. At the beginning of 1944 I was able for the first time to give a fairly accurate description of the set-up of the British Intelligence service in Izmir, the correctness of which was confirmed by statements made by Intelligence officers from Izmir who were caught by the German I.S. in Greece. Neither Missir norI had anything to do with that incident. I merely obtained a summary afterwards of the intelligence in their statements. I do not know Missir's sub-agents. I believe his information was derived chiefly from Italian sources.[20]

The sixth source was

> a journalist, German citizen editor of the *Boyoglu*. Actually, Streiter was never an agent of mine. I add him here because on one occasion he put me in contact with a very good contact namely:-
>
> Stanislav Opiensky, an employee of the Polish Consulate-General in Istanbul, and a National Democrat. In the spring of 1944, Scheffter whom I knew slightly through his friend Ehrnau (KONO II) came to see me and said that he had become acquainted with a certain Opiensky from the Polish Diplomatic Staff who had disassociated himself from the present policy of the Polish Government and was on bad terms with the Consulate. It was possible that he might be transferred to Palestine, which Opiensky in no way desired. Streiter was of the opinion that Opiensky could be useful to the Germans from the point of view of espionage, and later politically. I agreed with this suggestion and said I would be prepared – if Opiensky so desired – to bring about his departure for Germany en route to Poland. At the same time I asked Streiter to sound out Opiensky in a discreet manner, from the point of view of the Intelligence Service. Shortly after that Streiter produced a complete list of the Polish Intelligence Service in Turkey which, however, did not give agents but only people in the Consulate who were working for the Intelligence service with their real and their cover-names. Beyond this, there was not much important material of a III/F nature forthcoming

> because Opiensky frankly did not know very much. Thereupon he wrote to his Consulate saying he was handing in his resignation and thinking of settling down in Istanbul as a private individual. A few months later Opiensky was arrested by the Turkish police and deported to Bulgaria. I made arrangements for him to be sent to Vienna where it had been agreed he was to be run by Streiter. In the meantime I was interned and heard nothing further, from Streiter or from Opiensky.

In addition, Ludwig mentioned two other sources, one of whom was codenamed HILFIS:

> I do not know his real name. Had been an agent of the Naval Attaché for many years and was apparently a police official. In addition to purely naval intelligence he produced III/F information regarding personalities, intelligence centres, the organisation of the police and of the Turkish Intelligence Service. Also original correspondence which had to be photographed and returned immediately. Further, occasional lists showing travel arrangements.[21]

The second source was codenamed UTUBRAND:[22]

> Information from this source was passed by an agent of III/F who was a sleeping-car attendant. Who he is, even IDEZ [corrupt] does not know, It consisted of photographic extracts of English correspondence which contained a part of the interrogations of Vermehren, Hamburger and Kleckowski (for example, there was no mention therein of me or my work). Quite obviously they were those extracts from the investigation which the British service passed on to the Turkish service. This correspondence carried neither addressee nor signature. From the same source I received an English instruction on the handling of double agents and other agents which was not particularly interesting nor enlightening as it contained nothing but universally-known principles.[23]

During his interrogation Ludwig expanded on the problems created by the Abwehr's requirement to obtain a clearance from Berlin for every item passed to a double agent.

> It is strictly forbidden for all III/F officers, under threat of severest punishment, to give out any item of information before it has been submitted for specific approval to the appropriate department in Berlin, i.e, Referat, III D (Oberst Dr. Schlaufer). In exceptional circumstances – so long as it was not a matter of military information – this approval could be applied for subsequent to the event. It is obvious that, in a Stelle

> situated abroad with a courier leaving only once a week, this process quickly leads to an exposure of the agent. Further, where the missions concerned troop dispositions or movements or armament production, the information supplied was generally of an inaccurate or insufficient character, and it was generally quickly realised that this was 'feed' material. In order, therefore, to avoid this difficulty, I instructed my agents to suggest that they did not have contacts of a military nature and thus were not given missions of that type which could not be successfully carried out. Material suitable for my purposes I was able to prepare and issue on my own account, and approval from Berlin followed later, in the ordinary course of business.
>
> In the year 1943 when Canaris was still in office, the SD were given sanction to give out 'feed' material to their Stellen which never came to the knowledge of IIID of the Abwehr. This procedure must have led to exposure of the agents, since the main Stelle was at times supplied with entirely contradictory material.[24]

* * *

Apparently eager to assist his captors, Ludwig described the entire German intelligence structure in Turkey, and provided profiles of his former colleagues, beginning with Herbert Rittlinger, the author of several popular pre-war travel guides who had served at the KO Belgrade. He had arrived in Istanbul in 1943 to act as a handler on behalf of KO Bulgaria.

In total Ludwig identified the true names, cover-names and handlers of sixty-four agents of all nationalities, and naturally the British were keen to learn more about any individuals he had suspected of being double agents. In May 1945, in preparation for his interrogation MI5 drew up a questionnaire, which included:

> Details of double agents run by Ludwig to penetrate British and Allied organisations in Turkey, Ludwig may be told that we know Alexander Nikolowitsch to be one of these. Does he know anything of such agents run by the SD? Estimate of the nature and value of information received from those agents. What other methods were used to penetrate Allied organisations, and with what success?[25]

Clearly, there was much concern about the 60-page SIME monograph on the handling of double agents which Ludwig acknowledged having read, as the ISLD double agent BLACKGUARD had reported on in April 1944. A security review at the time had shown two Roneoed copies to have been distributed in October 1942 to only two recipients in Istanbul, Section V's Nicholas Elliott and the Defence Security Officer Istanbul, Guy Thomson.

BLACKGUARD was an Iranian, Hamdi Khaqqay, formerly employed as an announcer on Radio Berlin. He had been supplied with five wireless transmitters to develop his network in Persia, Cairo and India, and in 1943 had been promised two radio operators, named Botetchi and Neshat, but the pair never completed their training. The issue was extremely sensitive because Thompson was a regular attendee at the Kutchuk Bureau, a highly secret joint Turkish-British forum on Axis counter-intelligence information.

According to his SIME file, BLACKGUARD was a 37-year-old businessman who had blamed the collapse of his firm, the Zoroastrian Company, on his political opposition to the government and not on his own mismanagement. In 1938 he had left for Berlin and in January 1943 he had tried to make contact with SIS in Switzerland through a Persian intermediary. In April he had turned up in Istanbul with a plan for the sabotage the Soviet supply route through Iran. Then, on 13 October, he contacted SIME to declare that he had been employed by the Abwehr to deliver

> five w/t sets to various parts of the Middle East, and that he was in personal contact with Leverkuehn, Zaehringer, and von der Marwitz. He had informed the Germans of his ability to send w/t sets to Tehran through the Persian diplomatic bag as a result of his friendship with the Persian vice consul in Istanbul, Fotuhi. Of the five sets available, three were destined to be located in Persia and were to be in direct contact with Berlin from Tehran, Ahwaz and Tabriz, respectively. The first was to be operated by Akbari who was in fact working with one of the German groups in Persia until his arrest by the British authorities in August 1943, while the second was to be operated by KISS, a young Persian who had been recruited by BLACKGUARD and trained by the Abwehr in Berlin. The other two Persians, Botchetchi and Neshat, were introduced by BLACKGUARD to Leverkuehn in July for training as w/t operators, one of them being designed to replace Akbari. The Abwehr then asked BLACKGUARD to send a set to Egypt ... [26]

KISS was a 30-year-old Persian electrical engineering student, Mohamed Salmassi, who had lived in Germany since 1936 and been in occasional contact with the Abwehr since January 1942. Although the Germans had been told that KISS had been arrested in Aleppo in November 1943, and subsequently released, he had in fact been incarcerated continuously since January 1944 at 50 Internment Camp at Sultanabad, outside Arak, and run by SIME's local organisation,

Combined Intelligence Centre Iraq. Far from resisting his interrogators at Aleppo, as BLACKGUARD claimed to his Abwehr handlers, KISS had 'broken' and confessed after three days, based on information supplied by BLACKGUARD himself. Thereafter his transmitter was operated by a SIME officer imitating KISS's rather amateurish style, KISS himself being unaware of this development. KISS proved to be an important case because it required direct liaison between the NKVD, which was active in Soviet-occupied northern Iran, and SIME.

* * *

Three of the key objectives of German intelligence collection in the Middle East were the Allies' regional military headquarters in Cairo, Allied naval activity in Alexandria, and the Suez Canal, a waterway universally recognised as strategically vital for the survival of the British Empire. Following the arrival of Rommel's Afrika Korps in Libya in January 1941, considerable efforts had been made to address the vacuum created by the expulsion of suspect Germans upon the outbreak of war, and then in 1940 by the wholesale internment of Italians residents who were shipped to camps in Australia. Specifically, the Abwehr had lost the benefit of PASCHA, the DNB correspondent Dr Reichert. His replacement was Renato Levi, an Italian agent recruited by Hans Travaglio in Rapallo before the war and then handled by Clemens Rossetti for a mission to Paris in anticipation of the May offensive. Levi, who had the advantage of a genuine British passport through his father's citizenship, apparently performed well, and in December 1940, codenamed ROBERTO, was offered the opportunity to undertake another assignment, this time in Cairo. He accepted, and travelled from Brindisi to Sofia and Istanbul, finally reaching Egypt in February 1941. There Levi established radio contact with an Abwehr station in Bari in July and this link was maintained more or less uninterrupted until the end of hostilities.[27]

With ROBERTO concentrating on I/H material, the Abwehr appointed I/L's Nikolaus Ritter, formerly of Ast Hamburg, to establish a network capable of exploiting local nationalist sympathies, and a plan was drawn up to exfiltrate a senior army officer, General Aziz Ali al-Misri, from Cairo and bring him to Berlin to mobilise a Fifth Column and create a 'Free Egyptian Army'. The same mission was intended to deliver two Arabic-speaking volunteers, Klein and Muhlenbruch, who were to ride an Italian motorcycle into Cairo. The scheme required a Luftwaffe He 111 transport aircraft to land behind British lines, rendezvous with General al-Misri and send Klein and Muhlenbruch on their assignment, but in the event the plane was unable to find the designated airfield, was redirected to Benghazi, ran out of fuel and ditched in the Mediterranean. Although the crew survived, Muhlenbruch was killed, Klein was injured and Ritter, who had insisted on participating in the operation, suffered a broken arm.

Meanwhile, SIME learned from ISOS of al-Masri's intended defection and took him and his two companions into custody on a pretext to protect the source. His co-conspirators, Flight Lieutenant Hassan Ezzat of the Egyptian Air Force and a Signals Corps officer, Captain Anwar al-Sadat, were also court-martialled in October 1942 and interned for the remainder of the war.

The pressure on the Abwehr to rebuild an organisation in Egypt escalated significantly as Rommel, heavily dependent on COMINT, led the Afrika Korps over the Egyptian border towards Alexandria. The greater Rommel's success, the more he demanded reliable intelligence about Allied troop reinforcements brought in from Palestine, Iraq and India, and the level of supplies reaching Egypt from the Red Sea.

The next effort to infiltrate Cairo from Libya, supervised by I/H's Major Franz Seubert, took place in May 1942 when Johannes Eppler, aged 25 and codenamed SALAAM, accompanied by his radio operator Heinrich Sanstede, reached Cairo. They crossed the desert in an epic 1,700-mile journey in two captured Ford V-8 trucks from Tripoli to Assyut with the Hungarian explorer and cartographer Count Laszlo Almassy acting as guide, in just three weeks. A former Egyptian government surveyor, celebrated desert explorer and author of *The Unknown Sahara*,[28] Almassy achieved his objective but Eppler and Sanstede's adventure had been monitored on an almost daily basis by ISOS and therefore was doomed from the outset. Both men, fluent in Arabic and very familiar with Egypt, were ideal candidates for the operation, but they were arrested at their houseboat on the Nile at Agouza by SIME in July 1942 after just a month at liberty. The intervention had been triggered by Eppler and Sanstede making arrangements to return to the German lines, and their denunciation to SIME by an Austrian, Viktor Hauer, to whom they had turned for help with their failed communications.

Under CSDIC interrogation conducted by Harry Shergold, Eppler and Sanstede, with an offer to be treated as prisoners of war and not enemy spies, gave their full cooperation and named the people they had been instructed by Berlin to contact, among them Prince Abbas Halim, Eppler's half-brother Hassan Gaafar, Viktor Hauer, an Austrian employed by the Swedish legation who was in touch with a Viennese physician Fatima Aher, and Abdel Moghny Said Salama. In their very full confession the pair described how they had reached

Assuit from Libya, and then caught a train to Cairo where they had stayed first at a brothel, the Pension Nadia, and then at a rented flat before moving to a houseboat. Their mission had been handicapped, they claimed, by dwindling funds, poor communications, and their inability to exchange messages with their controller at Rommel's headquarters. Since their purpose was to liaise with local pro-Nazi elements who could seize control of the city in the event of a British withdrawal and hold it until the Afrika Korps arrived in force, the pair had decided to abandon their mission. When confronted with some very incriminating entries in Sanstede's diary relating to details of Tobruk's defences, it was claimed that they had been instructed by Rommel's intelligence chief, Colonel Ernst Zolling, to 'obtain plans of the fortifications of Mersa Matruh', a task they had demonstrably failed to accomplish.[29]

Hauer was interned under an alias, to prevent the disclosure of his role in the betrayal of Eppler and Sanstede, and in January 1946, having been arrested in Lauterbach the previous May, Seubert was interrogated in Salzburg by the US CIC. Commissioned just before the end of the First World War while serving in an artillery regiment in the Carpathian Mountains, Seubert, who was fluent in several languages, worked as a travel agent and had joined the Abwehr in 1939 to run its courier services to Italy, Spain and Portugal.

Seubert had been appointed to I/H West in early 1941 and was responsible for Abt. I operations in North Africa, so had been in an excellent position to provide context for what had happened to the SALAAM mission. He recalled that the 'Abwehr I-H strongly suspected that the two men might have gone over to the British'.

Seubert, who had played a supervisory role in the operation, explained how the Abwehr had expanded its coverage of the region, and effectively divided responsibility for the theatre into three distinctly separate chains of reporting. The first was through KOS in Madrid, headed by Wilhelm Leisner, who ran Nests in San Sebastian, Algeciras, Tangier and Ceuta, staffed mainly by Abt. II sabotage personnel.

> Reports on North Africa which came via Spain were usually reliable and frequently of a pessimistic and alarming nature. The strong influence of the high-ranking officers of the German Armistice Commission at the High Command in Berlin caused these reports to be considered as exaggerated. In one instance, a report obtained through high Moroccan personalities, via the outpost at Ceuta, pointed out that British or American landings were expected in the Casablanca region, and that preparations lead to believe that these landings were planned for a

> certain period . . . not far off. This report was ridiculed, torn up, and thrown away in the I-H office; the Allied invasion did take place at the predicted time and location.[30]

Understandably, these Meldestellen concentrated on Gibraltar and were not focused on the collection of military intelligence, a task that fell to Ast St Germain, an important location subordinate to Ast Paris, because of the number of agents recruited from local PoW camps. The prisoners were promised their liberty and free travel back to their homes in North Africa, but most promptly deserted or 'disappeared with valuable equipment'. St Germain improved its performance when Hauptman Pretzel took control of agent recruitment. A former Roman Catholic priest from Bavaria who had converted to Islam and lectured on Semitic languages at Munich University, Pretzel would be killed in a plane crash in 1942.

In March 1941, in support of Rommel's campaign, the Abwehr established an aussenstelle at Tripoli codenamed WIDO under a former cavalry officer, Witilo von Griesheim. As well as liaising with the Italian SIM, WIDO was responsible for intelligence collection across Algeria, Tunisia and French Equatorial Africa. As the Afrika Korps progressed, WIDO moved to Nalut in western Libya, and then to Zuara, near the Algerian frontier.

> WIDO reorganised and intensified the Italian monitoring service in western Libya (Nalut, Gadames, Murzuk, Ghat) and obtained valuable information from the territory of the French colonies, through Arabian agents and through members of the Tuareg tribes. Griesheim's interpreter was a young native of one of the latter tribes. Information on the secret armament of the French Colonial Army, on the establishment and preparation of airfields, and on troop movements was thus obtained. [....]
>
> Most of the time WIDO's personnel consisted only of three radio operators and a driver, who all spoke Italian fluently. They wore civilian-type tropical clothing, associated freely with the Italians, and as a result gained excellent cooperation. The Italian Intelligence Service, like the average Italian officers and troops, was considered inefficient by the Germans. It showed little or no interest in the prosecution of the war. Von Griesheim's appearance at Zuara led to great improvement of the service, partly by his diplomatic behaviour toward the ranking personnel, partly due to his generosity expressed in money and cigarettes directly to subordinate Italian soldiers, as well as to agents and civilians who volunteered information. While von Griesheim's little organisation continued to work in the zone of Libya and Tripolitania it assisted in the

preparation and direction of two separate undertakings, which were in connection with the last big Axis drive to the East eventually stopped at El Alamein.[31]

After the SALAAM operation, WIDO embarked on another ambitious undertaking, codenamed DORA, under the command of Colonel Haeckel and planned from Ast Munster where an I/H headquarters had been accommodated in Rheda Castle in Westphalia.

Air and sea traffic from the American continent to French Central Africa had been carefully observed and the frequent press reports about the formation of a French army under de Gaulle in French Equatorial Africa caused the German High Command to evaluate the seriousness of a threat from that direction. The OKM, as well as Luftwaffenfuehrungsstab, wanted to be informed about the possibility of moving sizeable bodies of troops, particularly mechanized units, from the south against Rommel's flank. The maps of Libya (which had proven to be unreliable) could not be used to answer this question. A special detachment THEODORA of the Ast Munster had already begun a somewhat academic examination of poorly cartographed African territory. Following a suggestion of the young scientist Schulz-Kampfhenkel and based on thorough study of geographical works and maps, a considerable amount of information was gained. The tedious work of piecing together such information was largely performed by university professors who wore assigned to this task as Sonderführers. Interrogation of prisoners from French colonial troops also brought some useful results. The High Command however, was not satisfied with this theoretical approach to the problem. It wanted quick and reliable on-the-spot exploration of the territory between Equatorial Africa and the North African zone of operations, and for that purpose the command DORA was organised by I-H (West). With the consent of the Italian Ministry of War and the assistance of WIDO, the expedition was equipped in Tripoli in the spring of 1942. It was based in Hon, Central Libya and consisted of approximately 30 to 40 men under the command of Colonel Haeckel of the Luftwaffe, with Leutnant Schulz-Kampfhenkel in charge of the scientific work. The latter established an office in Berlin called detachment THEO equipped with the most modern instruments of its kind which compiled and evaluated the results of the expedition DORA as they were transmitted from Africa. The expedition itself used several desert-going armoured cars, two reconnaissance planes, and a glider plane in its work.

After three months of this kind of combined research, the OKW was satisfied that a deployment of enemy troops from French Equatorial Africa into the German flank was extremely unlikely in view of the geographical and geological conditions and could be discounted . . .

While the two special commands SALAAM and DORA were in operation WIDO continued its assigned intelligence work, besides assisting in matters of communications with the two groups. When the British Eighth Army threatened Tripoli, von Griesheim received orders to move his post WIDO to Gabes, Tunisia, which had been occupied by the Germans after African invasion of the Allies. Although the military situation was dangerous and confused von Griesheim succeeded in reaching Gabes, and on his way liberated a part of the Italian Armistice Commission to Tunisia, which had been captured by the French. Upon arrival at Gabes, Dienststelle WIDO was re-activated under the direct command of Abwehrkommando Tunis. As the German-held area contracted von Griesheim was dispatched to Sicily in March 1943 to establish an echelon to which Abwehrkommando Tunis could withdraw. Further developments rendered these preparations futile, and in May 1943 his service for the Wehrmacht was terminated as far as source knows.[32]

Although THEODORA was intended to have a limited assignment and duration, the techniques developed proved valuable and Dr Schulz-Kampfhenkel continued his cartographic work under Colonel Mauer with a staff of 150, as was later recalled by one of his subordinates, Hans Berger, who was interrogated in March 1946.

The scientific work was directed by Dr. Voppel, who in peacetime had been the head of a state cartographical institute in Leipzig. The work was carried out in close cooperation with the Mil Geographical department of OKW. The THEO department enjoyed far greater powers than the Mil Geog department, in that it was allowed to issue completely new maps based on scientific surveyors reports, air photographs, etc, whereas the Mil Geog department could only issue revised editions of old maps.

The THEO department worked out new methods of map-construction, e.g. by making plastic models of the terrain, showing natural features and military targets. These models were particularly valuable for air operations. During the North Africa campaign the department did some particularly useful work on the production of up-to-date maps of the Mediterranean coastal area from Oran to Tripoli, and in the publication of technical data, illustrated by drawings and photographs, on the Algerian-Moroccan railway system.

[.....]

Operation DORA later received a more extensive commission. After the North African Campaign, Colonel Haeckel took some other post outside the Abwehr, but Dr. Schulz-Kampfhenkel was made Reichsförschungsrat and took over the scientific leadership of DORA in the Western and Eastern theatres. The new tasks of DORA were to

> discover the best methods of camouflaging defence-works by means of foliage; to investigate the practicability of the Russian swamp areas for tanks, as illustrated on Russian maps; and to produce new and reliable maps. All these tasks, according to Prisoner, were carried out with great success.[33]

Both during and after the war the Abwehr would be widely criticised by Allied commentators for undertaking essentially short-term missions and employing poorly-trained and ill-equipped personnel, but the reality is that the adverse comment was often made on a fundamental misunderstanding of the organisation's designated role in the Reich's military machine, one that was entirely subordinate to the OKW. Certainly in the Middle East theatre, the Germans were woefully disadvantaged by shifting demands, which reflected the speed of military developments, especially in North Africa, and the strategic decision taken pre-war not to establish long-term, deep penetration networks reporting by radio. Even though the Abwehr's transmitters were judged to be among the best in the world, long-distance radio signals were highly susceptible to atmospheric conditions, a handicap especially prevalent in the Near East. An additional factor was an innate German mistrust of the concept of advance intelligence. Frankly, like their Allied counterparts, few German commanders put much faith in advice based on agent information. The only source worthy of risk was COMINT, on which the OKW (and their Allied adversaries) set much store. It was timely, likely to be accurate and could easily be verified.

The aggressor, as in a Blitzkrieg scenario, needed only tactical reconnaissance and an understanding of the opponent's order of battle, their strengths and weaknesses on a fast-moving battlefield. The stunningly successful Wehrmacht, employing unconventional tactics, had swept through Norway, Holland, Belgium, Denmark, France and the Balkans by exploiting the modern tactics of surprise, swift armoured advances, overwhelming force supported by coordinated ground-attack from the air, and avoiding static confrontations. In such circumstances a high-level political source was interesting, but hardly decisive. And so it proved. The further in distance from Berlin, the more academic the issue.

The Abwehr possessed a nuisance value across the Middle East and could stir up local resentment against Allied occupations, but was unlikely to have any lasting impact on the prosecution of the war. Indeed, just as the Allied commanders came to depend on COMINT, and were otherwise sceptical of most intelligence sources, their opponents also prized what SIGINT they received.

Chapter VII

SOUTH AMERICAN INTRIGUE

> The SD Group in the Argentine, despite warning from headquarters, is still more active and successful in intrigue than in obtaining intelligence
>
> MI5 B(1) Information Note, 1 March 1944[1]

According to information supplied by Herbert Wichmann, and circulated by MI5, South America had long been a priority target for Abwehr reporting. His interrogation in August 1945 prompted these observations from SIS:

> As far as we know, Hamburg had networks in Brazil, Chile, Mexico and the US. Subsidiary networks were organised from Brazil into Argentina, from Chile into Peru, Ecuador, Colombia and Venezuela. Agents in Mexico worked closely with agents in the USA and Chile. The South American network was largely directed by [Hermann] Bohny, German Naval Attaché Rio de Janeiro; Ludwig von Bohlen, German Air Attaché in Chile; and Dietrich Niebuhr, German Naval Attaché to Brazil and Argentina. By the summer of 1942 three networks had been largely liquidated and most of the leading agents had been arrested or deported.
>
> Since this time however, there has been evidence that Hamburg has maintained organisations in Chile and Argentina and Mexico and had attempted to re-establish reporting from Brazil. Briefly, this evidence is as follows:
>
> Chile
>
> A group of agents directed by Ludwig von Bohlen and, after his return to Germany in the autumn of 1943, by Bernardo Timmerman, reported air intelligence to Hamburg, using Spanish seamen couriers supplied by General Wolf, German Military, Naval and Air Attaché in Buenos Aires (now in Camp 020). A W/T link with Hamburg was set up for a time, but proved unsatisfactory. Kuhlenhauer was the W/T operator.

The group operated up to the summer of 1944 when Kuhlenhauer and Timmerman were arrested.

Brazil

Two agents, Kopff and Bauer, were dispatched to Brazil in the summer of 1944 by the yacht *Santa Barbara*. Both were arrested on arrival. Dr. Cadius, I/M Hamburg was associated with this mission.

Evidence from excepted material shows that in the summer of 1944 Hamburg sought to re-establish an organisation in Brazil. The project was given the cover name INNA and as far as we know, came to nothing.

Names of possible agents in Brazil and suggested means of contacting them were sent through SD channels in Argentina. The following persons were interested in the plan:

KLINKISCH	IMHER
BONI	HANS MICHAEL
HARKS	FRITZ AMERICO

Klinkisch is probably Dr. Klimkisch, I/w Hamburg; Boni possibly Bohny and IMHER possibly Erich Imhoff, I/w Berlin. The others may merely be Germans who had lived in Brazil and had contacts there. The material does not suggest them as Hamburg officials.

Mexico

Abwehr activities in Mexico were halted in 1942 by the deportation of Georg Nicolaus (MAX). Nicolaus is now being questioned in the USA and should provide useful information. Some months after his deportation, his work was revived by Joaquim Ruge, Edgar Hilgert, a Hamburg agent recruited probably by Hans Blum and Franz Buchenau, a Cologne agent. These characters are still at large.

As far as we know, no attempt was made to reinforce them, but recent reports have shown that Hamburg did on at least two occasions plan to send additional agents there.

Argentina

Abwehr activities in Argentina were revived in late 1942, probably under the direction of Niebuhr. From time to time until the summer of 1944 excepted material shows the existence of an organisation known under the cover-name BLAU which we believe to be a Hamburg shipping intelligence service. We have little information as to its composition but suspect it was directed by General Wolf and his assistants Martin Meller, Maumien, and Schumann. Ernst Schleuter, Eugen Langer, Lothar von Reichenbach and Heinrich Reiner may have been agents. Reports on these characters can be found in the Argentine Primer.

> As you may know, the SD and Cologne groups were broken up by a series of arrests in the summer of 1944. It is possible that some of the Hamburg group may still be at large.[2]

Wichmann's interrogation reports relating to South America were compared by MI5 to information supplied by another Ast Hamburg I/M personality, Harold Mandt, a pre-war insurance company executive who had done much business in London and had travelled extensively in South America.

> According to Wichmann, wireless traffic from the Argentine to Hamburg ceased in 1943. Wichmann maintains that prior to this time the traffic was routed to Hamburg from whence it was passed verbatim to Berlin without being deciphered. The reason for this routing was because of the great efficiency of the Hamburg W/T station. It is believed that some of the material was shipping intelligence which was possibly obtained from former Hamburg agents by the Naval Attaché in the Argentine. We would like to know whether any of this intelligence was made available to the Hamburg stelle and if it was we should be interested in the nature and sources of the material.
>
> We believe that the following may have been some of the agents who produced this material in the Argentine: Ernest Schleuter; Eugen Langer; Lothar von Reichenbach and Heinrich Reiners.[3]

The Allied forensic reconstruction of the various networks in South America, often run in parallel with each other but sometimes overlapping, would take some years to complete, and eventually relied on interrogation reports compiled post-war. Some of the key information came from German returnees who were repatriated with German diplomatic personnel in May 1945 on the SS *Drottingholm* which was required to undergo an inspection in Liverpool while on her voyage to Sweden.

The Abwehr officer responsible for creating Ast Hamburg's first networks in South America was Friedrich Obladen, a very successful, cultured, cosmopolitan businessman who had made his fortune manufacturing a chemical disinfectant for medical use and had worked pre-war in New York, Chicago and London. With a reputation as something of a playboy, Obladen had used his commercial contacts to recruit two well-established businessmen, Ottomar Müller in Rio de Janeiro and Friedrich Kempter in Buenos Aires, and a legation official in Quito, Walter Giese, to build local networks able to collect shipping intelligence.

An accomplished yachtsman, skier and international hockey player, Obladen impressed his post-war interrogators but he was unaware that MI5 had opened a file on him in September 1937 at a time when he was a frequent visitor to London and suspected of collecting naval intelligence.[4] In his interrogations conducted in June 1945 and February 1946 he denied having engaged in espionage before the war and confirmed that in March 1941 he had been posted to Greece, and thereafter had played no part in Ast Hamburg's South American operations. Of his three original agents Kempter, a graduate of Tübingen University who had emigrated in 1923, would be arrested in March 1942. By the end of December 1941 he had transmitted over 400 messages to Hamburg, and had received more than 200. Giese escaped to Europe in April 1942, having been granted a safe-conduct passage from Chile, and Müller was arrested in November 1942.

* * *

The extent of German espionage in Latin America, as manifested by the amount of illicit radio traffic generated, was immense, and in August 1940 the US Federal Bureau of Investigation created a Special Intelligence Service (FBI-SIS) to meet the challenge. Initially the FBI-SIS concentrated on Argentina, and the organisation's official history records that SIS coverage in Argentina was inaugurated on 25 September 1940 when the first undercover Agent was sent to Buenos Aires. In the following years coverage was expanded until October, 1943 when fifty-one Special Agents and Special Employees were assigned to various parts of the Republic.[5]

Buenos Aires was always the centre of German intelligence operations in the western hemisphere, and as well as communicating by radio the Abwehr made use of the LATI Italian airline route to Rome via Recife and Dakar, until it closed in December 1941. This channel carried airmail to Italy, and Ast Hamburg's channel terminated with deliveries via Bolzano and Innsbruck while the Berlin traffic completed its journey in the Rome diplomatic pouch. However, Allied pressure on President Vargas resulted in the air route's termination, which placed even greater strain on the Abwehr's radio links.

In December 1942 radio interception conducted by the US Coast Guard identified a clandestine transmitter with the call-sign PQZ which led to the arrest of sixty suspected German agents, of whom thirty-four were charged, among them Bernardo Timmermann, Augusto Kroll, Hans Heincke, Eugenio Ellinger, Guillermo Kunsemueller, Raul

Malvino García and Anna Bradenkamp de Hellemann. In addition, five transmitters were recovered, together with currency amounting to $200,000.

The investigation had begun in Chile in August 1941 when an FBI-SIS officer, Dwight J. Dalbey, gathered information about the call-sign PYL, which was traced to the Cerro Alegre home of a licensed amateur, Wilhelm Zeller. However, the Chilean secret police, the Direccion General de Informacion e Inteligencia (DGII), failed to find the apparatus, which had been dismantled. PYL went off the air until October 1942 when it was triangulated by direction-finding equipment to a farm outside Quilpue, near Valparaiso. It was directed by the German air attaché, Major Ludwig von Bohlen, who had himself been born in Chile but had fought in the First World War. Also implicated in PYL was the Compania Transportes Maritimos, which before the war had been a local Norddeutscher Lloyd subsidiary. Indeed, von Schulz-Hausman had been the Norddeutscher Lloyd agent in Chile before he had moved to Argentina, and had been replaced by Bruno Dittman. Other former Norddeutscher Lloyd staff incriminated in PYL were a radio technician, Hans Blume, and his brother-in-law Heinrich Reiners, formerly of Norddeutscher Lloyd in Panama, later based in Valparaiso.

By the time Chile severed relations with the Axis in January 1943, PYL had been silenced by a DGII raid in November 1942, but another transmitter, call-sign PQZ, continued to operate from Santiago. When Ludwig von Bohlen returned to Germany in September 1943 he entrusted his organisation to his co-conspirators Timmermann and von Schulz-Hausman. The station had been established in April or May 1941, apparently by von Bohlen, but sufficient espionage and cipher paraphernalia had been recovered from the PYL site to compromise him as well, and he was arrested in February 1944.

The PQZ investigation laid the pattern for further counter-espionage cases based on the location of transmitters which, because of the vagaries of long-distance radio reception, often had their signals relayed through sites in the United States where the Coast Guard alerted the FBI, which in turn mobilised its Special Intelligence Service personnel posted in Latin America who were instructed to liaise with the local security apparatus, principally the DGII in Chile and the Direcao da Ordem Politica e Social (DOPS) in Brazil, to help locate the source of the illicit transmissions and participate in the apprehension of the spies. Invariably the agents turned out to be members of the very large local German expatriate community. One of the first channels to be monitored was a link from Chapultepec in Mexico to Rocky Point,

Long Island and then to Nauen in Germany, a chain that justified the FBI-SIS's activities in Latin America, and appeared to demonstrate a link between spy-rings in the United States and Brazil.

Although the FBI would not admit it at the time, the Rocky Point station was under the FBI's control and was part of a counter-espionage investigation into a spy-ring headed by Frederick Duquesne in Manhattan which would be rounded up in July 1941. In the meantime the FBI's operators relayed the encrypted messages to Germany, unaware of their content.[6]

Running in parallel to the Abwehr networks was an SD spy-ring headed by Johannes Becker who was established in Buenos Aires in May 1940. Assisted by Heinz Lange, Becker's mission was intended to be primarily sabotage, but this assignment as dropped in the face of opposition from embassy-based diplomats, and in September 1940 he decamped to Brazil and made contact with Albrecht Engels, the AEG representative in Rio de Janeiro who had been recruited by I/w's Jobst Raven in Genoa in 1939. Originally employed by Siemens, Engels had fought in the First World War before emigrating and acquiring Brazilian citizenship. His network, largely managed by Herbert von Heyer and a Portuguese immigrant Antonio Gama Pinto, extended to Mexico where Karl von Schleebrügge and Georg Nikolaus collected economic intelligence. Engels also recruited some of his own staff, among them Beno Sobisch and Ernst Ramuz, to work as radio operators.

The Allies monitored Engels' wireless traffic, transmitted with the call-sign CEL from Sao Paulo, and learned more about him from a British double agent, Dusko Popov, who travelled down from New York in November 1941 to receive money and radio communications instructions. With the benefit of this evidence, which supported the highly secret radio intercepts, Engels and his organisation, codenamed BOLIVAR, would be arrested in March 1942.

Another network active in Brazil was headed by Ast Hamburg's Josef Starziczky, a former Kaisermarine officer who, based in Rio de Janeiro, developed a large organisation until he was detained in March 1942.

Other independent networks detected by the US Coast Guard included LIR in Rio de Janeiro, which was spotted in May 1941 and operated a net across Brazil, Argentina, Uruguay and Ecuador. The source of the signals turned out to be a commercial information service, the Informadora Rapida Limitada, managed by Heribert O.J. Müller who employed Friedrich Kempter as his W/T operator. Another key figure in the LIR group was Herbert von Heyer, of the Theodor Wille Company in Recife, who was also active for CEL. In June 1941 this commercial cover started transmitting as CIT, and was followed three months later by another Brazil-based group run by Fritz Noak and Herbert Winterstein.

When in March 1942 the DOPS began its round-up, Becker was back in Berlin to confer on future plans for South America, and three fugitives, Johnny Hartmuth, Heinz Lange and Wolf Franczok, fled to Paraguay. When Becker returned to Brazil Lange was assigned to Chile where von Bohlen had avoided arrest and, from his diplomatic base in Santiago, was in touch with Bruno Dittman in Valparaiso, Friedrich von Schulz-Hausman at Buenos and Georg Nicolaus in Mexico.

Following the 1942 debacle, the Abwehr attempted to re-establish its networks with two entirely new organisations that were to be run by individuals uncontaminated by earlier contact with the compromised networks, and be infiltrated into Latin America by a route what would avoid the hazards of Allied inspections. The first, codenamed MERCATOR II, involved the delivery to Brazil in June 1943 of two agents, Wilhelm Kopff who had lived in Peru, and William Baarn, a black merchant seaman from Dutch Guinea. They were delivered by a 46-ton French-registered yawl, the *Santa Barbara*, which, with a I/M crew of six, under the command of a celebrated Hamburg yachtsman Heinz Garbers, who had been employed previously on two voyages to land agents in south-west Africa. The pair sailed from the French port of Arcachon and reached Sao Joao da Barra without incident, but quickly surrendered to the local police. They were put on trial in March 1945 and sentenced to 25 years' imprisonment, even though Kopff had cooperated with the Brazilians and for a period had operated his transmitter as a double agent in an unsuccessful attempt to dupe his German controller.

A second scheme, codenamed JOLLE, was supervised by Amt. VID's Kurt Gross who selected Walter Hansen, alias Walter Burckhardt, an experienced radio operator, and Josef Schroell, a merchant seaman originally from Luxembourg, for a mission in Argentina, delivering the pair at the end of June 1944. As part of their covert communications plan involving microdots and secret writing, they were indoctrinated into a group in Spain headed by Karl Arnold.

A former volunteer in the French Foreign Legion in Morocco, Schroell had joined the SD in 1938 and had been arrested in February 1940 while on a mission in Alsace-Lorraine. He was sentenced to death for espionage at Chalons-sur-Marne but was liberated by the Wehrmacht. Thereafter he worked in Paris as an interpreter, but was then recruited by Gross for a mission to Argentina under the alias Alfonso Chantrain.

Accordingly, Hansen and Schroell landed at Mogotes, near the resort of Mar del Plata, and were escorted by Gustav Utzinger to a Buenos Aires suburb where they lodged with Walter Schweiger. Also safely delivered was an estimated 50 tons of materiel, including radio transmitters and weapons, and a large strongbox containing some £200,000 in £10 banknotes.

Having completed half its assignment, the *Santa Barbara* returned to Europe carrying three fugitives, Heinz Lange and the two radio operators Felipe Imhoff and Jurgen Sievers, who were all considered too badly compromised to be useful. Instead of their intended destination of Bordeaux, Garbers docked in neutral Vigo in September and the three passengers were able to make their way to Berlin via Madrid and Barcelona. Meanwhile Schroell, by now in contact with Johannes Becker, was arrested by the Coordinacion Federal in Buenos Aires in August 1944, detained until June 1946, and then deported on the SS *Rio Teuco* in May 1947 with Utzinger, Juan Harnisch and five other German spies. When interviewed in the United States Schroell tried to make a deal with his interrogators, offering to find the elusive Becker if he could be returned to Argentina, and he acknowledged having been in touch with Hansen until November 1946. Schroell's interrogation was never completed because he escaped from the Wannsee internment camp in September 1947 and, although scheduled to be returned to the French authorities, was never recaptured. In June 1947 MI5 commented

> we feel that Utzinger, Harnisch and Chantrain should be considered as three-star characters. Utzinger is probably one of the most remarkable assets to the German Intelligence Service and was, as you know, head of the SD and W/T organisation in Argentina. Harnisch was head of the Nest Cologne organisation who had important political contacts in Buenos Aires, and Chantrain was one of the last SD agents to be sent out to Argentina in *Santa Barbara*.[7]

The post-war investigation into Schroell revealed that his half-brother was Karl Steffen, with whom he jointly owned a shoe shop in Luxembourg. Steffen was also an Abt. III/F officer formerly based in Bordeaux and was described as 'very dangerous'.

* * *

The picture that finally emerged of German espionage across Latin America was large in scale and complex because of the numerous organisations which sought to deploy personnel and mount operations.

Initially, the Allies had to rely on three principal sources of information: communications intelligence, which was never shared in its entirety (known internally as 'excepted material' and withheld from the Americans); a handful of double agents run by the FBI, MI5 and SIS; and the interrogation of prisoners seized from neutral ships during Contraband Control inspections.

The first senior enemy intelligence asset to fall into British hands while travelling from South America was Osmar Hellmuth who was arrested in October 1943 when his ship docked in Trinidad while on a voyage to Spain. A wealthy insurance broker, Hellmuth's relationship with the SD's Johannes Becker and his assistant Hans Harnisch had been compromised by ISOS. Under interrogation at Camp 020, Hellmuth made a detailed confession and described the SD's activities in Argentina.[8]

The interdiction of Hellmuth was the culmination of a chain of counter-intelligence events which had been prompted by an FBI-SIS agent Jesus Aguillar, a cabin steward on the *Cabo de Buena Esperaza*, who had served as a courier until March 1943 when he had deserted his ship in Buenos Aires to be employed by Jose Valles as an intermediary between General Wolf and the Spanish consulate.

Aguillar gave the FBI-SIS an insight into the German organisation and led the American investigators to another member, Ramon Quevedo, who was recruited, and also José Olivera del Rios, telegraphist on the SS *Habana*.[9] In turn, Olivera was arrested in October 1943 by a Dutch patrol boat and flown to England for interrogation. When questioned, Olivera had implicated the Spanish telegraphist radio operator on the SS *Monte Monuich*, Diego Beltran, as a senior and trusted courier, a prominent ISOS personality.[10] At the end of October 1943 his ship was stopped by HMS *Lady Hogarth* and escorted to Gibraltar where he was found to be carrying rolls of exposed undeveloped films with eighty-six incriminating messages from Buenos Aires. Under interrogation at Camp 020 Beltran admitted his true role, describing his recruitment in November 1941, and examination of the items entrusted to him revealed a long list of SD agents in Argentina. Like dominos falling, Aguillar had compromised Olivera, who then had incriminated Beltran. As his MI5 interrogator observed, 'The outstanding feature of the case of Beltran however, is a list in code which was found among the photographic material carried by Beltran during his last journey. It seems almost too fantastic to be true, but when the code was broken the list disclosed the names and personal particulars of no less than forty German agents.'[11]

A qualified radio operator who had served on the destroyer *Velasco Ceuta* before joining the merchant fleet, Beltran was a Falangist and had been recruited by an Abwehr representative introduced to him as 'Otto' in November 1941 while on shore leave in Barcelona. MI5's verdict was that the Abwehr correspondence entrusted to Beltran 'helps considerably to piece together the jigsaw of German espionage in the Argentine'.[12]

* * *

Until his very public exposure and expulsion by the Argentine government in January 1943, Dietrich Niehbur had headed the Abwehr's espionage operations across most of South America. The catalyst for his expulsion had been embarrassing references to him in the trials of Hans Napp, Walter Freiwald, Martin Schneider, Thilo Martens, Ottomar Müller, Lothar von Reichenbach and Elvezio Ortelli. When the embassy declined to allow him to appear as a witness in the prosecutions, he was declared *persona non grata* and he left the country within hours on a Spanish freighter.

Having commanded the submarine *U-21* in the First World War, Niebuhr had emigrated in 1918 to represent a German shipbuilder. Three years after his recruitment into the Abwehr by its then chief, Conrad Patzig, in 1933, Niebuhr was chosen to represent his organisation in South America, and he had been responsible for a great coup in December 1939 when he had rescued the *Admiral Graf Spee*'s crew from internment in Uruguay and spirited them away to Argentina, thus allowing a large number to return home to Germany and re-join the Kriegsmarine. Other members of the crew who remained in Argentina found themselves working for Niebuhr, and when in June 1946 the time came to round up the ship's complement for repatriation of the troopship *Highland Monarch*, only 264 out of 1,150 turned up for embarkation.

After the outbreak of war Niebuhr's intelligence-gathering duties had been shared with two colleagues, Bohny in Rio de Janeiro and von Schulze-Hausmann in Chile. He was also responsible for the Kriegemarine's Etappen organisation which supported German U-boats and blockade-runners with information about Allied shipping. The Etappen was represented in Santiago by Schulze-Hausmann; Walter Geise in Ecuador; Edgar Hilgert in Mexico; Nils Christensen in Brazil; Heriberto Schwartau Eskilbsen in Colombia; and Claus Waljei, Ferdinand Westihoff and Hans Christian von Busch in Peru.

Niebuhr was interrogated by the US CIC at Darmstadt in June 1946, when he described his expulsion from Argentina and his promotion, upon reaching Berlin in June 1943, to head Abt. III. In the meantime, in April 1945, a comprehensive report on the Argentine networks was placed in Niebuhr's MI5 file, identifying three distinct organisations:

(1) Ebassy Group – or BLUE directed by Captain Dietrich Niebuhr alias DIEGO which had at its disposal a radio transmitter in Hamburg.
(2) The Becker Group – or RED run by Juan Sigfrido Becker alias SARGO which had at its disposal a radio transmitter in Berlin.
(3) The Harnisch Group – or GREEN directed by Juan Rudolfo Leo Harnisch alias BOSS, which had at its disposal a radio transmitter in Cologne.[13]

All three networks had been severely disrupted by the Coordinacion Federal's intervention in January and February 1944 when seven transmitters, ten suitcase transmitters, thirty-two portable sets, ten shortwave receivers and fourteen long- and short-wave receivers were confiscated. Also seized were three enciphering devices, three cars and a micro-photography apparatus.

Gustav Utzinger quickly reorganised the networks under his control with two transmitters within the Buenos Aires city centre, three in the suburbs and two held in reserve, in Santa Fé and Uruguay. Niebuhr's replacement was Friedrich Wolf who acquired his predecessor's three principal assistants, Martin Müller, Federico Grimm and Franz Mammen. Similarly, Becker attempted to rebuild his compromised group but that was largely closed down by police action in Uruguay in January 1945 when his associate Jose Pfeffer was arrested.

With Niebuhr hopelessly compromised, direction of the South American networks passed to Friedrich Wolf, with Becker remaining in charge of the SD presence. An infantry officer who had served on the Western Front in the First World War, Wolf was not an Abwehr professional and had been acting as a military adviser to the Argentine army since 1937. He took the role when he was appointed to Santiago in July 1940, and he transferred to Buenos Aires in July 1943.[14]

Wolf's extended interrogation at Camp 020 from May to October 1945 was leveraged by documents retrieved from his private safe at the German embassy in Buenos Aires, and information relating to his private life. Wolf's long-term mistress, 28-year-old Adriana Barahona, whom he had met while serving as military attaché in Santiago before the war, lived in an apartment on the ninth floor of a building in the Calle Correintes in Buenos Aires that he paid for, although his wife was unaware of the arrangement. An added detail, disclosed to demonstrate to Wolf that cooperation with MI5 was advisable, was that Adriana shared the apartment with a girlfriend, Ernestina Arias, who was conducting an affair with the Japanese military attaché, Colonel Toshikazu Suzuki.

Wolf was withdrawn from Buenos Aires, along with the rest of the embassy staff, in July 1944, sailed to Lisbon on the SS *Rio Pachal*, and remained in Portugal until May 1945 when he was evacuated on the *Drottningholm*, never expecting to be detained when the ship reached Liverpool. During his many hours of interviews Wolf was pressed on his relationship with Becker, whom he admitted having met just once, unintentionally, and acknowledged him as the SD's senior representative in South America. Becker himself was arrested by the Argentine police in April 1945, to whom he made a detailed statement which was later circulated by the FBI as a 51-page report.

According to his own account, Becker had worked as a commission salesman or commercial traveller, representing various German firms in Buenos Aires from his arrival there in April 1937, but he had returned to Berlin in April 1940 where he was inducted into the RSHA by Amt VI's Major Rossner and given a six-week course in intelligence tradecraft. Although he had previously served briefly in the army with the rank of lieutenant, having gained a diploma from Leipzig University in military instruction, this was Becker's first introduction to espionage, and in June he flew back to Buenos Aires via Rome in the guise of a diplomatic courier with instructions to supervise Heinz Lange and his embryonic network. His main mission was to build an organisation to collect economic and political information, and his principal method of communication was by letters written in secret ink and couriered by a team of LATI pilots through Rome, by arrangement with the airline. Another channel was provided by Gustav Utzinger at the Telefunken company in Rio de Janeiro. Having completed his mission, Becker flew back to Italy in October 1941, and remained in Berlin until May 1942 when he was given a second assignment to Buenos Aires, which he reached on the SS *Rita Garcia* in February 1943.

Becker managed his networks through Lange and Utzinger until April 1944 when he was directed by Berlin to establish a third network. Fearing police surveillance, Becker arranged for the reception of two new arrivals from Berlin on the *Santa Barbara*, and took the opportunity to evacuate Lange. Although over the next few months he took the precaution of moving from one safe-house to another, he was arrested by the police in April 1945 and confronted with an album containing photographs of thirty-five of his agents. In the weeks that followed, his notebooks and extensive financial records were examined, leading the police to compile a list of 119 of Becker's contacts across South America, together with numerous cover-addresses in Europe. Evidently Becker's organisation was well funded, receiving large amount of cash through Hellmuth Strehmel, a cut-out with an office in the same building as the embassy. In the opinion of SIS's Section V,

> the SD was extremely fortunate in their choice of Johannes Siegfried Becker as chief of their organisations in South America, as is shown by his energy and ingenuity in keeping their services going. His laborious system of cut-outs and his care in keeping his different sections in water-tight compartments undoubtedly directly contributed to his success in this connection.[15]

In spite of the huge advantage offered by ISOS and the difficulties the German networks experienced with their clandestine communications, under considerable harassment from the local police, neither the British nor the Americans fully understood the scale of Axis espionage until the cessation of hostilities when some of the key players were interrogated.

Chapter VIII

THE WESTERN CAMPAIGN

> The higher the position held in the German Intelligence Service, the more likely as a general rule that the incumbent was more than an opportunist, i.e. a Pan-German or outright Nazi.
>
> Eric W. Timm, OSS X-2 Interrogation of Murat Farid, 2 August 1945[1]

A War Room assessment of the Sicherheitsdienst in France, circulated in October 1945, painted an unflattering picture of Amt VI B's operations in France, explaining that the organisation had not enjoyed the benefit of any pre-war preparation, and found the occupied population's climate of hostility unconducive for its activities.

> The first Referent for France chosen by Hermann Bielstein, Gruppenleiter of the original VI F, was Marcel Zschunke, to whom was assigned the task of preparing V-Men for despatch into that country. Zschunke had no easy task; since prior to the outbreak of war the SD had not even attempted to install agents in France, nor was there, as in Eastern Europe, any pro-German minority in France which could be exploited to advantage. In addition, little background material regarding France was available to the Gruppe, so that Zschunke had virtually virgin territory to exploit. The SD-Abschnitte in the West had nothing to offer in the way of agents, and Zschunke's efforts at recruitment met with failure.
>
> There was however one exception. In November 1939 Zschunke took over a prospective Abwehr agent, Fritz Lorenz, who had been destined for a mission in Paris. Zschunke was successful in providing Lorenz with false papers of sufficiently high standard to enable him to get to Paris through Italy in March 1940, armed with three W/T sets and sabotage material. Lorenz was a failure in his mission, but on his return in April claimed to have obtained through a telephone operator in Paris details of a conversation between Reynaud and Chamberlain regarding the dispositions of Weygand's Near East armies. The story was an invention

on the part of Lorenz, but was accepted on its face value and passed direct to Hitler himself. The story was given great prominence in the German press for propaganda purposes, and was the first success claimed by Amt VI. It was a success of a rather ominous quality.

When the French campaign began Zschunke passed what little material he had on France to Amt III as occupied territory was considered by that Amt to be its concern. The fall of France and the occupation of Paris however opened up new possibilities for Amt VI, but contrary to what might have been expected, there was no coordinated plan for such an eventuality. Filbert, Gruppenleiter VI A, but in effect directing the work of the Amt, sent both Zschunke and Lorenz to Paris to carry on their work there. Their stay did not exceed a fortnight as Helmut Knochen, the new BdS Frankreich, had his own ideas, and sent them quickly packing. The conflict between Amt III and Amt VI on occupied territory was an added complication. It was not an auspicious start. Soon two lines of development emerged – the steady growth of Abteilung VI in the Paris Dienststelle with Knochen as BdS and Hastuf Nossek as Leiter of Abt. VI, side by side with the despatch by the Amt itself of individual representatives in different parts of France.

Of the two tendencies mentioned in the previous paragraph the more considerable was the strong development in Amt VI work from Paris; it also yielded least results. Knochen, the BdS, was ambitious and jealous of his reputation, largely based on the Venlo incident; he personally undertook to send reports on France and Vichy direct to the BdS, thus circumventing Gruppe VI B. This relationship continued when Ernst Kaltenbrunner became DdS. Meanwhile Nossek developed his VI Abteilung, but on lines hardly profitable to Amt VI, The results achieved under the Jost regime were negligible. By the end of 1941, however, Schellenberg had become Abtschef, and some attempt at improvement was made, though it is to be noted however that Schellenberg had little faith in Amt VI work carried on under a BdS normally ignorant of what secret intelligence meant and unsympathetic towards it, especially when it dealt with political matters.

Ostbaf Bernhardt was appointed by Schellenberg as Referent for France in January 1942. By now the Paris Dienststelle had grown to the extent of having its own Abteilungen. It became indeed the largest Dienststelle under Amt VI in Europe. It extended its interests beyond the borders of France itself, and thus we find an Abteilung VI B responsible for France, Abteilung VI C under Hastuf Alisch collecting information on the Iberian Peninsula, Abteilung VI D under Hastuf Zuchristian working against England and the USA (Zuchristian was in fact a Gruppe VI D officer), and a section under Hastuf Doehring responsible for North Africa. This section was later to become VI B 4 (Parseval). This organisation however was impressive rather than effective. No results of any importance were achieved and the Dienststelle was more concerned in combatting Resistance Movements than in collecting political information. Nossek in July 1942 was replaced by Stubaf Haagen, who showed himself equally Resistance minded. Bernhardt's attempts at improvement of a rapidly deteriorating situation failed, and the failure was due to the everlasting problem of finding personnel of sufficient ability to carry out the work.

Further attempts at improvement were made in the course of 1943. An added impetus was the order to prepare I-Netze in the event of an Allied invasion of France, which preparations are dealt with in the following paragraphs. By April 1943 Haagen, whose conception of Amt VI work continued to be operations against the Underground, became personnel Referent to the HSSUPF Frankreich, and was replaced by Staf Bickler who remained in command until the evacuation of Paris. In the same month Ustuf Bourjeau took over from Nossek who was given the special assignment of concentrating on Vichy and North Africa, for which purpose he exploited the PPF. In this work Nossek employed as specialist Leopold Vorlkrt (later despatching officer for agents as Leitstelle Siegfried). A certain amount of success was achieved, especially through contact with those PPF delegates who attended the conference in Paris in 1943.

A serious start on the preparation of the stay-behind organisation in the event of an Allied invasion was begun by March 1943. For the purpose additional staff was sent to Paris, the actual task of preparing the networks being in the first instance given to Ustuf Rissman. Later Hastuf Koengi, Stubaf Lang, and Haschaf Zuang were sent, and a training school established at Rue Desbordes-Vallmore. Ustuf Zagh of VI F became the W/T expert at the school By June 1944 agents had been placed with W/T sets at Rennes, Paris, Bordeaux, Montpelier, Marseilles, and Toulouse. The proportion of agents rejected in training had however been exceptionally high and the comparatively small number of agents ready by June 1944 was a small return for more than one year's work. It is to be noted too that apart from this activity, the Paris Dienststelle as an Amt VI station had almost ceased to function, the chief contributing factors being the continued poor quality of officers and the attitude of Knochen himself. The Dienststelle therefore had its last chance of justifying its existence.

The I-Netze in fact failed completely; soon after the breakthrough in Normandy the first of the stay-behind agents was arrested in the second week of August. Before the end of the month five more were picked up, and the faults in training were now apparent. Little attempt had been made to segregate agents in training, close contact between the agents and the officers themselves had been allowed, and the agents themselves were unreliable and easily swayed by the fortunes of battle; the inevitable result was that before the end of August an almost complete list of agents in training together with the names, functions, and ranks of the officers responsible for the organisation of the network was available to the counter-espionage forces of the Allies. The liquidation of the network became comparatively simple. When Bernhard visited Paris just before the evacuation two W/T links were still available while three more agents could be reached by courier. By February 1945 one W/T set in Montpelier (MARCAUD) was still operating, but on MARCAUD's arrest the network ceased to function. The information achieved by the network had been negligible.

Early in August 1944 the BdS Paris split up and retreated into Germany in sections. Abteilung VI withdrew to St Die and then to Strasbourg where it underwent reorganisation. After some initial confusion it was decided to set up a new organisation to work against France from Germany making use of the subversive elements which had withdrawn from France – the Dorlot and Darnand groups. The organisation vas placed under the command of Staf Bickler and was known as Leitstelle Walter.

Leitstelle Walter set up its headquarters in Baden-Baden in October 1944. The personnel was largely composed of the personnel of Abteilung VI of the BdS Paris, while Stubaf Hubig from the Amt was sent as Bickler's second-in-command. The stelle was divided into some nine Kommandos, each Kommando recruiting its agents from one or other of the French subversive organisations, each Kommando having a cover name. These Kommandos were as, follows:-

I-BAER under Nossek recruiting from the PPF.
I-TAGEL under Moro recruiting from the PPF.
DACHS under Detering recruiting from the Milice.
FUCHS under Bourjeau recruiting from mixed sources.
MARDE under Moritz recruiting from Groupe Collaboration.
HIRSCH 1 and II under Kunze as the central W/T school.
SIBER under Wild recruiting from the Breton Group.
ELCH under Wenzel recruiting from mixed sources

The Stelle recruited both for line crossing and, parachute operations. The Moritz Kommando concentrated on sending its agents through Switzerland while Nossek worked in collaboration with Stubaf Gohl in Milan. In March 1945 Doehring of VI B LI (parseval) also joined the unit.

The results achieved by Leitstelle Walter were meagre in the extreme – of the line-crossing operations about a 20% degree of success was achieved in agents reporting back. The parachute operations were a dismal failure; one plane crashed on the take-off, another left but missed its course, a third dropped its agents who were immediately arrested. At the end a further batch of eight agents was ready for despatch but no planes were available.

Eventually the Stelle itself was overrun by the speed of the Allied advance and instructions were given to the remaining officers and agents to disband. The Stelle evacuated from Baden-Baden to Horalberg and finally to Heiligenberg, where it dispersed. This dispersal brought to an end the history of the Dienststelle in Paris, the end of five years of continuous failure.

It was noted in paragraph B(1) above that the growth of the Dienststelle in Paris was one development of Gruppe IIIB activities against France from 1940 onwards. The other independent development was the dispatching of representatives to different parts of France reporting directly to the Amt and not through a BdS. This development had its beginnings with Zschunke in 1940, not because Zschunke considered such a method superior to working through the BdS; but because no other method was open to him since Knocken had regarded control of his work by the Gruppe as unnecessary. By the time Schellenberg took command however in late 1941, the system became a matter of policy and not of convenience, as Schellenberg considered that Amt VI work such as he envisaged it was much more likely to succeed through the activities of a single well trained officer working under proper cover than by a large and self-advertising Dienststelle. The trouble as ever, however, was to find the competent, well-trained officers.

It is to Zschunke's credit that he was instrumental in recruiting the most successful VI B officer to operate in France in the person of Ostuf Dr. Reiche. In the Autumn of 1940 Zschunke sent Reiche to Vichy under cover as the representative of the German Embassy in Paris. Soon after his arrival in Vichy in October 1940, Reiche was given a W/T operator through whom his reports were sent to Amt VI. Reiche was successful in making good contacts in official Vichy circles, and until his departure in 1942, was able to submit reports of a consistently high standard on political trends in Vichy. Reiche had only one paid agent – a Swiss newspaperman. His information was obtained almost entirely through social and diplomatic channels. Reiche left Vichy in 1942 and was transferred to the Eastern Front where he was killed in action. He was replaced by Hastuf Schmidt, whose work was not of the same high standard.

Zschunke's other venture was hardly so successful. Ostuf Gross (alias Grunde) was sent as an ordinary civilian to Biarritz armed with a W/T set. He did not have Reiche's advantage of any kind of official cover. Gross was quite unsuccessful in his work, falling foul of the Abwehr, in the first instance his W/T set, of which the Abwehr had had no notification, being taken to be an enemy set, and secondly becoming involved in a drunken brawl, which led to his recall early in 1941.

As explained in paragraph 1 above, Schellenberg was not long in deciding that proper Amt VI work through the BdS in Paris was not to be hoped for, and his efforts were concentrated on finding single officers of suitable ability for work at outstations. The following officers were given special assignments:

(a) Ostubaf Schneider was sent in the Spring of 1942 to Strasbourg with the task of exploiting Corsican circles. Schneider was a failure in his work and achieved nothing. He was eventually recalled in the Autumn of 1943 and dismissed from the Amt.

(b) Stubaf Freise, the Gruppenleiter before Steimle, was appointed at the end of 1942, did little to redeem his past failures. He was sent to Portugal in 1943 but was expelled before the end of the year. On Schneider's recall from Strasbourg, Freise went as replacement. Freise attempted liaison with the Paris Dienststelle, but only succeeded in arousing jealousy and suspicion there. His work achieved nothing and he too was recalled in 1944 to be transferred eventually to Amt IV. His assistant, Kriminalrat Uhring, was arrested on the fall of Strasbourg.

(c) Hastuf Senner at Marseilles was a more serious effort. Senner was sent under consular cover to Marseilles early in 1942. He succeeded in recruiting a network of some 20–30 agents, finding his material among the Groupe Collaboration. The Senner network covered the South of France and extended into Spain. The results achieved however were negligible owing to the very poor standard of agent available: Senner remained in Marseilles until the retreat, and after his return to Germany was sent to Milan to work with Gohl in the Unternehmen BERTRAM.

(d) Stubaf Fanselsa at Metz is the last of this group. Fanselsa was a complete failure and it is only necessary to record his name.

Senner returned to Germany from Marseilles in August 1944. He had not attempted a stay-behind network before the invasion. It was decided by Steimle to send Senner to Milan in order to operate against his former territory of Southern France from the Italian side of the border. Senner accordingly established himself at San Remo in October 1944 and made tentative plans to utilise subversive French groups for frontier-crossing operations into France. These efforts came to nothing; by the end of the year Stubaf Gohl was sent to San Remo to become head of espionage activities against France and the enterprise now became the Unternehmen BERTRAM and TOSTA. Senner's function was to organise the crossings into France either direct through Switzerland or by sea. The agents were sent to him from Berlin already briefed for their missions. The agents were chiefly from the PPF groups. Altogether Senner had nine agents to despatch, the majority were arrested soon after reaching French territory. Senner himself surrendered to the French soon after the collapse.[2]

Following the swift German military success of 1940, the Abwehr expanded its activities and enhanced its operations based on the existing stellen. Thus Ast Vienna, which had been established with staff from Ast Munich and Ast Nuremberg, took responsibility for much of south-eastern Europe and created a liaison relationship with the Hungarian military intelligence service. Similarly, the Asts Wiesbaden, Cologne and Munster moved to France, leaving a core staff which concentrated on Abt. III work.

For the next three years Allied counter-intelligence attempted to develop a wiring diagram of the enemy's occupation organisation, based on ISOS interception which exploited German reluctance to entrust sensitive communications to landlines that were vulnerable to eavesdropping and sabotage. In the absence at that time of knowledgeable defectors or prisoners, the results were quite poor, as SIS Section V's John Day conceded in his 1943 assessment of the Abwehr and SD in France, following the occupation of the entire country in the previous November, and their preparations for the invasion. He began by describing the Nazi power structure in France, and the role of the Higher SS and Police Leader (HSSuPF):

> 1. Functions and Powers of the HSSuPF
>
> The system of control by police authority invented by Himmler for Germany can be more ruthlessly and uniformly employed in occupied territory. Supreme power in police matters is placed in the hands of the HSSuPF, who acts as:-
>
> (a) Delegate for police and security questions of the military administrative commander or Reichcommissioner, whichever is appointed.
>
> (b) The representative of Himmler in all his capacities, *viz.* Chief of Police, Minister of the Interior and Reichsführer SS. The HSSuPF for France is SS Gruppenführer and Major-General of Police Karl Albrecht Oberg.
>
> The Zone Nord, which is fully occupied, is controlled by a German military administration under General von Stuepnagel; the Zone Sud (unoccupied until November 1942) is a so-called 'operational zone' in which the Vichy Government has a greater independence, and which is under the direction of the German operational commander in the West, Field Marshal von Rundstedt, through his delegate in Vichy. Oberg is responsible for police measures and for the 'security of the interests of the Reich' in its widest sense in both zones. As a result, the control of security and repressive measures by the German police and SD

throughout France is centralised in Paris, while administrative control remains divided between Stuepnagel and Rundstedt's representative; and this situation no doubt strengthens Oberg's position as the direct representative of Himmler, to whom he can appeal against decisions of the military authorities and the Foreign Office. His powers are so designed as to give him in time of emergency maximum powers of control over the French people and dangerous groups, parties and individuals in France, and in addition to having the German police under his command he exercises full control of the French police through its Secretary-General.

As commander of the SS he can employ Frenchmen recruited for the Germanic SS on repressive tasks within Metropolitan France. Further, through his Abt. VI of Sipo and SD he can indirectly ensure that pro-Fascist and para-military groups share in the work of repression. The use of such powers in time of emergency was well illustrated by the virtually dictatorial measures of Rauter, HSSuPF for Holland, during the strikes of April 1943.

2. The two Befehlshaber. Oberg's functions are exercised except in matters of high policy, through two officers who are the executive equivalent of the HSSuEF[1]s Inspectors in Germany:-

(a) A Befehlshaber der Orpo, Oberstleutnant Schweinichen (acting), responsible for the German uniformed police (Schupo and Gendarmerie), fire and ARP services and 'Teno' in France, and for the employment and control of their opposite numbers in the French police. The duties of Orpo are those of a normal police force and will not be dealt with further here.

(b) A Befehlshaber der Sipo und des SD, SS Oberführer Knochen, who is responsible for directing the work of Gestapo, Kripo and SD and controlling the indigenous security police. The Grenspolizei stationed on the various frontiers also come under the orders of the BdS, since they are adjuncts of the 'Gestapo'. The separate organisation of the Zollgrenzschuetz and the Verstaerkte Grenz-aufsichtsdienst Kueste (VGAD-K), whose customs inspectors perform many security duties although they are recruited and paid by the Finance Ministry in Berlin, is under the orders of the Sipo and SD through its HQ in Paris.

3. Sipo and SD

(a) General Organisation. Whereas in Germany the Kripo, Gestapo and SD, though under a common HQ, remain almost entirely separate, abroad their identity is much less distinct. Knocken in France controls central offices in Paris which reproduce the main divisions of the RSHA, and has established in both Zones Sipo and SD Einsatzkommandos under the direction of Dienststellen at the capital towns of each Vichy administrative region, (i.e., in the Zone Nord: Laon, Chalons-sur-Marne, Paris, Orleans, Rennes, Angers, Poitiers, Bordeaux, Dijon, Nancy; and in the Zone Sud: Toulouse, Limoges, Clermont-Ferrand, Lyon, Grenoble, Marseille, Montpellier). The Lille region, which is controlled by the German administration in Brussels, may possibly be an exception. Both these regional units and the special Einsatzkommandos formed for particular duties (e.g. the mobile EK which operated at the time of the total occupation, and which was responsible for taking Mandel and Daladier from Fort Portalet to Germany), are commanded by a Kommandeur der Sipo und des SD. The regional Dienststellen reproduce the main departmental divisions of the RSHA. This unification is made more easy by membership of the SS which is common to all three services. It remains true, however, that Gestapo and Kripo personnel are State officials, and members of the Kommandos and Stellen still refer to one another as 'Gestapo', 'Kripo' or 'SD' rather than as members of Abteilungen III, IV and V. They can probably be distinguished on occasion by the police titles they bear in addition to their SS rank. Many members of regional Kommandos are, however, wartime recruits of the Sipo and SD, and continue to identify themselves more closely with the SS than with a particular type of police activity.

(i) Aussenstellen. The regional stations establish out posts in departmental towns or in dangerous areas such as the 'Maquis' district of Haute Savoie, to carry out investigations, make arrests and supervise the work of the French police. Evidence from other countries confirms that such Aussenstellen consist of ten or twelve men representing between them the interests of the main sections in IV and V

(ii) Mobile Einsatzkommandos perform executive tasks for all departments alike, and although there is no detailed evidence of their composition in the west, it may reasonably be assumed that they are similar to the Einsatzkommandos in the East and other occupied countries. In the East they work both in large groups (Gruppen) in areas of partisan activity or where a large force is specially required, as direct executives of the Befehlshaber der Sipo, and in small Kommandos, for his Dienststellen. They are highly mobile and well armed (c.f. the battalions of Schupo for lees specialised police duties) and are administratively controlled by the SS Headquarters, although their activities are directed by the RSHA. They consist of about 70 SS personnel picked for their suitability and knowledge of languages. They wear Waffen SS uniform, often with an SD badge, and they may include Waffen SS men for guard duties.

It is interesting to note that in Yugoslavia, mobile Einsatzkommandos gradually changed their role to a more static one comparable to that of the French regional Kommandos described above, and it may well be that the French Kommandos themselves started life as mobile rather than static units.

(b) Duties of Sipo and SD Departments in France.
Sections are styled 'Abteilungen' and not 'Aemter' as in the RSHA.

(i) Abt. I which is concerned with administration, has been definitely identified in the Sipo and SD Kommando, Marseille, and by inference in Paris and other regions. It has no special counter-espionage interest. In a Kommando its officer clearly performs the duties of adjutant.

(ii) Abt. II at Marseille is the liaison section with the French police. This may well be the rule in France, but does not seem to agree with the duties of the parent section of the RSHA.

(iii) Abt. III. Not identified.

(iv) Abt. IV ('Gestapo'), is responsible, both at HQ and regional Stellen, for the duties normally associated with the Gestapo in Germany, i.e. combatting threats to German interests of every kind, and therefore impinges more than any other on the daily life of French men and women. Its head in Paris, Obersturmbannführer Karl Boemelburg, is Knochen's most formidable lieutenant, and was a resident in France before the war. The following sub-sections can be considered as generally identified: IVA.1 deals with Communist, and IVA.2 with Gaullist matters. IVB is concerned with Semitic problems. IVE, of which Sturmbannführer Kiefer is probably the head in Paris, runs a number of French organisations for penetration by agents provocateurs and stool-pigeons, and deals with cases of sabotage and attacks upon Germans. IVF and IVH deal with arrests. This should not be taken as a full list of the functions of each named sub-section. IVC, on the analogy of Norway, is presumably in control of frontier police. Religious, Czech, Austrian and Polish sections which have also been reported in Paris, and were presumably responsible for watching specific categories of persons in France, date from the days of the old Sonderkommando and have not been reported since its re-organisation. The following analysis of the tasks which fall to the lot of Section IV will give some idea both of its interests and methods.

A It studies the whole problem of Communism as an enemy of National Socialism and as a powerful member of the Action Secrete alongside the Gaullist resistance movements. This is probably the reason why Gaullist affairs have been included in the duties of sub-section IVA in France, since in other countries this section is usually confined to Communist and other left-wing parties. Through the regional Dienststellen it supervised the French Police Judiciaire and assists them to penetrate and round up resistance groups organised by both Communists and Gaullists. (Section IVA)

B It organises the internment and removal from France of Jews, probably in close collaboration with the French Police Juive. The internment camp at Drancy, formerly run by the French, is now staffed and run by Sipo and SD personnel until recently under Dauenekker. (Section IVB)

C It deals with cases of suspected espionage, except where strictly military personnel or establishments are involved, when Abwehr III is the responsible authority. (Section IVE)

D It vets agent recruits for the Abwehr, and co-operates closely with Abwehr III F on general counter-espionage policy in France.

E It issues identity documents, checks visa applicants, and through the Grenzpolizei and VGAD-K prevents undesirable persons from crossing frontiers and the demarcation line. Subversive literature is equally subject to control at the frontiers.

F Through Section IV2, it runs a number of organisations for the penetration of resistance movements and escape routes, e.g. that run by Moog, a German officer of IVE at Lyon, who is in charge of a large band of French agents provocateurs, mostly disreputable or criminal types; and that of Lappguyade, a Frenchman who runs a similar party at Perigueux. The most dangerous of all is that of Lafont © CHAMBERLAIN, who also works for Abwehr III and covers most of Metropolitan France. Details of these organisations will be found in the personal index. It seems possible that political movements such as Paparin's Phalange Raciste Francaise in Bordeaux are sponsored by Abt. VI for the S.D. political service, though their main function at the moment is the penetration of pro-Allied groups.

G It controls a D/Fing service for clandestine wireless sets, which possesses mobile detector vans. A unit for this kind of work was operating in Lyon in close co-operation with Abwehr III F several months before the occupation of the Zone Sud.

H It supervises security inside the Organisation Todt. A special 'Gestapo' officer named Hoepnagel has been appointed for this duty in Marseille. The Organisation Todt, with its large numbers of French and other foreign nationals, presents excellent opportunities for sabotage of German constructional work and espionage in important defence areas.

All these duties may be expected to concern regional Dienststellen throughout France. Apart from specific organisations mentioned in sub-paragraph (p) above, Abt. IV controls a great number of individual agents who spy on the French population and inform against anti-Nazis and pro-Allied sympathisers. Most of these agents, who are of all nationalities, are venal and not particularly intelligent, many of them will no doubt change their colours at once with a change of masters in France, but there are no doubt some who have been briefed to watch Gestapo interests after a possible withdrawal of German troops from France.

In order to co-ordinate the work of the Sipo in the Unoccupied Zone, Hauptsturmführer Kurt Geissler was established in Vichy at least as early as 1941 under cover of a police delegation. His duties were liaison with the French police authorities in order to secure the maximum facilities for the German police at a time when the French were still in a position to offer resistance to German penetration. Thanks to his efforts, considerable parties of Sipo and SD moved into Unoccupied France before the total occupation in November 1942, and Geissler himself was given permission to be present at interrogations of British agents captured in the Zone Sud, although another source denies that he in fact did so. After the occupation, Geissler remained at Vichy as Oberg's and Knochen's representative who has concealed his identity as an Amt VI officer under Foreign Office cover. Geissler co-ordinates the activities of the regional Kommandos in the Zone Sud, and is a useful link with the General Secretariat of the French police at Vichy, although the regional Kommandanturs of course take their orders direct from Paris. Geissler is assisted by a small staff, and no doubt his reported functions as local representative of Sipo and SD afford Reiche a better cover for continuing his operations unobserved.

(v) Abt. V. There is no definite information about this section. As the section in control of criminal police, it cooperated with the French Police Judiciare and no doubt also takes a great part in the organisation of arrests and the proclamation of suspects. It is known to have a large card and finger-print index in Paris, and appears to include a central detective bureau (Zentral Fahndungstelle) for the occupied territories of France, Holland and Belgium, which issues a monthly list of 'wanted' persons largely supplied by the Reichskriminal polizeiamt (i.e. Amt V of the RSHA) in Berlin. This book is issued to the Police, GFP, Feldgendarmerie and the military administrative authorities. One source reports that Abt. V includes an economic section. If true, this may mean that in some way or other the Kripo concern themselves with economic levies and impositions on French commerce and civilian life.

(vi) Abt. VI. The functions of Amt VI of the RSHA or the SD foreign political service vary greatly from country to country. Its political information is often conveyed by Himmler direct to Hitler as an alternative to that supplied by Ribbentrop, and in Italy since the fall of Mussolini it has been responsible for all political policy. Elsewhere it has conducted sabotage and political espionage by individual agents and mobile Einsatzkommandos. In France it is represented by Abt. VI of the Sipo and SD, which, though nominally subordinate to Knochen as BdS, maintains a close direct link with the RSHA. Its HQ in France is at 11, Boulevard Flandrin, Paris, and it is likely that its activities are much more centralised than those of Abt. IV, since it is concerned with major issues of a political kind, and its agents are directed mainly beyond the French border, e.g. against Africa and neutral countries such as Spain in which Alisch of the Paris Abt. VI is much interested. It has a training school for agents, probably run by Hauptsturmführer Nossek, at 11, Boulevard Flandrin, An example of this kind of work was the dispatch of two agents to Spain with the task of discovering the sympathies of the British and American Embassies there, and the intentions of their Governments towards Spain.

Before the total occupation, Berlin maintained, under cover of the Consulate General, a representative at Vichy – Reiche – whose main function was to inform Amt VI of the RSHA, often for the benefit of Himmler and without the knowledge of the Foreign Office, of the trend of events in Vichy and elsewhere. He had direct communication with Berlin. Reiche's mission may be assumed to continue at Vichy, although there is no direct evidence of his presence there since December 1942. Keiche also ran high-class agents (e.g. Hans Kurth in Marseille) to investigate the sympathies of Vichy politicians and groups, as well as to operate in Spain. While the activities of Abt. IV do not require a specific form of cover, those of Abt. VI generally do; but it is safe to assume that some Abt. VI functions are in fact entrusted to regional Sipo and SD Commanders, since Luther, Kommandeur of Sipo and SD at Bordeaux, is said to control the exploitation of the Basque separatist movement. Another regional Commander is said to be interested in the Breton separatists. At Bordeaux a small party called the Phalange Raciste Française has been organised by Paparan and includes a Garde Speciale, whose members are known to receive their pay from the Sipo and SD Kommando. It seems reasonable to suppose that this is a specimen of local work by Abt. VI, and the members of the Garde Speciale are clearly expected to be useful during an Allied invasion.

(c) Relations of Sipo and SD and Abwehr

Some instances of collaboration between Sipo and SD and Abwehr have already given. It remains to consider their relative responsibility for security and espionage in France

Abt. IV and Abwehr III. As in Norway and other European occupied countries, so in occupied France in the initial stages of occupation, a large number of GFP, the executives of Abwehr III were attached both to the field troops and to the static Kommandanturen which were quickly established to direct the French authorities and to exploit the country. A detachment of GFP was to be found with each Feldkommandantur – i.e.

at each 'Chef lieu de departement'. They were assisted by the Feldgendamerie or Military Police, and were no doubt mainly occupied with the control of civilians and the investigation of cases of attempted espionage directed at the forces of occupation. They also directed the controls established at the limits of the various 'restricted areas'. At least as early as 1941, according to a recent report, their duties were in part taken over by SS Sonderkommandos, representing the advance parties of the Sipo and SD and by July 1942 the majority of GPP had been withdrawn and proper Sipo and SD Dienststellen established at the main regional centres, not without resentment by Keile of Abwehr III. In the coastal restricted zone, which runs along the entire Atlantic coastline of France, the GFP are still frequently reported, but they are more and more concerned with purely military security duties. The repressive control of the French population, supervision of the French police, and all the duties described in paragraph (b)(iv) are now entirely in the hands of the Sipo and SD Kommandeur, a transference which is quite in accordance with the German policy of extending SS and Police authority over all except operational areas. The Sipo and SD Kommandos receive in this work the assistance of German uniformed police units.

It would be incorrect, however, to interpret this development as implying that Abwehr III has been relegated to a subordinate position vis-a-vis the Sipo and SD. Systematic repression is not the function of this branch of the Abwehr, nor has it the necessary staff to undertake it. It is a counter-espionage section, and continues to work as such. Abt. IV does indeed frequently use captured agents to penetrate resistance and escape organisations within France itself, but here it is acting within its province. On the other hand, there is no evidence that it uses such agents for the penetration of Allied intelligence services at home – work which it leaves to the Abwehr. It may be assumed that Abwehr III frequently turns over the results of its counter-espionage activities for executive action by the Sipo and SD, which is in any case its executive arm in the Reich; and this accords with the diminution of activity by the GFP already mentioned above. The extent of the Sipo and SD's repressive powers was well illustrated in Holland in April 1943 when Raute, the HSSuPF, became virtual dictator of a country under police law. Holland, however, has a civil and not a military administration such as exists in France, where presumably the military authorities, and with them the Abwehr, would in a crisis maintain a close hold over the situation. Since in France Abwehr III is a very active section, it would seem that at least in counter-espionage, as opposed to repression, it retains considerable power. There is no evidence to suggest continued bad relations between the two services, though according to more than one account there was considerable friction in the early days of occupation, especially in Paris; latterly there have been many instances of collaboration between the two services in the detection of enemy agents, especially in the areas of Lyon, Toulouse, Biarritz and Perpignan.

Abt. VI and Abwehr of the Sipo and SD in France is, as has already been explained, chiefly concerned with political espionage and the manipulation of political opinion. Despite the fact that both it and the Abwehr have been in touch with separatist movements, such as that in Brittany, there is no evidence that they have come to blows. Abwehr officers have taken the chief part in recruiting from the PPF agents for work in North Africa and Metropolitan France but Oberg, as Himmler's representative, has attempted to assist the party to political power at the expense of the Vichy Government. From its Vichy link at least the RSHA has required information rather than action. Sabotage, which has been a main interest of Amt. VI in the East, has been left entirely to Abwehr II. Furthermore, no one can fail to be struck by the great disparity in scale between the operations outside France of the Abwehr and the SD: a disparity which is undoubtedly a fact and not due to relative ignorance of the latter. The SD in France has undoubtedly operated in neutral or Allied territory such as Spain, and French North Africa, but on nothing approaching the scale of the Abwehr.

(d) Some Possible Cause of Confusion

Attempts to assess the importance of Sipo and SD in France have been made more difficult by the general lack of knowledge which informants possess of its organisation. Thus it has been necessary to distinguish between the loose use of 'Gestapo', (which may be applied by the uninitiated to any German espionage or counter-espionage service, to Waffen SS units, to the purely military Feldgendarmerie, or to the battalions of uniformed police which are to be found wherever the German armies have invaded), and the correct term 'Sipo and SD'. Only where knowledge of the source or internal evidence justifies it, has the exact term 'Sipo and SD' been used. Where further definition has been possible, this has been done by adding to the words 'Sipo and SD' the Abteilung responsible – e. g. an officer engaged on Communist matters is described as 'a member of Sipo and SD Abt. IVA'. It must be remembered, however, that inside a Kommando the Germans still speak of themselves as Gestapo, Kripo and Sicherheitsdienst personnel, and that, since they generally wear the SD badge, the term Sicherheitsdienst has come to be used loosely outside Germany as an equivalent of Sipo and SD. A further confusion has arisen from SS ranks being reported in military terms. The badges of rank worn on the shoulder straps of SS field uniform are identical with those worn by military NCOs and officers, so that a Hauptsturmführer is often loosely reported as a Hauptmann and a valuable identity check thus lost.[3]

This Section V summary encapsulated everything that SIS had accumulated, from ISOS, agents in the field and double agents run by MI5, relating to the German organisation in France and although it appears superficially impressive, it would be redundant within weeks, a reflection of a dramatic change in the tide of war. The OKW's abject failure on the Russian Front signalled to many the inevitability of defeat, and triggered a distinct change in attitude among those intelligence officers who understood the strategic implications. Consequently, from the last months of 1943, the atmosphere changed and Abwehr professionals, the nest of vipers, began to think treason.

Appendix I

Abstellen in Germany

Centrally based in offices in the Wilhelmstrasse, next to the High Command's Berlin headquarters, the Abwehr operated through individual offices in each of Germany's military districts. Each Abwehtstellen (Ast) ran branch offices, known as Neberstele (Nest). In addition, there were two other centrally-controlled operational units, the Meldeköpfe (MO) and semi-autonomous Kriegsorganisationen (KO) which operated in neutral or occupied countries.

Abstellen in Germany

I	Königsberg	XI	Hanover
II	Stettin	XII	Wiesbaden
III	Berlin	XIII	Nuremberg
IV	Dresden	XI–XVI	(Did not exist)
V	Stuttgart	XVII	Vienna
VI	Münster	XVIII	Salzburg / Protectorate Prague
VII	Munich	XIX	(Did not exist)
VII	Breslau	XX	Danzig
IX	Kassel	XXI	Posen
X	Hamburg		

Appendix II

MI5 Assessment of German Activity in the Iberian Peninsula, dated November 1941

Assembled by Camp 020's Eric Goodacre, described as an officer of 'considerable ingenuity and patience'.

LIMITING CONDITIONS IMPOSED BY ITS GEOGRAPHICAL AND POLITICAL SITUATION

The essential feature of all German espionage directed from the Iberian Peninsula is that it is restricted in its communication facilities by two facts: the first is that Spain and Portugal are separated from the United Kingdom by over a thousand miles of sea, and the second that both are still nominally neutral. In other words, it cannot be used for the introduction into this country by air of parachute spies equipped with wireless transmitters. It is hardly necessary to say that it should be impossible for such apparatus to be imported through the Customs but the DRAGONFLY case suggests that a careful watch should be kept for portable gramophones and that these should automatically be confiscated by the Customs if it is not already the rule.

Consequences of these conditions

It follows from the above that:-

(a) Practically all traffic to and from the Iberian peninsula must be slow traffic, since an airmail letter to or from Lisbon takes about seven days.

(b) The Iberian peninsula has become the clearing-house for all communication between the United Kingdom and the continent of Europe. Furthermore, all such communication must pass through the bottle-neck of Lisbon.

(c) The German organisation in the peninsula must be swollen by the inclusion of a liaison service to handle transit mail, for Paris, Brussels and other centres.

(d) Whereas German agents exported from the peninsula consist either of seamen and pseudo-volunteers sailing for the United Kingdom via Gibraltar or of diplomats or of such-like affluent individuals entering the United Kingdom by the air-service from Lisbon, information filtering back through Lisbon will include not only all that gathered by the above categories but also occasional messages from wireless-equipped parachutists dropped in this country and obliged for some reason or another, to resort to communication by letter; hence the immense importance of efficient censorship of the Lisbon mail.

Extent of the German Organisation in the Iberian Peninsula

So far as present information goes, the German intelligence centres are, in Spain, Madrid and Barcelona, with an agency or subsidiary organisation in San Sebastian, and, in Portugal, Lisbon. Little is known of this organisation, and at any rate up to February last it was handicapped by the lack of wireless communication with the control station, but it may be of considerable operational importance since its head is reported to be a German engineer in charge of harbour development works there, which latter might of course have some connection with submarine activity.

Personnel of the German Organisation

The one outstanding point about the personnel of these espionage centres is that their most active members appear to be without exception Germans of comparatively long residence in the country – say, five or six years at least – and about whom we ought therefore to know everything. Spanish is not too widely known a language in Germany and for that reason the enemy has evidently been far-seeing enough to provide an adequately-equipped nucleus some years in advance of requirements. Whether or not these people were established in Spain before the Civil War remains to be determined, but is quite obvious that many of the busiest agents now operating there were Condor

Legionnaires who have become the local representatives of German industry and commerce. This generalisation does not necessarily apply to the directional heads of the Madrid and Lisbon organisations, shadowy figures about whom no conclusive information is yet available, but, as will be seen from the analysis that follows, it does cover all the rest of those who have so far come to our notice.

(1) MADRID

The Madrid Stelle is a fairly elaborate organisation which quite possibly controls, to some extent at any rate, the activities of the Barcelona, Lisbon and North African stations. HERMANN, a member of the Madrid staff, travelled to Barcelona last December and was then expecting to visit 'his agents' and was then expecting to be appointed to North Africa; Van Wijk was sent by PABLO to Tangier to make enquiries there; while in both the Del Campo case and others, vague 'chiefs from Madrid' have been reported in Lisbon.

Except for the curious case of Del Campo, Madrid has so far concentrated on recruiting and training secret ink agents as distinct from wireless operators. Moreover, it seems likely that even Del Campo, as soon as he got his wireless going, would have had to work with Lisbon rather than Madrid.

In considering the personnel of the Madrid and other centres, attention will be concentrated on the active elements, the host of individuals hovering about the fringe of each organisation being dealt with more summarily.

(i) German Personnel

(a) PABLO

Apparently one of the most important members of the Madrid stelle is a German known as PABLO; a description of him is as follows:

> Age 39/40; height 5' 9"; straight thick brown hair parted on the left and brushed back; sharp blue eyes; oval face; fresh complexion; straight or slightly aquiline nose; carefully manicured nails; well-dressed, usually wearing blue or grey double-breasted suits; professes an enthusiasm for tennis; claims to have lived in France; speaks good French and Spanish.

Up to the present PABLO is known to have been actively concerned in one case only, that of van Wijk, but is possibly identical with the individual introduced to Del Campo by EMILIO as 'my chief' who, in return, strongly resembles SOMMER, the chief pointed out to THE SNARK. A notable common characteristic of SOMMER and Del Campo's chief is that both men walk with a stoop. It seems nevertheless unlikely that PABLO is actually the head of the Madrid organisation, if only for the reason that it was he who made the first direct approach to Van Wijk.

PABLO uses an office, No 8 on floor H of a tall building opposite the Hotel Nueva York in the Avenida Jose Antonio. This is possibly No 31 (formerly Pi y Magall, 9) in which HISMA has offices. He also uses an apartment, which may or may not be his private residence, on the third floor of a large modern block faced in polished grey stone on the right-hand side of the Calle Ayala going from the Castellana (now Avenida Generalissimo Franco). It was to this address that he took Van Wijk on 25 March 1941. The German Consulate is at No 10 in the Calle Ayale, but this block is some distance beyond that, probably between Nunez de Balboa and Castello. PABLO owns a maroon-coloured Citroen four-seater with folding roof, and sometimes uses a small closed German car, BMW or DKW. He is known to have been in Madrid, with occasional absences, from 15 October 1940 to 26 March 1941.

(b) EMILIO

Another very active member, and one closely associated with PABLO, for whom he occasionally deputized, is EMILIO who has been encountered in three cases, those of van Wijk, Del Campo and THE SNARK. A description of him is as follows:-

> Age about 40; height, 5′ 4″; getting fat; straight dark hair turning grey and brushed back; sometimes wears horn-rimmed spectacles; sallow complexion; often wears a belted brown leather coat; speaks excellent Spanish and some French.

EMILIO is an established resident of Madrid, married to a Spanish woman, has two children and is said by Del Campo to occupy an apartment in the Calle Infantas above the Paris and Oro bars, i.e. at no. 22; a certain Jorge Helmut Lange is recorded in the telephone directory as living at Infantas 22, telephone number 10366. EMILIO has a drop-head two-door four-seater Opel with luggage chest and spare wheel behind, beige coloured canvass hood and dark coachwork, Madrid registration. Sometimes he uses a dark-coloured closed two-door, four-seater Fiat Balilla with a small Spanish flag (red, yellow, red) on one wing.

According to the same source, he has an office in the Paseo de Hecelatos opposite the Banco Hipotecario and over the Café Dijon.

This is no. 21 Avenida Calvo Botalo (formerly Paseo de Recolatos. The Madrid telephone directory for June 1941 shows an Emilio J. S. Kiechle here as a subscriber for the number 17134. It is interesting to note that the same address and telephone number are given for the firm entitled La Hispanense Industrial y Comercial S.A. agents, among other things, for Skoda. In the advertisement section under 'haqquinaria' of the December 1939 directory this firm appeared as Erhardt & Seymer La Hispanense Industrial y Comercial S.A. telephone number 17134 but this may mean nothing more than the latter firm were agents for Erhardt & Seymer.

THE SNARK thought that EMILIO lived at the Hotel Nacional and was employed at the German Embassy. He was reported in Madrid as late as the end of this summer. His precise relationship to PABLO is a little uncertain but he would appear to be his junior while being himself senior to HERMANN, a leading figure in the Del Campo case.

(c) HERMANN

HERMANN is particularly interesting on account of his long and close association with Franco's party; a description of him is as follows:

> Age, 35; height 6 ft; broad-shouldered; strongly-built; fair hair; broad round face; ruddy complexion; heavy jaw; big fat hands; short fingers; big feet; often wears plus fours; of military habits; speaks excellent Spanish.

Del Campo was introduced to HERMANN by Jose Maria Bolivar, a connection of Del Campo's by marriage, in March 1937 at Badajoz. At that time HERMANN was serving as a 'volunteer' in the Flechas Negras, with which and with the Condor Legion he fought throughout the Civil War. Towards the end of 1937 Del Campo came across him in San Sebastian, where he heard he had been appointed by the Falangist Revilla to assist Colemares in organising the new Spanish Labour Syndicates on the German-Italian model. Del Campo's next encounter with him was in Madrid in the early summer of 1940 i.e. before the collapse of France. On this occasion HERMANN suggested to Del Campo that he should undertake the job of German courier between Madrid and Paris. Nothing came of this scheme and later in the year HERMANN handed Del Campo over to EMILIO, who he described as 'my chief' and who put before Del Campo the Azores plan.

HERMANN lives at the Hotel Moderno, Calle del Arenal no. 2. At the beginning of December 1941 he went to Barcelona and returned to Madrid by air on the 8th January 1941. He has not been heard of since the Del Campo case.

It may be observed here that HERMANN is not improbably this agent's correct name, since Del Campo has known him by that name since 1937. But from the mere accident that he could not well assume some other name in dealing with Del Campo, it does not follow that he will necessarily be known to other recruits by that name. The case of Dr Hacke @ Martin Haustein (see section VIIII(a)) or inversely, is worth pondering in this connection.

(c) FEDERICO

The fourth German member of the Madrid organisation who has had the handling of agents is known as FEDERICO. He has recurred in the Ejsymont and THE SNARK cases, so that our information about him relates to summer 1941; a description of him is as follows:

> Age about 27; height 5′ 9″; slim; well built; fair wavy hair brushed back; large nose; long thin face; pasty complexion; clean shaven; well-dressed; speaks Spanish and French.

FEDERICO is attached to the German Embassy where he usually works and where he was put in charge of Ejsymont by Colonel Bruck. He has lived in Spain for some considerable time and his parents also lived there. He occupies a large, well-furnished apartment in a block in a street newly-planted with small trees somewhere off the Calle Bravo Murillo on the left-hand side (?) going from the Puerto del Sol and owns two cars, one a small grey Mercedes cabriolet and the other a Ford V8 cabriolet.

(e) ALFONSO and an unnamed secret ink instructor

Both Ejsymont and THE SNARK were given lessons in secret ink writing by a middle-aged German who was a friend of FEDERICO. It has not been established, however, that the instructor was the same man in each case.

Ejsymont's man, whose name he does not know, occupies a poorly-furnished, second-floor apartment in the Pinar quarter, while THE SNARK was taken to see her man ALFONSO, in an apartment which she thinks may be FEDERICO's at Colonia del Calle de Viriato No. 73, second floor (right) a street running off the Calle Bravo Murillo, over on the other side of Madrid. Moreover, Ejsymont was taught to write with Pyramidon and THE SNARK with a solution made from prepared cotton wool.

Apart, however, from the fact that Ejsymont's man could not speak French, while THE SNARK, who is no great linguist, thinks ALFONSO could speak Spanish, French, and English as well as German, there is a certain resemblance between the scanty descriptions which are as follows:-

ALFONSO	UNNAMED INSTRUCTOR
Age about 45/50	Age about 44
Height 5′ 6″	Height 5′ 5″
Fat	
Round face	Full red face
Broad but not large nose	-
Dark upper teeth	-
Clean shaven	-
Mouse-coloured hair	Light brown hair
Speaks English, French and Spanish	Speaks bad Spanish and no French

(ii) Non-German Personnel

(a) Miodrag Ljubomir Jevrenovic @ EMILO @ DARGO

This Yugoslav ex-journalist was working as a talent-spotter in Madrid during the early summer of 1941. It was he who picked up THE SNARK.

On 5 May he took an apartment at Alcala No. 108, 3rd Floor, where on 13 or 14 May he was visited by a distinguished-looking white-haired German old gentleman. He left Madrid hurriedly for Paris on 15 May without paying the rent. A description of him is as follows:

> Age, 30; Height 5′ 7″. Fair wavy hair; blue eyes; scar under chin; speaks German, French and Serbo-Croat.

(b) Jose Aiguabella Bustillo

Aiguabella was the Spanish courier who escorted Timmerman from San Sebastian to Huelva via Nanclares and Madrid in August 1941. He is a doctor (physician) and lives at Calle Charrucca No. 20 and his telephone number is 26082. The circumstances that his telephone number on the wall of the obscure hotel in the Arenal to which he took Timmerman to in the first place suggests that this was not the first time he had been employed on such duties. Furthermore, it is perhaps significant that he took Timmerman next day to the hotel Moderna in the same street, the hotel in which HERMANN lived. A description of Aiguabella is as follows:

> Age 26; height 5′ 5″; medium build; black hair; dark eyes; thin face; dark-skinned; well-dressed; speaks very rudimentary French.

(c) Julia Van Reigersberg Versluys @ FLORA
Julia, a friend of Van Wijk, Spanish by birth, married to a Dutchman, alleged now to be in a German concentration camp, served as a 'link' for telephonic communication between Van Wijk and PABLO. Moreover, when Van Wijk left Madrid he was told to write to her if he wanted to get in touch with PABLO again. She thus appears so far to be merely a passive instrument.

Financial difficulties and expensive tastes may have got her into the clutches of PABLO. She is thought to be the mistress of Joaquin Reig, a suspect film agent. She now lives at Calle Serrano no. 176 though up till recently she lived with her parents at Calle Nontalban No. 7, telephone number 10822.

When passing on telephone messages from Van Wik to PABLO she used the cover-name FLORA. A description of her is as follows:

> Age about 30; small and plump; dark hair now died fair; has two young children aged 4 and two respectively. Speaks excellent French.

(d) Unknown girl messenger
Once, while Van Wijk was in Julia's house, a girl called, bringing him money from PABLO. She may or may not have met Julia before, since she addressed her as 'FLORA'. A description of this girl is as follows:

> Age 25; height 5′ 4″; slim build; fair wavy hair down to shoulders; strikingly beautiful; spoke fluent Spanish but with a foreign accent; nationality uncertain.

(2) BARCELONA

Present indications suggest that the Barcelona Stelle is mainly concerned with wireless and that it was on this account that FATHER was taken on to Barcelona instead of being left in Madrid. There is no evidence of it being a centre for recruiting and training other types of agent in the way that Madrid and Lisbon are. As a wireless centre Barcelona seems to work in closer cooperation with Lisbon than with Madrid.

(i) German Personnel

(a) PABLO
Since practically the whole of our information about the Barcelona organisation is derived from the FATHER case it is obvious that the data available are insufficient for any proper assessment of the relative

importance of the individuals encountered. PABLO must nevertheless be one of the principal figures there. A description of him follows:

> Age 39/40'; height 5' 9"; solidly built; fair hair brushed back; clean-shaven; bears a strong resemblance to the airman on Moss Bros (?) poster; speaks Spanish and French, good knowledge of English.

PABLO has some sort of business which cannot be identified from the telephone directory, at No. 29 Rambla de Cataluna, the office, to which he goes for a couple of hours every afternoon at about four o'clock, is on the first floor.

He also has an office, which may be the headquarters of the Stelle, in the Calle Descartes. This office includes a wireless station which communicates not merely with European cities such as Berlin and Lisbon, but also with the United States. The whole of the house is occupied by the German organisation and PABLO was certain the fact that it was 'a German house' must be generally known.

PABLO lives in a small detached house or villa in a residential street where last December either new building or re-building was going on; it is about five or seven minutes' walk from the Calle Descartes office, going away from the city. There are no indications that PABLO is married. He owned a small Fiat saloon but it was stolen towards the end of November 1940.

The telephone number which FATHER used to ring PABLO, or indeed any other member of the German organisation was 77047. FATHER thought this must be the number of the Calle Descartes office but in the February 1940 edition of the telephone directory it is assigned to a certain Bagenski, B. of Calle Lincoln. The address is a few hundred yards from the Calle Descartes but in the opposite direction from PABLO's private house.

From his knowledge of Spanish and his understanding of the Spanish character it is evident that PABLO has lived for some considerable time among the Spaniards. At one time it seemed just possible that he might be identical with Del Campo's HERMANN of Madrid, who as already mentioned, is known to have gone to Barcelona in December 1940 'to visit his agents there' and to have stepped out of the Barcelona 'plane at the Madrid airport on 8 January 1941.

PABLO was not in Barcelona when FATHER arrived there on 4 November 1940, and only turned up about the 10th. He was then in Barcelona continuously until 21 December when he left by an afternoon train for some destination unknown, but probably not Madrid since the Madrid train did not leave until much later in the evening.

(b) PEDRO

Of PEDRO, deputy to PABLO, little is known except that he works in the office in the Calle Descartes. He fought with the Condor Legion during the Civil War and also claims to have lived in France. He speaks fluent French though with a German accent. A description of him is as follows:

> Age 30/35; height 5′ 7″; heavily built; brown hair; prominent nose; clean shaven; speaks fluent Spanish and French.

(c) Mohre @ CARLOS

Mohre, or more probably Maurer, also known as CARLOS, like PEDRO fought with the Condor Legion in the Civil War and lived for some time in France at Toulouse. He speaks fluent French but with a pronounced Midi accent. He acted as FATHER's guide in Barcelona and obtained for him his residence permit which enabled him to leave the apartment of the German proprietor of the Carveceria Hispano-Akleman and move to the Hotel Regina. A description of him is as follows:

> Age 50/55; height 5′ 8″; fair hair; clean-shaven; wears gold-rimmed spectacles; has lost lower front teeth; speaks Spanish and French.

(d) TOMAS

TOMAS, an unimportant young man, accompanied PEDRO when they came to meet FATHER at the Parador de Hidalgo café the night they arrived in Barcelona. FATHER subsequently saw him quite frequently. He appears to be a minor Consular official. A description of him follows:

> Age 30; medium build; black hair; thin face; clean-shaven; speaks good French and Spanish.

(e) Wireless operator, name unknown

It was from this man, who was in charge of the wireless station at the Calle Descartes office, that FATHER learnt that Lisbon was in direct communication with the United States. A description of him is as follows:

> Age 26/28; height 5′ 7″; slim build; brown hair brushed back; blue eyes; clean shaven; sharp, slightly twisted nose; generally wears a blue gabardine raincoat; speaks fluent Spanish but only scraps of French.

(f) Müller

Ejsymont was picked up in Barcelona towards the end of April 1941 by a Yugoslav known as MUNK, who introduced him to the German consular official named Müller; the latter in turn sent him to Madrid. Müller is said to be married and to have two children living in Barcelona; a description of him follows:

> Age about 30; height 5′ 10″; strongly built; light brown hair; clean shaven, two gold teeth in upper jaw; always wears a green suit; speaks French.

(ii) Non-German Personnel

MUNK

This man, who claimed to be a Yugoslav, picked up Ejsymont outside the Café Espana in the Plaza de Cataluna at the end of April 1941. He appears to be employed by the Germans as a talent-spotter. During the Civil War he fought for Franco, was badly wounded and is now in receipt of a disability pension. He lives at No 10 or No 12 in a small street off the Ronda san Antonio, possibly the Calle Principe de Viana or the Calle Candia. The house is one of four identical blocks recently erected by a building society and is next door, or next-door-but-one to a church. A description of him is as follows:

> Age 30/32; height 5′ 10″; dark brown hair plastered back; scar on forehead; square black moustache; sometimes wears glasses; speaks German, French, Spanish, Magyar (?) and some unidentified Slavonic language.

(3) LISBON

As the main recruiting centre for seamen sent to this country as agents and jumping-off ground for the majority of others, except those landing clandestinely, Lisbon is obviously of the greatest importance from the counter-espionage standpoint. The size of the German organisation there cannot be accurately gauged yet, because it seems to be constantly changing and probably includes a large proportion of Portuguese and other pro-Germans. Furthermore, it is continually being reinforced by visiting officials from other centres. Lisbon is also, like Barcelona, an important wireless station.

(i) German Personnel

(a) CARLOS

The first important German agent in Lisbon to come under notice was CARLOS to who de Jaeger and Verlinden were taken by HOFFMAN at the end of August 1940. CARLOS gave de Jaeger the telephone numbers 63170 and 63179, and since these prove to be German Legation numbers it is evident that CARLOS was employed there. Nothing has been heard of him since that date, so, considering that the scar on his right cheek must have made him a conspicuous figure, it is a fair assumption that he has long ago left Lisbon. A description of him is as follows:

> Age 46 / 48; height 5′ 8″; broad-shouldered; strongly-built; fair hair; clean shaven; prominent scar on right cheek; speaks good French.

(b) HOFFMANN

CARLOS's energetic subordinate was an agent named HOFFMANN who lived at the notorious Pensao Estrangeira. HOFFMANN sailed as a stowaway in the *Pilote 16* from Bayonne and met de Jaeger on the boat which arrived at Lisbon about 26 June 1940.

HOFFMANN recruited both de Jaeger and later Laureyssens, in the latter case using Verlinden as an interpreter, but has since disappeared. A description is as follows:

> Age 34; tall; light brown hair; blue eyes; high cheekbones; clean-shaven; projecting ears; broad shouldered; slender build; deaf in left ear; speaks French.

(c) Horst Raider (?)

Associated with HOFFMANN was a German or Hungarian (nationality uncertain) named Horst Raider who also lived at the Pensao Estrangeira. He was present at HOFFMANN's conversation with Verlinden, de Jaeger and Laureyssens. After Verlinden had signed on the SS *Portugall* and sailed to Setubal HOFFMANN hired a car and sent Horst Raider and Laureyssens in it to Setybal to find Verlinden and give him some secret instructions HOFFMANN had forgotten to convey to him before the *Portugall* left Lisbon. When they got to Setubal Horst Raider went to find Verlinden while Laureyssens waited in the car. This must have been in September 1940. A description of Horst Raider is as follows:

> Age 28; height 6 ft. or more; athletic build; black wavy hair; greenish eyes; swarthy complexion; clean-shaven; had been a cinema operator in Angola; speaks German and a little Portuguese but no French or English.

(d) Madame Julie Seele @ SILVA

The third member of the triumvirate engaged in the suborning of seamen in the autumn of 1940 was the German woman who kept the Pensao Estrangeira at No. 10 rua Braamcamp, Madame Seele. Since HOFFMANN's disappearance it is not known who is her link between the German controlling organisation at the Legation or Consulate but THE SNARK reported that in January 1941 the Portuguese used to visit the Pensao on the look-out for likely material.

By January 15th this year Madame Seele had left the Pensao Estrangeira and moved to an apartment at Avenida Miguel Bombarda No 54, already known as a cover-address. A description of this lady is as follows:

> Widow; age 55/60; short and stout; brown hair turning grey; brown eyes; healthy complexion; wears spectacles for reading; speaks French and Portuguese.

(e) Merkel, (Otto) @ MARCEL @ Mr Matthews @ AEGER

Throughout 1941 the most active agent in Lisbon seems to have been MARCEL who has been concerned in the DRAGONFLY, FATHER and Ejsymont cases. Like his counterparts in Madrid and Barcelona, he has been some years in the country having, according to DRAGONFLY, lived six years in Lisbon.

The first agent to encounter MARCEL was DRAGONFLY to whom, on 30 November 1940, he introduced himself as 'Mr Matthews'. At a later stage MARCEL told DRAGONFLY to get in touch with him by telephoning 26268, the number of the Victoria de Belim Insurance Company, Praca do Municipalo No 7 and asking for 'JAEGER'.

At the end of December 1940 or the beginning of January 1941 FATHER, who had been instructed in Barcelona to get in touch with Dr Schott, was introduced by the latter to MARCEL who, for the next four months, looked after him in Lisbon. FATHER's rendezvous with MARCEL were nearly always at the Café Colonial in the Rua da Palma. On one occasion, however, he was taken to MARCEL's private apartment, a third-floor flat, the address and telephone number of which he gave to an SIS representative in Lisbon, Mr Gill; this valuable information has not yet been communicated to MI5. MARCEL got FATHER to draft a dozen commonplace letters in French for the use of other agents writing in secret ink from England.

On 14 July 1941 Ejsymont, acting on instructions given him by FEDERICO in Madrid, called at the German Legation and saw MARCEL who, he had been told on the telephone, was only to be found there at certain specified hours. MARCEL gave Ejsymont some money and his telephone number. Ten days later Ejsymont took Sukkienik to see MARCEL and he also received some money and was given a telephone number which he thinks was 63015. The registered subscriber to this number is: Joao Batista Tavares d'Almeida Arez, Rua da Impresna National No. 77, ground-floor left.

MARCEL did not drive a car but did employ a taxi-driver named Nunes da Costa, a bearded mulatto, whose address is Praca de Automoveis de Rua S. Domingos (a Lapa) – corner of Rua Garcia da Horta – telephone number 62622.

A description of MARCEL is as follow:

> Age 32/35; height 5′ 9″; strong but slim build; long face; thick brown wavy hair; brown eyes; clean-shaven; often wears blue jacket and grey trousers; fond of dancing; thought to have been born in Mainz; speaks good French.

(f) Dr Schott

Dr Schott served as the channel for communication between FATHER and MARCEL. He was a member of the Firma Brinnett Ltda, Praca Duque de Terceira No 24, fifth floor, where he had both an office and a private apartment. It was in this apartment where FATHER's first meeting with MARCEL was arranged and took place.

Dr Schott spends his whole time at this address and his Secret Service connections are thought to be limited to passive roles similar to the above. A description of him is as follows:

> Age 30/35; height 5′ 9″; slight build; fair hair brushed back; aquiline nose; clean-shaven; assiduous patron of night-clubs, especially the Olympia Cabaret; understands very little French.

(g) Werner Pankow

Del Campo arrived in Lisbon by 'plane from Madrid and on 8 January 1941 and next day, disregarding his instructions, called at the German Consulate and asked to see Pankow, with whom he had been told by EMILIO to get in touch after a couple of days. He subsequently saw Pankow on three occasions, either at the Consulate or at his own pension. Towards the end of January Pankow was evidently out of Lisbon for a few days and returned on 2 February.

Pankow must have been in Lisbon for some years and lives at Avenuida de Berne No 120, ground floor, telephone number 43977. A description of him is given below.

> Age 30/35; height 6 ft.; broad-shouldered; strongly-built; fair hair, thin at the temples; ruddy complexion; big nose and feet; walks as though he had some shoulder injury; speaks excellent Spanish.

(h) LEON

LEON was the wireless operator at the German Legation in Lisbon. FATHER saw him both at the Legation and at MARCEL's apartment where there were a couple of wireless sets, but had already met him several times in Barcelona, the first being when he (FATHER) went with the Barcelona operator to the Iberia office to book a seat in the Lisbon 'plane. A description of LEON is as follows:

> Age 30; height 5′ 11″; strongly built; brown hair; clean-shaven; spoke fairly good French.

(i) LEOPOLDO

The 'friend of EMILIO' who came to see THE SNARK on 25 June 1941, told her his name was LEOPOLDO. He gave her a cover-address in Lisbon and telephone number – 51780 – which does not appear in the November 1940 directory and has presumably been allocated since that date. A description of him is as follows:

> Age 40; medium height and build; dark hair brushed back; dark eyes; thick hanging underlip; looks Portuguese; speaks German.

(j) Kramer

Lenihan was told, in the event of his ever getting to Lisbon, to hand in at the German Consulate a letter asking to see the representative of Dr Schultes, the letter to be enclosed in an envelope simple addressed 'REMARK' which is just 'KRAMER' written backwards.

(k) FRITZ and FRANZ

In the late summer and autumn of 1940, two men were used by the Germans to pick up seamen at the Café Rotal and take them to the Casa

Elama where they were plied with drink and pumped for information. One of these men, known as FRITZ, was a German; the other, FRANZ, was a Dane. Both frequented the Pensao Estargeira. Descriptions of them are as follows:

FRITZ
Age 40/45; short; very fat; brown hair; bald on top; very red face; small brown moustache, shifty eyes; wears glasses for reading; long resident in Lisbon; never been to sea; speaks English, French and Portuguese.

FRANZ
Age 45; height 5′ 6″; slim build; brown hair; small brown moustache; turning grey; pointed face; nervous trembling hands; malarial; former ship's cook; speaks German, French, Dutch, some English and Portuguese, and presumably Danish.

(ii) Non-German Personnel

(a) An unknown Portuguese
When THE SNARK was staying at the Pensao Estrangeira, ie 15 January to 10 March 1941, a Portuguese used to call for the purpose, she thought, of recruiting agents, A description of this man is as follows:

Age 45/50; height 5′ 4″; small; thin; dark hair with a fringe in front and going bald on top; no front teeth in upper jaw; simian appearance; poorly dressed; spoke English and Portuguese.

(b) An unknown Portuguese (?)
On 14 April 1941 Van Wijk got a trunk call from Julia telling him not to leave the Hotel Europa till 'a friend' called to see him. The visitor duly appeared and warned Van Wijk to be careful to carry out his instructions. He spoke French, English and Spanish, but the hotel porter assured Van Wijk that he was Portuguese. A description of him is as follows:

Age 45; height 5′ 6″; stocky build; dark hair; brown eyes; clean-shaven; prosperous appearance; plump hands; pleasant voice.

(c) Verlinden
Verlinden is a doubtful case in that there seems to be some uncertainty as to which side he is double-crossing at any given moment. His history, in so far as it concerns Ham, is briefly as follows:

About 26 June 1940 he arrived in Lisbon on the Pilote 16, a Belgian boat which had brought about forty refugees from Bayonne. There he and de Jager were suborned by HOFFMANN, a German agent who had boarded the *Pilote 16* at Bayonne disguised as a British soldier. Arrangements were made for Verlinden to come to England and collect information for the Germans which would be taken back to Lisbon by de Jaeger. One job he did in the meantime was to act as interpreter between HOFFMANN and Laureyssens. Shortly afterwards he sailed from Lisbon on the SS *Portugall* and at Setubal was given secret instructions by Horst Raider on behalf of HOFFMANN. De Jaeger's description of Verlinden is as follows:

> Age now 23; height 5′ 6″; dark red curly hair brushed back; eyes set close together; no glasses; oval face; reddish complexion; narrow aquiline nose; ears rather large; clean-shaven; athletic looking; well built but not stout; high-pitched voice; well-dressed; has high insteps and has to have boots made specially for him; speaks Flemish, French, English and German.

SUSPECT INDIVIDUALS

In addition to those whose activities prove conclusively that they are German agents, numerous individuals have from time to time been reported as possible German agents, sometimes on slender enough grounds, the degree of guilt attributed to them varying with the mentality of the denouncer. To give a description of all these individuals would create a false impression of the extent of the German organisation or at least of the extent of our knowledge of it, so a few brief details must suffice.

(a) A German at Perpignan

Nothing is less unlikely than that the Germans have agents at the principal point of entry into Spain from unoccupied France. Ejsymont was accosted in the Grand Hotel in Perpignan by a German who apparently took an interest in his movements against whom he was warned by the hotel-keeper. This man was looking for a villa in the neighbourhood. In addition to his German passport he had a special pass signed by de Brinon, authorising him to travel freely between Occupied and Unoccupied France. About the end of March 1941 he left by car for Paris, intending to be away for some four or five weeks. A description of him follows:

Age 36/37; height 5′ 6″; strongly built; light brown hair brushed back and cut very close at the sides; hazel eyes; wears glasses for reading; clean-shaven; one or more gold teeth; slightly Jewish-looking; was wearing a tweed coat and trousers; is thought to be a native of Tangier; spoke French and German and a little Czech.

(b) A German at Peligros No 2, Madrid

A day or so after his arrival in Madrid ie about 30 October 1940, FATHER was taken by Hacke to an office above the Restaurant Bilbaino at Peligros No. 2. Just inside the entrance was a large painting of Junkers 52s bringing the 'Terceio' over from Morocco during the Civil War. The occupant of the office, a German, was an old friend of Hacke who had previously told FATHER that this man would put him up in his apartment in Madrid should there be any difficulties over hotel accommodation. FATHER remembers little about him except that he was over 35.

This man may conceivably be a German businessman named Müller, a fellow-passenger of Van Wijk's in the Madrid 'plane from Berlin on 20 November 1940. Müller, a native of Hamburg, had lived a long time in South America where he had two sons, but the card he gave Van Wijk was Peligros 2, Madrid. From the Madrid telephone directory it appears that there is a firm, H & C Wilmer, agents, telephone numbers 16335 and 15262 at this address. Van Wijk subsequently saw Müller fairly often in Madrid usually in the company of members of the German Legation or of Carlos Lippmann, a suspect German Jew sometimes Netherlands Consul in Madrid. A short description of Müller is as follows:

Age about 50; very tall; very fair hair, red face.

(c) Joaquim Reig (Madrid)

Joaquim Reig, a Spaniard educated in Germany, formerly Zeiss agent in Madrid, is now the agent for UFA-Newsreels, the office of which – Actualidades UFA – is on the seventh floor of Avenina Jose Antonio No. 48. He lives in the Hotel Nueva York which is in the same building.

Van Wijk learned that Reig was listed by the Spanish Secret Police as a German agent. Other grounds for suspecting him are that Van Wijk heard him telephoning someone called PABLO, a significant point in view of the association between Reig and Julia, and that Van Wijk once saw on Reig's desk a copy of secret-ink writing instructions similar to those used by PABLO.

Besides being the UFA representative, Reig is a member of the German Club. A description of him is as follows:

> Age 41; height 5′ 6″; narrow shouldered; thin, wavy black hair brushed back; thin face; olive complexion; wears glasses; wears a gold signet ring; gesticulates when talking; fond of women.

(d) ENRICO (Madrid)

ENRICO, concierge of the Palace Hotel, Madrid, since early 1939, having previously been concierge of the Condestable Hotel, Burgos, is a naturalised Spanish subject of Austrian origin and a Falangist. He is believed to have spied on Van Wijk and communicated information about his movements to PABLO. A description of him is as follows:

> Age 48; height 5′7″; broad shouldered; heavily built; hair turning grey; wears glasses for reading; married to a Spanish woman and has several children, his oldest about 23; seems fairly well educated and speaks Spanish, French, English and Italian as well as German.

(e) Jose Maria Bolivar

In the spring of 1937 Del Campo was introduced to HERMANN at Badajoz by Jose Maria Bolivar, a connection of his by marriage. Bolivar is thought still to be in touch with HERMANN, now an active agent in Madrid. His means of livelihood are a little obscure but he is believed to be a dealer in the Black Market. He lives on the top floor at Velasquez No. 55, Madrid. And also has, or had, an apartment at the Hotel Nacional. He is, of course, a Falangist 'old shirt'. A description of him is as follows:

> Age 35; height 5′ 8″; broad-shouldered; plump; dark wavy hair; round face; clean-shaven; big hands and feet.

SUSPECT GERMAN COMMERCIAL ORGANISATIONS

(1) MADRID

(a) HISMA

Van Wijk had an interview with PABLO at an office on floor H of a large block in the Avenida Jose Antonio. From the fact that there was a stationer's shop on the ground floor and that it was practically opposite the Hotel Bueva York, this block is identified as No. 31. Among the tenants at No. 31 (or No. 9, according to the system of numbering adopted) are HISMA, the Transradio representative and the British Chamber of Commerce. HISMA have another office at the Avenida Generalisimo No. 13, telephone numbers 36637 and 26657and in Barcelona at Paseo de Grasia No. 44 (telephone numbers 13133 and 10601).

Some months ago Del Campo mentioned a certain Alfonso 'Esteimer' who had been employed in 'a German office called HISMA in the Avenida Jose Antonio, above the Café "Zara" (Zahara) and subsequently in an office in the Paseo de Recoletos above the Caje Gijon, opposite the Banco Hipolotecario'. ALFONSO, his brother CARLOS who works at the German Embassy, and his sister, now a nurse in Germany, are the children of Carlos 'Esteimer' the elder, uncle to J. Alonso Colemenares who often flies to Germany. Though there is as yet nothing to show that any of these three is actively engaged in intelligence work, their descriptions are probably worth noting:

> Carlos 'Eister' the elder:
> Age 40/50; tall; broad-shouldered; strongly built; dark hair turning grey and getting thin at the temples; wears glasses; round red face; clean-shaven; small plump hands; wife died on 8 January 1939; Del Campo says he is Spanish and comes from Navarre.
>
> Carlos 'Eistemer' the younger:
> Age about 28; tall; broad-shouldered; dark hair; clean-shaven; large hands with long thin fingers; big; fat; a fanatical Nazi and violently anti-British.

(b) La Hispanense Industrial y Comercial SA

The offices of this German agency are at Evenida Callvo Sotelo (formerly Paseo de Recoletos) No 21 (telephone number 17154. From the advertisement section of the telephone directory appears that they are agents for Skoda, Goerz-Zeiss-Eikon. Buettnerwerke, Erhardt y Seymer, Walther Calculating Machines, and all kinds of machinery.

In section (a) above Del Campo's reference has been quoted to Alfonsa 'Esteimer' who was employed in an office in the Paseo de Racoletos above the Café Gion; that office is La Hispanense Industrial y Comercial SA. Not only does Alfonso 'Esteimer' work there, but, according to Del Campo, EMILIO also. It may be observed that the firm's telephone number – 17134 – is also that of Emilio J S Kiechle of the same address.

(2) LISBON

(a) Firma Brinett Ltda. Praca Duque de Terceira No 24 (fifth floor)
These premises have been used so frequently as a cover-address that little more needs be said about them. Dr Schott, a member of the firm of Brinett, served as an intermediary between FATHER and MARCEL and as his postbox for as long as he was in Lisbon.
(b) Victoria de Berlin Insurance Co. Praca do Municipio No 7 (telephone number 26268)
This firm cropped up only as a telephone number for MARCEL under the alias 'Jaeger'. It has an office in Madrid at Carrera Sn Geronimo No 13 (telephone number 21061).

SUBSIDIARY NON-GERMAN ORGANISATIONS AND PERSONNEL

A sinister feature of German activity in the Iberian Peninsula is the extensive assistance it receives from organisations directly or indirectly controlled by the Spanish and Portuguese governments.

(1) Spanish Government Services
(a) Security Service (Direccion General de Seguridad)
By arrangement with the Spanish authorities, Timmerman, a German agent, was taken to Nanclered concentration camp for three days and on his release on 8 August 1941 was given a certificate to the effect that he had been detained there for three months. This certificate was issued at German instigation for the sole purpose of deceiving the British authorities into believing that Timmerman was a victim of Falangist persecution and a bona-fide refugee.
(b) Passport Office
Some at any rate of the Spanish passport offices, both in Madrid and in Barcelona, are in German pay. Both HERMANN and EMILIO told Del Campo as much, and EMILIO did in fact obtain exit visas for Del Campo and THE SNARK with the greatest ease and expedition. In the case of THE SNARK he brought a Spanish official along with him to the rendezvous at Jevrenovic's empty flat. Del Campo gives the following description of a man, either a Secret Police agent or a passport officer, whom he saw frequently with EMILIO at the Cerveceria Correos:

> Age 25/28; short; thin; wavy black hair; white face; dark eyes; thick black moustache.

(2) Other Spanish Organisations

(a) Falange Postal

The only information about this secret censorship organisation comes from Del Campo and dates from January 1941. It is controlled by its founder Jose Mora Garcia, his lieutenant, De Frances, and Velasco, all three of whom are more violently pro-German and anti-British than the Falange. During the Civil War Mora and Colmenares, on the instructions of General Martinez Anido, Falangist Minister of Public Safety, established a secret mail censorship at San Sebastian which overrode the military censorship. Since the war Mora, now one of the heads of the Post Office, has developed his service as a subversive organisation in German interests. If Tangier were taken over by Spain, Mora expected that either he or his lieutenant De Frances would be appointed Controller-General of Communications there. If there were a coup d'etat in Spain by the extreme pro-German party, Mora would take over the postal and telegraph system immediately on their behalf.

(b) Colmenares and his friends

An equally dangerous group is constituted by Colmenares and his friends, Joaquin Alonso Colmenare, employed at the Direccion General de Sevuros, Serrano No. 69, is an exceedingly violent 'Old Guard'. Falangist and friend of Medilla whose abortive coup was, according to Colmenares, supported by the Condor Legion. His late father, Don Dario Alonso Colmenares, was chairman of the Lascaris-Comneno Committee, a curious organisation formed to promote the claim of the Lascaris-Comneno family to the throne of Byzantium, while Joaquin himself was a claimant to the throne of Albania! Of his two sister, one, Maria Isabel, married to Escequel Murietta de la Cases, living at Espartinas No 5, is, like her husband, a Falangist and a pro-Nazi; the other, Pilar, married to Dr Jose Manuel Herrero Corjita, living at Alcala No 161, is, like her husband, anti-Fascist and pro-British. In fact Dr Herrero and his friend Carbonell, who took a friendly interest in Del Campo and lives at Velasquez No 53, are suspected by Colmenares of being British agents.

Colmenares, whose uncle Carlos 'Esteimer', is mentioned in Section VI (i)(a), regularly visits the German Military Attaché, and is as aggressively anti-British as he is pro-Nazi. Del Campo gives his address as Calle Particular de la Sud America No 2, ground floor.

Of his many anti-British and pro-Nazi friends the most conspicuously active is Luis Fernandes del Pino, formerly one of the heads of the Falange Intelligence Service. During the summer of 1940 he discussed with Herrero a scheme he had devised for a Nazi Intelligence Service in Spain to be run by himself. Del Campo believes he has agents in Tangier and North Africa and in January this year was about to visit

Tangier 'to clean it up'. He used to live in the Chamartin de la Rosa district of Madrid, possibly at Calle Jose Picon No 3 la Cuindalera, but the June 1941 directory shows he is no longer at this address.

(3) Portugal
Lisbon International Police
Ocana's experience suggests that the International Police behave as though Portugal, instead of being neutral territory, were governed by Franco and they were his appointed agents for the apprehension of escaped Republicans. Despite the fact that Ocana has been signed on a Swedish boat, with the sanction of the Swedish, Spanish and British Consulates, the International Police refused him an exit permit until they had received his assurance that during the Civil War he had fought for Franco.

VISITING SECRET SERVICE OFFICIALS

The Iberian stations receive periodic visits from outside officials. Some of these visits have clearly been for the purpose of supervising the instruction and disposal of agents under their control and it is quite possible that, if sufficient data were available, every one of them could be linked up to the movements or activities of some particular agent.

(a) Hacke @ Martin Holstein and Rademacher
On 4 November 1940 FATHER arrived in Barcelona, having been escorted the whole way from Brussels by Hacke and Rademacher. From Bairritz they had travelled by car via Burgos, where they stayed at the German-managed Hotel Condestable, and Madrid, where Hacke and Rademacher stayed at the Hotel Gran Via and FATHER at the Hotel Derby in the Calle Arlaban. From Madrid they flew to Barcelona where Hacke and Rademacher put up at the Hotel Majestic while FATHER was accommodated for the first few nights in the apartment of the German proprietor of the Cerveveria Hispano-Aleman and then at the Hotel Regina.

Hacke never had any difficulty over such things as visas or residence permits in Spain because wherever he went he merely showed his Condor Legion card, the perfect 'open sesame'. In Spain he was known as Martin Haustein, the name under which he had fought as a legionary.

After making the necessary arrangements for FATHER with PABLO, Hacke and Rademacher left Barcelona for Madrid on their way back to Brussels about 13 November 1940.

Descriptions of Hacke and Rademacher are as follows:-

Hacke
Age 37/38; height over 6 ft; slim but powerful build; light brown hair; thin face; clean-shaven; good teeth; qualified wireless operator; speaks English, French, Spanish, Italian and possibly Russian. Hacke knew Madrid well and may have worked there before the war as an agent for the Lorenz Landing Beacon Co.

Rademacher
Age 40; height 5′ 7″; plump; round face; black hair; clean-shaven; brown eyes; no glasses; engineer by profession; speaks French.

(b) Kliemann @ Kielburg
Kliemann, under the name of Kielburg, saw DRAGONFLY in Lisbon in December 1940. He told him that he was attached to the Paris station which controlled all espionage against England. (In July 1941 Kliemann, in representing Dr Shultes of Paris, flew from Schipol to Buc with Lenihan.) A description of him is as follows:-

Age 45; height 5′ 7″; dark brown wavy hair slightly graying; dark brown eyes; rather thin face; small brown moustache; dark complexion; long nose; nominally a Luftwaffe officer; speaks French; born in Vienna and educated at Klagenfurt.

(c) Schultes, WERNER, WITZI and VOGEL
In addition to Kliemann, the above four members of the Paris Dienstelle are all reported by Lenihan as having visited Spain and Portugal within the past twelve months. The precise sequence of their visits is as follows:-

Dr Schultes was in Lisbon just before Christmas 1940 and probably also at the end of April 1941. A description of him is as follows:-

Age 47; height 5′ 5″; brown eyes; fair healthy complexion; large head; square face; mouse coloured hair; speaks perfect English.

WITZI (wireless instructor) was in Spain for about a week at the end of February 1941, travelling via Bordeaux. He cannot speak English. A description of him is as follows:

Age 35; height 5′ 7″; fair hair; blue eyes; pug nose; Germanic appearance.

WERNER was in San Sebastian in May 1941. A description of him is as follows:

> Age 41; height 6' 1"; brown eyes; long face; long nose; loose mouth; stoops when he walks; dandified in dress; officer in the last war; drives a Chrysler car; speaks excellent Spanish, Italian, English and French.

VOGEL was in San Sebastian in May 1941. A description of him is as follows:

> Age 23; height 6 ft; stout; black hair; puffed out face; very flashily dressed; speaks English.

(d) Francisco Garcia
This man escorted Timmerman and two other Belgian agents from Paris, whence they set out on 26 July 1941 to Bayonne; here he left the two unnamed Belgians at the Naval Barracks and went on alone with Timmerman as far as San Sebastian where they arrived on 4 August and where he handed Timmerman over to Aiguabella. Garcia, who is presumably employed by Paris, gave Timmerman the following address and telephone number: Francisco Garcia, Calle Francisco Rojas No 2, Madrid, telephone number 26082. There is no Francisco Garcia recorded at this address in the Madrid directory, while 26082 is Jose Aigubella's telephone number.

TELEPHONE ARRANGEMENTS

(a) MADRID
The system of telephonic communication with agents applied in Madrid suggests a more elaborate organisation there from a precautionary standpoint, than in Barcelona and Lisbon. The Van Wijk case affords a clear illustration of the working of the system. PABLO gave Van Wijk a telephone number – 58062. When Van Wijk rang this number he was to say: 'This is ERNESTO;I want to speak to DON PABLO'. A Spanish girl would answer the 'phone, take the enquiry and in due course ring back a reply. Van Wijk never spoke to PABLO direct.

On no account, however, was Van Wijk to ring 58062 from a public telephone or call-box. If he wished to speak from, say, a café, he had to ring Julia at a workman's bar near her house – she had no telephone of her own – and get her to transmit the message. Julia herself would then call 58062 and say: 'This is FLORA. I want to speak to EMILIO'. When she got a reply she would telephone it back to Vann Wijk. This curious arrangement led Van Wijk to suppose that PABLO and EMILIO were one and the same person.

The number used, 58062, proves to be that of a subscriber named Rufino Diaz Castellano, living in Cuidad Jardin, a villa district on the outskirts of the city just beyond Chamartin. It seems likely that it is used as a private Secret Service telephone exchange.

Ejsymont's experience was similar. FEDERICO gave him a number which Ejsymont thinks began and ended (?) with '62' and told him to ring if possible between 1300 and 1430 hrs, using the words 'This is EDUARDO. I want to speak to FEDERICO'. Ejsymont was never able to speak to FEDERICO direct; his message was always taken by a woman who would tell him to ring again to get a reply.

Both Van Wijk and Del Campo, while in Lisbon, had calls from Madrid. Van Wijk from Julia on behalf of PABLO and Del Campo from some unknown individual on behalf of EMILIO. In no single case did any of the leading German Secret Service officials speak on the telephone himself.

(b) BARCELONA

FATHER was given by PABLO the telephone number 77047 through which he could get in touch with any of those members of the German organisation with whom he habitually spent his time. The 'phone was answered by a girl who had great difficulty in understanding French and was probably Spanish. After some delay she would either connect PABLO, PEDRO, TOMAS or whoever had been asked for. There is then quite obviously a private exchange at that number.

The address of this number FATHER had always assumed to be the house in the Calle Descartes, but according to the Barcelona telephone directory it is the number of a certain Bagesnki, B of Calle Lincoln No 52 who can be identified with some degree of confidence as Baron Bogislav von Bagenski, a German officer who lived in Madrid from 1929 to 1934 and ex-husband of Mrs Montgomery, now in Holloway. A photograph of Bagenski, taken some years ago, will be found in Appendix S.

(c) LISBON

There is no evidence as yet of the existence of any central telephone exchange for the German Secret Service staff in Lisbon, the majority of whom appear to be attached to the Legation or the Consulate and to be accessible at those addresses. It is nevertheless possible that MARCEL's number, 63015, serves as a private exchange.

COVER ADDRESSES

The following sixteen cover-addresses, arranged in chronological order, have been given to ten agents within the past twelve months:

1 August 1940 (Caroli and Schmidt)

Daisy Lopez
Santo Amaro d'Cirfas
Marius Silvas 33
LISBON

2 September 1940 (de Jaeger)

Mlle Flora de Conciego de Gomez
Rua de Gavias 59-3, right
LISBON

Mlle Maria de Lourdes Gomez
Rua de Gavias 59-3°, right
LISBON

Mme da Silva
Av Miguel Bombarde 34-4°, right
LISBON

5 October 1940 (Laureyssens)

Maria Jose Santos
Rua 20 April, 48
LISBON

6 December 1940 (DRAGONFLY)

Antonio Marthos
Paco d'Arcos
Rua Davonte Mayo 27
Portugal

7 December 1940 (FATHER)

Francisco Jorba Bueno
Calle Caspe 37
BARCELONA

Tomas Aiscorve
Calle Marimon
Villa Maria
BARCELONA

9 January 1941 (Lenihan)

Siegfried Aehner
Hotel Maris Cristina
SAN SEBASTIAN

10 March 1941 (Van Wijk)

Baroness Jule von Reigersberg Versluys
Serrano 176
MADRID

11 May 1941 (Ejsymont)

Manuel Rodriguez Inglesas
Apartado 179
MADRID

Luis Fernandez
Flordia 10
MADRID

13 June 1941 (THE SNARK)

Sta. Carmen Rodriguez Ingelias
Lista, 91
MADRID

Carlos Ramos
Rua Actor Taborda, 46
LISBON

16 June 1941 (Lenihan)

Don Luis Fernandez Heredia
Plaza de Jesus 3
LISBON

16 August 1941 (Timmerman)

Ampareo de Melo
Praca de Flores 24 bis 1°
LISBON

Appendix III

German Penetration of SOE, SIS and Allied Organisations

The MI5 report dated April 1943 and compiled by Jack Curry, as requested by the Director-General,Sir David Petrie, amid growing concern about enemy penetration of Allied intelligence networks in Europe.

Introductory Remarks

1. It is proposed to attempt to set out the facts relevant to the problem of providing a 'protective umbrella' for the operations of SOE and SIS, as far as they can be studied from the material available at present in this office. It should be emphasised that this is written without any knowledge of the organisation and policy of SOE. SIS presents a different problem and is not dealt with in any detail.

2. In the first place it is desirable to explain what is meant by a 'protective umbrella'. The idea underlying this convenient cliché is to provide for counter-espionage and security arrangements which will facilitate the successful operations of these organisations and their agents, and obstruct or prevent their detection by the enemy in so far as this is possible by preventive measures. These preventive measures must here include such steps as may be necessary to counter the moves of the enemy counter-espionage organisation when they succeed in getting SOE or SIS agents under their control.

3. The facts relevant to this problem fall under five main heads:

i) those disclosed by actual cases of penetration by the enemy,

ii) those concerning the system and technique employed by SOE and SIS in training, controlling and directing the activities of their agents,

iii) the policies followed by SOE and SIS in this connection and the policies of the British and Allied Governments, which lie behind the departmental policies and are directed towards sustaining the national resistance movements in occupied territories,

iv) the problems presented by the relations between SOE, SIS and MI5 among themselves and their relations with the Allied Intelligence services,

v) the facts, as far as they are known, regarding the methods and organisations of the enemy, i.e. the Abwehr, the Sicherheitsdienst, the Geheime Feldpolizei (Secret Field Police) and the Gestapo.

4. In the present report it is not proposed to deal with any of these heads in any detail, except under (i), but it will be obvious that the question of counter-espionage arrangements is inseparable from that of the policies, methods and systems followed by SOE and SIS. It will be sufficient for present purposes if the fact that the other heads have a bearing on the problem is kept in mind.

5. The following details which relate to Belgium, Norway and France are not intended to be comprehensive. They are merely to be regarded as an illustrative cross-section of some of our information and have not been selected to prove any particular point of view. All the cases are dealt with very briefly and as a rule long and complicated stories have necessarily been simplified. There is information on our records relating to other cases in these countries; and also regarding Abwehr III, Geheime Feldpolizei or 'Gestapo' and Sicherheitsdienst operations against SOE or SIS organisations and indigenous resistance movements in other countries, such as Holland, Greece and elsewhere, but our records are far from being exhaustive and often leave us in doubt as to whether an organisation is primarily British (SOE or SIS) or indigenous.

II Belgian Cases

6. In view of the complicated nature of the problem it seems desirable to treat one particular aspect of it in some detail by way of making a fairly close examination of a small part of the field, as an illustration of the

kind of problem which arises for consideration. For this purpose SOE operations in Belgium have been selected. Belgium, however, is not a typical case, in the sense that the SOE section dealing with Belgium has met with exceptionally serious setbacks and it is understood that the question has arisen of taking drastic action to curtail activities in that country, at any rate for a time, owing to the fact that nearly all the SOE agents who have been sent there are known to be compromised or are regarded as doubtful. In consequence of these facts steps have been taken to examine the causes of failure and to avoid some of them by arranging for more complete records to be kept about each agent and of all the circumstances connected with him, with a view to making it possible to check all the relevant facts and also to impose workable identity checks whenever an agent is suspected to be under the control of the enemy.

7. Special difficulties which have arisen in the case of SOE operations in Belgium are stated to arise from the fact that the Belgian Prime Minister, M. Pierlot, and the Belgian Suretė are inclined to give independent instructions to SOE agents without keeping SOE informed. Another outstanding cause of failure has been due to the marked tendency of Belgian agents to make contact with one another when in Belgium. This tendency is to be attributed to various causes, among them being the fact that they are trained as SOE agents in groups; that they have sometimes been given instructions to make contact with one another; that they have at other times made unauthorised contacts – a tendency which is promoted by the special conditions in Belgium – and that whenever a man has been recruited from the Belgian Army for SOE duties a notice is posted announcing that he has been seconded to the British for a special mission. An even more important source of difficulty is to be found in the fact that while SOE have in some cases given their agents a sabotage mission, the Belgian authorities in this country are believed to have given contrary instructions and to have been anxious to discourage sabotage because they did not wish their factories to be damaged and they prefer to support a policy of 'go slow'. (If there is this cleavage in a fundamental question of policy, it would seem to be necessary that a compromise should be arrived at on a high level.)

Jean Prosper Cassart and the LUÇ organisation

8. As an illustration of the extent of the material it may be mentioned that there are no less than 41 files, roughly representing some 40 persons who have passed through the LRC and given information

about the LUC organisation (and this is typical of many other cases). In spite of this, there is no complete picture of the LUC organisation, although very detailed information has been extracted from the 41 files and put on the Information Index (the principal object in view being to supply data useful to LRC interrogators who examine people coming from Belgium). Many of these files deal with the penetration of the organisation connected with the case of Jean Prosper Cassart, an SOE agent who was arrested in Belgium on 13 December 1941, but there is no sufficient material on record in this office to show whether that case has been fully investigated, nor is it possible to arrive at the exact facts about the penetration at that time. It seems probable that fuller information is available in SOE than we have in this office. Further information, again, is undoubtedly available in the Belgian Sureté, but if SOE and the Sureté have conducted a full investigation into the cause of the breakdown, the precise results do not appear to be available here.

9. The LUC organisation is closely connected with other SOE and SIS organisations, as shown in the Appendix, and with the extremely important and very large organisation based on the Belgian Army.

10. As mentioned in the Appendix, the LUC organisation shows signs of having been penetrated more than once, the most important instance being in connection with the case of Jean Prosper Cassart. Cassart was a Belgian officer who refused to surrender with the Belgian Army and eventually made his way to England, where he became an agent of SOE. He had already given evidence of his zeal by collecting military information about the German occupation of Belgium and France. He was dropped in Belgium by SOE on 3 October 1941 with Henri Verhaegen, who was to act as his W/T operator. Cassart was arrested by the Germans on 13 December 1941 and Verhaegen eventually made his way back to England through France and Spain. According to one report some 200 people in Belgium, as well as the Société Generale, were involved after Cassart's arrest, although it is also stated that Cassart, in spite of very brutal treatment, refused to make a statement to the Germans.

11. Among the events which preceded Cassart's arrest the following stand out. On or about 10 October 1941 Cassart and one Bernard, a leading member of the organisation, met another member named Jamart at Brussels. Shortly afterwards Jamart left for Paris, where he met a Luxembourger named Richir. Jamart very indiscreetly gave Richir a lot of information about the whole organisation and Richir

then admitted that he was a German agent. Jamart returned to Belgium and warned various members, including Bernard and Leclercq but, presumably because he did not tell the whole truth and they did not regard him as very reliable, they did not pay much attention. Early in October the German Secret Field Police, (Geheime Feldpolizei) searched Jamart's house. On the next day Jamart told one of his colleagues named Deschamps that one Jacobs was a traitor. Glazer, describing himself as the founder of the Legion Belge, has stated that a great deal of harm was done to the Legion by the personal treachery of Jamart. A suspicion of being concerned in treachery which led to Cassart's arrest also fell on one of the members named Nessu, in whose house Verhaegen's W/T set was at one time kept. Verhaegen, however, says that he enquired into the allegations and decided that Nessu was not guilty. According to one Libotte, Nessu sold the W/T code to the Germans and he alleges that the Germans thus got to know Verhaegen's code and tried to send messages to the UK, i.e. at some time shortly after the middle of October 1941.

12. After Verhaegen's return to this country he made a long statement giving an account almost from day to day of the events which preceded and followed Cassart's arrest. Five days before the arrest, i.e. on 8th December, Cassart, Verhaegen and two others were attempting to arrange for a Lysander to land near Neufchateau when they were interrupted by some German soldiers, after which the Germans appear to have got on the track of both Cassart and Verhaegen. The whole incident has been the subject of discussion between officers of B1, SOE and the Belgian Sureté, as well as Captain Brooke-Booth of E Division who commented that it seems that the whole unfortunate affair was due not to treachery, but to the normal risks attached to such an enterprise. Presumably this is the result of a more or less formal enquiry, but precise details are not available on the files relating to Cassart or Verhaegen and there is no indication that the affair connected with Richir and Jamart has been fully probed. In the circumstances it is not possible to form a definite opinion on the cause of the penetration, or to discuss steps which could have been taken to prevent it, but presumably this information is available in SOE. (The LRC files of the 40-odd people who have referred to the LUC organisation have not all been studied for this purpose.)

13. Some slight indication of the character of Cassart had the nature of the LUC organisation may be obtained from the fact that Cassart had arranged a body of released convicts, under the supervision of

a Belgian police officer, who were to kill Germans and bury them secretly in Belgian graveyards. Again, this Belgian officer when arrested showed presence of mind by giving a signal to two of his confederates, which prevented them from falling into German hands. When Verhaegen was arrested at the time when they were attempting to arrange for a Lysander to land, he escaped by wresting his rifle from one of the German soldiers and, although wounded, ran for 5 or 6 kilometres through the snow until he became feverish from the wound. One of their associates named Debroeu had Verhaegen's W/T set in his house at the time of Cassart's arrest. A German officer and three soldiers came to search Debroeu's house. His wife, knowing that he was going to fire on the Germans, fainted and in spite of this fact he attacked them, killing or wounding three of them and escaped into the road in his pyjamas, where he met Verhaegen, and then the two went quietly to a friend's farm to obtain clothes and to make arrangements to warn other of his associates. In spite of the fact that the Germans were looking for him, Verhaegen remained in Belgium and carried on the work of the organisation at great personal risk. On one occasion he and two Belgian police officers, believing that the Germans were after Verhaegen, walked through the streets of Liege fully prepared to shoot at any German who interfered with them.

ANDREE Escape Organisation

14. The LUC organisation, among others, made use of the ANDREE organisation, which was established immediately after the capitulation by Andree pére and his daughter for the purpose of setting up an escape route. It ran from Brussels, through Paris and Bayonne, to the Spanish frontier where a British organisation took over from it. In May 1942 the Brussels end was broken up by the Germans and Andree escaped to Paris. A Baron Jean Grundel in Brussels then re-established the Belgian end. In consultation with ANDREE it was agreed that henceforward they would confine themselves to passing RAF men or highly skilled air mechanics out of Belgium. The new arrangements functioned satisfactorily until the middle of November, 1942. About that time two individuals who are regarded as being undoubted German agents got into touch with the organisation in the guise of American airmen. Immediately afterwards a number of members of the organisation were arrested and the Brussels end collapsed again. This escape route was used by other organisations, such as the Dame Blanche.

15. In July 1942 the extent of the German knowledge of the ANDREE organisation was proved by the way in which the Abwehr made plans

to use it to send one of their agents, a Belgian named Gabriel Jules Emanuel Pry, from Belgium via Spain to England and the Congo. For this purpose the Abwehr utilised Mme Fiorina Dings, an important double agent, whose chief function was to constitute the link between the Abwehr and patriot circles in Belgium which had been penetrated by the Germans and were being used for their own purposes. Pry obtained a number of letters from Gildon, a distinguished patriot and statesman in Belgium and General Secretary of the Association des Interets Coloniaux Belges. These letters were addressed to the Governor General of the Congo and the Colonial Minister of the Belgian Government in London. They were long and contained a quantity of information about the national morale in occupied territory and proposals for sustaining the spirit of resistance. The Abwehr evidently hoped to gain valuable intelligence about the Congo and no less valuable information about the activities of Belgian patriots in the Congo, in England and inside Belgium, by a plot, according to which Pry was to use these letters from Gildon to enable him to travel between the three countries, having gained the confidence of the Belgian authorities concerned.

16. From all these circumstances it would appear to be possible that the penetration of the ANDREE organisation has given Abwehr Abteilung III in Belgium a very considerable amount of information about Belgian resistance movements and SOE agents, and the extent of the penetration cannot easily be assessed.

17. (The information which reaches us often stops short at such points as the introduction of the two German agents in the guise of American airmen, but we do not know how the Germans obtained the information which enabled them to effect the penetration which made this introduction possible. The explanation may often lie in the use of agents, as in the case of Mme. Fiorina Dings. If Pry had not been suspected by the Belgian Legation in Lisbon, and therefore sent to London for further enquiry, he would probably have been an extremely important agent for penetration by the Abwehr. The reason for suspicion falling on Pry at the Belgian Legation in Lisbon was that he had German documents in the shape of a passierchein and a durchlasschein.)

18. As mentioned above, Mme. Fiorina Dings was used by the Abwehr to make plans to send Pry via the ANDREE organisation in July. This information reached us at the LRC in October and the full story was

known after interrogation at Camp 020 in December. There is nothing on Pry's file to show that we have communicated this information to SOE although it seems possible that if they had possessed it in October they might have been able to prevent Andree's daughter from being arrested by the Germans in November (or later). We have no other information about Fiorina Dings, except that contained in Pry's statement, but we know that the Belgian Sureté know her as the mistress of one Dezutter, alias Captain Coll, alias Jack Colen, a Belgian who has been naturalised as a German and is known to penetrate escape organisations by sending young Belgians through them. This information is stated to have been confirmed by Ugueux, mentioned in the Appendix as connected with the ZERO organisation.

19. (It therefore seems that our information is incomplete on many points where more detailed information is available in SOE or the Allied Intelligence organisations, and the question suggests itself whether it is not desirable for more complete information on such matters to be recorded centrally and to be at the immediate disposal of LRC interrogators, as well as for subsequent interrogation at Camp 020.)

Oscar Katherine

20. The story of one of the most important disasters in connection with Belgium has been told in a report by Mr. Harvey of B1(a) dated 28 November 1942. While the report shows that the conditions under which the SOE agents were controlled from this country and the conditions under which they worked in Belgium have been such that no counter-espionage arrangements of a purely protective kind could have prevented the disasters, the first essential was great care and careful organisation in making the arrangements for the despatch and control of agents and, if that is possible, steps to ensure that they carried out instructions. It appears that in certain cases they have failed to carry out instructions, even when their own lives were in the balance. The story in the above mentioned report deals with the cases of a number of SOE agents sent to Belgium, many of them having been recruited from the Belgian Army or through the Belgian Sureté in London. The details are extremely complicated and the report itself does not purport to be complete, but the following are some of the outstanding points. M. Pierlot, the Belgian Prime Minister, desired to arrange for a Belgian named Marc Delforge to leave Belgium and come to the United Kingdom and, without informing SOE, the Belgian Sureté gave instructions to Oscar Katherine of the Belgian Army, who was dropped by SOE by parachute near Mons on the night of 28-29 January 1942 together with Maurice Aarens, also recruited from the Belgian Army,

who was to act as his W/T operator. The B1(a) report shows that they were furnished with admirable cover stories and suitable documents to match them. It appears, however, that at an early date Aarens fell into the hands of the Germans and his W/T set was operated under their control. This fact did not become known to SOE until several months later, i.e. after Marc Delforge arrived in this country on 21 August 1942. Delforge was interrogated at the RVPS, which he left on 29 August 1942, but it was not until nearly a month later that SOE learnt of it, and they learnt it from PID, who sent them a copy of a report in which he disclosed details not mentioned by him at the RVPS. When interrogated at the RVPS he had, however, stated that he had met Oscar Katherine, who had come to inform him on or about 3 February 1942 that Pierlot desired him to make his way to the UK and this fact was also mentioned in the PID version which gave more elaborate details. In the meanwhile, however, in April 1942 a message had been received from the W/T operator Aarens to the effect that he – i.e. presumably Oscar Katherine – had not had time to get in touch with Delforge. That is to say, this message was sent under German control, but the fact was not appreciated at the time. In this connection, the B1(a) report shows that in the light of after events it might be possible to pick holes in the traffic, but allowing for the circumstances of the case, it can hardly be said that there were any definite indications prior to the arrival of Delforge that Aarens was under control. The consequence of the fact that Aarens was under control not being realised was to bring disaster to a number of other agents, regarding whom instructions were sent to Oscar Katherine. Oscar Katherine's mission to Belgium is stated to have been largely a propaganda one and he was also to send political information and to make contact with existing organisations, in particular with the publishers of secret newspapers, and to engage in sabotage as a side-line when opportunity offered. In addition to all this he was to arrange 'reception committees' for the arrival of supplies and to reconnoitre landing grounds for Lysander operations. Apart from this, as already indicated, he received elaborate instructions from the Belgian Sureté, including the names of many useful contacts in Belgium. The function of the 'reception committees' was to show lights to enable Lysanders to land supplies or agents at a spot prearranged on the traffic and selected by the 'reception committee' as suitable. It follows that various supplies, including arms which were dropped on 30 April 1942, and three agents dropped in May, June and August fell into German hands after they had Aaren's W/T set under their control. On 10 May 1942 Aarens – under German control as explained above – reported that various people with whom he had concealed the arms dropped on 30 April 1942 were getting nervous and asked for somebody to whom they could be delivered. He was given the name of Major Gaston Ohain. (This undoubtedly gave the Germans information of special importance, and if they have penetrated his organisation by keeping it under observation and obtaining statements about it from Ohain or other members, the consequences may be very far-reaching but the exact facts are not available here.) On 28 May 1942 Aarens reported that Ohain was too nervous to receive the arms and asked for another name: he was given that of a man called Potter. The agents dropped in May and June were instructed to organise passive resistance and carry out sabotage. The man who dropped in August, Pierre Rauld Osterreith, appears to have had a more important mission, evolved by the Belgian Sureté with the consent of PID. He was to influence prominent Belgian industrialists to develop a 'go-slow' movement and he was furnished with powerful letters from the Belgian Government in favour of their policy. His mission had been approved by the Foreign Office. He was actually dropped on 27 August 1942 and had the significance of Delforge's statement at the RVPS on 25 August 1942 been appreciated Osterreith's life could have been saved. It was not appreciated because there was no one at the RVPS who had any knowledge of the significance of the fact that Delforge had received his instructions from Pierlot through Oscar Katherine in February and that the Aarens W/T set had reported in April that Katherine had not yet got into touch. Steps have been taken to remedy this kind of gap in the protective arrangements by the issue of instructions that copies of statements made at the LRC are in future to be sent without delay to the country sections of SOE. A difficulty which apparently has not been got over is that SIS insist that references to SIS agents shall not be sent in this way to SOE. In this particular case Deforge did in fact mention an important SIS agent and he does not appear to have made it clear – even if he knew – whether Oscar Katherine was an agent of the Belgian Surete, SOE or SIS. In view of the operational importance of SOE activities, it would seem necessary that in such matters first priority should be given to the need for SOE to have the fullest and promptest possible knowledge of information obtained at the LRC, or from any other security source, in matters where the safety of their agents may be at stake.

21. The B1(a) report mentions that from the security point of view the general picture is extremely disquieting and suggests that any refugee who claims to have come from Belgium by any of the escape routes in recent months may at some time have been in touch with one of the SOE agents or their contacts, and as these agents are in frequent if unauthorised touch with each other and since a considerable number of them are or have been in German hands, the suspicion arises that any refugee arriving in this way may be acting for the Germans.

22. In view of the connection between some of the important Belgian organisations mentioned in the Appendix, such as LUC, Les Mousquetaires, the Belgian Military Organisation (including the Legion Belge) and the Zero organisation, and the fact that some of the captured agents have contact with them, it seems possible that the Germans (whether Abteilung III or the Gestapo are principally concerned, or most probably both) have penetrated Belgian organisations to an extent which may have an important effect, not only on SOE operations which may be timed to coincide with an invasion of the Continent, but also on the conduct of the military operations and on the future of our relations with Belgium, or even on the future of Belgium itself.

23. The reason for thinking that all this might have such serious consequences is to be found in the way in which the Nazi leaders and their instruments, such as the Gestapo, have acted in the past. For instance, these Belgian cases and others have shown that the Abwehr having once penetrated an organisation will hold on to it for a very long time without taking action to break it up. They will gradually penetrate further and further into the organisation by watching it and making occasional arrests, or by turning an agent round to work for them. There can be little doubt that on the 'Night of the Long Knives' they acted on information which had been accumulated over a period and then, on Hitler's orders, took drastic action by executing hundreds of Germans. Hitler himself has proclaimed that this is his method; that he watches for a long time and then pounces when the time is ripe. In view of the possibility that several Belgian organisations have been penetrated it may not be too far-fetched to suggest that there is the possibility that the Nazis may be preparing to act against the numerous Belgian organisations, including that based on the Belgian regiments, in a similarly dramatic way and that the most probable occasion for such action would be at the time of an Allied invasion of the Continent. There is no direct evidence of this, but it would seem to be worthwhile to suggest that the possibility should be kept in mind.

III Norwegian Cases

Small boat cases

24. Two cases occurred in 1941 and one in 1943 in which in which the Abwehr attempted to penetrate Norwegian or British organisations in this country by sending agents on small boats.

25. On 16 March 1941 the MV *Olaf* arrived at Lerwick from Trondheim with three Norwegians on board. Two of them, named Johansen and Solem, were subsequently employed by SOE. In November 1941 reliable information showed that Johansen had come here on an Abwehr mission. The exact circumstances have never been fully cleared up, but there can be little doubt that the Abwehr intention was to penetrate SOE, and the case is instructive as showing the difficulty in the way of the detection of such cases by interrogation at the LRC in the absence of definite information.

26. On 8 July 1941 the MV *Hernie* arrived at Lerwick from Bergen. In this case prior information had been received that one of the three Norwegians was an Abwehr agent and Helmik Wallem, the man in question, confessed on being interrogated here. It was a straightforward attempt to penetrate SOE and was planned by Abwehr Abt. III. Helmik Wallem was a qualified wireless operator and the Abwehr apparently believed that this would result in his having no difficulty in obtaining employment as a British agent. The difficulty of detecting agents of the type of Wallem is enhanced by the fact that it is not necessary for them to carry any incriminating material.

27. On 8 January 1943 the MV *Melder* arrived at Lerwick from Aalesund with three Norwegians on board. One of them, named Arnold Evensen, confessed that he had been an agent of the Abwehr in Trondheim and that his mission was to proceed to England in the guise of a refugee with the other two who were unaware of his intentions. One of them, Lewis Westrum, wanted to obtain a wireless transmitter in England in order to establish contact with a resistance organisation in Norway. His intention had become known to the Abwehr and Evensen's instructions were to ingratiate himself with Westrum in order to get himself sent back to Norway by the British Intelligence to supply the required transmitter to the organisation with which Westrum was in contact. The above is a greatly simplified account of a very involved case.

The Bergen Organisation

28. Early in 1941 a number of Norwegian groups were working in Bergen collecting information. They eventually came under the leadership of Johan Hefsdahl and were in contact with the Military group escape organisation. An important part was played by Eystein Henrik Magnus who among other activities managed a photographic department for the organisation. He employed one Rolf Bonnevie in this photographic department and later removed Bonnevie on account

of his lack of discretion, but gave him some other work to do. In August 1941 very reliable information was received that a German agent was in touch with Bonnevie and had his confidence. It appeared that this agent was Olaf Pjettursen. It is known that Olaf Pjettursen had been working for the Germans in 1940, 1941 and 1942. In the summer of 1941 he was responsible for the arrangements by which the MV *Hernie* was sent to this country, as mentioned in para 26 above. Wallem, the German agent on the *Hernie*, was however unaware that Pjettursen was also a German agent and believed that he was a genuine organiser of Norwegian escape parties.

29. Refsdahl, who arrived in this country on 24 September 1942, reported on 24 June 1942 he saw Rudolf Hess, Bonnevie's successor in Magnus's photographic department, and that Hess told him that Pjettursen had made an offer through Bonnevie to supply him with a military map of certain German fortifications in Norway. Hess had refused the offer and Refsdahl told Hess not to have anything to do with Pjettursen as he had been warned against him by a member of the Oslo Police. On the following day Bonnevie was arrested and this was followed by a series of arrests of people whose names were known to Bonnevie. Further arrests also followed and, having done all they could to protect the remaining members of the organisation, Magnus and Refsdahl both came over to this country. They are both regarded as being completely loyal Norwegians, and they believe Bonnevie to have been an innocent dupe, not a traitor. Bonnevie was reported to be an SOE agent and presumably the facts about his connection with Pjettursen were communicated to SOE by SIS in 1941. As far as can be seen, it is not possible to say from the information on record whether Pjettursen penetrated the organisation only at the time of Bonnevie's arrest in June 1942, or had been watching Bonnevie, or getting information from him, from about the time of the *Hernie* affair in June 1941.

Tor Guldbransen

30. Tor Guldbransen is a Norwegian officer who was trained by SOE and sent on a mission to Norway. According to his own statement, he landed on 22 February 1942 at Televaag near Bergen and went to Brammen where his parents lived, on 28 February 1942. There he got in touch with a number of local people and a local organisation. He gave instruction in guerrilla warfare to a number of Norwegians. He went to his parents' house in Brammen early in May and the Gestapo learned of his presence and arrested him. He attempted to escape but was shot and badly wounded, and suffered from temporary and

partial paralysis. In a very weak state in hospital he was subjected to interrogation by the Gestapo and to what he described as mental torture, which consisted in part of being compelled to listen to what sounded like the screams of people being tortured. (There is a suggestion that gramophone records were used for this purpose.) For a long time he tried to conceal the truth or mislead his interrogators but eventually broke down. He states that his interrogators were in possession of a great deal of information about SOE, its training schools, methods and its officers, as well as about Norwegians who had been trained for dispatch to Norway as agents. When he made any misleading statement it was invariably carefully checked and he was made to suffer for departures from the truth. They also knew a good deal about his associates in Norway and had obtained possession of a code and some addresses which were in his possession.

31. Finally, under great pressure, he consented to return to England to act as a German agent, with a view to obtaining further information about SOE and sending the information back to the Germans in Norway and to find out what was known in England about the German agents in Great Britain. In the alternative he was to return to Norway as an SOE agent if that were possible. In order to obtain a hold on him, his parents, his fiancée and other relatives were put under arrest and he was also told that if he admitted on his return to England that he had agreed to work for the Germans he would be guilty of high treason.

32. The Germans staged a faked escape in a forest, in the course of which, in spite of not having fully recovered from his illness, he knocked down two Germans (who were playing their parts) and ran through the trees without being caught or hit by the shots they fired. He got back to England through Sweden where he arrived on 19 October 1942, having sent a message to the 'Gestapo' as an earnest [sign] of his good intentions and in the hope that it would lead, as promised, to the release of his mother. In the message he gave some information about Norwegians who had already escaped from their clutches.

33. Shortly after his journey to Scotland was arranged through the British Legation in Stockholm. On his arrival here he made a statement in which he concealed the facts as to the extent of the information he had given to the 'Gestapo' under pressure and pretended that the faked escape was a real one. SOE officers acted in consultation with B1(a) of this office in view of the fact that there was reason to believe that Guldbransen was serving as a double agent. The story of his escape was

regarded by B1(a) officers as betraying traces of German technique which had come to notice in connection with other reports of faked escapes, and the general circumstances of his case made it appear extremely probable that Guldbransen was holding back a true account of what had happened to him. Enquiries continued for some time without any success in the attempt to induce Guldbransen to tell the whole truth. Eventually information was received from another Norwegian, named Ernst Kirkeby Jacobsen, who had also been arrested by the 'Gestapo' and stated that Fehmer of the Gestapo had told him that Guldbransen had given them information and that arrangements were being made to send him back to England, his 'escape' having been arranged.

34. Finally, on 29 January 1943 a formal enquiry was arranged in which a Norwegian officer, SOE officers and Major Robertson of B1(a) took part. Guldbransen, having been confronted with the fact that information (as given by Jacobsen) had been received, made a statement in which he said in answer to questions that he had given more information to the Germans than he had previously admitted and that he had concealed the fact that his escape had been arranged. It appears that he was influenced not only by the fact that his relatives were held as hostages, but also by the German argument that if he admitted the real facts in England he would be treated as a traitor. The Germans had also attempted to influence him by arguing that by working for them he would be working in the interests of Norway as opposed to the interests of Great Britain.

35. The view was taken, and is understood to have been accepted by Guldbransen himself, that his duty compelled him to act without reference to the safety of his relatives who were held as hostages, but that an attempt to arrange for him to communicate with the Germans as if he were still acting as a double agent should be made and that this might save their lives. It was held that Guldbransen was a loyal officer and had eventually told the whole truth and had not at any time contemplated working genuinely for the Germans. One of the strongest motives on which the Germans had worked had been his sense of shame admitting to his superiors that he had given away as much as he had about the organisation with which he was concerned in Norway.

36. It is probable that if Jacobsen's information had not been received it would have been extremely difficult to obtain the full truth from Guldbransen and this illustrates the extreme complexity and difficulty of investigating cases of men who have been in the hands of the Abwehr

or the 'Gestapo' and returned to this country with stories of having escaped. It is not possible to go into all these complexities here but they are obviously greater in the cases of men with weaker character that Guldbransen.

37. The statements of individuals who have been in German hands, as in this case, are not always clear regarding the functions of different parts of the German machine, such as Abwehr Abt. III and the Gestapo, but the facts regarding Fehmer mentioned by Guldbransen as the Gestapo chief who dealt with him appear to show that he is in fact an official of the GFP or Secret Field Police.

IV French cases

Mrs Stella Lonsdale

38. Mrs Stella Lonsdale, British, arrived in England by air from Lisbon on 5 November 1941, having been abroad since 12 January 1940. Early in 1940 she had been in France where her husband was stationed, and she refused to leave when the Germans advanced. According to her own statement, they did not molest her and she used her liberty to collect intelligence for the benefit of the Allies. She was caught in flagrante delicto and rigorously examined by the head of the Abwehr counter-espionage at Angers. When she arrived in England Stella Lonsdale told a long story about her relations with an Abwehr officer, who she alleged had obtained her release on condition that she worked for them. While in unoccupied France, to which she proceeded on an Abwehr mission, she worked for MI9, although her conduct aroused the suspicion of other British authorities. She was also induced to work for the 2ieme Bureau. She alleged that the Abwehr officer who had obtained her release was a traitor to Germany and had given her information to pass on to the British Intelligence. This information was found on reference to SIS to be accurate and it was regarded as having been supplied to her as part of a plan by the Abwehr to build her up as a double agent. The enquiry regarding her case presented difficulty as it was not possible to rely on any uncorroborated statement she made. She made repeated requests to be sent back to France as an agent of the British Intelligence, in order to obtain further information from the above mentioned Abwehr officer. There is therefore a strong probability that this is to be regarded as an attempt to penetrate the British Intelligence Service on the part of the Abwehr.

Notes on the VICTOIRE Case

39. A brief summary of this case has been prepared by Mr. Harmer of B1(a) and it reads as follows:

40. 'During the period November 1940 to November 1941 a very successful Polish organisation worked in France under the name of INTERALLIE. It was run by a Polish officer, whose code name was WALENTY, and his second in command was a woman known to us now as VICTOIRE. In all, he recruited over 100 special agents. They sent periodic reports on the military situation to the Polish Deuxième Bureau in London, who passed them on to the British War Office. They in fact provided an almost complete Order-of-Battle of the German forces in France. At the beginning of November 1941 the Gestapo at Cherbourg got on the track of one of the sub-agents working in that district, arrested him, due to the betrayal of one of his former mistresses, forced him to write a letter to WALENTY asking for an interview, arrested the man WALENTY sent to attend the interview, and eventually tortured the latter into giving away WALENTY's address. On 18 November 1941 the principal members of the organisation were arrested. VICTOIRE immediately threw in her hand with the Germans and collaborated with them wholeheartedly. Her collaboration took the form of helping them to settle messages to be sent back to London via the W/T set and also acting as an agent provocateur to catch the remaining sub-agents. She was not allowed complete liberty, but instead Bleicher, the German 'Gestapo' official who was in charge of the round-up, became her lover and accompanied her everywhere, posing as a friend. Many sub-agents were arrested as a result of her efforts, which consisted in her sitting in cafes where they were due to meet and identifying them.

41. 'By Christmas, 1941 the whole of the INTERALLIE Organisation was in German hands. Then, through a contact of the organisation (a Polish lawyer living in Paris) VICTOIRE got in touch with an important SOE agent whose codename was LUCAS. The probability is that her contact with him was entirely fortuitous and that she reported it to the Germans to curry favour with them. From that time onwards she was allowed almost complete liberty, installed in a most expensive flat in Paris and used to penetrate the LUCAS Organisation. For a month LUCAS did not realise that she was controlled. His primary object in getting in touch with her was that he was without quick means of communication in London and was using her wireless link. He would, therefore, give her messages to be passed back to London and she would, of course, show these to the Germans who would also see the replies

before they were handed back to him. Several operations took place during January and February, whose object was to bring LUCAS back to England. The Germans were prepared from the outset to let him go, which was obviously taking a very big risk, but which they no doubt felt to be justified on the grounds that the messages they were seeing revealed that he was going back to England to be made the titular head of all the British underground organisations working in France. It was obviously, therefore, to their advantage to let him go and watch him on his return. VICTOIRE, therefore, went with him when a plane was expected and later during two unsuccessful attempts to take him off by sea. On each occasion she was kept under observation by the Germans but allowed her own, complete liberty. The Germans thus ran the risk of her betraying her mission to LUCAS and losing him, and she did in fact do this very thing at the beginning of February when she became his mistress. Finally, however, a sea operation at the end of February was successful and he arrived in England accompanied to everybody's surprise by VICTOIRE herself. (The Germans had not announced her coming in their messages.)

42. 'Parallel to the above but much less important, the Germans were using an ex-agent of the WALENTY organisation to penetrate an SOE organisation in northern France known as OVERCLOUD. Here again the agent was allowed complete liberty and the Germans took the risk of his double-crossing them. Again, however, they cultivated personal relations with him and stayed in his family and so on. They also allowed an operation to take place whereby the heads of OVERCLOUD, the Le Tac brothers, returned to England and came back again to France with fresh material and instructions. They did not close down this organisation until the Le Tac brothers were back in France.

43. 'The case provides a valuable insight into the methods employed by the Germans, in showing the risks and chances they are prepared to take in order to win substantial prizes. It will be seen from the above that they put their trust in two agents who had shortly before been working whole-heartedly against them in the first case they might well have missed their prize but in fact got it due to outside circumstances; in the second case they achieved what they wanted. The second lesson seems to be that, when using agents for penetration purposes, they allow them a very large amount of liberty and treat them very decently, to the extent even of making them personal friends. The third, and perhaps most singular lesson of the case is that in its broad outlines it was handled with great imagination by the Germans, whereas in

detail they were very slovenly and failed to take a great deal of care. Some of their messages, for instance, were very bad and they did not prepare VICTOIRE's cover story in this country with any care at all. One's general feeling on investigating the case is that the Germans are playing for results rather than for safety, and either by successful handling or by good luck they achieved them in this case.'

44. A very long summary of the case has been prepared by the same officer. It comprises some 60 pages and voluminous appendices. It does not purport to be more than a summary of the information available to us and our information is obviously a small part of the story of this important and widespread organisation in France. The facts are exceedingly difficult to assess, because we are in main dependent on VICTOIRE's version of them and it is impossible to be certain whether she is telling the truth at any point where there is no corroboration. It follows that a large part of this longer summary consists of speculation, which necessarily involves considerable uncertainty, although the whole case has been set out with great care and ability.

45. The INTERALLIE Organisation as we know it owed its existence to a meeting between a Polish officer and a French woman who made eyes at one another in a cafe. Within a short time she became his mistress and they set to work together to found the organisation. Their work has every appearance of being brilliantly done, but both of them and some of their colleagues were probably somewhat eccentric if not abnormal people. Personal jealousies between some of the women and their lovers possibly had some influence on the final catastrophe and it is obvious that no counter-espionage 'umbrella' could provide against factors such as these.

46. When the Germans broke up the INTERALLIE Organisation they appear to have succeeded for some time in deceiving SIS by the messages which they induced VICTOIRE to send to England on her transmitter, in spite of the fact that viewed in the light of after events these messages appear to have been badly prepared. The Germans were thus in possession of the facts regarding her W/T in November 1941 and from this case alone would have obtained useful information about the wireless technique of SIS agents.

47. WALENTY eventually arrived in England and told a story of escape as a result of a motor accident which enabled him to dive through a column of marching troops. This story aroused scepticism when he

was examined here. He ultimately reported to his superior officers that he had been given a mission by the Germans who had attempted to persuade him that in working for them he was helping his country. They also held his relatives and his fiancée as hostages.

48. The following are the details available regarding Bleicher who is described in this case as a Gestapo officer:

> Feldwebel Hugo Bleicher (This rank if correctly given implies that he was GFP).
> November 1941: Originally Commissaire de Gestapo in Cherbourg – now holding important position in Paris. Stated to have been European agent in Damstadt before the war. Spied in England during the last war. Arrested WALENTY on 18 November1941.
> It is known that Abt. III/F of the Abwehr was concerned with his work on the WALENTY case.

Jean Charles Pelletier

49. On 15 April 1942 Pelletier, who was an accredited agent of [SIS and] the Fighting French Forces, arrived at Liverpool from Vichy territory. He had previously arrived in this country as a refugee in August 1940, and after being trained as a W/T operator by SIS was sent to unoccupied France with instructions to get in touch with certain other agents in unoccupied France in order to assist them in their W/T communications with London. In June 1941 he received orders from London to go to Paris and in July he was arrested by the Germans and submitted to a rigorous examination. The main reason for the German success in breaking down his resistance was that they possessed a great deal of information about de Gaullist agents in the occupied and unoccupied zones, and that an Air Force captain, who was a wireless expert, disconcerted him by producing copies of practically every message that Pelletier had sent since he commenced practice in this country before he left for France. He stated that one expert was able to produce a large number of messages sent by every British or Fighting French agent in France and a mass of other information about the movements of sets and operators. It appears that he had been given a list of most if not all of these agents, in order to enable him to help them with their wireless sets. After he had made a full confession to the Germans they proposed to him that he should work as a double agent in their interests. He accepted this proposal because the Germans informed him that his parents were in their power and would suffer if he did not comply with their wishes. On 28.10.42 the Germans arranged

for his 'escape'. The plan was that he was taken from the prison by ambulance to hospital, pretending to be suffering from appendicitis, and later escaped from the hospital. He was instructed to return to the unoccupied zone, re-joining his network, and transmit to the Germans in Paris full information, especially W/T and cryptographic, about the operations and identities of the other agents. He was then told that he would be sent to this country to get into the wireless section of the British Intelligence organisation running agents in the free zone. From this point of vantage he was to transmit to the Germans by one of the British sets information regarding traffic arrangements, the identities of new agents in training, and identities in the controlling organisation in London. He stated that he proceeded to unoccupied France and it is significant that two Fighting French agents, his former colleagues whom he happened to meet shortly after his release, were immediately arrested by the Germans. On 17.11.41 he decided to make his way back to England for a reason which is not on his own statement entirely clear.

50. There is hardly sufficient material in the above cases to admit of an exhaustive analysis of German methods but the following facts stand out:

These cases in occupied territories are controlled by Abteilung III/F of the Abwehr, assisted by the G.F.P. or Secret Field Police. The agents who come into contact with the various officials are not always able to distinguish between those of the Abwehr, the Gestapo and the GFP.

The Germans are especially interested in W/T operators and W/T technique.

The ultimate means of German penetration are difficult to ascertain, but are probably to be found in the use of agents inside indigenous or British inspired organisations and in wireless interception.

Importance is also attached to their methods of turning Allied nationals round to work against Britain, by attempting to suggest that it is in the real interest of their own country for them to do so. In such cases 'escapes' are arranged and escape stories are therefore treated with suspicion when agents who have been in contact with the enemy arrive here.

Pressure is placed on captured agents by brutality combined with attempts at moral persuasion, including the holding of hostages.

After penetrating an organisation the Germans do not necessarily take precipitate action, but by watching and waiting effect further penetration and the extent to which this is done is not easy to gauge.

There is an inescapable security interest in cases in which an Abteilung III agent or an SIS or SOE agent who has been turned round is sent here by the Germans. The former includes cases like that of Wallem of the *Heernie,* mentioned in para. 26 above as an attempt to penetrate SOE and also cases where an unaccredited recruit in occupied territory is a double agent working for Abteilung III F. (The machinery for the detection of such cases is at the LRC and largely depends for its efficiency on having the most complete information possible regarding organisations and individuals working for the enemy or against them.)

51. There are other cases of penetration in Belgium, Norway and France, as well as in Holland, which have not been included in these summaries as they have not yet been fully examined.

Conclusions

52. The facts that have been set out above are a very small fraction of those bearing directly or indirectly on the question of counter-espionage and security arrangements for the protection of SOE or SIS operations abroad. The case of Belgium has been dealt with most fully but, as the appendix shows, there are a few important and a number of less important organisations which are working against the enemy, either by sustaining national morale by obtaining military information by working on behalf of SOE or SIS, or providing means of escape for British soldiers left there, or RAF personnel who make forced landings, for secret agents of SOE, SIS or indigenous Belgian organisations posing as ordinary refugees. The exact facts about many of these organisations are not available in this office and it is clear that more precise facts must be known to SOE or SIS, or to the Intelligence Service of the Belgian Government in London, especially in regard to organisations working directly for them, but the links between the various organisations appear to be numerous and this fact gives Abwehr Abt. III and the Sicherheitsdienst as the Intelligence organisation under Himmler, with the GFP and the Gestapo as executives, opportunities for penetration which cannot be fully assessed on our present material, and may prove extremely dangerous when the question of action on a large scale on the Continent comes to an issue.

53. The material available here regarding resistance movements in France, Holland and Norway is voluminous and no attempt has been made to examine it in detail, but certain cases have been briefly mentioned above by way of illustration. Nearly all the cases of penetration are, as already mentioned, extremely complicated and

the difficulty of understanding them is increased by the fact that very often more is known about them in SOE or SIS than to us.

54. One point which a study of the material so far dealt with emphasises most strongly is the overriding importance which attaches to SOE operations in occupied territories. (No reference is made to SOE operations in German territory.) While we do not know how far SOE operations are directed in pursuance of the strategical and operational plans of the Chiefs of Staff, it must be assumed that on broad lines if not in every detail they are co-ordinated with plans for military operations and that the most important SOE activities would be timed to coincide and to fit in with military plans for the invasion of the Continent. If, for example, there are five alternative plans for invasion, involving attacks on five points, a, b, c, a, and e, it follows that in the event of an attack, for instance, at c and e, SOE operations at those two points would follow a certain line, while those at other points would conform on different lines to the same conception. If, in pursuance of that general conception, the organisations of a country such as Belgium were expected to play an important part, either as diversionary move or in the enemy's rear, the liquidation over-night of the important leaders of the organisations would seriously affect the general strategical plan. Hitler's methods of watching and pouncing were mentioned in para. 23 above. For practical purposes it would not be safe to assume that they are not being applied to the various types of resistance movement in occupied Europe. In fact, the general indications which we receive in this field as a whole are in conformity with the view that they are being applied at the present time, but direct and authoritative evidence on such a point cannot easily be obtained. If this is correct, the protection of SOE organisations is clearly a matter of the highest importance.

55. There can be no question that sufficient information on matters of SOE policy and operational plans cannot be available in MI5 to enable the latter to take any great degree of responsibility for protective measures; and that the major responsibility for the safety of SOE operations must rest on SOE themselves. If this fact and the five main heads of the problem mentioned in para. 2 of this note are borne in mind, it is clear that ultimate decisions in all relevant matters can only be taken satisfactorily by those who are responsible for the carrying out of SOE operations.

56. Under the present system the functional relations between SOE and MI5 are governed by the geographical basis of the relations between

MI5 and Section V. The consequence of this is that MI5 officers tend to deal with an enquiry from the point of view of the case against a suspect (whether he is an SOE agent who has been turned round by the enemy or otherwise) and they do not necessarily pursue lines of enquiry which affect the operational interest of SOE. (For instance, in the case of the Belgian Pry, mentioned above, the MI5 officers concerned with the case against him did not feel that it was for them to follow up the indications regarding Mme. Fiorina Dings, the double agent who penetrated the ANDREE Organisation.)

57. Reverting to the simile of the 'umbrella', we have to deal with a constantly changing situation. The protective arrangements cannot be static. They must be as flexible in their movements as a squadron of aircraft protecting a battleship. It is necessary to meet the ever-changing situation of secret operations co-ordinated with military operations. One instance of changes which have to be taken into account is the recent series of indications that Himmler and the Sicherheitsdienst are increasing their influence in counter-espionage matters at the expense of Canaris and the Abwehr.

58. In dealing with such situations the difficulty of co-ordinating the plans of allies is notorious and, at the same time, there is a close relation between the operations of SOE and SIS and the measures of the Allied governments on British soil which aim at sustaining the resistance movements in their own countries.

59. It is not proposed to suggest remedies here. It is a matter which in most respects can best be dealt with – ultimately, if not directly – by the officers responsible for secret operations. The question of security measures in the field is one which is beyond the scope of MI5, but while various indigenous movements in occupied territory have their own counter-espionage arrangements in some cases, it seems clear that it is not feasible to direct such measures from this country.

60. So far as SOE and MI5 are concerned, there are various ways in which MI5 machinery and the intelligence obtained by various branches of this office, especially the LRC, Camp 020 and B1(a), can be of the greatest value for the purpose in view. In one sense it might be said that the texture of the 'umbrella' is already woven into the existing fabric: that is to say, co-operation between the security section of SOE and sections of this office such as B1(a) and B1(b) already goes some way towards facilitating the counter-espionage

protection which is required. This has been developed recently and is still being developed, but it is impossible to resist the feeling that something more comprehensive and closer in the way of co-ordination is required. This could be effected by the creation within SOE of a section or staff with a good knowledge of all the relevant information about the German machine and its methods, and of our own counter-espionage machinery.

61. The problem of SIS is more complex, if only because SIS have, in the shape of Section V, their own counter-espionage organisation outside the three-mile limit. This position involves a further complication after Allied landings in Africa or Europe, when the functional relations between Section V and MI5 seem to become more difficult to define and Section V, acting in co-operation with the provisional (or permanent) Allied government, presumably becomes responsible in British-occupied Africa or Europe for the security of SOE organisations and agents in the same sense that MI5 are responsible within the three-mile limit, e.g. for assisting with information obtained by interrogating suspects, as at the LRC, or by advising in cases of double-agents.

62. The following are among the causes of enemy penetration:

a) The unavoidable risks of such undertakings.
b) The avoidable risks taken by agents or the controlling authorities.
c) Lack of sufficiently close collaboration between the three British services on the one hand and between them and the Allied Intelligence services on the other.
d) The German success in reading agents' wireless messages (cf. in particular Cassart, VICTOIRE and Pelletier mentioned above). It is not known whether an enquiry into the extent of this success and its duration has been undertaken, nor what counter measures have been adopted. It is obviously a matter of major importance, which deserves close and constant attention. There have been references to a belief among agents that the Germans have a very efficient system of D/Fing their sets.
e) The German success in employing agents to penetrate resistance or escape organisations in occupied territory; their skill in watching organisations once penetrated over prolonged periods (cf Mme. Fiorina Dings in the ANDREE case); and their severe treatment of captured agents.

63. This report is based on information available in MI5. A full consideration of the intricate problems involved would only be possible in the light of the knowledge and experience available in SOE and SIS. The time at disposal or the preparation of this report has not been sufficient to allow of an examination of all the relevant files of MI5 and even less so for an extensive enquiry into the knowledge and experience of MI5 officers in this subject

2 April 1943

SOURCE NOTES

All MI5 files cited are available at the National Archives, Kew (www.nationalarchives.gov.uk); OSS, CIC and CIG files are at NARA, Suitland (www.archives.gov); CIA documents are at www.cia.gov; FBI records at www.vault.fbi.gov.

Introduction

1. Paul Hartman, CI Staff, Research and Analysis Group.
2. Ladislas Farago, *The Game of the Foxes* (New York: David McKay, 1971).
3. John Masterman, *The Double Cross System of the War of 1939-45* (London: Yale University Press, 1972). See also KV4/5.
4. See Tommy Jonason and Simon Olsson, *Agent TATE* (Stroud, Glos: Amberley, 2011).
5. COBWEB's autobiography *Gagnnjosnari Breta a Islandi* was published in Icelandic.
6. *Generalmajor Lahousen Reports on Canaris Secret Organisation*, OSS, 17 December 1945.
7. Klop Ustinov's January 1947 interrogation of Kauder as 'Mr Johnson' at KV2/1496.
8. CAB 21/3878.
9. Whitehall intervened to censor the memoirs of E.B. Gill, *War, Wireless and Wangles* (Oxford: Basil Blackwell, 1934) and Sir Alfred Ewing, *The Man of Room 40* (London: Hutchison, 1940).
10. TRICYCLE was Dusko Popov (*SpyCounterSpy* [London: Weidenfeld & Nicolson, 1972]); ZIGZAG was Eddie Chapman (*The Real Eddie Chapman Story* [London: Library 33, 1956]); TREASURE was Lily Sergueiev (*Secret Service Rendered* [London: William Kimber, 1968]); BRUTUS was Roman Garby-Czerniawski (*The Big Network* [London: George Ronald, 1961]); MUTT was John Moe (*John Moe: Double Agent* [London: Mainstream, 1986]); and GARBO was Juan Pujol (*GARBO* [London: Wiedenfeld & Nicolson, 1984]).

11. Eugn Steimle's PF at KV2/966. Whether coordinated or not, several MPs with wartime intelligence experience made speeches in the Commons debate about the 'missing diplomats' in support of MI5, among them Sir Rupert Speir, Kenneth Younger and Dick Brooman-White.
12. Ian Wilson.
13. List of assets.

Chapter I: Pre-war

1. My Eriksson's MI5 PF at KV2/535.
2. Hans Thost's MI5 PF at KV2/952.
3. Mrs Jordan's MI5 PF at KV2/3532.
4. See the Rumrich case in Ray Batvinis, *The Origins of FBI Counter-Intelligence* (Laurence, KS: University Press of Kansas, 2004).
5. Hermann Goertz's MI5 PF at KV2/1322.
6. Walter Simon's MI5 PF at KV2/1293.
7. Vera Schalburg's MI5 PF at KV2/14. See also David Tremain, *The Beautiful Spy: The Life and Crimes of Vera Eriksen* (Stroud, Glos: History Press, 2019).
8. Anna Chateau-Thierry's MI5 PF at KV2/358.
9. Mathilde Krafft's MI5 PF at KV2/701.
10. See also Madoc Roberts, *SNOW* (London: Biteback, 2011).
11. Eugene Horsfall-Ertz's Home Office file at HO45/25730.
12. KV3/7.
13. Dick White, KV4/240.
14. See also Nigel West, *Double Cross in Cairo* (London: Biteback, 2015).
15. Paul Borchardt's MI5 PF at KV2/2430.
16. Ludwig Warschauer's MI5 PF at LV2/1141.
17. See also Ray Batvinis, *The Origins of FBI Counter-Intelligence* (Laurence, KS: University Press of Kansas, 2004).
18. Max Betram's MI5 PF at KV2/3559.
19. Werner Unland's MI5 PF at KV2/1295.
20. Gunter Schutz's MI5 PF at KV2/1298.
21. Ibid.
22. Walter Praetorius's MI5 PF at KV2/524.
23. Ibid.

Chapter II: The Buro Jahnke

1. Winston Churchill, *Closing the Ring: The Second World War*, Vol. V (London: Cassells, 1952).

2. The Krivitsky allegations concerning the theft of British classified material, including papers from the Committee of Imperial Defence, would never be resolved. See Peter Wright, *SpyCatcher* (New York: Viking, 1987); Nigel West, *MASK* (Abingdon, Oxon: Routledge, 2005). Krivitsky's MI5 PF is at KV2/802.
3. The MI5 PF for Carl Marcus, codenamed DICTIONARY, at KV/2964.
4. Ibid.
5. Ibid.
6. Walter Schellenberg's MI5 PF at KV2/98. See also Walter Schellenberg, *The Labyrinth* (London: Andre Deutsch, 1956).
7. Christian Daufeldt's MI5 PF at KV2/142.
8. Ibid.
9. See also S. Payne Best, *The Venlo Incident* (London: Hutchinson, 1951).
10. Gordon Parry's MI5 PF at KV2/630.
11. Jack Hooper's MI5 PF at KN2/4347.
12. Herman Giskes' MI5 PF at KV2/962.
13. Carl Marcus' MI5 PF at KV2/2964.
14. Ibid.
15. Christian Daufeldt's MI5 PF at KV2/142.
16. Norman Baillie-Stewart's MI5 PF at KV2/174.
17. Carl Marcus' MI5 PF at KV2/2964.
18. Ibid.
19. Ibid.

Chapter III: Nest Bremen

1. Counter-Intelligence War Room Liquidation Report 206 / MI5 SF 52/16/12 *Abwehrstellen Bremen.*
2. Ibid.
3. Ibid.
4. Johannes Bischoff's MI5 PF at KV2/2749.
5. Albert Meems' MI5 PF at KV2/2428.
6. Simon Koedel indicted, *New York Times*, 25 October 1944.
7. Walter H.J. Lohrey's MI5 PF at KV2/1725.
8. References to John M. Kessler at KV2/1725.
9. References to John M. Joslin at KV2/1725.
10. Johannes Bischoff's MI5 PF at KV2/2749.
11. Carl Grundell's MI5 PF at KV2/320.
12. Paul Mulak's MI5 PF at KV2/2123.
13. Counter-Intelligence War Room Liquidation Report 206 / MI5 SF 52/16/12 *Abwehrstellen Bremen.*

14. MI5 SF *The Abwehr in Lisbon* at KV3/170.
15. MI5 SF *The Abwehr in South America* at KV3/154.
16. Ibid.
17. Henry Addicks' MI5 PF at KV2/1924.
18. Nikolaus Bensmann's MI5 PF at KV2/1328.
19. Herbert Wichmann's MI5 PF at KV2/103.
20. Ibid.
21. Ibid.
22. See also Carolinda Witt, *Double Agent CELERY* (Barnsley, Yorks: Pen & Sword, 2017). Walter Dicketts' MI5 PF at KV2/624.

Chapter IV: GOLFPLATZ

1. *Generalmajor Lahousen Reports on Canaris Secret Organisation*, OSS, 17 December 1945.
2. *German Secret Service Operations*, March 1942 at KV3/7.
3. Joseph Kelly's MI5 PF at KV2/359.
4. Donald Adams' MI5 PF at KV2/290.
5. *German Secret Service Operations*, March 1942 at KV3/7.
6. Ibid.
7. Walter Sensburg's MI5 PF at KV2/ 977.
8. Jose Waldburg's MI5 PF at KV2/107.
9. Charles Van den Kieboom's MI5 PF at KV2/11.
10. Sjiord Pons' MI5 PF at KV2/13.
11. Karl Meier's MI5 PF at KV2/12.
12. Simon Olsson and Tommy Jonason, *Goesta Caroli, – Double Agent SUMMER* (Unpublished manuscript. Stockholm, 2010).
13. TATE's MI5 PF at KV2/61.
14. POGO's MI5 PF at KV2/3851.
15. Renato Roque Laia's MI5 PF at KV2/4316.
16. References to *La Part Bien* at KV2/4316.
17. Karl Drucke's MI5 PF at KV2/18.
18. Robert Petter's MI5 PF at KV2/17.
19. References to GANDER in KV2/2593
20. Engelbertus Fukken's MI5 PF at KV2/114 (alias Jan Willen Ter Braak).
21. References to Gunnar Edvardsen at KV2/2593.
22. KV2/2893.
23. Reference to Karl van Gils and Joseph Laureyssens at KV2/109.
24. Josef Jakobs' MI5 PF at KV2/24. See also Giselle Jakobs, *The Spy in the Tower* (Stroud: History Press, 2019).
25. Gerth van Wijk's MI5 PF at KV2/1145.
26. Ibid.

27. John Moe's MI5 PF at KV2/1067.
28. Tor Glad's MI5 PF at KV2/1068.
29. *A Digest of Ham* at KV4/13.
30. Karel Richter's MI5 PF at KV2/30.
31. Helmik Wallem's MI5 PF at KV2/3282.
32. Florent Steiner's MI5 PF at KV2/1315.
33. Alphonse Timmerman's MI5 PF at KV2/3856.
34. References to Olaf Saetrang at KV2/3856.
35. Gustav Ronning's MI5 PF at KV2/727.
36. Henry Obed's MI5 PF at KV2/1296.
37. Gunter Schutz's MI5 PF at KV2/1300.
38. Werner Unland's MI5 PF at KV2/1295.
39. References to Axel Coll at KV4/13.
40. Ibid.
41. SNOW's MI5 PF at KV2/449.
42. KV3/7.
43. Stella Lonsdale's MI5 PF at KV2/733. See also David Tremain, *Agent Provocateur for Hitler or Churchill? The Mysterious Life of Stella Lonsdale* (Barnsley: Pen & Sword, 2021).
44. KV3/7.
45. Ibid.
46. Paul Morel's MI5 PF at KV2/1152.
47. KV3/7.

Chapter V: The Front Line

1. Marcel Schunke's MI5 PF at KV2/2747.
2. KV3/7.
3. Ibid.
4. Ernst Kleyenstuber's Foreign Office file at FO837/1167/1.
5. SAFEHAVEN Report: NARA OSS X-2 Record Group 226.
6. KV3/7.
7. Ibid.
8. Ibid.
9. Ibid.
10. Nikolaus Ritter's MI5 PF at KV2/86. See also Katharine Wallace, *Cover-Name Dr Rantzau* (Lexington, KY: University Press of Kentucky, 2019).
11. KV3/7.
12. Aloys Schreiber's MI5 PF at KV2/3568.
13. Ibid.
14. Fritz Cramer's MI5 PF at KV2/1742.

15. METEOR was Eugn Sostaric. See Dusko Popov's MI5 PF at KV2/661.
16. FREAK was Frano de Bona. See his MI5 PF at KV2/1069.
17. DREADNOUGHT was Ivan Popov. See his brother's MI5 PF at KV2/852.
18. GELATINE was Friedle Gaertner. See Dusko Popov's MI5 PF at KV2/851.
19. BALLOON was Dickie Metcalfe. See his MI5 PF at KV2/2070. See also David Tremain, *Man-at-Arms. The Making of* a *Double Agent* (Barnsley: Pen & Sword, 2022).
20. ARTIST was Johannes Jebsen. See Dusko Popov's MI5 PF at KV2/858.
21. KV2/742.
22. Ibid.
23. Ibid.
24. Carl Eitel's MI5 PF at KV2/383.
25. Ibid.
26. Ibid.
27. Ibid.
28. Ibid.
29. Ibid.
30. Lily Sergueiev's MI5 PF at KV2/466.
31. KV2/393.
32. Ibid.
33. Ibid.
34. Guy Liddell's Diary, 9 January 1942.
35. KV4/240.
36. WASHOUT's MI5 PF at KV2/2101.
37. Duncan Scott-Ford's MI5 PF at KV2/57.
38. Ernesto Simoes' MI5 PF at KV2/294.
39. KV2/383.
40. Ibid.
41. Ibid.
42. Ibid.
43. Ibid.
44. Ibid.
45. Ibid.
46. Ibid.
47. Rogeiro de Menezes' Foreign Office file at FO 1093/256.
48. Angel Alzazar de Velasco's MI5 PF at KV2/3535.
49. POGO's MI5 PF at KV2/3851.
50. Luis Calvo's MI5 PF at K2/713.

51. KV2/383.
52. Gottfried Taboschat's MI5 PF at KV2/93.
53. Alberto Koepke's MI5 PF at KV2/92.
54. Friedrich Knappe-Ratey's MI5 PF at KV2/101.
55. KV2/383.
56. Ibid.
57. Ibid.
58. Ibid.
59. Ibid.
60. Ibid.
61. Ibid.
62. Ibid.
63. Ibid.
64. Ibid.
65. Ibid.
66. Ibid.
67. Ibid.
68. Ibid.

Chapter VI: German Intelligence in the Middle East

1. Thomas Ludwig's MI5 PF at KV2/3653.
2. KV3/7.
3. Ibid.
4. Ibid.
5. Ibid.
6. Fritz Mayr's MI6 PF at KV2/1477.
7. KV2/3653.
8. Paul Leverkuehn's MI5 PF at KV2/2654.
9. KV2/2653.
10. KV3/4.
11. KV2/2653.
12. Ibid.
13. Ibid.
14. Ibid.
15. KV3/7.
16. KV2/2653.
17. Ibid.
18. Ibid.
19. Ibid.
20. Ibid.
21. Ibid.
22. Text corrupted in the original document.

23. KV2/2653.
24. Ibid.
25. Ibid.
26. KV3/7.
27. Nigel West, *Double Cross in Cairo* (London: Biteback, 2015).
28. Laszlo Almassy, *The Unknown Sahara* (Budapest: Franklin, 1935).
29. Johannes Eppler's MI5 PF at KV2/1467.
30. Franz Seubert CIC Interrogation Report, January 1946, No. SO65.
31. Ibid.
32. Ibid.
33. Hans Berger CIC Interrogation Report, March 1946.

Chapter VII: South American Intrigue

1. Herbert Wichmann's MI5 PF at KV2/103.
2. Ibid.
3. Harold Monat's MI5 PF at KV2/3422.
4. Friedrich Obladen's MI5 PF at KV2/521.
5. *History of the SIS Division* (Unpublished: FBI Archives).
6. Frederick Duquesne's MI5 PF at KV2/1953.
7. KV3/154.
8. Oscar Hellmuth's MI5 PF at KV2/1722.
9. Jose Olivera's MI6 PF at KV2/1938.
10. Diego Beltran's MI5 PF at KV2/1939.
11. Ibid.
12. Ibid.
13. Dietrich Niebuhr's MI5 PF at KV2/3301.
14. Friedrich Wolf's MI5 PF at KV2/1487.
15. Siegfried Becker's MI5 PF at KV2/89.

Chapter VIII: The Western Campaign

1. KV3/153.
2. Ibid.
3. Ibid.

INDEX

50 Interment Camp, Egypt 202
105 SCI (Special Counter-Intelligence in Paris) 24

A-2009, *see* Marc Aubert
A-2011, *see* Simon Koedel
Aarens, Maurice 276
Abaire 170
Abel, E. 6
Abendschoen, Willi 5
Aberle, Walter xxvi, xxix
Abwehr decrypts, *see* ISOS
Adams, Donald xxix, 60
Addicks, Gerhard xxix
Addicks, Henry xxix, 37, 58–59
Admiral Graf Spee 219
ADOLF communications system xxv
ADOLPHE xxix
Agat 127
Aguillar, Jesus 218
Aher, Fatima 204
Ahmed Bey (ARTHUR; DOLEFUL) 183
Akbari 202
ALARIC (Juan Pujol) 89
Alassi, Luigi (ANCHOR) xxix
Alcola, Colea 128
ALFONSO 202
Alhrichs, Heinrich xxix
Alisch, Hastuf 224
Allgemeine Eléktrische Gesellschaft (AEG) 215
ALLIANCE 185
Almassy, Count Laszlo 204
Almeida 122
al-Misri, Gen. Aziz Ali 203
Alseth, Sigurd xxix
Alter, Hans 34
Alvarez, Paul 176
Amado, Capt. 126
American Express 139
Americo, Fritz 211
Amirante, SS 146, 162
ANCHUR xxix
Andora, Lt 187
Andrade, Garvaho 140
ANDREE Escape Organisation 274–5
Anger, Paul 109
Anido, Gen. Martinez 261
Annes, Armando xxix, 146–7
ANTON 184–5
Arajuo, Alfredo 154
Arda, Gen. 108
Ardringa, Leonardus (TURNIP) 302
Arend, Pierre (FATHER) xxix, 63
Argentine Primer 211
Arias, Ernestina 220
ARMOUR, *see* Luigi Alassi
Arnold, Karl 110, 216
ARPA Verlag 15
Arrowsmith, Harold 36
ARTHUR (Ahmed Bey; DOLEFUL) xxix, 182
ARTIST, *see* Johannes Jensen
Aruajo, Assuncao xxix
Ast Brussels xxxii, 50, 62
Ast Dijon xxvi
Astor, Hugh ix

ASTRAY 177
ATOM xxix
Aubert, Marc (A-2009) xxix, 5, 33, 41–2
Auenrode, Ludwig Kramer von (alias Fritz Cramer; LUDOVICO) xxx, 120, 147
Auersperg, Prince Karl Adolph xxix
AUEST 195
Augener, Maj. 34, 41
AUGUSTA (Renato Roque Laia) xxix
AUGUSTO 151, 172
Augustus, Antonio 128
Ayvazyan, Josef 194

B Division, MI 2, 57
B1(a) (MI5's section handling double agents) 88, 104, 276, 278, 282–3, 292
B1(b) (MI5's German espionage research section) 292
B1(g) (MI5's Spanish section) 147
B2(a) (German analysis section) 124
B4(b) (industrial espionage section) 11
Baarn, William 216
Bad Blankenburg xxv
Bad Nenndorf 23
Bad Sulza xxvi
Bad Tolz, Bavaria 22, 27
Bagesnki, Baron Bogislav von 265
Baheshy, Robert xxix
Baillie-Stewart, Norman xxix, 25
Bakos, Louis xxix
BALLOON (Dicke Metcalfe) 76, 89, 92–100, 134
Balzer, Emma 12
Baptista 150
Barahona, Adriana 220
Barclay, Cecil ix, 33
Bartalsi, Col. 187
BASKET (Joseph Lenihan) 75
Batavian Oil Co. 23
Battye 58
Bau 108
Baumann, Dr Rudolph 137
Baumeister, Friedrich (alias Col. Rudolf) xxx
BBC 184
BCRA, *see* Bureau Central de Renseignements et d'Action
BD001 142
BdS (Befehlshaber der Sicherheitspolizei) 11, 224, 226–7, 230, 235
Beck, August 122
Becker Group (RED) 220
Becker, Johannes (SARGO) xxx, 215–29, 220–2
Beevor, Jack ix
Befesuklu 195
Behrens, Karl xxviii
Beigl, Kurt xxx
Belgian Sureté 271–3, 276, 278
Bell, Walter ix
Beltran, Diego 218–19
Bendixen, Hans 33, 41, 120, 142, 144
Benoist, Robert 30
Bensmann, Nikolaus 38–49
Benson, Arthur 154
Bentivegni, Egbert von 186
Benton, Kenneth ix, 102
Berg, Willie 109
Berger, Hans 207
Bermehren, Dr 123
Bernard 272
Bernardo, Jose Maria San 136
Bernhard, Obf. 226
Bernhardt, Prince 126
Bernhardt, Ostaf. 107–08, 224
Berthold, Herbert J. (JIGGER) xxix, xxx
Bertram, Max 11
BERTRAM 228
BEST 194
Best, Sigismund Payne ix, 23
Bey, Ahmed (DOLEFUL) xxx
Bibire xxx, 60
Bickler, Hermann 225–6
Bielstein, Hermann 223

Biermann, Sgt. 298
Billings, George 6
Bischoff, Johannes xxx, 34, 36, 38–49
Bischoff, Ludwig xxx, 34
BISCUIT (Sam McCarthy) xxxix, 69, 72, 82, 85–6, 93
Bishop, Sarah ix
BJ diplomatic decrypt 18
BLACKGUARD (Hamdi Khaqqay, alias Mirz Khan) xxx, 182, 201–02
Blake, George ix
Blaum, Wolfgang (alias Friedrich Baumann) xxx
BLAZE xxx
Bleicher, Hugo 288
BLIST 194
Blohm & Voss shipyard 23
BLUE 222
Blue Division 108
Blum, Hans 211
Blume, Gunther xxx, 185
Blume, Hans 214
Blunt, Anthony viii, xxx
Board of Overseas Trade 59
Boehme, Cornelle, xxx
Boehme, Eleanor 3
Boemelburg, Carl xxx
Bohlen, Ludwig von 210, 214, 216
Bohny, 210, 219
BOLIVAR 244
Bona, Frano de (FREAK) ix
BONI 211
Bonnevie 286
Book, Friedrich 23
Borchardt, Paul xxx, 10
Boreas 63
Borges, Joaquin Ferreira 150
BOSS 210
Botchetchi 202
Bourjeau, Ustuf 225
Bourriez, Pierre xxx
BOVRIL (Juan Pujol) ix
Boxshall, Eddie ix
Boyoglu 199
Bradenkamp de Hellemann, Anna 214
Brandenburg Regiment 24
Brandenstein 58
Brandes, Juan xxx, 134
Brandt, Dr 128
Brandy, Gertrud xxx, 5–6, 58, 60
Bremen, SS 35, 137
Breuer, Arthur xxx, 38
Bristow, Desmond ix
British Army Records Centre, Hayes xxv
British Council 21
British Secret Intelligence Service (MI6) ix, xiii–xv, xxxi–xliv, 14, 22–5, 28–31, 57, 65, 89, 120–1, 130, 134, 136, 140, 143–4, 148–50, 152–4, 156–68, 180, 185, 188, 202, 210, 218, 222, 229, 235, 253, 269–71, 278, 281, 284, 387, 289–3. Chief of, *see* C; *See also* Passport Control Office; Section V
British Security Service (MI5) *passim* *See also* B Division
British Services Security Organisation xxv
Brito, Alicia de 151
BRIZO SENIOR, *see* Georg Hansen
BRONX, *see* Elvira de la Fuentes
Brooke-Booth 273
Brooks, Tony ix
Browning, Mr 191
Brueckner, Fraulein 109, 245
Brugha, Caitlin 14–15
Bruhn, Harald xxx, 66
BRUTUS, *see* Roman Garby-Czerniawski
Buchenau, Franz 211
Buchenwald concentration camp 31
Buecking, Erich xxx, 142
Buenaga, Roberto xxx
Bunzing 26
Bureau Central de Renseignements et d'Action (BCRA) xxxiv, xxxvii

Burger, Karl xxx, 58, 60
Burgess, Guy 22
Burghard, Joachim 31, 216
Burman, Dr 192
Buro Jankhe xl, 17–21
Burt, Len ix
Busch, Hans Christian von 219
Bustillo 246
Butler, Richard 1, 7
Byford, Charles ix
Bygott, John ix

C (MI6 Chief) 29
CABANON xxx
Cabo Buena Esperanza 174, 218
Cadius, Dr 211
Cairncross, John ix, xxxi
Calca, Joachim xxxi, 156, 161
Calvo, Luis 163
CAMOUFLAGE xxxi
Camp 020 36–7, 53, 63–6, 102, 120–1, 142, 146–7, 163, 168, 220, 276, 292
Camp Ritchie, Maryland xxv
Camp WALDBURG xxv
Campbell, Francis P. xxi, 58–9,74
Campo, Jose Antonio del 164–6, 242–5, 253, 258–61, 265
Campos 144
Campsa Agency 173
Canarias III 170
Canaris, Joachim xxxi
Canaris, Wilhelm (GUILLERMO) xxi, xxvi, xxxi, 22, 33, 40, 55, 115–16, 134, 292
Cann, Marie 138
Carbinares Garcia 165
Carbonell 261
Carcellar 109
CARELESS (Edward Ejsymont) xxxi, 71, 94, 96, 171
Carl, Lt 44–5, 47
Carlo, Col. De xxviii
CARLOS 142, 166, 251, 259
Caroli, Goesta (SUMMER) xxxi, 62, 168
Carré, Mathilde (VICTOIRE) xxxi
Carrere, Jean (KEEL) xxxi
Cases, Eseequiel Murietta, de la 261
Cassart, Jean Prosper 271–3, 292
Castro, Fernando de 122
Catela, Rene 130, 145
Cavendish-Bentinck, Bill ix
Cecil, Robin ix
CEL 214–15
Celal Bureau 195
Celal, Col. 188, 195–6
CELERY (Walter Dicketts) xxxi, 55, 72, 129, 144, 153, 159
CHAMBERLAIN 253
Chamberlain, Neville 224
Chantrain, Alfonso 216
Chapman, Eddie (ZIGZAG) xx, xxiv
CHARLIE (Charles Eschborn) xxxi–xxxii
CHARLY 172
Chateau-Thierry, Duchesse Anna de 59
CHEESE (Renato Levi) xxxi, 9, 88, 182
CHESTNUTS 30
Chidson, Monty 24
Chilean secret police, *see* Dirección General de Informacion e Inteligencia
Cholmondeley, Charles xxxi, 8, 66, 91
Cholmondeley, Lady George 8
Christensen, Nils 219
Churchill, Winston 17, 104
Ciki 187
City of Antwerp 13, 176
City of Bremen 176
Claudius, Mathilde 8
Cloeren xxxvii
COBWEB (Ib Riis) ix, xx
CODAR 38
Codrington, John ix
Cody, Sebastian ix
Cohn, James 58
COLACO xxxi, 162
Coll, Axel xxxi, 65

Colmenares, Don Dario Alonso 165
Colmenares, Joaquin Alonso 165
COLOMBINE, *see* Hans Zech-Nennwich
Colville, Jock ix
Combined Services Detailed Interrogation Centre (CSDIC) 15, 204
Committee of Imperial Defence 18, 28
Compania Transportes Maritimos 214
Condor Legion 106, 108, 114, 249, 261, 262
Conte de Savoia, SS 35
Contraband Control 218
Corjita, Dr Jose Manuel Herrero 261
Cornell University 36
Corraux, Julie 21
COSSACK xxxi
Costa Silva, Maximo (RADIO) 131, 144
COSTA xxxi, 182
Costa, Jose xxxi
Costa, Jose Lucio Atayde 154
Counterintelligence Corps (CIC) xix, 130
Counter-intelligence War Room xix
Courcy, Kenneth de 21
Cowgill, Felix ix, 28–9, 121
Cram, Cleve ix
Cramer, Fritz xxxi, 130, 134–5, 143–4
Cressado, SS 125, 153
Cripps, Mrs Freddy 7
Crookes, Mrs xxxi, 58, 60
Crosby, Ken ix
CROW xxxi
CRUDE 31
CRUSE 169
Csarda, SS 64
CSDIC, *see* Combined Services Detailed Interrogation Centre
Cudell & Weltzein 146
Cuidad Sevilla 178
Cumano 123
Cunneen, Ingeborg 313
d'Aguilar, Marques 122, 150
D'Andria 198
d'Arcos, Paco 267
D'Hooghe xxvii
da Silva Martin, Guilherne 135
Dachau concentration camp 10–11
DACHS 226
Daily Herald 123
Dalbey, Dwight J. 213
Dalil, Said 195
Ddalley 214
Dalton, Hugh 23
Dame Blanche 274
Dargel, Editha 8
DARIEN xxxi, 130
Darragh, G.H. 143
Das Brittische Kriegheer xxiii
Daufeldt, Hans 20, 25–7
Daufeldt, Helmut 27
Daulfeldt, Hans Christian 20
DAVIT xxxi
Day, John 229
de Breuille, Alice (BLANCHE) 133
de Frances 165
de Freitas, Umberto 37
de Haas 196
de Lee 63
de Renzy 58
de Renzy-Martin, Edward 163
de Salis, Charles xxxii
Dearden, Kim ix
Dearden, Martin ix
Debroeu 274
Deeker, François de xxxii, 72, 84, 86
Deeker, Robert de 72
Defence Security Officer (DSO) 9, 164, 201
Deichmann, Max 21
Delforge, Marc 277
Delgrande ccvii
Delius, Dr (alias Col. Wagner) 194
Denniston, Alastair 28
Dennys, Rodney ix
DEPUTY xxxi

DERRICK xxxi
Derwent, Lord 7
Deschamps 273
DESIRE (Albert Gabas) xxxii
Detering 226
Deussen, Werner 134
Deutsche Atlantisch Linien 39
Deutsche Bund 36
Deutsche Nachrichten Buro (DNB) 203
Deuxieme Bureau xxii, 23, 30, 61, 130
Dezutter (alias Capt. Coll; alias Jack Colen) 276
DGII (Dirección General de Informacion e Inteligencia) 214
DICK 56
Dicketts, Walter (CELERY) 56
DICTIONARY (Carl Marcus) xxxii
DIEGO (alias Miguel Lopez) 177
Dieppe Raid (1942) xxiii
Dierks, Hans 53, 55–6
Dietel, Erich 109
Dietergartner, Otto xxxii, 65
Dings, Fiorina 275, 292
DINTER 179
Direcao da Ordem Politica e Social (DOPS) 214, 216
Direccion General de Informacion e Inteligencia (DGII) 214
Directorate of Operations (DO) xx
Dittman, Bruno 214, 216
DNB, *see* Deutsche Nachrichten Buro (German News Agency)
Doebler, Hans (alias Dorner, alias Duarte; MADEIRA) 125–6
Doebler, Henry 121–2
Doehring 111, 125, 227
Dohse, Friedrich xxxii, 113
DOLEFUL (Ahmed Bey; ARTHUR) xxxii, 182
Dollar, John 111
DOMINANT xxxii
Domine 179
DOMINO (DOLEFUL) xxxii
DON PEDRO (Bertie Koepke) xxxii, 165
DOOLITTLE xxxii, 63, 71
DOPS (Direcao da Ordem Politica e Social) 214, 216
DORA 207
Douro, SS 141
DRAGOMAN (Jean Frutos) xxii, 139
DRAGONFLY (Hans George) xxxii, 64, 75, 96–101, 129, 154, 167–8, 240, 252, 263
Draper, Christopher xxii, xxxii, 2, 4, 58
DREADNOUGHT (Ivo Popov) 134
Driessen 47, 49
Drottingholm 186, 211, 220
Drucke, Karl (alias François de Deeker) 63
Drummond-Hay, Grace 21
Drury, Victor 21
DSO, *see* Defence Security Officer
Ducidma, Hektor 187
Dugarde, Muriel 65
Dulles, Allen xx
Dumont, Mariana 198
Duncombe, William 6, 58, 60
Duqiesne, Frederick xxiii, xxxii, 59, 215
DURANT 189
Durrant, Bernard xxxii, 6–7, 58
Dutch Intelligence 31

Ebassy Group (BLUE) 220
Ebright, Col. 119
ECCLESIASTIC (Olga Zemanova) xxxii, 143
EDDA (Ib Riss) 20
Eden, Lady George 8
Eden, Sir Timothy 8
Edinburgh University 27
Edinger, Ellinger 21, 213
Edouards, Col. 191
Edwardsen, Gunnar xxxii, 63, 71
EGGS 147
Ehrnau 199

Eikens, John (PANCHO) xxxii
Eins Heer (I/H) 97, 158
Eins Luft (I/L) xxvii, xxxii, xxxvii–xxxviii, xlii, 16, 34, 39, 41, 43, 64,91, 95, 103, 116, 129, 158, 182, 184, 203
Eins Marine (I/) xxvii–xxviii, xxx, xxxii, xxxiv–xxxvii, xl, xliv, 33–4, 36–9, 42–3, 46–55, 103, 136–44, 163, 169–72, 182, 211–12, 216
Eisehorn 16, 66
Eitel, Carl (ELLERMAN) xxviii, 36, 43, 136–9, 141–3
Ejsymont, Edward (CARELESS) xxxii, 65, 164, 250, 253, 265
El Alamein (1942) 104, 306
ELCH 226
Eleka 193
ELLERMAN (Carl Eitel) xxxii, 138
ELLI 198
Ellinger, Eugenio 213
Ellington, Arthur 193
Elliott, Nicholas xxx, 188, 201
Elvedon, Lady 7
Elvedon, Viscount 8
Emba 173
Emig, Marianne 4
EMILIO 165–6, 243–4, 264–5
Empire Gale 156–7
Engelhorn, Heinz xxxii
Engels, Albrecht (ALFREDO) 215
Enigma xxiii, 172
ENRICO 166, 258
Eppler, Johannes xxvi, 204
Erikson, Vera xxxii, 59, 63, 84, 86
Eriksson, My xxxii, 7–8, 58, 68, 72
Erkunder 23
ERNEST 133
Eschborn, Charles (CHARLIE) xxxiii
Eskilbsen 37
Estranda, Jorge 120
Etappemdienst xxix, xxxiii, xxv–xxvii, vli
Europa Agency 135
Europa, SS 3, 123, 134
Evert, Ingebord 130
Evertsen, Cornelius 280
Evinsen, Arnold xxxiii
Ezzat, Hassan 204

F-7129 (Paul Morel) 102–04
F Section 30, 116, 129, 149
Fabian, Maj. (alias Dr Maier) 190, 193, 197
Fair, Mrs Richard (*née* Blanche Fiault) 104
Falange 163, 165, 261
Falk, Peter ix
Falselsa 228
FAN xxxiii
FANK xxxiii
Farago, Ladislas ix, xx
Farid, Murat 223
Farraoq, Josef (JUPP) 46
Farzad, Homayoun xxxiii, 184
Farzad, Massud 184
Fast, Waldemar xxxiii
Fastnacht 20
FATHER (Pierre Arend) xxxiii, 64, 71, 92, 94, 96–7, 164, 168, 247–8, 252–4, 257, 260, 262, 265, 267
FBI, *see* Federal Bureau of Investigation
Federal Bureau of Investigation (FBI) 2, 3, 5, 35, 61, 137, 218, 220
Director of, *see* J. Edgar Hoover *See also* Special Intelligence Service
FEDERICO (Friedrich Knappe-Ratey) xxxiii, 166–7, 248, 253
FEILAND 189
Feldman, Adolf von 23–4
Ferreira, Mario xxxiii
FHW, *see* Fremde Heere West
Fidrmuc, Paul (OSTRO; MAX; ERNST) xxxiii, 133, 149
Finck, Julius Joachim 149
Finck, Walter 149
Finkenstein, Ulrich von xxxiii, 66
Finland, SS 146
FISH xxxiii

Fletcher, Charles 27–9
FLORA 247
FLUNKI 55
Foester, Kurt 112, 162
Foge, Capt. Georges 129–30
Foley, Frank 29
Fordham University 4
FOREST (Lucien Herviou) xxxiii
FORGE xxxiii
Fort Leavenworth, Kansas 11
Fort Missoula, Montana 3
FORTITUDE 183
Fotuh 202
Franco, Francisco 108, 113
Franczok, Wolf 216
FRANK xxxiii
Frankfurter Zeitung 21
FRANZ 255
FRANZ 54, 158
FRANZ JOSEF 197
Frauedorf, Richard xxxiii
FREAK, *see* Frano de Bona
FREDERICKS 31
FREELANCE xxxiii
Freiland, Rof 198
Freise, Stubaf 228
Freiwald, Walter 219
Fremde Heere West (FHW) 183
Freund, Hans Milo 188
Fricke, Walter 38
Friderici, Rolf 120
Friederichi, Col. 140
FRITSCHEN (Eddie Chapman; ZIGZAG) 57
FRITZ 254–5
Frontaufklärungstrupp (FAT) 49
Fruhling 128
FRUTA 131
Frutos, Jean (DRAGOMAN) xxxiii, 34, 139
FUCHS 226
Fuentes, Ekvira de la (BRONX) ix
Fukken, Gilbertus (alias Willem Ter Braak) xxxiii
Fw-200 Condor 185
G-2 (Irish intelligence service) ix, xxii, xxiii, 134
G.W. (Gwylym Williams) 62, 72–3, 75, 82–3, 85–6, 101
Gaafar, Hassan 204
Gaertner, Lisel (GELATINE) ix, xxii, xxxiii, 134
Gaessler, Alfred xxxiii
Gamotha, Ramon 184
GANDER (Karl Gross) xxxiii, 63, 74, 85–7
GAOL xxxiii
Garbers, Heinz 216
GARBO (Juan Pujol) 89
Garby-Czerniawski, Roman (WALENTY; BRUTUS) ix, xxiv, xxx, xxxiii
Garcia 264
Garcia, Jose Mora 214
Garcia, Raul 154, 156
Gardner 6
Garner, William A. 6
Gärtner, Lisel (GELATINE) xxii, xxxiv, 76, 84, 100, 134
Gast, Hans Otto xxxiii, 5
GAT xxxiv
Gaulle, Charles de 30, 207
GC&CS, *see* Government Code & Cipher School
GeheimeFeldPolizei (GFP) 106, 235–7, 284, 288–90
Gehre, Ludwig xxxiv
Gehrts, Erwin 313
Geissler 243
Geitye, 38
GELATINE (Lisel Gaertner) xxii, xxxiv, 76, 84, 100, 134
GEORGE 140
George, Cyril V. 63–4
George, Hans xxii
Gerlach, Richard 213
German Commercial School, Ealing 13
German Intelligence Service - Use of Deception as an Aid to Military Operations xxv

German Officers League 191
German-American Bund 35
Gerschon 127
Gessmann, Wilhelm (alias Alexander) xxxiv, 130
GFP, *see* German Field Police
Giaever 66
Gibbs, Mary (EGGS) 147
Gibraltar 36, 48, 102, 114, 144, 150, 162–3, 179, 206, 218, 241
Gibson, Archie 5, 189
Giebl, Ignatz 4
Giese, Walter 212–13, 219
GILBERT xxxiv
Gils, Karel van xxxiv, 63, 71, 164
GIOVANNI 36, 46–7, 52
GIRAFFE (Georges Graf) xxxiv, 71, 85
GIRRANT xxxiv
Giskes, Hermann xxxiv, 24
Glad, Tor (JEFF) ix, xxxiv, 64, 69–70
Glanz 23
GLASS xxxiv
Glasser, Erich 3
Glazer 273
Gledhill, Cecil ix
Glover, Gerald ix
Glueck, Paul 190, 195
Goertz, Hermann xxiii, xxxiv, 4–5, 58, 65
Goetz, Willy xxvii, xxxiv
Gohl 227, 229
GOLD 194
GOLDFLAKE xxxiv
GOLFPLATZ 62, 65
Gollnow, Herbert 120
Gomez, Flora de Conciego de 265
Gomez, Maria de Lourdes 266
Goodacre, Eric ix, 240
Gordier 120
Gorenson, F.C. 6
Göring, Hermann 108
Gottingen University 188
Government Code & Cipher School (GC&CS) 28
Graefe, Dr 25
Graepe Hans 185
Graf, Georges (GIRAFFE) xxxiv, 63
Grandes 108
Gray, S.P. 58
GREEN 220
Gregory, E. 6
Grey, Charlie 136
Griesheim, Witilo von 206
Grille, Georg xxxiv, 109, 185
Grimaldi, Martin xxxiv, 66, 91
Grimm, Federico 220
Grimm, Hans 34, 37, 46, 51, 138
Groebel, Dr 20
Gronau, Baroness Marie von 130
Grosjean, François ix
Gross (alias Grunde) 227
Gross, Karl (GANDER) xxxiv, 216, 228
Grover-Williams, William 30–1
GRU (Soviet military intelligence) 29
Grundel, Baron Jean xxxiv, 35–6
Grundell, Carl xxxiv, 35–6
Gudenberg, Werner 3
Guensberg, Gerold viii, xxi
GUILLERMO (Wilhelm Canaris) xxxiv
Guldbransen, Tor 281, 283
GULL (Elie Haggar) xxxiv
Gumprecht 110
Gut, Hedwig 21
Guttjahr, Dr 27
Gwyer, John ix, xxxiv, 66, 91, 124, 147–8, 161
Gyorgy, Andre xxvi, xxxiv

Haatz, Col. 187
Habana, SS 218
Hacke 166, 245, 257, 262–3
Haeburn Little, William 145, 158–9
Haeckel, Col. 207
Haeften, Werner von xxxiv
Haffner, Luipold xxvii, xxxiv

Hagemann, xxvii
Haggar, Elie (GULL) xxxv
Haldiun 193
Halim, Prince Abbas 204
Hall, Pamela 14
Hamada Jawad xxxv
Hamada, Mahmoud (ROMEO) xxxv
Hamann, Dr 25
Hamburger, Willi xxiv, xxvii, xxxv, 200
Hammes, Ernst 106
Hanke 124
Hannestad 66
Hans Ruser (JUNIOR) xxiv, xxxvi, 125, 127, 129, 133–6, 144, 149
Hansa, SS 35
HANSEN, 115, 177, 194
Hansen, Bjame 64
Hansen, Georg (BRIZO SENIOR) xxv, xxvii, xxx, xxxv, 116, 238
Hansen, Hans 108
Hansen, Kurt xxxv, 110
Hansen, Walter (alias Walter Burckhardt) 216
Hanslope Park xxii
Harbers, Kurt xxxv, 184
Harding, Sir Alexander 104
HARDY (Wilhelm Hoffmann) xxxv
HARKS 211
HARLEQUIN (Richard Wurmann) xxiv, xxviii
Harmer, Christopher ix, 285
Harmer, Pam ix
Harnisch, Hans xxxv
Harnisch, Juan Rudolfo Leo (BOSS) 217
Harris, Enriiquetta ix
Hartman, Paul xix
Hartmann, Fraulein von 21
Hartmuth, Johnny 21, 63, 95
Harvey 27
HATCHET (Albert de Jaeger) xxxv, 63, 95
Hatchett's 66
Hauer, Viktor 204
Hecheveria, Pedro 63
HECHT 54
Heidschuck, Hauptman 172
Heincke, Hans 213
Hellmuth, Osmar xxxv, 217–18
HELMUTH (SCEPTIC) xxxv, 182
Hempel, Eduard 15
HENDLE 189
Hendle, Friedrich 189, 197
Hendrik, Harry 24
Henge, Dr 26
Heresvili 196
HERMANN 165, 242, 244–8, 258, 260
Hermann, Erich 34, 47
Hermans, Leo 23
Hernie 64, 70, 280–1, 290
Hervious, Lucien (FOREST) xxxv
Hesketh, Rob ix
Hesketh, Roger ix
Hess, Rudolf 29, 281
Heydrich, Reinhard 19, 22, 106
Heyer, Herbert von 215
Highland Monarch 134, 219
HILFIS 200
Hilgert, Edgar 211, 219
Hill, Pamela 14
Hill-Dillon, Stephen xxxv
Hinchley-Cooke, Edward 5, 7, 10
Himmler, Heinrich 22, 115, 123, 229–30, 234–5, 290, 292
Hinrischen, Otto xxxv, 148
Hinsrich Freese 66
Hinz, Walther 187, 195
HIRSCH I 226
HIRSCH II 226
HISMA 259
Hitler, Adolf 115, 198, 224, 234, 279
HITTITE xxxv, 77
Hoare, Sir Samuel 62, 163
Hochleitner 191–2
Hoeffig 35, 50–1
Hoel, 65
Hoessler, Albert 64
Hoffman, George 64

Hoffmann, Joanna 3
Hoffmann, Wilhelm (HARDY) xxxv, 130, 251–2, 256
Hohenloe, Max 107
Holl, Hans 34
Holland, Leslie 21
Holloway 21
Holm (alias Paul Thummel) xxxv
Holting, 109
Holzapel, Hans xxxv, 185
Homann, Otto 48
Hood, Bill ix
Hooper, Jack 23–4
Hoover, J. Edgar 2, 5
Hope, Peter ix
Horges 123
Horn, Boris 196
Hornfjell 65
Horsfall-Ertz, Eugene 8
HOSIERY (Willi Hamburger) xxxv
HOST xxxv
HOSTESS xxxv
Howard 30
Hubig 226
Huckreide-Scholz 13, 15
Huntemann, Gerhard xxxv
Hutchinson Camp, Isle of Man 11

I/H, *see* Eins Heer
I/L, *see* Eins Luft
I/LTW, *see* Eins Luft Technik
I-BAER 226
Ida Knudsen, SS 171
Ile de France 142
I-M, *see* Eins Marine
Imhoff, Erich 211
IMMORTAL (Juan Pujol) xli
Imperial Airways 140
Inaki, SS 146
Informadora Rapida Limitada 215
Ingersoll, Gen. 103
INNA 211
INTERALLIÉ 285–7
Inter-Services Liaison Department (ISLD) 180
ISLD, *see* Inter-Services Laision Department
Isle of Man 7, 11, 66
ISOS (Abwehr decrypts) 27, 63–4, 102, 129–30, 142, 144, 146, 149, 162, 167, 172, 174, 178–80, 204, 218, 229, 238
I-TAGEL 226
Itish Republican Army (IRA) 14–15, 28
Ivens, Jack xxxv
IVORY 38

Jacobs 283
Jacobsen, Ernst Kirkeby 283
JACQUES xxxv
JAEGER (Otto John) xxxv
Jaeger, Adolf xxxv, 63
Jaeger, Albert de (HATCHET) xxxvi, 71, 164, 168, 251, 256
Jakobs, Dietrich xxxvi, 273
Jakobs, Josef xxxvi, 64, 72–3
Jamart 272
Janhke, Kurt xxxvi, 17–19, 22–4, 31
Japanese Intelligence Service 19, 27, 181
Jarvis, Ralph xxxvi, 143, 147–8
Jazequel, Theophil 63
Jeanne d'Arc 33
JEANNOT xxxvi
Jeebsen, Johannes (ARTIST) xxiv, xxix, xxxvi, 140
JEFF (Tor Glad) xxxvi, 92–101
Jesus, Paulino de xxxvi
Jevrenovic, Mirodrag Ljubonur 246
JIGGER (Herbert J. Berthold) xxxvi
JIMENEZ 169
Jean Bart 141
JOCCA 131
Jodl, Alfred viii
Johansen, Invald xxxvi, 23, 280
John, Otto (WHISKY; JAEGER) xxiv, xxxvi
Johns, Philip ix, 145
Johnson, Herschell 18

JOLLE 216
Jonassen, Hugo 63
Joost, Otto xxxvi, 63, 86
Jordaan, Johan (TRUMPET) xxxvi
Jordan, Franz (alias Frank Walter) xxxvi
Jordan, Jessie xii, 2–3, 58, 60
Jose Almeida Jr, 122, 150
Josephine, MV 63
Joslin, John M. 35
Jude, Leon 36
JUNIOR (Hans Ruser) xxxvi
Junkers Ju-290 185

K. Joe (Kurt Ludwig) xxxvi, 35
Kaes, Amady 162
Kahn, David ix
Kaisermarine 6, 167
Kallab, Hermann 111
Kaltenbrunner, Ernst xxxvi, 20, 224
Kamler, Ottto xxxvi, 133
Karth, Bahr 194
Karl 33
Kassner, Hans 34, 36
Katherine, Oscar 276–7
Katz, Hillel (DUBOIS) xxviii
Kauder, Richard (KLATT) xxi, xxvi, xxxvi
Kautz, Hans xxviii
KEEL (Jean Carrere) xxxvi
Keinert 107
KELLER xxxvi
Kelly, Joseph xxxvi, 58, 60
Kemp, Peter ix
Kempter, Friedrich 212, 215
Kennedy, Joseph 28
KENT (Viktor Guryevich) xxxvi
Kenyon-Jones, Bill ix
Kessler, John M. 35
KEYNOTE xxxvi
Khan, Mizra (SHAROCK) xxxvi
Khaqqay, Hamdi (BLACKGUARD) xxx
Kieboom, Charles van der xxxvi, 62, 74, 83
Kiener, Bernie (RAINBOW) xxxvii, 66
Kilburg, Dr (alias of Emile Kliemann) 128
KILLIAN (Hans George) xxxvii
King, Andrew ix
King, W.J. Harding 10
King George V, HMS 72
KINGPIN xxxvii, 63, 71
KISS (Mohamed Salmassi) xxxvii, 202–03
Klaps, Lt 34
KLATT xxxvii
Kleczkowsky, Karl von xxxvii, 200
Kleczkowsky, Stella von xxxvii
Klein 36, 203
Klein, Dr Wilhelm 123
Kleyenstubber, Ernst xxviii, xxxvii, 113, 115–16
Kliemann, Emile xxvii, xxxvii, 64, 128, 263
Klinkisch, Dr 211
Kloos, Barend (LEEK) 302
Knapman, Thomas 178
Knappe-Ratey, Friedrich (FEDERICO) xxxviii, 167
Knochen, Helmut 19–20, 224–45, 230
KO Bulgaria xxvi, 187, 190, 193, 197, 199, 201
KO Portugal (KOP) 47, 129–30, 148–9
KO, *see* KriegsOrganisation
Koch, Paula 194–5
Koechel, Johann 4
Koedel, Marie 34
Knigge 149
Koedel, Simon (A-2011) xxxvii, 34, 43
Koengi, Stubaf 225
Koenig, Kpt 35
Koepf, Richard 36
Koepke, Bertie 166
Koester, Hans 123
Kohsen, Elisabeth 11
Kolbe, Hans 37

Koller, Haupt. 187, 196
Kollmorgan Optical Corp 4
KONA (Kommandeur der Nachrichtenaufklärung) 33
Kondgen, Ernst xxxvii, 185
Konieczny, Georg xxxvii
Konnecke 113
KONO (KreigsOrganisation Nehe Orient) 180
KOP (KriegsOrganisation Portugal) 47, 129–31, 148
Kopff, Wilhelm 211, 216
Korel, Karl xxxvii, 185
Korostowitz, Vladimir 21
KOS (KriegsOrganisation Spain) xxiii, 114–29
Kosnchik, Franz (DARIEN) 143
Kostov, Col. 187
Kraatz, Lillie 133
Kraeutzer, Karl 38
Krafft, Mathilde 67
Krafft, Carl 8
Kraft, Vinzenz 22
Krag, Peter 63
Kramer, Karl 125, 254
Krasinsky 26
Krieck, Dr 26
KriegsOrganisation (KO) 129
KriegsOrganisation Nehe Orient (KONO) 180–7, 194, 199
Krivitsky, Walter 18–19
Kroll, Augusto 213
Kron, Mr 2
Kronberger, Georg xxiv, xxxvii
Krueger, Hastuf 109–10
Krüger, Otto 24
Kruse, Ewald 109
Kuebart, Wilhelm xxvii, xxxvii
Kuhlenhauber 210–11
Kuhlenthal, Karl-Erich 167
Kuiper, Willem 38
Kunowski 26
Kunsemueller, Guillermo 213
Kunze 226
Kup 296
KUPPER 194
Kurrer, Natasha 131
Kurmes, Martin xxxvii, 184
Kurrer, Otto (alias Kamler) 131
Kurth 235
Kutchuk Bureau 202
Kuvett, Josef (MIMI) xxxvii

La Part Bien 63, 74–5
Lackner, Franz 37, 39, 109
Lady Hogarth, HMS 218
Lafont 233
Lahmann, Ernsy xxxvii
Lahousen, Erwin xxi, xxxvii, 57
Laia, Renato Roque (AUGUSTA) xli, 62, 151, 160–1
LANG 172
Lang, Fred xxxvii, 37, 121
Langbein, Alfred xxxvii, 38, 46, 49
Lang, Ilya xxxvii
Lange, Franz 216
Lange, Heinz 215–17, 220
Langer, Eugn 211–12, 225
Langner, Ogf. 50
LARK xxxvii
Latham, Andre (GILBERT) xxxvii
LATI 213, 221
Lauenstein xxv
Laurenco, Maj. 145
Laureyssens, Joseph xxxviii, 63, 71, 86, 89, 164, 168
Lawrence, Mrs M. 145
LAZY, xxxviii
Le Tac 285–6
Leadlay, Maj. 21
LEAGUE xxxviii
League of Nations 23
Leclercq 272
Ledebur, Josef xxiv, xxvii
Lee, Russell ixl
LEGION xxviii
Legion Belge 273, 279
LEHMANN 54
Lehmann, Col. 104
Leipzig Univserity 221

Leisner, Wilhelm (alias Lenz) xxviii, 113, 115–16, 129, 167, 205
Leitstelle WALTER 111, 227
LENA xxxviii, 61
Lenihan, Joseph (BASKET) xxx, xxxviii, 65, 168, 254, 263
Leon 23
LEON 254
LEOPOLDO 254
Letter Interception Unit 59
Leverkuhn, Paul 186, 195, 198, 202
Levesi 198
Levi, Renato (CHEESE; ROBERTO) xxxviii, 203
Liai, Renato Roque xxxviii
LIBERATORS xxxviii
Libot, Gerard xxxviii, 63, 273
Liddell, Cecil xxxviii, 13
Liddell, Guy xxxviii, 2, 4, 28, 144
Liebl 187
Liehtenthal xxi
Lima, SS 141
LINA 169
Linde, Christian ix
Lindenbarg 119
Linguists' Club 13
Lippold, Mani 187
LIR 215
LITIGANT xxxviii
Lloyd George, Gil xxii
Lloyd's Register 174
Lochner, Robert xxxviii, 183
Loewe, Lionel ix
LOGENBRUDER 54
Lohmann, Carl 35
Lohrey, Walter xxxviii, 35
London Reception Centre (LRC) 278, 290, 283
London School of Economics 21
London University 10
London War Room xix, 105, 223
Lonkowski, William 3
Lonsdale, Stella 90, 284
Loon, Jan van 14
Lopez, Daisy 266
Lorant, Michael 21
Lorenz, Fritz 74, 223
Los Solos 170
Lowschin, Boris 166
Loxley, Peter xxxviii
LRC, *see* London Reception Centre
LUC Organisation xxxviii, 271–3, 279
LUCAS 285
Ludwig, Kurt (Joe K) xxxvi–xxxviii 35
Ludwig, Laurentius xxviii
Ludwig, Thomas xxviii, 180, 186, 188, 190–5
Lufer, Salzburg xxv
Luftneidekopf Sofia xxvi
Luke, Bill ix
Lund, Legwald xxxviii, 63, 86
Lunda, George 64

Machaeo, Jose Carlos (JOCCA) 132
Mackenzie 30
Maclean, Donald D. xxii
Macphie, Maj. 7
Magallanes 174
Magan, Bill ix
MAGISTER 133
Magnus, Eystein Henrik 281
Mahon 58
Maier, Erich 38
Main Index xx
Maingot, Graham xxxviii
Maiwald 25
Majewitz, Johann 37–9
Malone, Richard L'Estrange xxxviii
Mammen, Franz 220
MAMMUT xxvi
MAMMUT II xxviii–xxix
Mandt, Harold 212
Manenfeld 25
Manhattan, SS 36
MARCAUD 226
MARCHAND xxxviii
Marcus, Carl (alias Marienfeld; DICTIONARY) xxiv, xxxviii, 18, 22, 24–5, 29–31

MARDE 226
Marek, Maria (THE SNARK) xxxviii, 65, 167–8
Marnegro 179
Marques des Commillas 172
Marriott, John 14
Marschner, Hans (alias of Gunter Schutz) xxxviii, 13, 65
Martens, Thilo 186, 219
Marthos, Antonio 266
MARTIN 172
Martinez, Juan 63
Marwitz, Adm. von der 191
Mason, Peter 25, 31
Masterman, J.C. xx, 104
Matschili, Hamal 196
Maude, John ix
Mauer, Col. 207
Maumien 211
MAURICE 38
MAURITZ 177
MAX xxi, 133, 177
Mayer, Friedrich W. xxxix, 59
Mayer, Helen 35
Mayer, Otto xxxviii
Mayr, Franz xxxviii, 184–5
McCarthy, Sam (BISCUIT) xxx, xxxix
McCartney 58
McQueen, Elspeth 21
MEADOW xxxix
Medical Corps 4
Meems, Aikne 34
Meems, Albert xxxix, 34, 38
MEHMERT 172
Meier, Carl xxxix, 62, 74, 83
Meinhardt (alias Weingarten) 128
Meissner, Otto xxviii
Meisstueffen xxvii
Melder, MV 280
Meller, Martin 211
Mendes 152
Menezes, Rogerio de xxxix, 162
MERCATOR II 216
Merckl xxxix
Merkel, Otto 252
Merskl, Otto (alias Marcelle) 121, 124–5
Mesquita, José 136
Messerschmidt, Dr 27
METEOR (Eugn Sostaric) 134
Meyer 110
Meyer, C.F. 589, 175
MI5, *see* British Security Service
MI6, *see* British Secret Intelligence Service
MI-14 xxviii
Michael, Hans 211
Mielitz, Theodore 122
MIGUEL 169
Mikojan, Michael 194
Milice 226
Mills, Cyril ix, xxxix, 14
Mills, John ix, xxiv, 64
MIMI (Josef Kuvett) xxxix
Ministry of Aircraft Production 84
MINT xxxix
Mirnig, Theresa 21
MISSIR 189
Missir, Emil 199
MIT, *see* Turkish Intelligence Service
Mitchell Field, Long Island 3
MODEL xxxix
Moe, John (MUTT) ix, xxiv, xxxix, 64
MOEDEK 132
Mohr 166, 249
MOLA 177
Momm, Eberthart 186
MONARCH xxxix
MONOPLANE (Paul Jeannin) xxxix
MONTAG xxxix, 171
Monte Albertia, SS 175
Monte Monuich, SS 218
Monteiro, Armando 133
Montgomery, Hugh ix
Montgomery, Mrs 265
MONUMENT xxxix
Moravec, Frantisek 5
Morel, Paul (F-7129) 102–04
Mori Aoki xxix, 187

MORITZ xxi, 226
Moritz Kommando 27
Moro 226
Morrow 58
Morse Patrol 17
Mosig 107, 109–10
Most Secret Sources (MSS) 149, 151, 156, 161
Mountjoy Prison 12
Mouths, Ferdinand 123, 128
Moyzisch, Ludwig xxxix
MSS, *see* Most Secret Sources
Mueller, Kapt. 54, 106
Mueller, Karl 35
Mueller, Ottokat xxvii
Muhlenbruch 203
Mulak, Paul 36
MULETER xxxix
Muller (alias of Dante Mario de Souza) xlii, 154, 160
Muller, Gottfried (TIGER) xxvi, xxxix
Muller, Heribert O.J. 215
Muller, Ottomar 212, 215, 219, 250
Muner 173
MUNK 250
MURAT (Otto Mayer) xxxix
Mure, David ix
Musik 127
MUTT, *see* John Moe
Muycos Grandez 108

Nachrichtenabteilung 17–18
Nachrichtendienst (ND) 121
Naiad, HMS 65
Nani, Maj. xxxviii
Napp, Hans xxviii, 219
Napp, Walter xxvii
NARA, *see* National Archives and Records Administration
Nascoucslhos, Antonio (FRUTA) 132
Nasserstein 112
National Archives and Records Administration (NARA) ix
Naval Control of Shipping Organisation (NCSO) xx, 154
NCSO, *see* Naval Control of Shipping Organisation
ND, *see* Nachrichtendienst
Neshat 202
Nessu 23
Nest Bremen 32–48
Nest Cologne xxvii, 217
Neuburg 107
New York, SS 4
New York Times 3
Nicolas, Walter 4
Nicolaus, Georg (MAX) 211, 215–16
Niebuhr, Dietrich (DIEGO) xxxix, 210, 219–20
Niemayer, Willen xxxix
Nieuw Amsterdam 142
Niklaus 25
Nikolovic, Alexander 187, 189
Nilsen, Ingard 64
NKVD (Soviet intelligence service) 203
Noak, Fritz xxxix, 37
Noble, John 11
Noehme, Corneille xxx
Nogueira, Eduardo 132
Nolte, Emily 128
NordDeutschen Handelgesellschaft GMBH 38
NordDeutscherLloyd Shipping Co. 41
Norden bomb sight 94
Nossek, Haupt 225
Novimar 179

O'Brien, Edward 21
Obed, Henry xxxix, 65
Oberg, Karl Albrecht 230, 234, 237
Oberkomuiondo der Kriegsmarine OKM)
Obladen, Friedrich xxvii, 212–13
Obladen, Michel 53
Ocana, Daniel xxxix
Odami, Ali Miri 190–1
Oeckel, Dr 121
Office of Naval Intelligence (ONI) xix

Office of Strategic Services (OSS) xix, 134, 137, 212
Official Secrets Act 4
Ohain 277–9
Olaf 280
Olchansky, Paul 178
Olivera 218
Olsen, Martin xxxix, 189
OPIENSKY 199–200
Opiensky, Stanislav 189
Oppenborn, Rittmeister 187
Oppenheim, E. Phillips 188
Organisation Grille 107, 109
Organisation of Military Counter-Espionage 5
Organisation of German Secret Service in Spain and the Spanish Dominions 168
ORLOFF (Wilhelm Gessmann) 130–1, 135
Ortelli, Elvezio 219
Oscar 170
Osmers 45
OSS, *see* Office of Strategic Services
Oster, Hans 10
Osterreith, Pierre 27
OSTRO (Paul Fidrmuc) 133
Othmer, Waldemar xxxix, 37
OUT, *see* Officer Training Unit
OVERCLOUD 286
OVERLORD 183
Owens, Arthur (SNOW) xxii, xxxix, 56, 60

PABLO xl, 165, 242–3, 247–8, 258
Paget, Hans 35
PAIR 167
Pan, Vaclav xl, 130
Pan-Am Airlines 136
PANCHO (John Eiikens) xxxii, xl
Pank, Capt. 163
Pankoff 127, 166
Pankow, Werner 253–4
Pannwitz, Heinz (alias of Heinz Paulsen) xl
Paparin 233
PAPS 166
Parczyck, Georg 37
Pariser Tageblatt 19
Parseval 225
PASCHA (Dr Reichert) xl, 203
Passport Control Office (PCO) 162
PASTURES xl, 64, 72
Patzig, Conrad 219
PAUL 153
PAULO 152
Paul-Taboschat, Gottfried xl, 166
Pazos-Diaz, Nicolas 63
PCO, *see* Passport Control Officer
Pearson, Norman Holmes 143
PEDRO (Alberto Koepke) xl, 167, 249
Peis, Gunter ix
Pelizaeus 140
Pelletier, Jean (alias Lacoste) xl, 288, 293
PENKNIFE xl
PENNANT xl
Perceira, Antonio Aruna 176
PERCY xl
Pereiro, Antonio (MAGISTER) 135, 176
PERRIER xl
Perry, Gordon W. 23–4
Perugi, Carlos (MOEOKKANER) 132
PESSIMISTS xl, 182
Petter, Robert (alias Werner Wälti) xl, 63
Pfeffer, Jose 26
Pfeffer, Pan 28
Pfeffer von Saloman, Franz 20–1
Pfeiffer, Augusta ('Gulla') 21, 27
Pfisterer 107
Phieffer, Erich (alias N. Spielman, Dr Erdhoff) xxviii, xl, 4, 28, 32, 25, 39–40, 51–2, 55, 143
Philby, Kim xl, 129, 147–9
Phipps, Joanna ix
PIE (Ferdinand Rodriguez-Reddington) xl, 185

Pierlot, Hubert 271, 276
Piert, Willy 23
PIGEON xl, 143
Pilderit, Isabel xl, 37
Pilote 16 251
Pinto, Antonio Gama 215
PIP xl
Piwonko, Kurt xl, 184
Pjettursen, Olaf 281
Plath 107
Podewils, Grafin 107, 109
POGO (Miguel del Pozo) xl
Pohl 146
Poils xxvii
Poliakoff, Vladimir 19
Policia de Vigilancia e de Defesa do Estado (PVDE) 123, 135, 162, 261
Polish Intelligence Service 191, 197, 199
Pomme, Maj. 19
Pons, Sjoerd xl, 62, 74, 83
Ponzo, Max xxviii
Popov, Dusan (TRICYCLE) ix, xxiv, xl, 63, 134, 215
Popov, Ivo (DREADNOUGHT) ix, 134
Popov, Marco ix
PORTO 130
PORTO II 130
Portugall, SS 251, 256
Portuguese Legion 131, 145
Pottel, Hans 23
Pozo, Miguel del (POGO) 62, 163
PPF (Parti Populaire Français) 22, 236–7
Praetorius, Walter xl, 12, 15, 53, 65
PRECIOUS (Erich Vermehren) xl, 182
Preetz, Willi 11, 14, 65
Pretzel, Haupt. 206
Price, John H. (WASHOUT) xli, 157, 161
PROSPER 30
Protze, Richard xxvi, 23
Pry, Gabriel Jules Emanuel 274–5
Pujol, Juan (ALARIC; BOVRIL; GARBO; IMMORTAL) ix, xxiv, xli, 167
PUMPKIN xli, 146, 162
Purvis, Juan da Silva xlii
Putlitz, Wolfgang zu xxii, 21–2
PVDE, *see* Policia de Vigilancia e de Defesa do Estado
Pye-Smith 58
PYL 302

QUALITY xli
Quanza, SS 149
Qudsi, Dr 185
QUEASY xli
QUEROL 178
Quevedo, Ramon 218

Rabagliati, Euen ix
Rademacher 166
Radio Berlin 201
Radio Security Service (RSS) xxii, xli, 9
RAF Lavenham 4
RAF Mildenhall 4
Raider, Horst 252, 256
RAINBOW (Bernie Kiener) xli, 12–15, 68, 73, 81–5, 96, 100
RAMESES 177
Ramon Alonso Ramos 179
Ramsbotham, Peter ix
Ramuz, Ernst 215
Ramzi, Nafti Rashid xii
Raposo, Candida Lacombe 37
Raposo, Genalho 37
Rapp, Percy W. xli, 58–60, 74
Rauh, Heinrich 193
Rauter 230
Raven, Jobst 215
RED 220
Red Cross 26
Reed, Nicholas ix
Refsdahl 281
Reich 55

Reich Security Agency (RSHA) xvii–xviii
Reiche 227, 234–5
Reichenau, Gen. Walter von 28–9
Reichenbach, Lothar von 211, 219
Reichert, Dr (PASCHA) 203
Reichsluftfahrtministerium Forschungsamt (Air Ministry Research Office) 208
Reimer, Heinrich xli, 37, 211, 214
Remmicke, Curt (alias Richter) 34, 44
REMUS 178
Reveoz 6
Reynaud, Paul 224
Rheda Castle, Westphalia 207
Rheinhaber, von 13
Rheinmettal 23
Rhilhausen 44
Ribbentrop, Joachim von 115, 235
Ribeiro, Jose 123
Richir 272
Richter, Karel xii, 64, 72
Rigo, Don 126
Riis, Iib (COBWEB; EDDA) ix, xx, xxiv
Ringhoffer 144
Rintelen, Franz von 21
Rio Pachal, SS 221
Rio Teuco 217
Rios, José Olivera del 218
Rissman, Hastuf 225
Risso-Gill, Christopher ix
Risso-Gill, Gene xii, 145
Rist, Jose xii, 37
Rita Garcia 221
Ritter, Kathleen ix
Ritter, Nikolaus xxviii, 7, 53, 56, 74, 125, 153–4, 203
Rittlinger, Herbert 187, 201
Rittmeister, Dr Johann 187
Ritzer, Heinrich 193
ROBERTO (Renato Levi) 203
Robertson, Joan ix
Robertson, T.A. ix, xii, 10, 283
Robles, Silvio 63
Rockstroh, Werner xli
Rodriguez-Reddington, Ferdinand (PIE) xli, 185
Roepke 35
ROF, *see* Royal Ordnance Factory
Rohde, Gen. 191
Rohleder, Maj. xxvi, 23
Rohrscheidt, Kurt von xli
Rolls-Royce 151
Rolph, William xli, 66
Romanov, George xli
ROMEO (Mahmoud Hamada) xxxv, xli, 123, 175
Ronge, Max 40
Rommel, Erwin 32, 203
Ronning, Gustav xii, 65, 89
Roosevelt, Franklin D. 25, 28
Roser, Rudolf xli, 181
ROSIE xli
Rossetti, Clemens 203
Rossner, Maj. 220
Rot, Mirko xxvi, vli
Rotet 202
Roth, Dr 123
Rothschild, Tess ix
Rothschild, Victor ix
Rottach-Egern xxv
Roussseau, Theodore 143
Royal Canadian Mounted Police (RCMP) 38
Royal Dutch Shell 23
Royal Geographical Society 10
Royal Ordnance Factory (ROF), Euxton 60
Royal Victoria Patriotic School (RVPS) 277
Roznicuk, Lt (FRANZ-JOSEF) 189
RSS, *see* Radio Security Service
Rudder 54
Ruge, Joaquim 211
Ruiz, Matilda 167
Rullhusen, Herman 34, 38
Rumrich, Guenther xxiii, xli, 2–3, 6
Rumrich, Gustav 5

Rundstedt, Gerd von 230
Ruser, Hans (JUNIOR) xii, 125, 127, 129, 134–5, 144
RUTHERFORD 146
RVPS, *see* Royal Victoria Patriotic School
Ryan, Frank 25
Ryde, Michael ix
Ryle, Gilbert xii, 181

S-2118, *see* TURCO
SABINE 168
SABOT xv
Sachenhausen concentration camp 30
Sadat, Anwar al- 204
Saetrang, Olaf xiii, 65
SAFEHAVEN 115
SALAAM 204–05
Salama, Abdel Moghny Said 204
Salazar 162
Salemann, Erich von 21
Salis, Charles de xiii
Salman 170
Salmassi, Mohamed (KISS) xiii
Salzinger, Hans xxvii
Samil, Sayed 196
Sanstede, Heinrich xxvi, 204
Santa Barbara 211, 216–17, 220
Santa Rosa 170
Santos, Carlos 145
Santos, Henriques 149
Santos, Maria Jose 266
Saygin, Tekin (A-2118; TURCO) xxi
SCEPTIC (HELMUTH) xlii
Schabbel, Klara xlii
Schacht, Dr 127
Schaeffer 113
Schagen, Peter xxiv, xxvii, xli
Schallburg, Vera von (alias Vera Erikson) xlii
Schallies, Gunther xlii
Scharf, Hans xxviii
Scharpf, Fritz xiii
Schatz, Erwin 36
Scheider 20
Scherr, Jennifer ix
Scheffter 199
Schell 111
Schellenberg, Walter xxv, xxviii, xlii, 19–20, 107, 111, 113, 224, 277–8
Schenker-Angerer, Gottfried xiii
Scheutz, Theodor 4
Schlattau, Hildegarde 14
Schleebrügge, Karl von 215
Schleuter, Ernst Eugn 3, 42, 211
Schloss Baruth 26
Schloss Schierensee 35, 53
Schmalschlaeger, Heinz 5
Schmidt, Else 7
Schmidt, Ernst xiii, 124, 146, 160
Schmidt, Hastuf 228
Schmidt, Wulf (TATE) xlii, 62
Schmitt, Dr 122
Schmitt-Lemere, Else 26
Schlauffen 200
Schmoele, Theodore 140
Schmuck, Hastuf 110
Schmuck (alias Schmeidow) 110
Schneider, Martin 187, 219
Schneider, Ostuf 187
Schnoele, Theodor 38
Schobius 121
Schoenbeck 111
Schoene 118
Scholz, Hans 34, 36, 38
Schott 253–4
Schreiber, Aloys xlii, 130–1, 228
Schroeder, Erich xlii
Schroeder's Bank 21
Schroell, Josef 216–17
Schubeius 121
Schubert 23, 144, 187
Schueddekopf 26
Schultz-Kampfhenkel, Dr 207
Schulze, Wilhelm xlii, 12
Schulze-Bernett, Walter 186
Schulz-Hausman, von 214
Schumann, Ernst 110
Schunke, Marcel 105, 223

Schutz, Gunter (alias Marschner) xlii, 11, 16, 65
Schwartau-Eskildsen, Heriberto xlii
Schwarz, von Berg 109
Schweinichen 230
Schwerdt, Otto xlii, 185
SCI, *see* Special Counter-Intelligence Unit
Scott, Olive 8
Scott, Stanley xlii, 58–9
Scott-Ford, Duncan xlii, 146
SD, *see* Sicherheitsdienst
SEBASTIEN 31
Sebes, Kendrik (HECK) 302
Section V xxiv, xxxi, xli, 9, 25, 31, 57, 102, 121, 129, 143–9, 167–9, 171–9, 188, 201, 222, 229, 238, 292–3, 295
Security Intelligence Middle East (SIME) 7–8, 180
Seele 252
Seevag 34
Seguridad 177, 260
Selle, von 21
Senner 228
Serhatli, Fauli (AVEST) 195
Sensburg, Walter 61
Sergueiev, Lilly (TREASURE) xxiv
Serrano Suner, Ramon 108
Service de Reneignements (SR) xxii
Sessler, Georg (alias Sinclair) 129
Seth, Ronald ix
Seubert, Franz 10, 205
Seydlitz, Gen. 191, 196
Seymour, Charles ix
Seyss-Inquart, Arthur 26
SHAEF, *see* Supreme Headquarters Allied Expeditionary Force.
SHAROCK (Mirza Khan) xlii
Shergold, Harry 204
Shumann, Mario xlii
Shwartau, Heriberto 219
SIBER 226
Siboni, SS 125
Sichel, Peter ix
Sick, Margarethe 38
SIDI 177
Siemens 215
Signal 123
Siegfried 221, 225
Sikorsky 3
Sil 170
SILBER xlii, 194
Silva Peralta, Antonio 37
Silver, Arnold xiii, 15, 130
Silverberg, Jacob 140
SILVIE 137
SIM, *see* Servicio Información Policia Militar.
SIME, *see* Security Intelligence Middle Eas
Simoes, Ernesto xiii, 144, 147
Simon, Walter xlii, 6, 14–15, 58, 65, 68
Simonsen 16
Singer 108, 110
SIPO, *see* Sicherheitspolizei
SIRENE 170
SIS, *see* British Secret Intelligence Service
SIS, *see* Italian Speciali Servizio Informazioni
SISYPHUS xliii, 63, 73, 85, 150–2, 160–1
Skardon, Jim ix
Skembry 198
SKULL (Jean Senouqu) xliii
Smith, Frank 7
Sneyers, Jean-Pierre 185
SNOW (Arthur Owens) xliii, 8, 68, 73–4, 78, 81–8, 97, 129, 153–4, 159
SOBAC 84
Sobisch, Beno 215
SOE, *see* Special Operations Executive
Sofindusorganisation 108
Soizic 65
Solborg, Robert xliii, 120, 136–7
Solem, Thorleif xliii, 280
Solms-Baruth, Frederick ix
SOMER xliii, 176

Sonderkommando 233, 236
Sorzano, Francisco Dalgado 170
Sostaric, Eugn (METEOR) ix
Southampton University 53
Souza, Dante xliii, 154
Spanish Civil War 113
Special Intelligence Service ix, 213
Special Operations Executive (SOE) 65
F Section 30
Speck xxvii
Speer, Albert 49
Speich, George xliii
Speir, Rupert ix
Spencer, Joe 184
Sperry Gyroscope 4
Stallforth, Alberto 21
Stallforth, Federico 21, 25
STANDARD xliii
Starziczky, Josef 215
Staudinger, Franzall 109
Stauffenburg, Claus von xliii
Steffen, Karl 217
Steimle, Eugn xxv
Steiner, Florent xliii, 64
Steinhurd, Lawrence 192
Stelle-P 22
Stephens, Robin 120
Steuer, Johann 4
Stevens, Richard 23
Stillwell, Victor 144, 156
Stockmann, Michel xliii
Stonehouse, Brian ix
Stopford, Richmond xliii, 28, 143–4
Stow, G.M.F. 143
Strandmoen, Johan 64
Strangeways, David ix
Strasser, Otto 22
Strehmel, Helmuth 272
Streiter 189, 188–200
Striepe, Adolf xliii, 37
STRIFE xliii
STRIPE xliii, 64, 71, 85, 95
Struenck, Theodor xliii
Stuart, Michael 138
Stubbs, Werner 134
Studies in Intelligence viii
Subtil, Joachim de Brito 152
Suez Canal xxi, 203
SUMMER (Goesta Caroli) xliii, 72, 82, 84–7
Supreme Headquarters, Allied Expeditionary Force (SHAEF) xix
Sylvan Arrow 145
Szelinski, Inge 33
Szymanska, Halina ix

Taanevik 54
Tamara, SS 36
Taria 179
TATE, *see* Wulf Schmidt (alias Harry Williamson) xliii, 13, 64, 72–3, 83–6, 154
Taylor, Jacqueline 130
Taylor, John ix, 24
Teeling, Edward 21
Teeling, William J. 21
Tennyson, Lord ix
Ter Braak, Willem (alias of Gilbertus Fukken) xliii, 73
Tester, Dr Arthur 192
Thanen 193
The Double Cross System of the War of 1939-45 (Masterman) xx
The Game of the Foxes (Farago) xx
The Manufacture and Use of Countefeit Currency by the RSHA xxv
The Navy 54
The Objectives in England of the German Secret Service, 1 October 1941 66, 89
THE SNARK (Maria Marek) xliii, 72, 95, 243–6, 252, 254–5, 260
The Unknown Sahara (Almassy) 204
THEO 207
Theodor Wille Co. 215
THEODORA 208
Third Army 27, 142
THISBE xliii, 65, 75–6, 90
Thomas Cook 23

Thomson, Guy 201
Thost, Hans xliii, 2
Thummel, Paul (alias of Dr Holm) xliii, 5
Tiburon 170
Tietz, Theodore xliii, 58, 60
TIGER (Gottfried Muller) xliii
Times, The 19–20, 55, 58
Timm, Eric W. 223
Timmerman, Alphonse xliii, 65, 71, 89, 168, 246
Timmerman, Bernardo 210, 213, 264
TOMAS 249
Torgersen, Henry 64
Toshikazu Suzuki 221
TransOcean News Agency 123, 194
Trauten 193
TREASURE, *see* Lilly Sergueiev
TRIANGLE (ISOS in the Middle East) 8–9
Tributh, Herbert xliii, 14–15, 65
TRICYCLE (Dusko Popov) xliii, 76, 83–4, 87, 95–101, 129, 144
Trues 194
TURCO (Tekin Saygin) xxi
Turkish Intelligence Service (MIT) 188, 195
Turkul, Anton xliii

U-21 219
U-38 65
U-213 xxxvii, 38
U-372 9
UGUATE 174
Ugueux 276
Uhring, 228
Uhrlatzlanu 187
Uhse, Hans 37–8
Ullstein Publishing 14
Ulmer, Al ix
Ulshofer, Robert xliii
United States Export Line 125
Unland, Werner xliii, 11, 15–16, 65
Untemehaen Sued 48
Unversagt, Werner xxvi
Urlatzlanu 192
Urzaiz, Angel 179
Ustinov, Klop (U.35 alias Mr Johnson) xxi, xliv, 21, 130
UTRILLAS 115
UTUBRAND 20
Utzinger, Gustav 217, 220

V-1 142
V-5007 170
Vaciago, Maj. xxviii
Valiente, Pedro Rodriguez (REMUS; V-611) 178
Valles, Jose 218
van t'Sant, François 31
Van Wijk, Gerth xliv, 64, 164
Vandam, Arie 63
Vanisttant, Sir Robert 18
Vargas, Getulio 213
Vaudreuil, Capt. 30
Vega 174
Vejarano, Carlos 172
Velasco 219
Velasco, Angel Alcazar de 163
Velicovic, Vladimir 196
Velikovsky, Vladimir 187
Venlo 23, 224
Verhaegen, Henri 272–4
Verlinden, Jack xliv, 251–2, 255–6
Vermehren, Erich (PRECIOUS) ix, xxvii, 133, 181–4, 188, 200
Verscheuren, Frank 144
Versluys 247
Vesle Kari 65
Vhibi, Haldun 193
VI/B Italy 26
VICTOIRE (Mathilde Carré) xliv, 285–8, 293
Vilar 54
Villa de Madrid 179
VIPER xliv, 130, 134
Visparia 170
Vivian, Valentine 28
Vogel 264
Volandia, SS 35

Volga 64, 70
Volkischer Beobachter 2–3
Vollbrecht, Hans 25, 112
Von Griebheim & Barranuilla 37
Voppel, Sr 208
Vorlk 225
Voss, Otto 3
Vrinten, Adrianus 22, 24
Vulcania, SS 35

Wacher, Otto 186
Waetjen, Eduard xliv
WAF & Co. 11
Wagner, Otto (alias Dr Delius) xxvi, xliv, 187
Waldberg, Josef xliv, 62, 74, 83, 86
WALENTY (Roman Garby-Czerniawsky) xliv, 285–8
Waljei, Claus 219
Wallace-Hadrill, Michael 31
Wallem, Helmik xliv, 64, 280, 290
Walter, 111, 226
Walter, David 138
Walti, Werner xliv, 72, 84, 86
Walton 198
Warden, Maj. 30
Warner Bros 26
Warschauer, Ludwig xliv, 10–11
Washington, SS 36
WASHOUT (John Price) xliv, 146
Wasserman, Joseph 21
Wassner, Adm. Erwin xliv
WEASEL (Dr Hilaire Westerlinck) xliv, 89–90
Weber, Waldemar xxvi, xliv
Weinberger 191
Weiss, Hans 109
Weiss, Haupt. 109
WELLINGTON 38
Weltzien, Kuno xliv, 123, 144, 146–58, 161
Wenzel, Hans ix
Wenzlau, Haupt. 34
WERNER 263–4
Westerlink, Hilaire xliv, 37
Westihoff, Ferdinand 219
Weston, Edward 3
Weygand, Gen. Maxime 224
Wheeler-Hill, Kurt 58–9
WHISKY (Otto John) xliv
White, Dick ix, 8–9, 64, 104, 120
Whyte, Jock 8, 27
Wichmann, Herbert xxvii, 53–5, 210, 214
WIDO 206
Wiedemann Ostuf 111
Wijk, Gerth van xliv, 64, 164–6, 165, 242–3, 247, 255, 257–8, 264–5
Wild, Noel ix
Wilhelmina, Queen 31
Wilkinson, Peter ix
Williams, Bill ix
Williamson, Harry (TATE) x
Wilson, Ian xxv
Wilson, T. 8
WINCHESTER 140
Winchester, Tarleton xliv, 140
Windham, Sir Walter 7
Winsor, Rita xliv, 140–2
Winterstein, Herbert xliv, 37, 216
Winzer, Paul 106–08, 113
Wishart, William xliv, 58, 60
Wisner, Frank xx
Wissmann 126
WITCH xliv
WITZI 263
Witzke, Lothar 17
Wolf, Bruno xliv, 192
Wolf, Friedrich xliv, 211, 218, 220
Wormwood Scrubs 6
Wurmann, Richard (HARLEQUIN) xxiv, xxviii

X-2 (Counter-intelligence branch, OSS) xxix, 223
XX (Twenty Committee) xxiv, 223

Yachting 54–5
Yasa, Sefik 194

Yasssani 111
Yatamati, Col. 187
YODLER xliv, 77
Yolland, Edgar xliv
Young, George ix
Yumnu, Resid 198

Zaehringer, Kurt xliv, 194–7, 202
Zagh, Ustf 224
Zamanova, Olga (ECCLESIASTIC) 146
Zamboni, Guelfo xl, xliv
Zaya, Kamal 188
ZbV, *see* Zur besonderen Verwendung
Zech-Nennwich, Hans Georg (COLOMBINE) xxiv
Zechntner, Kurt 123
Zehntner, Kurt 123
Zeller, Willhelm 214
Zemanova, Olga (ECCELSIASTIC) xxxii, xliv
ZERO Organization 279
ZIGZAG, *see* Eddie Chapman
Ziya, Kemal 195–8
Zolling, Col. Ernst 205
Zossen (ZEPPELIN) 26, 137, 139
Zschinke 107
Zschunke, Marcel 223, 227–8
Zuang 224
Zuchristian, Hastuf 224
Zur besonderen Verwendung (ZbV) 118